A Concise History of Russian Literature

THE GOTHAM LIBRARY
OF THE NEW YORK UNIVERSITY PRESS

The Gotham Library is a series of original works and critical studies published in paperback primarily for student use. The Gotham hardcover edition is primarily for use by libraries and the general reader. Devoted to significant works and major authors and to literary topics of enduring importance, Gotham Library texts offer the best in literature and criticism.

Comparative and Foreign Language Literature:
Robert J. Clements, Editor
Comparative and English Language Literature:
James W. Tuttleton, Editor

A Concise History
of Russian Literature

Volume II

From 1900 to the Present

by Thaïs S. Lindstrom

New York · NEW YORK UNIVERSITY PRESS

COPYRIGHT © 1978 BY NEW YORK UNIVERSITY

Library of Congress Cataloging in Publication Data (Revised)

Lindstrom, Thais S.
  A concise history of Russian literature.

  Vol. 1 has also special title: From the beginnings to
Chekhov.
  Vol. 2 issued in series: The Gotham library of the
New York University Press.
  Bibliography: v. 1, p. 216-223 ; v. 2, p.
I Includes index.
  1. Russian literature—History and criticism. I. Title.
PG2951.L5   891.7'09   66-22218
ISBN 0-8147-4980-1 (v. 2)
ISBN 0-8147-4981-X (v. 2) pbk.

MANUFACTURED IN THE UNITED STATES OF AMERICA

PREFACE

HISTORY IS INDEBTED to Russia for enacting one of the most spectacular and far-reaching events of the twentieth century. The 1917 Revolution instigated social and political repercussions throughout the world, attempted a total reshaping of the human being in relation to his environment, and placed Russian cultural life in a state of permanent crisis. The great story of the gestation period, agonies, and birth of the cataclysm, and the postnatal fevers that have not yet abated would have been little known from inside the closed Soviet society if these experiences had not been communicated to art. In this respect, Russian literature continued the function within the 150-year-old tradition of a unique intimacy between writers and political action. But during the country's revolutionary development, this relationship evinced change in a radical way. The nature of the writer's work and his role in society has reflected and continues to reflect, more decisively than ever before in the history of modern literatures, the current political situation. The writer, in turn, as artist and man, has been deeply influenced by it. The importance of this metamorphosis, played out against the background of shifting political events and the drama of the country's adjustment to the new social order, cannot be overestimated.

Since 1900 the literature of Russia has passed through three distinct stages of achievement.

The century ushered in a brilliant period of creativity, peopled by a highly educated and talented group of poets, thinkers, critics, and prose writers who were vying with Western artists in their search for new symbols, myths, and language to redefine philosophy and the arts. During the seventeen-year span between the tsarist and Soviet regimes, an interim period when literary censorship was practically abolished, there was a real cultural explosion. Writers gave free expression to their urge for experimentation with forms and metaphysical thought and pursued fully their intellectual and artistic endeavors for no other purpose than aesthetic gratification and self-development. Living in a world of war and revolutionary ferment, their writings reflect a sense of impending catastrophe, nowhere more compellingly than in the work of Alexander Blok, Russia's foremost symbolist poet and the most talented representative of the age. Although Blok, with the rest of his gifted generation, passed out of history in 1917, his poetic legacy lived on for other poets, who, striking out in their own independent directions, followed him. Throughout the entire period under review, creative expression is poet-haunted. There is a persistent resurgence of poetry in twentieth-century Russian letters that ranges from such lyrical initiators of new trends as the Futurist Mayakovsky, or from the Imagist Esenin and the individual genius of Mandelstam and Tsvetaeva, to the skillfully polemical verses of Evtushenko and the vocal satire of the underground balladeers. Significantly, the era that resounded in its first decade to the musical rhythms of Blok was to reach artistic fulfillment forty years later in a poetic novel by Boris Pasternak, one of the most distinguished Soviet poets. It may well be that at a later, less self-consciously political moment in time, another literary assessment of the twentieth century in Russia will give first place to the poets.

The second phase of literary development took place immediately after the Civil War in the 1920s. It is known as the heady and tumultuous epoch of Revolutionary Romanticism. Following the chaos and devastation of seven years of war, an upsurge of creative forces responded to the purifying storm of the Revolution and its promise of a new reality to be expressed by a new art. The cultural scene was crowded with young writers and painters who were breaking away from traditional academic and humanistic moorings with prolific experimentations in form and content. Painters Malevich and Kandinsky were seeking to convey in pure line and color a cosmic vision of the world that announced in abstractions the Communist millennium; ego-Futurist Mayakovsky shaped his poems from the raw materials of language and sensations that he felt was the palpable new life; a brilliant group of short-story writers were recording in hyperbolic imagery and a modernistic style their Civil War experience dipped in the dynamics of violence. In literary criticism, another avant-garde step was made by the Formalists who denied all previous theories in a concentration on lingual and structural patterns of text. In contrast to these erudite critics, proletarian circles advocated a workers' and peasants' literature that would directly reflect the life of the masses.

It was not yet clear during these years that allowed for intellectual exchange with the West and the publications of pre-revolutionary writers, whether a Marxist orientation would be superimposed on cultural life. Preoccupied with economic and political reconstruction, the Bolsheviks were content to play referee among partisan and independent-minded literary groups where ideas and ideology were in a state of flux and the general submission to the Communist ethos was mitigated by the richness and variety of individualized imaginative experience. The dominating voice was that of Leon Trotsky who characterized the twenties as an age of transition and wrote unprophetically in *Literature and Revolution* (1923) that when the new art would be capable of expressing the fantastic Revolutionary reality "it would make its own way and by its own means . . . the domain of art is not one in which the Party is called upon to command."

Within less than ten years, Stalin had successfully launched his "second revolution" with the First Five Year Plan and imposed a socio-political aesthetic on all literature that eventually sealed off the writer's creative initiative. The writer was mobilized into the country's labor force to serve in the construction of the socialist state. His function was to achieve in his writings, beyond aesthetic enjoyment, a successful presentation, in accessible form, of Communist principles and ideals to the newly literate masses of Soviet society. He was to be guided by the principles of Socialist Realism, eschewing subjectivity, individual psychology, and innovations of any kind that might bewilder the untutored public and that were considered by the Communists as decadent vestiges of the bourgeois West. This propagated an unusual brand of realism that was to portray in contemporary language and settings an optimistic and even enthusiastic concept of the new life under socialism in its revolutionary development, glorifying real-life heroes in their military and labor feats. Even as science was to provide the weapons of defense and material abundance for the Soviet Union, art and letters were to create for the Soviet mass man a new mass culture. Stalin sincerely believed, as did Lenin, in the printed word as an instrument of power. He was heir to the nineteenth-century revolutionary literary critics who saw in the ideational content of literature a great influence on public affairs, and he was determined to subjugate literature to party doctrine and party policy. In addition to the writer's primary task of enlightening, encouraging, and exhorting the nation's utopia builders, he was called upon to express his dedication to such constant party directives as the worship of the Leader and anti-Westernism, and in his creative effort was obliged to unfailingly fulfill some specific propaganda aim. A situation developed on the literary scene that is unique in modern times. The artist was not only compelled to obey current social commands and devote his art to the glorification of the state but he was also forbidden to use his talent in any direction, even one that was harmless, if it was simply irrelevant to the interests of the state.

The surrender of creativity to totalitarianism did not occur at once, nor has it been completely successful. In the last three sections, dealing with the Stalin and post-Stalin periods, the present study emphasizes the long and tenacious struggle between state directive and the writer's need to affirm his artistic integrity. The conflict is taut with tensions and difficulty; it is an unprecedented social and intellectual phenomenon of our day. In various attempts at maintaining allegiance to their talent and craftsmanship, writers like Ehrenburg and Alexei Tolstoy practiced superficial compliance to popular themes. Others, such as Pilnyak, Fadeyev, and Kataev were obliged to rewrite already published novels in obeyance to injunctions from above. Sholokhov wrote a semi-didactic piece of fiction in praise of forced collectivization at the summit of that tragedy of haste and waste in order to allay official criticism of his sovereign epic. Bulgakov and Akhmatova composed for many years "for the drawer" waiting for a more lenient period in which to publish. Pasternak submitted to steady Kremlin harassment for his defiant gesture of publishing his censored novel abroad. These individual efforts at self-emancipation from conformity swelled into an articulate public protest during the post-Stalin epoch. Taking advantage of the party's temporary indecisiveness in cultural matters after the feral dictatorship and Khrushchev's denunciation of it, liberalizing trends took shape in literary polemics between dogmatists and the progressives and in the works of such rising authors as Dudintsev, Panova, Kazakov and Solzhenitsyn. Heretical views were aired in a hitherto forbidden exposure of Philistine government circles, a vindication of the inner world of private emotions and doubts as to the qualifications of party critics to judge literary merit. An original and vigorous new form of protest against the negation of creative freedom by the authorities and the stifling cultural climate in the Soviet Union has been gaining momentum in the past decade among writers who have been privately disseminating their uncensored works by means of a widely flung network of self-publishing enterprise. The pendulum continues to swing from politically hazardous aesthetic achievement to officially approved writings, and a new kind of literary production has emerged, intermittently illuminated with works of indubitable artistic value but on the whole unequal in merit.

This book traces the development of Russian-Soviet literature in the works of the major writers. The burden of the investigation rests on the assessment of the creative act and its effectiveness in the pre-revolutionary period and the relatively permissive 1920s, as contrasted with the regimentation of art during the past fifty years that has endured to this day. In this regard, the problems of the Soviet writer in his confrontation with the concept of the collective versus the self, and his determination to express, imaginatively and independently, his moment in time will be examined against the background of Soviet political history and in the perspective of his art.

CONTENTS

PREFACE   v

1. A Russian Renaissance   1

        Nihilistic Sensualism: The Decadents   4

    Bryusov (1873-1924)   4
    Balmont (1867-1943)   8
    Sologub (1863-1927)   10
    Gippius (1867-1945)   14

            Aesthetes Versus Mystics: The Symbolists   15

    Vyacheslav Ivanov (1866-1949)   21
    Bely (1880-1934)   23
    Blok (1880-1921)   28

                    Acmeism   35

    Gumilyov (1886-1921)   37
    Akhmatova (1888-1966)   38
    Mandelstam (1891-1938)   41

                    Futurism   45

    Khlebnikov (1885-1922)   48
    Mayakovsky (1893-1930)   50

Independent Poetic Ventures   57

Esenin, (1895-1925), a Peasant Poet   57
Tsvetaeva (1892-1941), An Inveterate Romantic   60
Pasternak (1890-1960), A Modernist Synthesizer   62
Zabolotsky (1903-1958), A Surrealist-Soviet Style   66

2. Dry Run of a Revolution: Prose Experiments
   of an Era in Ferment   71

Korolenko (1853-1921), a Populist Writer   74
Kuprin (1870-1938), a Zestful Storyteller   75
Bunin (1870-1953), a Last Classic Realist   76
Andreyev (1871-1919) and Artsybashev (1878-1927);
   Seekers of Sensations   78
Remizov (1877-1957), a Stylistic
   Ornamentalist   81
Gorky (1868-1936),
   An Embattled Proletarian   83

3. 1917 Revolution: The Civil War   93

Zamyatin (1884-1937),
   A Pioneer of Modernity   100

Young Writers of the Twenties   104

REVOLUTIONARY ROMANTICS   105

Vsevolod Ivanov (1895-1963)   105
Pilnyak (1894-1938)   107
Babel (1894-1941)   112

SATIRISTS   118

Bulgakov (1891-1940)   118
Katayev (1897-   )   121
Ilf (1897-1937) and Petrov (1902-1942)   121
Zoshchenko (1895-1958)   123

PSYCHOLOGICAL REALISTS   128

Fedin (1892-   )   128
Leonov (1899-   )   130

Olesha (1899-1960) 134
Kaverin (1902-   ) 138

4. Stalinization: a Soviet Metamorphosis of Literature 141

    Literature by Prescription: Three Early Modules 150

Furmanov (1891-1926) 150
Fadeyev (1901-1956) 152
Gladkov (1883-1958) 153
*Sholokhov (1905-   ), A Paragon of
    Soviet Letters* 155

TWO CONFORMISTS 164

Alexei Tolstoy (1883-1945) 165
Ehrenburg (1891-1967) 169

Pastoral and Exotic Escapes 174

Prishvin (1873-1954) 175
Grin (1880-1932) 175
Paustovsky (1892-1968) 176

Socialist Realism in Action 178

War Literature 180

Zhdanovism: The Darkest Chapter 185

5. Post-Stalin Era 197

    Immediate Consequences: The First and Second Thaw 197

Vladimir Dudintsev (1918-   ) 202
The Day of Poetry: Literary Moscow Vol. II 204
Boris Pasternak: Dr. Zhivago 207

New Lyrical Voices from the Soviet Union 217

Rehumanized Images of Soviet Society 225

Instances of Modernistic Writing 232

"Country Prose" Writers 238

6. Literature of Dissent   243

   Samizdat   243

   Alexander Solzhenitsyn (1918-)   264

   The First Circle   268
   Cancer Ward   270
   August 1914   272
   Gulag Archipelago   273

7. A Glance at the Present-Day
   Literary Scene   279

   CONCLUSION   291

   BIBLIOGRAPHY   295

   INDEX   307

A Concise History of Russian Literature

1 · A Russian Renaissance

THE RUSSIAN twentieth century did not arrive at its appointed time but made its appearance in the 1890s when it triggered off the first of a series of cultural explosions that resulted in a thirty-year period of unprecedented literary and artistic brilliance known as the *Silver Age.*

It was precipitated by the revolt of the young against the doctrine of sociological betterment and utilitarian positivism, the exclusive property of the old intelligentsia which still dominated Russian thought and supported a societal realism that in second-rate fiction of that time had long outlived its day. The homogeneous structure of classical realism that had attained its apogee in Tolstoy, was crumbling; there seemed to be no call for a literature of social progress in a society that in the last decade of the century was becoming aggressively capitalistic, increasingly prosperous and urbanized, catering to the materialistic demands of a rising bourgeois class. Younger writers and artists withdrew from this reality which they could not accept or transform and turned to a reassessment of all values and a redefinition of the artist's function and his art.

During the years between 1898 and 1904, the first translations of Stefan George, the English Pre-Raphaelites, Oscar Wilde, and Edgar Allen Poe, the French poets—Baudelaire, Mallarmé, and Rimbaud—and the studies on Nietzsche began to appear in Russia. The impact of this humanism, which rejected subservience to the social group in favor of personal creative caprice and will, inspired the younger generation to forge a new

1

aesthetic that endorsed individualism, self-expression, imagination, subjectivity, and a great concern with form.

This was a concept of art diametrically opposed to the remorseless realism and doctrinaire ideology that had dominated the past half-century. What followed after the initial reaction of derision and scandalized surprise among the conservatives, was an irresistible surge forward in literature, the fine arts, the theatre, and philosophical thought that explored the potential of modern man in history, in religious myth, in his inner self, and encoded the promise of his ability to transform the world. To do this, the most educated and talented men drew upon ancient art, Western humanism, native traditions, and universal myth. The leaders of the movement were for the most part humanists, versed in languages and much travelled. Many of them also were interchangeably scholars, poets, thinkers, and connoisseurs of the arts.

More philosophical works were published between 1890 and 1910 than during the entire nineteenth century. A plethora of small avant-garde magazines succeeded each other—*The Northern Herald* (1889-1898), *Questions of Life* (1905-1906), *The Scales* (1905-1909), *Golden Fleece* (1905-1906) *The Torches* (1906-1907), *Apollon* (1909-1917), *The Scythians* (1917-1918)— that polemically expanded the new and changing views and served as a forum for literary and philosophical information and criticism.

To foster an enlightened curiosity and appreciation of the most advanced art in the Russian public, a cycle of exhibitions of contemporary European painters (Degas, Monet, and Puvis de Chavannes) and Russian moderns (Bakst, Benois, Golovin, Serov, and Somov) were staged in Moscow, St. Petersburg, and in the provinces between 1899 and 1901. Its organizer, Serge Diaghilev, also conceived the ambitious Tauride Palace "Exhibit of Russian Portraiture" in 1905 and programmed many other art shows in Russia and abroad. He also was the editor in chief of the *World of Art*, published in St. Petersburg from 1898 to 1904. This splendidly printed and illustrated monthly offered its readers spectacular discoveries in the contemporary world of the creative arts. Diaghilev and his staff of young and enthusiastic associates (critic Alexander Benois, modernist painters Bakst and

Somov, literary aesthete Filosofov) revolutionized the taste of
the Russian public and created an awareness of the sources and
the evolution of old and modern art. Diaghilev wrote editorials
that censured all didacticism. He propagandized for the art of
the "exquisite craft" that with line, mass, and color was to create
the supreme human expression. He exalted the synthesis of musical and visual media that he found in Wagnerian opera,
Scriabin's tone poems, and Rimsky-Korsakov. All this rhetoric
was illustrated with full-page reproductions of Russian moderns
and French impressionists and expressionists.

It is difficult to overestimate the civilizing influence of the
section in *World of Art* concerned with art criticism. It was
authored by Alexander Benois (1870-1960). He was an art historian, painter, and talented stage designer steeped in the history
of new and old art, and one of the most learned men of his time.
In his essays, which are models of lucidity, erudition, and cultivated prose, he discussed such diverse art forms as the stylization
of Russian mythology in the canvases of V. M. Vasnetsov (1848-
1926), the masterpieces of Velasquez and Michelangelo, Kievan
iconography, and eighteenth-century architecture and sculpture
(that with persuasive skill he rediscovered for his compatriots in
the beauty of the St. Petersburg landscape). The magazine was
primarily concerned with the visual and performing arts, although literature was considered as well. Among the regular
contributors were the poets Balmont, Zinaida Gippius, the
critic-novelist, Dmitri Merezhkovsky, and Valery Bryusov, leader
of the avant-garde literary school known as the Decadents.

The artistic phenomenon of the French symbolists had sparked aesthetic revivals all over Europe during the transitional
decades of the two centuries. In England, Germany, Italy, Pol-
and, and Russia, symbolism stood at first for Baudelaire, Verlaine, Rimbaud, and Mallarmé; then there was a gradual drawing
away from this direct influence as poets reached back to native
sources of earlier romanticism. Stephen George, for example,
turned to Holderlin and Novalis for inspiration; Oscar Wilde,
Swinburne, and Beardsley claimed Blake, Shelley, and Edgar
Allen Poe as precursors. This neo-romantic trend was discerned
quite early by young Dmitri Merezhkovsky in his essay "On the
Causes of the Decline and on the New Currents of Contempo-

rary Literature" (1893). He described how contemporary poetry in Russia, just rising from the nadir of the 1880s, was influenced by the Western *fin de siècle*; the Russian poets also relied on native writers of the past, Turgenev, Dostoevsky, Goncharov, and Tolstoy. The earliest young poets, called themselves Decadents or symbolists, and some confusion about these two appellations still exists.

The movement did split around 1903, and it became possible to distinguish between the older leading Decadents, Merezhkovsky, Bryusov, Balmont, Sologub, Zinaida Gippius, and Rozanov, and the later symbolist poets, Vyacheslav Ivanov, Andrei Bely, and Alexander Blok, who achieved a more spectacular and lasting popularity. The Decadents remained more social and political, whereas the symbolists became more truly neo-romantics, drawing upon Lermontov and the poets Tyutchev and Fet who, in turn, were steeped in German romanticism. Their art aspired for the most part to a form of mystical idealism alien to the nihilistic and sensual tendencies of the Decadents. However, there was no body of doctrine or aesthetic principle to distinguish the Decadents and the symbolists. In Moscow and in St. Petersburg they lived and worked in close association, meeting at the many gatherings of their literary circles, influencing and being influenced by the critical writings from either camp.

NIHILISTIC SENSUALISM: THE DECADENTS

BRYUSOV (1873-1924)

Bryusov has been called the Peter the Great of Russian letters. Within a decade, almost single-handed, he westernized Russian poetry, and had himself proclaimed by the most talented young writers as the leader of the symbolist movement. He was the son of a wealthy Moscow merchant and had been brought up in a literary-minded atheistic milieu. He received a good education, and at the age of fourteen was already passing out to his schoolfellows his own translation of a Maeterlinck play and some poems by Verlaine and was determined to make his name known by creating a similar mode of writing in Russia.

By 1894, Bryusov had gathered around him a group of

enthusiastic individualists who called themselves "Decadents," in the European fashion. He published three pamphlets, *Russian Symbolists*, himself. They contained translations of the more provocative poems by Baudelaire, Rimbaud, Maeterlinck, and Mallarmé with imitative verses of his own, some under a nom de plume. They met with a unanimously jeering reception; the critics called him a "hooligan," a "broken-down boulevardier," a literary mountebank. Rather pleased with the notoriety, Bryusov brought out another slim book of his own poems the following year, impudently entitled *Chef-d'Oeuvres*. In the Preface, the author claimed that "this was perfect work to be bestowed on eternity." He was again derided by the public and the press. Further, it was judged a threat to artistic form and to the morality of art.

Undaunted, Bryusov persevered. He plunged into an intensive study of major Russian poets, Pushkin, Lermontov, Fet, and Tyutchev. He also published more of his own poetry (*Me Eum Esse*, 1897, *Tertia Vigilia*, 1900) at his own expense. His use of a clear and more controlled language reflects the impact of nineteenth-century tradition. With the publication of two volumes of verse, *Urbi et Orbi* (1903) and *Stephanos-Wreath* (1906) Valery Bryusov was acknowledged as Russia's leading poet.

He managed to enlist the financial support of a wealthy amateur of letters in order to found the Scorpion Press in Moscow, and become de facto editor of its monthly journal *The Scales*. He then attracted the most creative avant-garde writers in Russia and the West. It was in a large measure due to the organizing abilities of its editor, his immense energy, self-discipline and extraordinary self-confidence that *The Scales* became one of the most prestigious European literary magazines of the period. Bryusov also was a born leader, and he literally "hypnotized" young writers into believing in him and his undertaking. Andrei Bely wrote that "Bryusov was for us the only master, a fighter for all that was new, the organizer of propaganda; we obeyed him as a leader and a fighter." This was in 1903, just a year before *The Scales* was launched.

Urbi et Orbi and *Stephanos-Wreath* represent the summit of Bryusov's creative achievement. Favorite Decadent themes predominate—eroticism, nihilism, a Baudelairian fascination with evil and the beauty of evil, and the "dérèglement des sens," in the manner of Rimbaud. His verses celebrate the mystic ritual of carnal love, predict the imminent collapse of civilization in apocalyptic tones, or pursue the image of what was then an excitingly new phenomenon—the emergence of the modern metropolis. Bryusov had just discovered Emil Verhaeren and inspired by his *Villes Tentaculaires* had constructed *Orbi et Urbi* around the movement, sounds, lights, and vices of the city. For the Belgian poet the city was like an octopus with grasping tentacles sucking humanity's blood; for Bryusov it was a dragon "enmeshed in a wiry net of brick, steel and glass" waiting for its prey. The poems in this collection seem to throb to the industrial urban beat or capture in the lilting accents of a folk song the mood of a factory crowd. Thematically, the cycle of poems in *Stephanos* evokes the classical world of myth and legend and is more interesting. There is hardly any trace of the musicality and suggestiveness of an inner reality that Bryusov attempted to bring into his earlier verses when he was absorbing the work of the contemporary French poets. Rather, his mature style recalls the chiselled stanzas of Gautier, or Leconte de Lisle, or Pushkin. Bryusov wrote verse after verse in traditional meter consisting of massive and sonorous lines, encrusted with the rhetoric of big words. He produces an effect at once gorgeous and solemn but also cumulatively monotonous and chillingly deliberate. This may not be poetry, but it is an impressive demonstration of literary craftsmanship. Bryusov adopted symbolism as a literary method to express sensations and moods. The poet that he willed himself to be was to live in such a way as to engender this method as often as possible, that is, to subject himself to the maximum number of emotions in order to transpose them into poetic form. Hence life is for art's sake; that is, basically, you should watch yourself live, and these telling lines from Bryusov's much-quoted advice "To the Poet" (1907) confirm his artistic formula: "Impassively view all" and "In the moment of love embraces, free yourself to remain unmoved." This may explain in part why the many erotically charged love passages convey no more than a sense of cold impersonal sensuality despite the fact that Bryusov, who had had passionate and unhappy love affairs, must have drawn on his personal intimate emotional experience to compose them.

Predictably, Bryusov's verse writing (that continued until 1917) was gradually reduced to sterile, laboriously polished exercises. In 1910, when his reputation as a poet had declined considerably, he addressed one of his most simple and poignant lyrics to his poet's soul that was "a withering flower and like a large sea fish was cast out on the burning sand" about to die. But his prodigious industry as critic, aesthetic pundit, translator, and editor went on unabated. He tried writing fiction, several stories and two novels (*The Fiery Angel*, 1908, and *The Altar of Victory*, 1912, the latter action packed, laced with horror episodes of every kind of perversity) probably to frazzle Philistine nerves, recounted in sober and objective prose. The historical backgrounds are variously set in Rome of the fourth century A.D., the Italian Renaissance, and Luther's Germany. The scenes are powerfully reproduced, animated by the colorful and authentic detail of the inspired scholar. Particularly fine is the description of medieval sorcery and the witch trial in the *Fiery Angel*, the most successfully sustained and executed prose work. The most important episode recalls the unsavory ménage à trois entanglement that severed Bryusov's friendship with Bely.

The mainsprings of Bryusov's intellectual being were scholarly rather than creative, and his main passion was books. He was at home in most domains and periods of Western humanism *humanis*, with a solid knowledge of the philosophy, religions, and lore of preclassical antiquity. He did contribute greatly to raising the cultural level of creative and critical literature of the age. Gorky called him the most cultured man in Russia.

Of the writers of his generation Bryusov was one of the very few who immediately and eagerly espoused the Bolshevik cause in 1917. Had this apolitical and asocial man of letters been hostile to the czarist regime as one of his best known poems, "The Coming of the Huns," seems to indicate? It was a prophecy of the destruction of civilization by invading Eastern hordes that would free the enslaved peoples who in their gratitude and joy would burn the books of former masters—and the poem ends with a hosanna and hymn to the Huns. Bryusov may have hoped to reassume his position of leader on the basis of his numerous writings and his former prestige, this time among the proletarian literati. He did obtain a small government job but remained practically unnoticed by the rulers of the new order. At fifty-one, he died a lonely and embittered man. Until the end, he went on writing highly technical articles on the structure of poetry, metrical innovations, and the evaluation of the uses of poetic language.

BALMONT (1867-1943)

"I have broken through the glass of sound," wrote Konstantin Balmont, summing up in this terse, immodest phrase his unequaled gift for creating verbal music from an extraordinary manipulation of assonance, alliteration, vibrant consonant clusters, richness of rhythm, and a variety of rhymes that pressed new vocal patterns onto the Russian tongue.

Like all the Decadents, Balmont explored in his poetry the sensations of sin, sexual excess, neurotic sensuality (Nero's wish for buildings to burn, a conquistador's yearning to see the blood spurt from an enemy's breast) and plunged alternately into depths of passion or dallied in shoals of sentimentality, espoused an ardent faith or professed nihilism, exuded life-hatred or life-love.

His life teetered between extremes as well. At seventeen, the ideal of universal happiness transported his entire being to immeasurable heights, as recorded in his autobiography. Five years later he attempted suicide. As an ardent supporter of modernism and Bryusov's literary comrade-in-arms, he engaged in sharp polemic with the reactionary press. Meanwhile he developed his art in successive collections of poetry (*Under the Northern Sky*, 1884, *In the Boundless*, 1895, *Stillness*, 1898) and a series (*Houses on Fire*, 1900, *Love Only*, 1903, and *Let Us Live Like the Sun*, 1903), that brought him wide acclaim. All over Russia he became known as "The Poet" to crowded lecture halls, where now arrogant, now spontaneous, and engagingly childlike, this short, violently gesticulating man with a mane of red hair, dramatically recited his sonorous verses. Youth worshipped him. The events of the explosive year of 1905 turned him into a revolutionary. He wrote one fiercely anti-czarist book of poetry in Paris, but politics could not sustain this aesthete. He next looked for new experiences in travels to Mexico, to South Africa, and the Pacific Islands. After the Bolshevik revolution, he settled in France, endured great hardship during the Nazi occupation, and, after a long illness, died in a mental institution.

Balmont's best poetry borrows little from prevailing Decadent trends. In *Let Us Be Like the Sun* he disavows the fashionable pessimism of the avant-garde with exuberant images of color movement and sound. The hypnotic effect of these poems is doubly powerful: It dazzles in a display of verbal fireworks that is melodious and structurally taut. He notes, with the uninhibited, exultant poet's wonder, the power and beauty of such diverse phenomena as a snowflake, the amethyst-hued torso of a python, a sleeping girl's smile, the roar of the sea wind. For the life of the elements in northern and southern climates—waters, wind, sky, the cosmic spiraling of the sun with its heat and light—Balmont reserves his deservedly most celebrated lines. There is a diaphonous quality about them, they seem irreal, edged with cosmic mystery, probably not unlike an astronaut's first impression of outer space. To attempt to analyze them is like trying to cut through a cobweb with a blunt knife.

The very prodigality of Balmont's production led to his creative undoing. Bryusov first criticized his "frivolous garrulousness," and the poet admitted with disarming candor in the well-known "How I Write Verses" (1905) that lines came to him unbidden; words effortlessly guided him along and suddenly the stanza, which he did not compose, took on life. Balmont shared this verse-spinning facility with Pushkin. Pushkin, however, recognized the danger of such virtuosity and discarded much of what came to his pen. Balmont, in contrast, was unrestrained by critical awareness and happily surrendered to verbal acrobatics even when he had nothing to say.

By 1914, he had a host of imitators but was little read. He was best known at home, and by the 1920s in émigré circles, for his literary translations. These include Calderon's theatre, numerous poems from antiquity in living and dead languages, and folk poetry that comprise two thick anthologies, Walt Whitman's *Leaves of Grass,* all of Edgar Allen Poe, Hoffmann's stories, Ibsen's plays, a large selection of modern Bulgarian,

Lithuanian, and Polish poetry, and innumerable translations of Western poets (Shelley, Wordsworth, Byron, Oscar Wilde, Swinburne, Leopardi, Baudelaire, Rosetti, Coleridge, Goethe, and Heine). For the sheer bulk and variety of foreign authors introduced into Russia, Balmont surpasses Bryusov and is comparable to Zhukovsky and Pasternak in bringing about a heightened and more cosmopolitan awareness among his compatriots of international literary movements and changes in creative expression and artistic tastes.

Zhukovsky's translations, however, suffused as they were with the essence of the romantic spirit, were judged by a number of critics to be superior to the English and German originals and Pasternak's total mastery of the iambic pentameter and rich verbal texture appear to Soviet audiences today, to equal Shakespeare's art. Not so for Balmont who remained faithful to himself. "Balmontism" so labelled by the Russian critic, Chizhevsky, permeates the translations. They are delightful and refreshingly replete with melodic sounds and unexpected movements. However, he was careless, occasionally feeling his way to solid meanings, as in Shelley's *Skylark* and *To Night*, but failing to grasp the inner vision of the English poet. He was more successful with works that had some kinship to his own, as for example in transmitting Whitman's rhythms that celebrate the life force surging through his own poems to the sun or in the rendition of Swinburne's effortless musical flow that also distinguishes major portions of Balmont's poetry.

SOLOGUB (1863-1927)

In the work of this greatly talented neo-romantic poet-novelist, the Decadent movement found its absolute expression.

Sologub was mainly concerned with struggle in his poetry, a struggle against the human God's universe that is as evil as its creator, and the sun that perpetuates its life. He warns against the deceptive lures in that life of matter and desire that mishape and make trivial the poet's dream. Finally, the need emerges to construct a refuge from modern men who, for Sologub, were but living corpses. He fled into the vision of a kind of subsphere, between life and death, peopled by witches, devils, and other monsters, where the poet becomes a sorcerer to work his spells on the lower creatures and attained self-divinization—the summit of subjectivity and individualism to which the new poets aspired. Sologub's underworld, that was for him the only habitable one, is controlled by Satan whom once he called The Father in opposition to the evil of men; it is complicated by the ambiguity of the demonic forces. At times they are benign and even submissive to the poet's will, elsewhere they symbolize human sordidness, vulgarity, and vice. One is reminded of Gogol's devils that wreak spiritual devastation upon mankind. But Sologub lacks the magic of Gogolian grotesque. Sologub's depiction of the human condition remains unrelievedly petty, cruel, ugly, and dull, indeed, closely resembling the existence of the provincial schoolmaster whose frustrations, nursed in quiet despair, bear an unmistakable autobiographical imprint, and were portrayed in Sologub's first novel, *Uneasy Dreams*, 1896.

Feodor Sologub, born in Petersburg as Feodor Teternikov, was the only commoner among the writers of his generation. His father, a shoemaker, died young, and his peasant mother became a chambermaid, whose masters helped the boy to complete his studies at a teacher's institute that secured him a post in a small town school. For over twenty-five years he eked out a penurious and obscure existence. The morbid and perverse complexes he developed as a result of hiding his haughty and passionate spirit behind the facade of a self-effacing, bespectabled provincial pedagogue, led him to explore a negativity that fertilized his art and to find creativity in violence.

In 1896, his first three works were published: a collection of poems, some stories with a few lyrics, called *Shadows*, and *Uneasy Dreams*. In 1904 he brought out another volume of *Collected Poems*, followed by his best-known verse in *The Circle of Fire*, 1908 and *Pearly Stars*, 1913. These poems stake out the distance between the ideal of the Good, the Calm, and the Beautiful that the poet may find only within himself and the pressing external evil, abhorrent yet fascinating, that is the real master serviced on all sides in grotesque, cruel, perverse, and erotic images. The only outer beauty is that of the human form, now platonically idealized, now sensuously suggested in voluptuous lines that rival Bryusov and which possibly were inspired by Baudelaire. The fashionable longing for death—a theme that commands some of the finest lyrics—is handled with extreme sobriety and persuasively integrated into Sologub's philosophy in which the purity of the hatreds expressed equals the classical purity of the poetic form. The line is gracefully even, flowing easily to traditional meter, and the vocabulary is reticent and clear. In a rare reference to his own art, Sologub wrote in the poem "Amphora" of the splendid vase carried carefully upright on a slave's shoulder, so that no drop of the poisonous liquid that it contains, would be spilled.

The nihilistic poison that had been served in small doses of elegant verse is generously splashed across the pages of *A Petty Devil*, a novel that brought instant acclaim to the poet in 1907 and established his reputation as a writer of fiction. It had taken ten years to complete; it was rejected by publishers for another five. Its success, when it was finally published, allowed Sologub to resign from the school inspector's job he had held since 1912 and devote himself to writing.

A Petty Devil is a hallucinating, obsession-driven story. The external reality is that of a low-level provincial town, commonly vulgar, bored, slothful, and petty minded. It is obviously modelled on the "society-out-of-joint" in Dostoevsky's *Devils*, and dominated by the figure of Peredonov, a schoolteacher who covets a promotion and uses and abuses his entire entourage to obtain it.

There are few heroes in fiction to equal him in brutishness and meanness of spirit. He is like Feodor Karamazov in his constant exhibitions of crudity and reminds one of Saltykov-Shchedrin's Yudushka in his leaden insensibility to others. He excels in wanton and arbitrary viciousness: tormenting his pupils with no provocation, leaving his room systematically befouled, spitting at his mistress, soiling and pulling off wall paper, sending besmirching anonymous letters about friends, and stealing food from the kitchen to show up the cook as thief.

Sologub uses his words, in *A Petty Devil*, as symbols of gesture to indicate the novel's intent. The outrages on the norm of behavior that shocked and excited Sologub's readers as evidence of the moral filth in which Peredonov seemed to wallow become the more forceful and credible as he gradually succumbs to his diseased psyche, bloated with the complex of insecurity and paranonia. He feels threatened on all sides, gouges out the eyes of the kings and queens on playing cards because they seem to laugh at him. He paints a huge red P all over his body that would identify him if he were kidnapped, and loses hold on reality in hallucinations that release the stuff of nightmares not the least of which is a small, gray female being, Nedotymka (the Untouchable One), who slips in and out of his vision, until in a fit of madness, he kills his best friend.

Peredonovism has entered Russian to indicate moral disease, but Sologub was not done. He needed yet another form of wickedness to round out his concept of a universe from which human qualities are banished. In apparent contrast to the crushing horror of the main plot, a love affair is started between young Sasha and the slightly older beautiful Ludmilla that would appear idyllic if it were not for her sly seduction of the boy. The author lingers over scenes suffused with wanton sensuality and an adoration of flesh with a leitmotif of voyeurism and transvestism that match in perversion and a certain heartless passion Peredonov's spiritual blight. This is another way of recreating the real world as it exists in the poet's understanding of it and that is the object of his loathing.

The most ambitious and longest work is a trilogy of novels written between 1908 and 1912. *Drops of Blood* centers on the activities of a retired chemist and poet Trirodov who is endowed with supernatural powers and becomes a revolutionary in 1905. Black-magic rites in his country home alternate with horror scenes of torture and pillage when the rebellion is stamped out. In *Queen Ortruda* we are transported to an imaginary kingdom on a volcanic island where the queen and her consort are kept busy with political intrigues and erotic happenings in a secret cavern until the volcano erupts killing the queen. This event may be a symbolic prophecy of the Russian monarchy's demise or a symbol of sexual orgasm, the revolution and death. The author links *Smoke and Ash* and *Queen Ortruda* by setting them on the same island. Trirodov leaves Russia to take over the vacant throne and arrives in a spaceship with promises to build a new world. The trilogy's title "A Legend in the Making" is apt. With this bewildering amalgam of legend, political beliefs, poetic visions of rare beauty, and pieces of realistic and science fiction, Sologub is trying to create, so he announces in his preface, "sweet legend" out of coarse reality. But nothing quite holds together. On a primary level, the fiction would appeal for the interest of the many dramatic, action-filled episodes. But the clear-cut symbols are unrelated, and, on the whole, the work lacks unity and ultimate meaning.

Sologub's last years were darkened by his rejection of the new regime and the difficulties of obtaining an exit visa that led his wife to suicide. Her body was not recovered from the Neva until the spring thaw. He died a few years later, in poverty and isolation.

GIPPIUS (1867-1945)

Between 1905 and 1917 poet-critic Zinaida Gippius (equally well-known as the wife and intellectual partner of poet-novelist-moralist, Dmitri Merezhkovsky) held sway over the modernist elite that on Thursdays gathered in her St. Petersburg salon. Not a few among them were at some time in love with the vivid and beautiful green-eyed and flaming-haired hostess, and everyone was fascinated by her coruscating intelligence that took upon itself to wrestle with all major mind-stirring issues of the day. This cerebral quality, that was also laced with a mordant and subtle wit, admirably equipped Zinaida Gippius as a sophisticated and exciting commentator on the age. She did so in literary and social critiques and psychological portraits that aimed occasional venom at well-known personalities such as Blok, Bryusov, Bely, and Rozanov under the name of Anton Krayni (Anton the Extreme). These essays were collected and published in two volumes in Paris in 1925, where the rabidly anti-Bolshevik Merezhkovskys settled after the Revolution. Two novels (*The Devil's Doll*, 1911, and *Roman-Tsarevich*, 1914) are complex studies of character under political stress. The earlier one is drawn for theme and mood from *The Devils* by Dostoevsky. However, it is flawed by a predilection for abstract analysis where ideas are rigorously and compelling projected but individuals do not come alive.

The poetry, however, is of a high artistic order and the successive influences that were at work on it are of great interest. For at least one critic, Vladimir Markov, Zinaida Gippius should be ranked as the greatest religious poet of Russia, although her poetic output is placed among the Decadents. As we read the poems—minor masterpieces of tautly metered and disciplined lines—we realize that she is both and neither, that the poetry represents the moment of transition between the Decadent movement and the later symbolists who were to follow. The fashionable Nietzschean refrain of singularity and the theme of withdrawal from the detestable external world, beloved by all the poets of the nineties, informs her verses of those years. By 1903, Dmitri Merezhkovsky's general revolt against materialistic and utilitarian concepts had crystallized into a religious messianism. The Merezhkovskys became luminaries of a new religio-philosophical circle where Zinaida, espousing her husband's creed, played the part of both sorcerer and apprentice, and her poetry began to reflect the new metaphysical direction. The poet's self-imposed solitude now becomes an abyss, an emptiness, a grave; she is concerned for her deadened, coarse-skinned, hideous soul that like a snake (a favorite symbol) is coiled around its own vacuum, and there is the urgency to learn to know and love God. The expression of spiritual search, for the most part, does not equal in potency and verve the picric utterances of chronicled despair. The latter contain rich verbal rewards in a choice of unsavoury epithets emitting with startling precision the viscousness, foulness, and crassness of quotidian existence or they dazzle with brilliant epigrammatic forays into descriptions of satanic lures. What is lacking, finally, is feeling. Sologub's overpowering hatreds are reduced to impersonally calculated effects. The mind alone seems to be at work in the invention and refinement of suitable symbols and devices. One such is the image of the circle that with studied repetitiveness is used to represent in metaphysical poems the divine orb and the eternal life while in others it suggests that of demonic forces that surround and imprison the human spirit.

AESTHETES VERSUS MYSTICS: THE SYMBOLISTS

The cleavage between the higher and lower world and the poet's failure to find his bearings in either one that haunts the poetry of Zinaida Gippius is at the core of the Decadent outlook. It incorporates and responds to yet another "uprooted and homeless" leitmotif, cast in the dynamics of Russian history. Almost to a man, the most sophisticated and cultivated avant-garde belonged to the class of the landed gentry that was facing extinction. The sense of impending catastrophe mingled with visions of another, higher culture that will be built on their ashes pervades their writings and gives them a peculiarly vibrant and paradoxical character. There is tragic urgency in the dialectic that, on the one hand, advocated Nietzschean narcissism, dark descent into Self and the Western European preoccupation with new aesthetic forms and, on the other hand, grappled with spiritual questions of ultimate universal import that would lead to a new reality in spectacular intellectual debate between aesthetes and mystics, critics, philosophers, novelists, and poets.

Among them, critic Dmitri Merezhkovsky (1866-1941), essayist Vasily Rozanov (1856-1919), and Vladimir Solovyov, philosopher (1853-1900), must be singled out as the most articulate and persuasive spokesmen for a religio-philosophic world view that made a deep imprint on the younger symbolist poets. There was a shift in perspective from Western-inspired aesthetics to a metaphysical probe into man-God relationships that in Russia had stemmed from Slavophile doctrines, and which Dostoevsky had imaginatively projected and transformed. There was a veritable cult of the great writer at the start of the century. Solovyov, whom Dostoevsky had known as a young man and had cast as Alesha Karamazov, had launched it with *Three Addresses in Commemoration of Dostoevsky* (1881-1883). Rozanov had contributed to an understanding of Dostoevsky's philosophy with probably the most astute comment to date on *The Legend of the Grand Inquisitor* (1891) and Merezhkovsky's *Tolstoy and Dostoevsky* (1901) that posited the two truth-tellers as irreconcilable opposites, Tolstoy as "seer of the flesh," and Dostoevsky as "seer of the spirit," was instantly successful and is still widely read.

This Hegelian pursuit of antinomies became Merezhkovsky's formula in his major work. Messianic religious beliefs, centered on the coming third and last world of the triumphant Holy Ghost, are concerned with pagan and Christian faith in his many extremely popular historical novels. In them, pagan antiquity is pitted against the Christian faith (*Julian the Apostate,*

1896). Leonardo da Vinci, in a novel of the same name (1896), wavers in his art between Christian and pagan inspiration. In eighteenth-century Russia power-intoxicated Peter the Great confronts his deeply Orthodox son, Alexis in *(Peter and Alexis* (1902). All these are versions of the Christ-Anti-Christ drama that shapes Merezhkovsky's vision of mankind. As works of art, the novels are inferior to those of Bryusov, although they are informative on the period and seem to summarize the author's extensive readings. There is little attempt made, however, to animate the action or flesh out the characters; they move about like costumed abstractions. The learned glitter of generalities in the many philosophical prose works, and in essays on Gogol, Nekrasov, Tyutchev, and Lermontov fascinated his contemporaries. The disarmingly simple explanations of a world of consistently interconnected poles appeared less a flirtation with intellectual irresponsibility than valid answers to the "accursed" questions. Half-hidden in a deep armchair, puny Merezhkovsky would propound his favorite theory in an unexpectedly strong and warm voice at meetings of the Religious-Philosophical Society that he had organized with his wife in 1903. It became the center of the "Godseeking" intelligentsia. Merezhkovsky also founded the prestigious *New Paths* journal where such prominent writers as Blok, Bely, Bryusov, and Rozanov were brought together with members of the more enlightened Orthodox clergy to discuss the burning religious issues of the day.

Although Vasily Rozanov yields points to Merezhkovsky's social prominence and writing productivity, he was by far the more serious and talented writer. His collections of essays *(Around the Walls of the Temple,* 1906, *The Dark Face,* 1911, and *Moonlight Men,* 1913) first appeared as articles in the daily press. They revolved around his lifelong love-hate relationship with the Orthodox Church.

Rozanov was a profound believer who understood the essence of dogma and thrilled to the beauty of ritual. He abhorred the ascetic monkish ideal of sterile sadness and suffering imprinted on the cowled "dark face" that dims God's world and denies man's natural rights to the happiness of sex, family, and procreation. In intensely subjective and naked language, trenchant and provocative with startling paradox, Rozanov exalts warm, fecund flesh that he finds in primitive religions and in the Old Testament. It appears to be a link to God since it is the root of the spirit. He celebrates the open enjoyment of sex that brought him acclaim from the Decadents. Outwardly staid, extremely conservative in politics, and a respected parishioner, he seemed to live in his writing on the knife edge of personal obsessions. Nowhere is this clearer than in his attack on the "unnatural" marriage conditions sanctioned by the church that tolerates illegitimacy and the difficulty of divorce. This recalls immediately his own unhappy experience with the "infernal" Paulina Suslova, Dostoevsky's ex-mistress. She left Rozanov after torturing him for three married years and refused a divorce to legalize his harmonious union with another who had to remain his unofficial wife.

Alone, among the religious thinkers of his day, Rozanov placed the total human personality at the center of his creed. His intuitive understanding of utterly human, vulnerable man was extraordinary, on a par with Dostoevsky's that, in another context, as one of the great writer's most sensitive critics, he was the first to discern and analyze.

It follows that in the last three and most notable works (*Solitaria*, 1912, *Fallen Leaves*, 1913, 1915, and *The Apocalypse of Our Times*, 1918) the supreme subjectivist would extol a return into the deep intimacy of self. It is an impressionistic flow, uninhibited and richly, emotionally sincere, of fragmented musings on art, writing, and religious misgivings, and, in the last book, his reactions to the Revolution that convey the texture and varying colorations of a powerful and original mind.

Vladimir Solovyov expressed a new spiritual awareness in a positivist, utilitarian-minded, nineteenth-century Russia. At the turn of the century, he dominated the religious revival of which he had been the apostle and the pioneer. Steeped in ancient and modern philosophy, widely travelled, and with broad European interests, he was the first Russian philosopher—in a professional sense—who had evolved a unified system of speculative thought. In articles, literary criticism, conferences, poetry, and lectures, in large halls all over the capital that his magnetic personality filled to overflowing, he continued to develop his metaphysical doctrine. He finally affirmed the ultimate union of heaven and earth that emanates from the mystical vision of a restoration of cosmic harmony to be realized in a total unity. The unity is God the Creator, and the multiplicity is nature that He had created. Man is the link between them, bearing within himself the two aspects of the divine and the creaturely. In God's great cosmic design for mankind, as Solovyov conceived it, man by his reason and also by his action, elevates earth to the heavens and by him also heaven must descend and fill the earth. This progression toward union may only be realized by the perfect functioning of the church, but this may not happen until all the churches unite into a solidarity of a collective theocracy that man will freely and joyfully join. He expounded and elucidated his views ceaselessly and unstintingly in a series of brilliant polemic tracts (*The God-Man*, 1881, *Religious Foundations of Life*, 1884, *Russia and the Universal Church*, 1889, and *Justification of Good*, 1897).

Solovyov argued for the collective good implicit in his tenet of mystical idealism that, he argued, was already integrated in the moral imperatives of the Russian populist tradition. His ecumenical plan for the first time in Russia freed a religious concept from Slavophile chauvinism. This gained him a large following among progressive groups, numbers of would-be-Marxists and Marxists, among them Nikolay Berdyayev (1874-1948), who became an important religious thinker. Berdyayev who had been attracted to the economic Marxist theories, wrote an article in 1898 giving primacy to spiritual and aesthetic values, collaborated with Merezhkovsky in *New Paths*, and later in exile authored several works on his evolution from Marxism to idealism that gained him international prominence.

Solovyov's monistic statement of faith and action turns away from the nihilism of the Decadents toward absolute good, where evil is nonexistent or transitory. The attainment of what he calls "Godmanhood" is to come through a peaceful evolution with the aid of Sophia, the incarnation of Divine Wisdom and the archetype of the Divine Feminine. The image of Sophia haunts Solovyov's poetry. In a repetitive transport of her name he invokes her as the embodiment of man's striving for one-ness and through her man is filled with a longing for union with God. The famous *Three Meetings* poem describes his mystical experience of three visitations from Sophia: She appeared before him when he was a nine-year-old boy at a church service, then thirteen years later in the British Museum, where he was studying occult literature, and the third time, when he was bidden to repair to the Egyptian desert.

The philosopher's transcendental postulates, that cut through historical theology to the essence of man's cosmic and divine potential, revitalized the more emancipated Russian clergy and also won the allegiance of numbers of agnostics to his kind of Christian humanism. His religio-philosophical approach made a profound impact on the symbolist movement. The younger generation of poets, spiritually parched by utilitarianism and the nihilistic narcissism of the Decadents, was yearning for fresh sources of emotional sustenance that would transmute externality and transpose it to a higher level of being.

This was the romantic dream of earlier, German idealistic philosophy that nourished the poetry of Lermontov, Tyutchev, and Fet. The modernists rediscovered it as the dual concept of the City of God and the City of Man that is interpreted by the poet in symbolical correspondences. But for Solovyov and all the symbolists who called him Master, the poet's penetration into the larger, hidden reality is that of an intermediary between the human and the divine; he communicates with the ideal archetypes of Truth and Beauty that reside outside the subjective illusion of human imagination and invests the creaturely world with reflections of them in pure and ardent images. Hence the cult of the Feminine, so cherished by Solovyov and his disciples, of the Heavenly Sophia who may be symbolized in an earthly, delicately sensuous feeling. Or it is a real woman who inspires a potentially divine love and stirs the poet's mystical sensibility to evoke the other, haloed object. The ecstasy of the nerves that assails Solovyov when he pursues these mystical, at times erotic, images finds its psychic counterpart in the ecstasy of prophetic revelations and invocation of supernatural forces that relate particular phenomena to the single principle from which they derive their being.

This interaction between divine and materal worlds became the instrument of higher purpose for the symbolist leaders, Alexander Blok, Andrei Bely, and Vyacheslav-Ivanov. And

Vyacheslav-Ivanov was inspired by Solovyov's ideas to formulate a coherent aesthetic of the movement.

VYACHESLAV IVANOV (1866-1949)

An aura of intellectual grandeur surrounds the work and personality of Vyacheslav Ivanov. He studied at the University of Berlin under the guidance of the renowned historian Theodore Mommsen, completed training in classical philology, and spent years abroad pursuing humanistic research. He spoke flawless Latin and Greek and moved assuredly, with the passkey of erudition, among the great writers of antiquity and such preferred companions as Dante, Goethe, and Nietzsche. He returned to Russia at thirty-seven, giving up a high-ranking professor's career for poetry and philosophy. He was discovered by the avant-garde poets when he published his first poetical work, *Pilot Stars* in 1903. A second collection, *Translucency* (1906), brought him to the forefront of the symbolist movement.

He became its grand hierophant from 1905 to 1911, presiding each Wednesday evening over large gatherings at his sixth-floor "Tower" apartment in St. Petersburg. All the modernist intellectuals met there to listen to his views on poetry and religion. They were mesmerized by the magnetic personality of the host who looked somewhat like a Biblical prophet and by his utterances on the mysteries of ancient rituals and the Dionysian cult which, according to Nietzsche, in its ecstasy and pain had initiated the birth of tragedy with its binary concepts of death and life, both equally regenerating. Vyacheslav Ivanov relied upon this tradition to transform the Christian symbolism of immortality after death into life on earth within the plenitude of life itself. A complex mythology emerged. Polarities met across the stretch of a mystical vision. With some oracular obscurity Vyacheslav Ivanov intended to confront multiplicity with unity, fire with water, Lucifer with Ahriman, Earth with the Sun. Andrei Bely recalls when the "Master" would weave for his fascinated public a "huge luminous cobweb with delicate threads that brought together everything that could not be united" and that constituted his world view. Put simply, his interpretation of the living cosmos, learnedly explicated in *The*

Hellenic Religion of the Suffering God (1904), *By The Stars* (1909), *The Testament of Symbolism* (1910), *Furrows and Boundaries* (1916), and in other collections of philosophical essays, is an attempt to fuse all the ancient and recent experiences of man, his sciences, knowledges, and intuitions into one non-analytic comprehension of the world. Again, as did Vladimir Solovyov, he draws his sources of strength from one syncretic religion.

All culture is an ascent toward God, from reality to the real reality, and it is the artist who illuminates the way by his intuitive knowledge of symbols in the external world that indicate and reflect the invisible, higher reality. This concept of the arts became the core tenet of the symbolist creed. Unsurprisingly, Solovyov designated poetry as "the incantatory magic of rhythmic speech, mediating between man and the world of divine things." For Vyacheslav Ivanov "mediating" is of the essence here and assumes a talismanic potency. The poet becomes the priest, the prophet, the announcer of the truth; his "mediation" is an awareness of the interconnection of all existing things and the meaning of every kind of life. But his poetic function is neither solipsistic nor subjectively creative. Rather it is a faithful and therefore realistic revelation of potential heavenly values and images on earth. The "autonomy of art" propagated by Bryusov and his fellow Decadents is rejected by the Russian symbolists, who derive their religious coloration from Tyutchev and Dostoevsky. The symbolists maintained, as well, that the artist was responsible for guiding others to a higher truth that enjoins poetry and religion and affirms the aesthetic convictions of Tolstoy.

The poetry of Vyacheslav Ivanov reflects, in its many mystical accents and ardent, imperatively intoned evocations of natural and spiritual forces, the theurgic aspiration of his art. A number of poems ecclesiastical in language and tone, bring to mind the fact that the author, who came from a family of priests on his mother's side, had as a boy learned all the church services by heart. The overall impression is one of great rhythmic sonority and verbal ornamentation. There is a dazzling variety of closed forms in examples of the Sapphic strophe, the *shloka*, the *terza rima,* some two hundred Petrarchian sonnets and the first instance of iambic pentameter in Russian. Each poem, of a symmetrically premeditated design, is impeccably and self-consciously structured, and extraordinarily rich in language and style. Unprecedented similes and uncommon vocabulary vie for attention with an abundance of archaisms, Greek idioms, and classical allusions that had not appeared in Russia since the brilliant neoclassical odes of eighteenth-century Derzhavin. He was nicknamed Vyacheslav the Magnificent and with cause. But need the overwhelming scholarship have been so much in evidence? This is particularly true of the collections *Eros* (1907) and *Cor Ardens* (1911). *Cor Ardens* also contained some of his purest and most poignant lyrics, occasioned by the death of his wife, in which he expresses his belief in the soul's reincarnation.

An impressive recording of the revolutionary years appeared in the powerful, dirge-like poetry of *Winter Sonnets* (1919). This depicts the national cataclysm in terms of cold and starvation that threaten intellectual survival. Ivanov more searingly expressed his disaccord with his century in the six letters that he sent across a hospital ward of a rest home to the liberal critic and cultural historian, Mikhail Gershenzon (1869-1928). This famous exchange of opinion on the revolution was entitled *A Correspondence from One Corner to Another* (1921). To Gershenzon's approval of Russia's rejection of "oppressive transcendental speculations" of the past Ivanov answered with a strong defense of the Absolute and Western humanism that perpetuated spiritual and moral values. In 1924, he settled in Italy. Two years later, in a cycle of poems, *Roman Sonnets,* that are suffused with the beauty of Rome, the impassioned apologist of a universal religion, describes poetically his conversion to Catholicism.

BELY (1880-1934)

The experience of the symbolist movement with the excesses that imperiled it, is reflected in the work of Andrei Bely, its most restless and exciting creative spirit. He was almost too richly endowed with a limitless potential for absorption and learning, too uncritically open to new influences and counter-influences, that were eclectically put to use in his writings. His impassioned search for ultimate meanings finally splintered in his poet's failure to create a habitable spiritual world.

A difficult childhood: born Boris Bugaev (pen name Andrei Bely) to an eminent mathematician, Moscow University Dean of Faculty, physically ungainly and extremely brilliant and to an emotionally unstable, beautiful socialite, thirty years her husband's junior. The hypersensitive boy was caught in a constant feud between the two parents who could not agree on his upbringing. The mother protected him from the "ugly" bookish professor's influence with a ban on almost all reading matter that extended, when he was already at prep school and drawn to science, to works on zoology, anthropology, and mathematics that filled his father's study. By chance, he walked into the Ostrovsky library to while away a boring hour. The very first books he saw—some Ibsen dramas—lost him to the world on that day and for fifty successive days when he devoured Hauptmann, Sudermann, Dostoevsky, Turgenev, Goncharov, Goethe's *Faust*, Hegel's *Aesthetics*, Nadson, Pushkin, Nekrasov, Fet, Sologub, Gippius, and Bunin. Like a child that, imprisoned since infancy within monastery walls, one morning climbs up a tall tree and sees for the first time with wonder and awe the limitless expanse of the world outside, so was young Boris shaken by the intellectual wealth that he had suddenly come upon. Like a recurring fever it addicted him to extreme and volatile enthusiasms.

First among them and most personal was Vladimir Solovyov's mystical doctrine that was reverently studied in the household of Michael Solovyov, the philosopher's brother who lived in the apartment below the Bugaevs and who had befriended Boris. His son, Sergei, became Boris's constant companion and both young men lived in an ecstatic expectation of Sophia's presence among them. This is the major theme of Bely's earliest prose poem, *Dramatic Symphony* (1902) and in a collection of lyrics, *Gold in Azure* (1904). It is the coming of the Divine Feminine Vision that is signaled and celebrated in a burst of magnificent colors. To sustain this mystical belief proved impossible for a young writer who had spent eight university years studying natural sciences that called for rational evidence. Thus, it is the post-realist Nekrasov who serves as a model in the next collection, *Ashes* (1909) where wretched, beggarly, peasant Russia is now cursed, now pitied by the wrathful poet who beseeches his motherland, out of his anguish for her destiny, to disappear into space. In 1917, when Bely was embracing the advent of the Revolution as the renewal of faith and hope, he changed the plea for Russia's disappearance to a blessed recognition of its Messianic force. In *The Urn* (1909) Bely uses a quiet, reflective tone to ruminate on neo-Kantian metaphysics. It is the last volume of poetry until the two justly memorable post-Revolution poems, *Christ is Risen* (1918) and *First Meeting* (1921). The former was composed under the influence of the scythian messianism of Ivanov-Razumnik, a leftwing member of the Social Revolutionary party that had joined the Bolsheviks and who prophesied Russia's imminent return to her ancient Slavic traditions. The poem is a symbolical identification of the Revolution with Christ's teachings. The second poem is reminiscent of Vladimir Solovyov's *Three Meetings* in its delightful interplay of seriousness and humor; it is a backward glance at the author's early spiritual and cultural encounters. It is also a brilliant final display of the remarkably interesting stylistic innovations that give to a page of Bely's prose or poetry an instant impression of power, exciting intricacy, and originality.

Like Blok, like Balmont, Andrei Bely believed music to be the dominating sister art. But he went further than they by modelling his very first prose poems, entitled "symphonies" on the theory of musical composition, and written with phonetic and rhythmic sounds. The four "symphonies" treat, respectively, an eschatological vision of Sophia, the world's destruction brought about by grave diggers, satirically perceived as the "decadent" Ibsen, Huysmans, Oscar Wilde, Maeterlinck and Nietzsche, occult themes, and in the last, *Goblet of Blizzards*, a whirlwind of personal despair (Bely's hopeless love for the unattainable Lyubov Blok, the poet's wife) is merged with the fury of a Russian winter storm.

In the poetry it becomes even clearer that the Wagnerian dictum of the unity of word and music is operative, as it was for other symbolists. Seemingly hypnotized by the tremendous unexplored potential of the Russian language, Bely vitalizes it with vibrant, startling neologisms and practically invents a new inner pace for successive stanzas with slower and accelerated meters, alternating consonances and assonances, and irregular rhyme breaks.

No one understood better than he that the new immaterial images required new poetic forms. In numerous articles, later collected in *Symbolism* (1910), Bely expounded his structural techniques, stressed the occult power of the word freed of its conventional meanings, suggested new combinations of verbal and sound patterns. His theories were adopted by the Futurists and greatly influenced later Soviet poets.

Although Andrei Bely is primarily known as a poet, it is for his trilogy of novels *(Silver Dove,* 1909, *Petersburg,* 1903, *Kotik Letayev,* 1915, and published in 1917) that he will be remembered, as well as for the magnificently rewarding memoir, *Recollections of Alexander Blok* (1922-1923), a portrayal, simply and subjectively written, of the fascinating personalities that created the Silver Age.

When *The Silver Dove* was published in *The Scales* it made a great stir in symbolist circles. Bely demonstrated his virtuosity with language again in the ornate descriptions of the Russian countryside. He also depicts nature's shifts of mood in a tone of sustained ecstasy that recalls the uplifted rhetoric of passages in *Dead Souls.* Elsewhere, a Gogolian blend of the extravagantly unreal and the homespun mitigates, in the manner of the great satirist, the Gothic buildup of sexual orgies that take place in a remote Russian village. The hero, Darlyansky, a student of Greek antiquity, comes to it to visit his fiancée. But he also has a social conscience and courts the villagers. He becomes attracted to sensuous, pock-marked Matrena, the local carpenter's wife, works in his shop, and through them is drawn into "The Doves," a peasant sect of sex-worshippers. At first their practices appear to him not unlike the Eleusinian mysteries, but the crudities of the sadistic and masochistic debauchery finally sicken him. Profoundly disturbed by the "darkly Asiatic" character of the revels, he attempts to flee. Fearing his betrayal, the "Doves" kill him, wrap his corpse in bast mats, and bury it in a vegetable patch.

Bely is concerned with the timely "East or West" theme in *The Silver Dove.* After the disastrous Japanese war of 1905, the spector of advancing Asia haunted many Russians. Bely also seemed particularly obsessed by the postwar tide of peasant revolts that for him signaled the collapse of the Empire, that is, of order and culture, and the surfacing of a diabolical force from within the masses that was not European nor pagan but profoundly Asiatic and, to Bely, Mongolian.

Petersburg stands at the center of the triptych. It is one of the most powerful novels of the twentieth century and the most wildly original one. The whole heraldry of Bely's imaginative behavior blazons this extravaganza of irreality. Peter's city has perished under the burden of its political and social past. It is but a mythical deformation of itself, an abstraction of geometrical streets and squares crossed and recrossed by phantom carriages and figures that only exist in the consciousness of its inhabitants. Against the background of spectral Petersburg, Bely constructs an oneirical scenario of chaos and disorder in a gripping sequence of illogical and incredible events that harrowingly blur into the hallucinations and dreams within dreams of the characters caught in revolutionary terrorism and near parricide. The party has ordered one of its young members, Nikolay Ableukhov, to kill his father, a conservative, high-ranking government functionary. Suspense builds up in an atmosphere taut with impending crisis as Bely burrows into the son's mind, racked with decisions and counter-decisions, while the time bomb somewhat absurdly placed into a sardine box, ticks away in his desk drawer. The ticking disturbs the older man's sleep and the situation resolves into Gogolian grotesque when it harmlessly goes off in an empty room where the father had placed it.

That Bely had planned *Petersburg* thematically as a sequel to his first novel becomes clear through the Ableukhov surname that is of Tartar origin. It carries the burden of Bely's dark forebodings about Russia's future. Seemingly opposed, father and son are in fact unconscious allies. At the crossroads of revolution and Mongolian anarchy (the father's Europeanization was only superficially superimposed as was that of the city now returned to its original marshland of "mists, moss, mess"), they represent together the roots of Russian nihilism. Dudkin, the party leader and the most delineated character in the novel, conveys this in his thirst for death and his wish "to reduce everything to nothingness, to zero."

In 1914, Bely's interest in the occult took him to Dornach, Switzerland where he settled in a community directed by Rudolph Steiner, founder of anthroposophy. He became immersed in this doctrine, which taught that, through practice, a gradual disembodiment of personality could be achieved, so that the soul, freed of the interference of the senses, could attain to the truth. At this time he also was composing *Kotik Letayev*.

Drawn from the author's immense store of childhood memories, *Kotik Letayev* is a portrayal of subjective experience that traces the growth of consciousness in a child between the ages of three and five. Based on the mystic belief that a newborn spirit is a reborn spirit, the work starts with a memory of prenatal life that develops on the level of real existence and in that of the "spheres." Although the analogy of a world soul and a child's within an anthroposophical framework is at times unwieldy, Kotic's earliest factual cognitions are masterfully conveyed as a process that crystallizes hazy, confused swarms into orderly, circumscribed shapes. With the child's increasing awareness of objects and situations and distinctions between various modes of being, the greatest problem for the writer to overcome was the narrator's adult speech. Bely's extraordinary penetration into language and the uses to which he could put it are brilliantly demonstrated in his invention of new techniques and even a new vocabulary to credibly express a child's imprecise and halting perceptions. Every conceivable aspect of the word comes into play—sound, rhythm, detonation, morphology—as Bely "melts" words down to "the fluidity of movement, gesticulation, mimicry" to give it the child's meaning. Preceding Proust and Joyce, *Kotik Letayev* is a unique psychological novel in Russian literature that pioneered the evolution of intellect and perception.

BLOK (1880-1921)

Alexander Blok leads and culminates the poetic revival of the Silver Age. His lyrical art, in the romantic tradition of Novalis, Keats, and Lermontov, is that of a poet who interprets human experience through a subjective vision and intuition and turns inward to create an unattainable ideal that is revealed to him in earthly images which drive him alternately to ecstasy or despair. His solitary life ends tragically in a world that he no longer finds habitable.

Blok fulfilled this conception perfectly even in his looks (tall, slender, with a face like an Adonis, and a grave manner) and his family background in that they encouraged him to become a poet. His father, a jurist, taught public law at Warsaw University, had a brilliant but unbalanced mind. He was divorced early by Blok's mother, daughter of a University of St. Petersburg Rector and well-known botanist, Beketov. She brought her three-year-old son back home into an affectionate and highly cultivated family of a mother and sisters. Two of them were translators, and all were accomplished linguists and enlightened readers of world classics. From his aunts young Alexander first learned the beauty and importance of the "word." His somewhat exalted mother shared the intellectual explorations of the moody, high-strung, extremely intelligent boy who only tolerated school as a perfunctory exercise and was happiest during the summers at Shakhmatovo, the family estate near Moscow. There he learned to ride, took solitary walks across the fragrant fields and in the deep woods that were to landscape much of his early poetry, and spent long evenings under the ancient lilacs in conversations about life and literature with his relatives and vacationing friends of the neighborhood, among them the family of the famous chemist, Mendeleev.

At eighteen, he fell in love with their young daughter, Lyubov. Seemingly, it was a boy and girl affair between two strikingly good looking and talented young people (both showed histrionic ability in staging amateur theatricals and later Lyubov became a professional actress). For Blok it was also an awakening of his poetic imagination. During the years of his courtship, between 1898 and 1903, he composed some eight hundred poems of which ninety-three appeared as *Verses to a Beautiful Lady* (1904). They comprise his happiest and most profound mystical experience. All the poems are reverent, ecstatic, humble, contemplative, and self-doubting. They are addressed to a supernatural Feminine Being from Beyond, whose presence the poet actually feels. She appears to him now distant, now near, veiled in mists, golden haloed on a garden path, or dimly outlined against a house window in images that flicker, gleam, and dissolve into shadows. He projects this symbol of the invisible world made visible and concrete to him and abandons himself to it in seemingly effortless, extraordinarily musical verse.

Music for Blok, possibly the world's most auditif poet, was the creative principle of life, an inexhaustible spiritual and organic force that caught the movement of the universe in timeless rhythm and discordant orchestration. Like Shelley who could not carry a tune, he responded to music with an inner and varying exaltation. Slighting formal versification techniques, he would depend on a sort of continuous song within him to create primarily musical symbols. This produced a text, frequently obscure, but sonorously dazzling in a kind of magical fusion of cadence, rhyme, intonation.

Blok wrote about his poetry that it was from the beginning an intimate lyrical diary, and it is this intensely personal creative expression that sets him apart from the other symbolists. Vyacheslav Ivanov was more intellectual, Bely excelled in lingual techniques and startling images; both were indebted to other writers for some aspect of their art. Blok remained among the modernists the greatest lyricist and the most spontaneous and subjective writer. He had a compulsive urge for self-sacrifice in his vocation, and in his own words he affirmed that "only the author who burns himself to ashes can achieve greatness." There is little discernible influence in his work with the exception of Vladimir Solovyov's vision of Sophia that corresponded to the yearning for the Beautiful Lady. In 1901, when over two hundred and forty of his mystical poems had already been written, Blok discovered Solovyov and for an entire summer was enraptured by his poetic mysticism. But he turned away from the philosopher when he decided that art was incompatible with religion. His private revelation of an idealized reality, to which the key was love, warred with Solovyov's religio-mystical dogma of the transformation of our world into a heaven and of man into God. By 1903, his marriage to Lyubov Mendeleev had settled into the ambiguous relationship of a couple who deeply care for each other but allow for other intimacies. He also began to have recurrent forebodings that the Beautiful Lady might change and leave him. Clearly, the seraphim innocence of the

Verses could not be sustained. He did not lose faith in a higher reality, but he felt betrayed, bereft, emptied; he returned to earth and its mire, plunged into debaucherie and drink.

In a collection of poems, *The City* (1906-1908), Blok describes the quagmire of the Neva and the gray, rain-streaked buildings of cement, brick, and stone, porous with disease and dirt. In "artificial paradises" of pleasure among creatures of sin, the poet searches for The One among the many. *The Stranger,* the best known and one of the most flawless poems in that collection, is a subtle profanation of the ideal woman. Blok gives an impressionistic portrait of an elegant veiled prostitute seen in a drink-sodden hour at a vulgar suburban bar. Her magnetism quickens the poet's passion and stirs mystical longings. But she is splattered with the sordidness of the surroundings, and finally the poem explodes into the savagely ironical line that only in wine is there truth. In this mood of disillusionment, Blok composed three symbolic dramas *(The Puppet Show, The King on the Square, The Stranger* [unrelated to the poem]) that were produced by Meyerhold between 1906 and 1908. The first and most successful is a mummer's tale of a romantic Pierrot made of cardboard courting a doll-like Fair Lady in vapid dialogue, that Blok intended as a fiercely blasphemous parody of his own astral dream. It shocked Andrey Bely and led to Blok's estrangement from the Moscow symbolist group.

Andrey Bely played to Blok the role of Boswell to Johnson and Salieri to Mozart. He was Blok's closest friend, but also his one-time enemy (coveting for several years his wife's affections), and his most lucid interpreter. Bely's comment that the poet was a maximalist and "interested only in direct experience" is confirmed by the deep gloom that pervaded much of Blok's work between 1908 and 1917. In poem after poem the former happiness has changed to desolation. The world that he has attempted to escape from into Her Presence overpowers him; it is loathsome, stagnant, vulgar, futile, and inhabited by the "dead souls" that had filled Gogol with horror. Out of his personal revulsion he composes *Dance Macabre,* a piece of spectral sculpture that places a corpse alongside the living; it functions successfully in a pursuit of work and pleasure and projects a powerful symbol of the deathlike torpor of existence. Here Blok acquires new artistic strength in simplified and compressed verse. It is instanced by a two stanzi masterpiece of anthology fame that with the staring directness of an Edward Hopper canvas depicts the fixed tedium of a city evening with the inevitable "street, lamp and a chemist's shop."

From 1901 to 1918, the ascending movement of the poet's art is oriented toward a supernatural Feminine Figure or a mystical feminine symbol. His poetry is inspired by love for a woman and in later years by love for his country. Each time the abandonment to the elemental force that contained and generated his passion was total; it was never more frenzied than in the thirty poems of *Snow Masks* (1908) written in the sixteen days after he had met the darkly beautiful actress, Natalia Volokhova. By the very intensity of his emotion, that transcends a manageable human experience, the poet seemed transported to another mode of being no less unreal than his relation to the Beautiful Lady. The affair with the exciting, wayward, faithless Natalia is described in feverish rhythms and repetitive rhyme that like approaching drums sound warning of chaos and annihilation. The imagery of radiance, stillness, rapturous waiting that suffused *The Verses* becomes primordial movement; the shooting star, the north wind, a torrential storm and a huge conflagration symbolize the paroxysm of passion. There is no more vibrant and compelling verbalization in Russian poetry of the demonic sexual urge that topples the world, shatters it, breaks the poet on the wheel of orgiastic self-destruction. What gives particular poignancy to the lyrics is the recurring confession of the poet's frailty, the inability to withstand the terrifying world that he has created and to which he surrenders.

The poet continues to play the tragic role in a cycle of poems, *Carmen* (1914) that were inspired by Lyobov Delmas, the prima donna in that opera, for whom Blok conceived a desperate infatuation. It is again transformed into a mystical world, where Carmen appears through a fiery mist as a night star in flight toward other planets. The lover hears dark music and longs for death in a fugue of tumultuous gypsy songs, dances, and flowing wine. Some of the more delicately sensuous verses, sober and objective in tone, are among the most exquisite love poems in the language.

It is significant of the rift between Blok and other symbolists that a reading of poems from these collections at a "Tower" evening produced bewilderment, even derision. When the poet wrote that "azure is hidden from the intellect" he was giving the lie to a theoretical concern with aesthetics that he considered mere cabbalistic word-spinning among his fellow writers. They, however, were only dimly aware of the essence of his creative genius that derived almost exclusively from a state of ecstatic "in-loveness" that reaches toward an idealized image. When these illusions darken and disappear, he finds himself locked in a forlorn solipsistic solitude and begins to search for the sovereignty of another vision to shape and fulfill his creative need.

In a poetic cycle, *The Native Land* (1906-1916), Blok celebrates his impassioned discovery of his country in multiple images. Mother Russia is personalized as an impetuous Tartar-eyed mistress or a shy, shawled peasant girl, as Nekrasov also drew her. He also portrays Russia as a savagely beautiful primordial vastness, girdled by rivers, surrounded by black forests and immense frozen wastes; desolate sadness emanates from blue steppe distances, the lonely troika's bell that haunts Grigoriev's romances, and the poverty-stricken villages that Turgenev painted and Tolstoy mourned. In increasingly forcible and direct symbols, emerge wild, beggarly, restless, unfulfilled Russia. In her protean and conflicting moods the poet reads signs of an approaching catastrophe that he believes will purge Russian life of all that is "ugly, deceitful, filthy" and beget a "gay, clean, just and beautiful" world.

The memorable poem "On the Kulikovo Field," where in the fourteenth century the Russians finally overcame Mongolian strength, is prophetic of the 1914 debacle. In the same year Blok also gave an impassioned speech to an audience of the intellectual elite warning them of imminent collapse of their class that had failed to bridge the gulf between them and the masses. With dark eloquence he predicted that Gogol's troika—the symbol of the Russian people—was rushing headlong to its destiny and the intelligentsia would be crushed under its hoofs. This poetry, which projects the poet's emotional involvement with Russia and his apocalyptic vision of its destiny, is directly related to writers from Pushkin to Dostoevsky whose apprehensions, hopes, and despair about their country reverberate through *The Native Land.*

Blok was the last great embodiment of the belief that life can look entirely to literature for its ideal. His greatest, most famous poem, *The Twelve,* is a culmination of his intuitive poetic genius. It responds to the fearful events of "the days that shook the world" with a vision of a revolution of cosmic sweep and purging redemptive power. For Blok, revolution was a mystical entity whose approaching roar he heard in the elemental rhythms of the spirit of music. It seemed to dictate to him *The Twelve* that he composed in a kind of trance from the 8th to 28th of January, 1918. While he was writing, he heard great, confused sounds around him that he thought was the noise of the old world crashing.

The twelve sections of the poem are written in rough ballad style pitted with street language that suits the twelve heroes of the Red Army night patrol, trigger-happy young ruffians of the new order who are marching down the blizzard-swept Petrograd streets. A carriage passes by with a guard's sweetheart now in company of one of their comrades in an officer's military coat, and when they see it again, the twelve almost casually open fire and the girl is killed. Her erstwhile lover is momentarily stricken but forgets his grief in the fun of looting the city's cellars. As taut with symbol in this turnabout of history are figures from the old world: a lady in a lambskin coat, a fat priest, a shivering bourgeois, hiding his nose in his coat collar, with a scrawny dog standing beside him. In the last stanza the Red soldiers stride forward with a blood red flag ahead. Through the bullet-streaked snow appears, beyond them, walking gently, rose-crowned Jesus Christ. The action, direct and brutal, is admirably recorded in incisive octosyllabic couplets whose regular rhyme beats out the steps of the patrol or becomes deliberately dissonant as starkly white or black images break, splinter, come together again. But above all, it is the resolute and ruthless marching of the guard that fills the frozen air. They forge ahead, exhilaratingly destructive, trampling on the black mud of the old world, not knowing what they are doing or where they are going. But the poet implies that, driven along by the cleansing white blizzard, they will meet the force that transcends them and become twelve apostles with crime-stained hands led by Christ. Through blood and suffering the revolution will bring about redemption and a new truth.

Within a few days, shaken by the humiliating Brest-Litovsk treaty, Blok wrote the *Scythians,* with a belligerent rhetoric that recalls the prophetic strains of Bryusov's *Coming of the Huns.* In a poetic rage, the poet warns Europe of an Asiatic invasion that the Russians will not ward off if now in her hour of need his country is not helped by the Old World.

This was his last poem. For the next three years, he worked on translation projects for Gorky, edited many of his own poems, served on state committees, but could not write. He said that he no longer heard the music of the world and for him there was no return. Spiritually defeated by the "filth and baseness" that continued to exist in the untransformed post-Revolutionary life, he was also weakened by physical hardships—lack of fuel, of transport, finally of food. He fell seriously ill in 1921 and died in August of that year.

ACMEISM

By 1910 the symbolist movement had lost its innovative and exclusive character. It was becoming popularized by a hoard of minor talents and its leaders, Vyacheslav-Ivanov and Blok, publicly recognized that the fabulous experimental years had come to an end. Blok wrote in the same year that "having completed a certain part of our journey, we stand before new problems . . . and must learn anew from the world."

In the period immediately before World War One when Russia was becoming rapidly industrialized and urbanized, bourgeois readers began to favor, in preference to other literature, the green-covered "Znanie" books which under Gorky's aegis were promoting the canon of literary realism. It was inevitable that reaction would set in against the mysticism, cultivated metaphysics, and conscious predilection for the obscure, the occult, and the suggestive identified with the symbolists. The new generation of poets was drawn to a palpable and visible reality.

This movement was similar to the Anglo-American Imagism

led by Pound and T. S. Eliot. It was a revolt against *fin-de-siècle* Romanticism and opted for a renovation of poetic techniques in the use of firm, unambiguous language, orderly planned composition, clear-cut images, and the celebration of publicly acknowledged, concretized beauty. A rose was to be admired, not as a symbol of mystical purity, but for the color and shape of its petals.

Innokenti Annensky was a formative influence on this new aesthetic. He was a classical scholar, translator, and little-known modernist poet. His posthumous poetry collection, *Cypress Box* (1910), was an early model for the opposition to the reigning symbolist school that became known as Acmeism (from the Greek "acme" for peak, perfection) so dubbed disdainfully by Andrei Bely and eagerly adopted by the chief advocates of the movement—Nikolay Gumilyov, Anna Akhmatova, and Osip Mandelstam.

The Acmeists formed a Poet's Guild, and in 1912, Gumilyov, the self-proclaimed Acmeist leader, published their manifesto in *Apollo*, a new literary and artistic journal. It was begun as a symbolist vehicle, but, by its very name, it indicated a new direction that led away from the Dionysian coloration of the older group. Gumilyov reiterated that the poet replace the vagueness and fluidity of musically inspired visions by concrete images fashioned of the impersonal materials of marble and metal, in the manner of Theophile Gautier whose "L'Art" the author had just translated.

In their varying approaches to life—Akhmatova's feminine confessions, Gumilyov's virile courting of physical danger, and Mandelstam's complex verbal reconstruction of cultural monuments—these three best known and most talented Acmeists had little in common. What united them was their firm, exact, conventionally metered verse. In addition, they all turned against the solipsistic, unreal visions of the symbolists and the Futurist school that stressed empiricism, freedom of verbal shape and sound, and the newness and idiosyncrasy of modern dynamics.

There was another resemblance among the three Acmeists. They were early tragic examples of the unequal struggle that was to ensue very shortly between individual creativity and political dictatorship. After the Revolution, thirty-five-year-old Gumilyov, who may have participated in an anti-Communist conspiracy, was arrested. Despite the pleas of his friends to spare a gifted poet, he was executed by a Bolshevik firing squad in 1921. His wife, Akhmatova, suffered recurring persecution, and their son spent a third of his adult life in concentration camps. She was refused the right to publish her work because her poetry did not reflect the proper ideological attitudes. Mandelstam's lapse into official disfavor stemmed from a like reason. In 1934 he wrote a caricature of Stalin that pictured the dictator as a bestial creature who beats the half creatures that surround him on the head, the belly, and the groin. When it was discovered, he became a "non person," and he was deported in the middle thirties. He returned to Moscow for a short reprieve but was sent again to a concentration camp, dying in transit, probably in 1938, from illness and spiritual and physical exhaustion.

GUMILYOV (1886-1921)

If Russia had been a colonial empire, Nikolay Gumilyov would have been its Kipling, nationally adulated for daring explorations of dark continents with risk, adventure, and war that was shared in the company of strong, unscrupulous men. His virile verses that celebrate these experiences in resounding rhythm and forceful images would have made all the school anthologies. As it was, he had to mastermind his own life: overcome psychological and physical obstacles (a father's and older brother's rivalry for his mother's love, a peculiarly elongated skull, slightly crossed eyes, thick lips, and a lisp), and create the kind of picturesque, bravura personality that would insure among fellow writers the attention that he craved. He was physically brave, even to excess. He was intelligent, compulsively active, and he had a poet's gift. Following a brief flirtation with philology at the Sorbonne, he returned to St. Petersburg to enter the fray of the Acmeist movement, married the delicately beautiful Anna Akhmatova in 1910 (they were divorced eight years later), and, hoping for Russian conquests in Africa, journeyed there that same year. He later went to Abyssinia and Somaliland as director of ethnological and geographical expeditions.

Alone among his intellectual peers, Gumilyov volunteered

as a private in 1914 in the dangerous cavalry units. He was decorated twice for bravery, all the while continuing to write poems (*The Quiver*, 1916, *The Pyre*, 1918, *The Tent*, 1929). In Paris when the tsarist regime fell, he came home voicing monarchial sentiments, proclaiming that he had faced wolves, and that Bolsheviks had not frightened him. In possibly his most interesting complex poem, *The Lost Tram* (1919), Gumilyov predicts his own early death in a surrealist vision of the Revolution, as a bloodstained greengrocer chops off the poet's head. In the posthumous collecttions of *The Pillar of Fire* (1922), *To the Blue Star* (1923), and the numerous "machismo" verses, Gumilyov dwells on prescient evil and man's unavailing tragic stoicism. But in most of the poetry, words are instruments of action; strength and indifference to physical danger are idealized. For this careful reader and translator of Heredia and Leconte de Lisle, it is the primitive exoticism that attracts. He does not use this exoticism as the French Parnassians had, as a decorative background, but to convey an exciting, challenging world to be lived in where man develops psychic and physical ties to animals and finds escape from the ordinary.

AKHMATOVA (1888-1966)

When at seventy-seven, Anna Akhmatova was at last allowed to travel abroad, she was personally honored with the Etna-Paormina prize in Italy and an Oxford honorary degree. She was acclaimed in prefaces to collections of her translated work and in the Western press as a foremost lyricist of the twentieth century. This was a world echo of the reception in Russia in 1914 of her second volume of poems, *The Rosary*.

It was a sensational literary event. The most diverse Russians learned her brief poems by heart (few exceeded twenty lines). Despite the war and the social and political upheavals, a new edition of *The Rosary* appeared annually up to 1922.

There could be no more dramatic counterpoint to the masculine escapist overdrive of her poet-critic husband's verses who condescendingly rated Anna's early writing as "poetical exercises." She made quiet, intimate statements of a woman undone by love. *The Rosary* hints in brief epigrammatic verses at the ordeal of the unhappy marriage to Gumilyov with moods of anguish, desolation, a sense of guilt, and hope for inner freedom. The undying theme of love, tyrannical, excluding, intensely emotional, continued to pervade her poetry *(The White Flock,* 1917, *Wayside Grass,* 1921, *Anno Domini MCXXI,* 1922).

Across twenty centuries, Russia's foremost woman poet meets Sappho who also lived, suffered, and wrote her passion. But Akhmatova's approach to the love experience lacks the Sapphic celebration of desire's urge and its fulfillment. The dominant tone is that of recollection, as in Proust, of the moment past or one that had been expected in the daydream of the nameless beloved who remains a shadow or wish of her thought. The original quality of this writing is charged with sentiment that liberates it from sentimentality; it is personal to Akhmatova as a signature. She makes oblique use of the lyrical thrust, expressed in a gesture, a laconic line, an object, and with the greatest economy of verbal means. This leap from the psychic condition to a concrete image becomes a marvel of emotional compression that controls the poem in an authoritative, modern way. Unforgettably, gloving the right hand with a left glove contains the confused frustration of a last lovers' tryst. Jealousy is a two-line cry of not wanting to know how the other is kissed; that a first encounter will end in pain is heard in the "inexpressibly sad" music of the café where they will meet. A whole winter's early mood is held in the "gaily dry leaves." Young Pushkin is unerringly caught on a path in Tsarskoye Selo where he went to school with the mention of a swarthy lad, a tricornered hat, and a dog-eared copy of Parny. Feeling is further muted in low-keyed descriptive fragments of a hamlet, a river's curve, a linden park, and of ordinary things such as a dark skirt, blue pipe smoke, a hammock, the sea smell of oysters on cracked ice. Acmeism receives its full due in these realistic passages in words selected for their fundamental, rather than their symbolical or transitory, sense.

Given permission to publish only for the one year immediately after the World War Two victory, Akhmatova had lived as an inner émigré during the Stalin period, surviving in conditions of great physical hardship by making translations from numerous languages. She was persecuted by the authorities and in 1946 was expelled from the Union of Soviet Writers and publicly insulted by Stalin's lieutenant, Andrei Zhdanov, as a "mixture of nun and whore" whose poetry was "utterly remote from the Russian people." She continued to write four or five poems each year that she bravely and proudly claimed were a link to her time and to the new life of the Russian people. In fact, this almost last member of a remarkably gifted pre-revolutionary generation of poets was upholding with Boris Pasternak the progressive humanism of the Russian nineteenth century. After the Civil War, she shifted her talent to reflect beyond purely intimate sensations the effect of social and political events upon her beloved country; epic edged on lyrics attempted to explain and justify the enduring national calamities. When her second husband and only son were caught in the purges, Akhmatova felt swept up into the stream of common destiny and began to explore, artistically, the concept of time that she now recognized as history. In many poems about deserted houses—a recurring image—that are haunted by the past, in a recreation of pre-Soviet Petersburg, the subject matter is the theme of time, the sudden dislocation caused by its violent passage, the erosion effected by swift historical change, desolateness brought on by the sense of lost time in one's own life. These themes, prevailing in later poetry, shape a densely wrought and exciting work, *The Poem without a Hero*, conceived during the Russian retreat in 1940 that a great many Russians thought was to be the end of the Soviet era. Akhmatova returns to 1913, the terminal year of a whole age, that she places in the brilliant solipsistic, self-indulgent literary and artistic world of the capital. The central episode of a young poet's suicide at the doorstep of a beautiful, fashionable actress set against the backdrop of masquerades, balls, and a midnight cabaret symbolizes in subtle patterns the frivolity and foolishness of the period just before the cataclysm. For some fifteen years the poet returned to the work, again and again. She searched for clues in her own less-than-innocent life of the time that would relate to the disasters that followed and offer hope and the promise of eventual expiation. Critic Max Hayward astutely notes Dostoevskian echoes in the interweaving religious motifs of the intricately structured poem where time is moved backward and forward in an endless continuum. In one dramatic, compression of time, New Year revellers that resemble those of the *Devils* usher in 1913, at the same moment surround the poet on the eve of 1940 reminding her of her past misdoings that precipitated the poet's death.

The *Requiem* (1935-1940), still banned in the Soviet Union, is Akhmatova's most powerful work and, as a searing historical indictment, one of the most memorable. Personal grief is transcended by the assertion of a common humanity as the poet identifies her own despair—near madness, wish for death, frenzied prayer, resignation, and willed stoicism—with all the suffering women who press in silent crowds against the barred iron gates of Leningrad Prison waiting for news of their loved ones. Intense emotional lyricism surges through the cycle of ten short poems that attain extraordinary pathos through the familiar technique of the complex, laconic simplicity, and the conversational, even colloquial language. An historical stanza, couched in the old Russian lexicon, brings back another Terror with wailing wives beneath the Kremlin walls watching their guardsmen husbands executed by the Great Czar. Among them, the poet finds her place. The most important Acmeist, Osip Mandelstam, who admired Akhmatova absolutely as a human being and artist, pointed to the dirge-like motifs and structure of her poetry. She borrows from oral tradition and reveals through literary idiom the peasant girl in the sophisticated twentieth-century woman of letters. *The Requiem*, a culminating work, throbs with the rhythms of folkloric lament and projects most forcibly the image that is central to her poetry. It is that of the Russian woman—patient, long suffering, deeply religious, faithful to her feelings and to her country as she faces the adversities of history, private circumstance, and her own nature with resignation and endurance. No other major poet has recorded with such clairvoyance and compassion the hard female destiny.

MANDELSTAM (1891-1938)

The rediscovery of Osip Mandelstam as a major twentieth-century poet is a memorable literary event of our time. In the West, he had been best remembered for the inexpressible conditions of horror that led to his death in a Siberian concentration camp. In Russia, where, as he once said, poetry was really important because people were killed for it, his work was banished, and it was not until the post-Stalinist era that some of it began to appear in samizdat (Soviet underground publications). A steadily increasing number of his poems in manuscript that had been preserved by friends and those that his wife had been able to save or had learned by heart, made its way to the West. A Russian-language edition of all the poetry published in his lifetime was printed in New York in 1955. It included the two collections *Stone* (1913) and *Tristia* (1922). It was then updated and expanded to three volumes between 1967 and 1971. His work was introduced to the English-reading public in a definitive scholarly edition of all his 417 poems, *Complete Poetry of Osip Emilievich Mandelstam* in 1973. He was immediately recognized as ranking among foremost contemporary poets, such as Mallarmé, Eliot, and Rilke, for the wrought density, lingual force, and modernity of his verse. This impression is enhanced and confirmed by a translation into English by his foremost interpreter, Clarence Brown, of the poet's prose pieces, *The Prose of Osip Mandelstam* (1925). *The Noise of Time* (1925) is a poeticized autobiography; *Theodosia* (1925) and *The Egyptian Stamp* (1928) are fictional memoirs of the period of bourgeois Russia between February and October 1917. They are cast in a mythic mold; they fragment reality through an interplay of film techniques and, in a manner almost unparalleled in Russian fiction, project an inner world of surrealist nightmares that foreshadow the fashion set a decade later by the French novelist, Julien Gracq.

Shy, frail, bird-like young Osip with his difficult manners was born into a Jewish leather merchant's family, attended the famous progressive Tenishev gymnasium in St. Petersburg, studied, between bouts of European travel, at the capital's university and when he failed to obtain a degree his father stopped supporting his "dilettante" son. Penniless and professionally rudderless, surviving on miniscule returns from an occasional translation and his writings, Mandelstam at nineteen was already immersed in poetry and never managed to establish a personal existence outside of it. He derived his paper-thin contacts with reality from the St. Petersburg circle of poets to which he was drawn by his adolescent admiration of the erudite Vyacheslav Ivanov until he himself became an Acmeist. He was befriended by Gumilyov, the poet Kuzmin, Akhmatova and gained entry into the columns of the *Apollo* magazine. On the human side, this oversensitive young man who was always "fatally" falling in love with someone, had the great fortune to meet, in 1919, a beautiful, intelligent, twenty-year-old painter, Nadezhda Khazina, from whom he never again separated. (She wrote a passionate tribute to her husband in a best-selling memoir, *Hope Against Hope*, in 1970. It records the poet's unshakeable inner freedom and stubbornly maintained creativity despite incessant persecution by the authorities, harrowing physical hardships and the exile that during the last years of his life they shared together.

There was no question for Mandelstam of submitting to any of the current political maelstroms that raged about him and imperilled his very life, or even to an irreversible decision, such as emigration abroad. He believed, simply and totally, in the poet's right to obey his own exclusive laws and in his poet's power. He asserts this in one of his most beautiful poems, *The Age* (1923), as "the flute" that alone may free "My century, my beats" from its prison and give birth to a new era.

What informs the cosmos of the poet's earliest poetry, considered by many his finest, is the mood of absence—in color, movement, sound—transmitted in a plethora of low-keyed, "non" words that recalls the white-upon-white blocks in the space-swept canvases of the early-twentieth-century Russian painter, Kasimir Malevich. If these poems may be regarded as poetic versions of the Suprematists' efforts toward nullity of content, one might wonder whether the two "architectural" poems, "Hagia Sophia" and "Notre Dame" in *Stone*, greatly admired by Mandelstam's avant-garde public, do not parallel the Constructivism movement in painting. The poet describes the two great buildings with the graphic precision of Acmeist approach. They represent for him a sacred succession of interlinked events, "a nostalgia for world culture" and monuments to the dynamic process that constructs a perfect whole from the thrust and counterthrust of interplaced stones, even as interdependent words shape and support the good building of a poem. It was not understood at that time that with his Western contemporaries— the Imagists Ezra Pound, Richard Aldington, Wyndham Lewis, and others—this vatic poet was already reacting against the impending chaos of the century with a call for an impersonal, opaque, solid art and the evocation of the classical order out of his vast literary reference and discipline derived from Italian, Greek, and French models. Hence, an early obsession with the harmony of visual line, volume, weight in depictions of monasteries, bell towers, casinos, the perfectly arched line of sky over a forest that gives the poet a feeling of surprise and elevation, the triumphant portrait of St. Petersburg's majestic perspectives of palaces and granite quays that he contrasts to his own "Judaic" disorder. Central to this was the preoccupation with language and its poetic structure where "stone" words as such, one after the other, were carefully placed to construct form that glints with startling verbal associations, teases the core subject with turns of phrase and fluid metaphors into mixed levels of meaning, and within a conservative metrical system devises new sound patterns with rare assonances, occasional sprung rhythm in the manner of Gerald Hopkins, and broken lines.

This modern exercise in "pure" poetry, which is frequently couched in a curious mingling of archaic rhetoric and colloquialisms, makes additional demands on the reader, for the author draws upon sources of literary reference from the past that are not well known to illustrate a current instance. The surrealist-tinged poem, *Solominka* (1916), for example, seems to mourn the passing away of beautiful Solominka in her immense bedroom flooded with the black December waters of the Neva as "the 12 moons sing the hour of death." In the fifth stanza her name is mingled with the "blessed words" of Lenore, Ligeia, and Seraphita. If the reader is not familiar with the first two ladies, Edgar Allen Poe's heroines, or with *Seraphita*, a little-known philosophical novel by Balzac, it might not be clear to him that the major theme of the poem is the poet's joyous recovery of his beloved after death in a resurrected image of the love ideal. But this poetry invites close and repeated reading. There is the excitement of unearthing at second and third perusal yet another meaning in a seemingly straightforward stanza, discovering fresh ambiguities in juxtaposed verbal play, rousing a tamed metaphor to further significance in the lingual complexity and diversity that characterizes a Mandelstam poem.

Another aspect of the poet's art that may outlive the recorded pressures of his age are moments of sudden delighted awareness of the earth's organic magic as in the savoring of orange peel scent *(I Regret That it Is Winter Now,* 1920), an evocation of forms in matter in an imaged progression of liquids to textiles *(The Flow of Golden Honey from the Bottle,* 1917), a masterpiece of one-to-three-word lines catching the sound of falling fruit in the silent woods *(A Careful and Mute Sound,* 1908).

To live, for Mandelstam, in this confused age, when the air is muddled like water and "fragile chronology has ended" *(Finder of the Horse Shoe,* 1923), is to resist with "the blessed, meaningless word" the "Soviet night" *(We Shall Meet Again in Petersburg,* 1920-1928), lift the ordinary daily joys above social or political missions *(Twilight of Freedom,* 1918), experience personal estrangement within a familiar city *(Where to Go in January,* 1931), stumble, lucidly in a Prufrockian hesitation between involvement and withdrawal *(#394,* 1937), pursue with muffled militancy the existential ambivalence of Being, with the poet situating Self as predator and victim—a quest that casts shadows across all his work. His later poetry, thematically, is richly relevant to the contemporary Western reader. Unlike the best of his more subjective fellow poets, particularly some of the Futurists, he reflects the broader sensitivity of a totally sophisticated twentieth-century mind.

FUTURISM

Literary and artistic tradition was the enemy of the Futurist movement, the other bold and most far-reaching modernist deviation simultaneous to the rise of Acmeism and the final corollary of the Silver Age. It was instigated in Russia by its Italian founder, Marinetti. His 1910 lectures in both capitals were acclaimed by numbers of avant-garde poets. They subsequently formed one group in St. Petersburg called the Ego-Futurists and headed by Igor Severyanin (1887-1941). In Moscow they formed the Cubo-Futurists, who rallied around the poet painter David

Burlyuk, their organizer, and the poets Khlebnikov and Mayakovsky.

The key word was modernity. For Severyanin, a facile weaver of melodious verses, this meant exciting appendages to "high living" such as rapid travel, mechanized gadgetry, and exotic luxuries (lilies in champagne, lilac motor cars) that he celebrated in topiaristic, narcissistic poems with a profusion of foreign-flavored neologisms. The perfumed glamor of his poetry, that, during the war years, had a spectacular but short-lived success, was the opposite of the boisterously crude posture of the Cubo-Futurists who were waging war against the "dirty" Philistines in a campaign of shock tactics. The Cubo-Futurists included the "hooligan" poets who walked single file with outrageously painted faces, in outlandish attire, through Moscow streets, catcalling at passers-by. They staged raucous discussions in cafés and public halls of the capital and "recital" tours through the provinces where they would declaim what to their large, gleefully jeering audiences seemed like incomprehensibly bombastic, shockingly colloquial, violent verses and challenged individual spectators to abusive debates that often ended in fist fights. Finally the aggressive anti-traditionalism of the pronouncements that the Cubo-Futurists made, was depicted by Mayakovsky in a 1914 poem as stamping "nihil" "on everything that has gone before." In their 1913 manifesto, significantly titled "A Slap in the Face of Public Taste," they expressed the need to cast overboard "from the ship of Modernity" Pushkin, Dostoevsky, Tolstoy, and all the outworn rhetoric of private love, lyricism, nightingales, beauty.

This seemed close to the Italian slogans which were stirring the international world of art with a call for the glorification of the age of technology and the rejection of the "suffocating" past. However there was a difference. The exhortations of Marinetti and his young followers to destroy museums and burn libraries made little sense in Russia where there was a scarcity of both. Besides, the anger of the young "déclassé" Futurists was directed primarily against the elite erudition of the symbolists, themselves members of the hated bourgeois establishment, and not against "culture," which, as an embattled radical-minded minority, they were committed to promote and disseminate among the masses. One purpose of these rowdy gatherings was the attempt to bring to their mass audiences an appreciation of literature by what appeared to them to be poetry that would be accessible, public, and "of importance to every man in the street." This was a revolutionary step that prefigured a major literary goal of the new social order. Not unexpectedly, the Futurist school, in the sense of an unmixed belief in the future, alone among the modernists, welcomed the revolution. It even merged with the state in a brief, brilliant honeymoon when some of its members were chosen to edit *Art of the Commune*, the official journal of the Commissariat of Education. In 1917 the Futurists became recognized directors of Soviet literary and artistic life. Conversely, the cultural nihilism that was already implicit in the Italian manifestos became an expanded and entrenched ideological tenet of fascist states.

What was of the essence for the early Russian Futurists behind the show of exuberant exhibitionism, and which was already evident in the radically different free verse of many of Mayakovsky's poems, was the discovery of universal dynamism and new principles of form to express it in poetry and the plastic arts. Kandinsky, Malevich, and Yavlensky led the way with the first powerful nonrepresentational painting. They discarded the traditional concept of a still, isolated object and integrated its essence and existence into a dynamic sensation of the entire environment. The poets and philologists experimented with all aspects of semantic and linguistic possibilities for poetry. They initiated a revolutionary reversal of lingual usages that eschewed syntactical and intellectual relationships to create a new "transmental" language. They highlighted the vast power of the word itself, freed it of conventional associations, and examined it for all possible self-contained values in each letter, each sound, which carried its own relevance and meanings. The art of poetry became the art of the word, as was explicated by the first Futurists, A. Kruchonykh in *Trio* and Velimir Khlebnikov in *The Word as Such* in 1913. It was strikingly illustrated by the latter in an etymological poetic "tour de force," *Smekh* (1910), that produced from the title word, meaning laughter, a dazzling series of derivatives. It attempts to renovate semantically, in a poetical system, a word's long forgotten relationship with other closely related words.

KHLEBNIKOV (1885-1922)

Velimir Khlebnikov, philologist, poet, historian, was a dedicated student of the history of the Russian language for which he had an almost mystical attachment. He endeavored to break away from literary patterns, made smooth and colorless through overuse, and to return—not unlike Kandinsky who drew upon Russia's old woodcuts in his early work—to a rough pristine idiom drawn from the earliest lingual archives that included tribal, Church, Slavonic, pre-Petrine speech. Borrowing from all the languages of the Russian empire, he arbitrarily manipulated disparate elements of the word, made metalogical links between roots and prefix-suffix expansions and created in this way something of a verbal legerdemain.

Khlebnikov's linguistic experiments reached out, beyond his mother tongue, to the possible rediscovery, through poetry, of a universal tongue whose common identity could be reestablished with letters of the alphabet. For him, as for another daring language explorer, James Joyce, the letters represented not only signs for sounds but also nonverbal signs that are symbolically related. An early death in conditions of extreme poverty, cut short his fascinating explorations into a whole new poetic language where, as Kruchonykh put it, "the creative shaping of speech throws everything into a new light."

Khlebnikov's rejection of ideological and emotional emphasis that had orchestrated most previous Russian prosody held great appeal for the Formalists. This was a group of young literary critics and philologists, among them Osip Brik, Boris Eichenbaum, Victor Zhirmunsky, Yuri Tynyanov, Roman Jacobson. They challenged the dichotomy of form and content and propagated a literature that would liberate itself from the Russian classical tradition, which subordinated words to meaning, in order to create aesthetically autonomous works of art. The basis for this reform had already appeared in the works of two nineteenth-century scholars, the literary historian, Alexander Veselovsky (1838-1906), and the linguist, Alexander Potebnia (1833-

1891), who had founded the school of historical poetics and the school of linguistic-psychological poetics. In their systematic investigation of literature, and in Veselovsky's writings of comparative literature as well, form and language prevailed over social and moral evidence. Their collected works, brought out in 1913 and 1914 by the Academy of Sciences, spurred the Formalists who had just banded into a Society for the Study of Poetic Language to attack the symbolist movement for its increasing religious and philosophical preoccupations. Nevertheless, it is to symbolist poetry with its new cosmic relationships and intuitive poetic images that the Formalists were deeply indebted. Even more, they were dependent on Andrei Bely's analyses of poetic language that highlighted many problems of literary form.

The Formalists were to treat similar literary questions in an impressive body of theoretical writings (between 1920 and 1930) dealing with numerous types of literary fact (poetical structure and language, prose styles, literary theory, major Russian novelists, comparative literary portraits, and entirely reconstructed literary periods) that define and develop the Formalists' approach to literary art. They negated all previously established theories and insisted on the preeminence of craftsmanship—a dictum that was taken up by the NEP fellow travelers. They also made exhaustive scientific investigations of linguistic creative patterns. What interested them most were the artifacts of style, the determinating potentiality of words, the possible structural unities of narrative and its deliberate disorganization. The latter was particularly favored by the leading Formalist theoretician and writer, Victor Shklovsky, who urged the creating of unusual effects to combat the reader's automatism of perception. Normal tension between content and form and opposition between meaning and verbal gesture disappear in the formalist concept of "lumped" artistic devices. These devices include theme, ideology, plots, characters, style, and language as part of the artistic equipment. Words are divested of all collateral meanings—psychological, social, moral, or philosophical. A work of art can thereby be created that is an object of aesthetic study. In effect, the main concern of the writer (who is always to remain outside of his work) is to engage in a creative process that assembles and manipulates all those artistic devices that will heighten and intensify the aesthetic quality only. The critic becomes something of a collaborator since he is to assess the work in a demonstration of *how* the devices are made to function.

From the start, when Shklovsky undertook to elucidate the theoretical principles of Futurist poetry (*Resurrection of the Word*, 1914), the Formalists, whose linguistic studies were to exert a large influence on Western European Structuralists, had been receptive to the Futurist movement. Some of their most interesting and original articles on a linguistic approach to Russian literary masterpieces (Tolstoy's *War and Peace*, Pushkin's *The Captain's Daughter*, among others) appeared in the magazine *LEF* that in 1923 had been organized by Vladimir Mayakovsky, the most famous Futurist poet and the acknowledged leader of the movement.

MAYAKOVSKY (1893-1930)

Criticism has exhausted the vocabulary of outsize words to describe the phenomenon that was Vladimir Mayakovsky. He has been called a charlatan, a genius, a monster, a supershowman, the most exciting figure in modern Russian literature, the loudest drummer of the revolution, the greatest Soviet poet, and, in the avant-garde Bohemia of prewar Moscow, the most flamboyant and active bourgeois-baiting Futurist.

A six foot five, eighteen-year-old with a boxer's build, a boxer's bruised good looks, tousled dark hair, and a thick lower lip insolently curled to the left, sporting a yellow tunic, a wooden spoon stuck in its buttonhole, he recited his verse to all and sundry in a stentorian voice. Mayakovsky made a tremendous impression on men like Pasternak, Kandinsky, and the stage designer Meyerhold, who were themselves caught up in the frenzy of modernism.

They felt that the uncouth, assertive youth who trampled with a primitive's careless ease on traditional values and sensibilities was an embodiment of the new movement in art. In fact, Mayakovsky was playing at Futurism, which reflected his own restlessness, exuberant aggressivity, and stance of hyperoriginality. It satisfied his temperamental craving for movement and excitement, much as the dangerous activity of distributing Bolshevik propaganda among small Moscow shopkeepers had.

In 1910, David Burlyuk met Mayakovsky at the Institute of Fine Arts where he was developing his gift for drawing by designing posters. Encouraged by the painter's interest, he showed him a poem "by a friend." At this turning point, Burlyuk yelled, "It is yours; you are a genius!" That evening, as Mayakovsky noted in his autobiography, he became a poet. Burlyuk "organized" his protégé by introducing him to scores of avant-garde poets and painters. He gave Mayakovsky fifty kopeks a day from his own meager funds to keep him in food and allow him to write so as not to make Burlyuk look like "an utter fool."

The early poems *(Cloud in Trousers*, 1914, *Backbone Flute,* 1915, *The Man,* 1916) are among Mayakovsky's best. They contain all his technical innovations and project in thunderously exuberant declamations the spectacular megalomania that is the essence of his art. "Handsome, twenty-two-year old" with "two fine arms, a precious mind, an extraordinary lump beating under the wool of the waistcoat" he struts across the pages now lashing out impassioned manifestos against society's cant, false religious beliefs, and romantic clichés about love, now emitting a jealous lover's howls of despair, "nailing himself to the paper with the nails of words" that turn to clowning self-mockery of the "huge clod . . . so large, so unwanted," or to a plea for the body of the beloved that he would guard as a crippled veteran does his only leg, or to self-pity, carrying his heart "like a dog carrying to the kennel a paw that a train has run over." The rather conventional young man's rebellion against suffering and injustice becomes a dazzlingly showy performance of the poet's insistent and uninhibited expansion of self. What largeness, magnitude, stock of emotions, and rage swagger in this "Mayakomorphism" as Trotsky wittily named it. The poet's elephantine ego populates the world with himself and treats its massive cultural and cosmic objects with gay irreverence and familiar or contemptuous blasphemy. Napoleon is led on a pig's leash; the sun is invited for tea to chat about this and that; "gray, curly locked" God is reprimanded for his negligence, and Heaven is told to take off its hat, for the poet is about to arrive.

The only unalterable and implacable enemy that the poet cannot overcome is *byt,* variously meaning mores, encrusted habits, social custom, or routine. The Futurist hated all of it as a symbol of the established bourgeoisie and hallowed reverence for the past, while Mayakovsky sensed in it the very principle of order and regulation that stayed his dishevelled self-rapture and limited the world that he felt was already too small to contain him. The theme of deadening and suffocating *byt* alternates repeatedly in his work with an urgent appeal to Time, not Time the preserver and ally of the Establishment, but Time the Destroyer who breaks, uproots, and clears the path to a new future. The poet hurries it along, predicting with the apocalyptic vision that marked his entire generation, the social cataclysm that took place within a year of the date he said it would.

Mayakovsky greeted the revolution with the impatience of a young heir coming into his estate. The abolition of all the old institutions corresponded to his destructive passions. His anarchic temper, like Bakunin's, reveled in the chaos and catastrophe even to the bloody events that had shaken Gorky. "Mondays and Tuesdays we shall color into holidays—with blood." The enormity of the tasks that faced the new regime was on a par with his organic giantism, and for five years he turned out propagandist verse (lampoons, marching songs, limericks, feulletons in rhyme) that glorified the builders of the socialist state and lashed out at the lack of fuel economy, lack of hygiene, malingering in industry, and black-marketeering that could destroy this state. When the Russian Telegraph Agency began to use its walls for news and propaganda in 1919, he designed some 6000 colored posters with rhyming squibs or titles of a satirical, informative nature that were sent out daily in hundreds of stencilled reproductions to all the major Russian cities.

This may have inspired him to write *Mystery Bouffe* (1918). It is significantly a huge political cartoon. It is farcical, but not humorous, with something of the grotesque, like that of Aristophanes, in the parody of the Biblical flood that topically presents a satirical Marxist version of the class conflict and the ultimate victory of the proletariat. The same simplistic political view prevails in the long poem *150,000,000*, (Russia's actual population in 1919, the year the poem was written), published anonymously to support his claim that the "We" of the work represents the entire country's voice. It vibrates with Mayakovsky's penchant for the colossal. "150,000,000 speak through my lips using a 90 mile super language." It depicts a combat between the gigantic Woodrow Wilson, expert at handling four-trigger revolvers and a seventy-blade sword, and the Leko, Ivan, whose arm is the Neva and whose feet are the Caspina steppes.

Mayakovsky's great popularity and his evident dedication to the state still did not endear him to the party chiefs. Lenin, an ultraconservative in literature, did not like modern poetry and professed not to understand Mayakovsky's. The artistically more enlightened Lunacharsky, Commissar of Education, admonished the poet for wasting himself on "trifling jingles." But Mayakovsky, who considered himself the standard-bearer of Communist culture, had organized a Left Front Movement with its own literary magazine, *LEF*, in 1923. The movement gathered many prominent and talented Futurists and Formalist critics. He proposed literary reforms that called for an end to "useless versification." This meant for him that art for its own sake had no place in the socialist state. Nevertheless, he remained lyrical in his poetry. He wrote *I Love* in 1922, which is a commemoration of his tumultuous and joyless affair with the coldly sensuous Lily Brik, wife of his friend and publisher, Osip Brik (with whom Mayakovsky lived in an uneasy ménage à trois). This is his gentlest collection of lyrics. It expresses the unresolved equation between private sentiment and public message that continued to harass him in the poignant *Homeward* poem, written in 1925, where "from poetry's skies I plunge into Communism."

The inner struggle sharpened into official dispute when the *LEF* publication came under fire for its Formalist-tinged program for purely factual literature that clearly skirted any political slant. Futurists were linked with "decadents of every stripe" in Lenin's letter on the Proletcult, and Mayakovsky was heckled by proletarian writers for his excessive individualism and "willful prankishness." The *LEF* magazine was discontinued in 1925, soon after the stories by Babel (who was purged in the thirties) had appeared in its columns. This seemed a propitious moment for Mayakovsky to gain temporary respite from official censure with a prolonged trip to Europe and America.

New York enthralled him as the incarnation of the Steel Age. He wrote an elegy on Brooklyn Bridge, "the mile of steel" fighting for construction rather than style and achieving "an austerity of bolts and steel" but he was also taken aback by the city's filth, its frightening "money-mad" pace, the imprisoning tunnels and elevated subway trains. He left the United States hoping that the "elemental American futurism" would learn to control its technology and enjoy a more cultivated and quiet existence.

Back home, he felt the noose of Soviet reality tightening around his neck, although he was still the idol of a huge public, and on the best-seller list. He was a spellbinder, and star of a film that he had written and produced himself. Gambling on this popularity and enraged by the encroaching Philistine bureaucracy that he had attempted to undercut throughout all of his creative life, he wrote *The Bed Bug* in 1928 and the *Bath House* in 1930, savagely satirizing the smugness, narrowness, and corruption of the party hacks. Of the two plays, both dramatically weak, *The Bed Bug* is the more interesting and complex. We are introduced in the early scenes to the vodka-drinking, romantically inclined hero, Pisypkin, who is a profiteer and ex-party member. Later in the play, time shifts to the future, fifty years hence, when Pisypkin is discovered, preserved with his bed bug, in a block of ice. The scientists of an efficient Communist utopia revive him and place him in a cage at the zoo. It is the wooden, depersonalized people of the socialist future that earn the author's contempt in a final scene when the warm-blooded, vulnerable hero appeals to the citizens, his brothers, to join him in his cage where he is alone and suffering. Castigating reviews in the party press foretold, despite Meyerhold's brilliant production, a forcibly short run of the play. It was not to reappear on the Soviet stage until 1955 when its message was appreciated by audiences of the post-Stalin era.

Mayakovsky tried to conform. That he was still unable to square his artist's conscience with a denial of his private sensibilities is expressed in an anguished review of his creative life in a last incomplete and splendid poem, *At the Top of My Voice* (1930). "As a latrine carrier and water carrier, by the revolution mobilized and drafted . . . I'd rather compose romances for you," declares the poet, and yet cries out in exultant despair that he is ready for martyrdom "in setting my heel on the throat of my own song." He deserted his gifted *LEF* friends to join RAPP, the official writers' association, but the writers kept him apart as if he carried an infection. He was convinced by the envy and spite of these mediocrities that the exciting and richly productive world of theatre and the arts, created by such talented producers as Meyerhold (purged nine years later), Hakhtangov, Tairov and the writers Zamyatin, Babel, Bely, Pasternak, Zoshchenko, and himself, was doomed.

He also suffered a deep personal grief in his loneliness and isolation. This was a lover's loss of a beautiful Russian émigré girl he had met in Paris. She had hit him "like a hurricane" but had finally married a Frenchman when she decided, despite the poet's ardent letters and telegrams, not to return to Russia, and the authorities, evidently curbing the poet's independence, would not grant him a visa to France.

These betrayals may have led to the "staging of my final performance." He predicted with an uncanny presentiment his untimely end fifteen years later. For the consummate showman, who had presented with such spectacular success the heroics of the alienated "poète maudit," it may have been the unendurable nonmeaning of existence that decided Mayakovsky, on the morning of April 14, 1930 to shoot himself. The socially dedicated writer had been made inoperative in the darkened and stifling theatre of Soviet reality.

News of the suicide shocked the Russian public. It was officially muffled, and his work was rarely mentioned until 1935, when Stalin proclaimed him the greatest Soviet poet. Statues were erected; railroad stations, squares, and streets were then renamed after him in major Soviet cities. His political poetry is featured in all school anthologies, and his work is read by millions of Soviet citizens. He continues to exert a great influence on Soviet writers, who are undeniably impressed by his self-proclaimed creed of the artist's submission to the needs of the state, and because of his official canonization as a supreme representative of socialist art. However, his contribution to literature has a much wider significance, and the style of such Soviet poets as Evtushenko, Brodsky, and Voznesensky probably would not have been evolved were it not for the revolutionary innovations that characterize Mayakovsky's work. What blazons every line that he wrote is the intransigently demotic form and spirit that anticipated the literary demands of late-twentieth-century mass society and that of the future. There are hundreds of subjects in the complete fifteen-volume collection among the intimate themes and those imposed by Soviet history. Mayakovsky's approach to life, however, is steadily single: It is the externalization of phenomena reduced to a simplified and rational point of view with emphasis on fact and physicality that leaves little room for imagination, ambiguity, or paradox. Contrary to poets like Mandelstam or Bely, who begrudge the reader entrance into their private world, Mayakovsky is obvious, accessible, almost agonizingly clear even in the realm of the most intimate emotion which he sometimes expresses in blatantly vivid, realized metaphor. His heart becomes an actual conflagration summoning hoses and fire chiefs; he compares himself to a sun-baked July pavement on which "she" throws cigarette stubs of kisses; speaks of a crowd as a hundred-headed louse bristling its legs and rubbing them against the butterfly of his heart.

The most immediate impact of a Mayakovsky poem is the language. It is concrete, calculatedly crude, colloquial, and for the first time in Russian poetry, systematically depoetized. With aplomb and skill, the poet removes all conventional poetical clichés and eschews romantic "melocrockery." He creates fresh tonality and flexibility through juxtaposed sounds and words and an abundance of suffixes and prefixes that variegate the root. There is rough beauty in this living idiom that is almost harshly palpable, just bordering on the excessively vernacular and enhanced with similes: "the dawn of my ultimate love, bright as a consumptive's flush"; "I rushed out like a curse." The absence of melodiousness affects the ear attuned to symbolist poetry no less than the new metrical order that permits an extensive use of free verse and allows rhyming freedom in line endings, assonances, and approximate phonetic associations.

Mayakovsky often filled most of the page with short broken lines that explode into one-word lines in capital letters. Like the mass media to which the poet was addicted, the typography offers its mass audience cultural and commercial images by means of a profusion of "headline" techniques. When Blok was asked what he thought was the outstanding feature of Mayakovsky's writing, he answered in his usual direct and laconic fashion: "Democratization."

INDEPENDENT POETIC VENTURES

ESENIN (1895-1925), A PEASANT POET

Vladimir Mayakovsky and Sergey Esenin were the first two highly gifted Soviet poets. However, Mayakovsky's empiricism and optimistic endorsement of urban technology as handmaiden of the Soviet state was opposed by Esenin who expressed fear of the city and the machine as the enslavers of men.

Sergey Esenin was a shepherd from Riazan province. He was a handsome lad with brilliant blue eyes and corn-colored hair, decked out in a vividly sashed peasant blouse. He began to appear at symbolists' gatherings in 1913, reciting melodious verse to a guitar with wistful folkloric references to haymaking, ploughing, birch woods, rye stalks in the field, countryside trysts, the evening's lowering light over the pond, and his father's humble hut. Against this rustic background he evoked primitive Christian figures of Jesus, a peasant-shawled Virgin Mary, and the kindly Church saints who in a halo of poetic superstition and homespun beliefs seemed integrated into the villagers' daily life.

He was identified early with the "peasant poets" group and particularly with the talented Nikolay Kluyev who was reconstructing in mystical poems the religious mythology of rural Russia. The spirit of Esenin's poetry was more spontaneous than Kluyev's, naïvely animistic, and met with greater popular success. He became known between 1914 and 1919 as "the poet from the people" with such collections as *Funeral Service, All the Blue of th Sky, The Village's Book of the Hours,* in which the pastoral motifs, featured in touchingly simple lyrics, were invigorated with the peasant idiom. He expressed a deep attachment to the patriarchial world where he was born, and its rhythm and flow of life, in his poetry, remained present and sustained.

Briefly, in 1919, when the avant-garde was still courting other literary movements, Esenin founded the Imaginist school that he believed would mark him as an outstanding modernist on a par with Mayakovsky and Blok. To judge from the Imaginist manifestos, there is some affinity between Ezra Pound's concept of the image as "an intellectual and emotional complex in an instant of time" and the Russian Imaginists' insistence on "the image . . . and nothing but the image . . ." that emerges from ". . . analogies, parallelisms, similes, contrasts, terse and drawn-out epithets . . . and is the tool behind the production of a master artisan of art." It is within its localized history, however, of Russia-in-Revolution, that the canon of Imaginism may be understood. It is another search for a new poetics that would allow for reciprocal freedom of content and form. (Esenin had already expressed his apprehension of "Marxian guardianship" of the arts in *The Keys of the Soul* in 1918.)

The Imaginists proposed the synthesis of colloquial and literary idiom as against the overerudite "un-Russian" terminology of the vulgarisms of the symbolists and the Futurists. They stated that it was possible to organize the structure of a poem around deliberately unrelated, self-sufficient images. In opposition to the "ideological opportunism" of the Futurists, they searched for ways to express the traumatic impress of catastrophies on the contemporary mind, and reached out beyond current issues into a hitherto unprobed cosmic awareness. It is not surprising to find that Esenin, more than the other Imaginists, tried to create the fulfilled image drawing upon the pure and the impure and palpable and corporeal consistently enough to "drive its splinter deeply into the reader's emotional response." The propensity for startling and strident images was a fundamental aspect of his art.

In his "Scythian" period Esenin composed a long poem, *Inonia* (1919). It is a depiction of an arcadian peasant utopia, untouched by the plague of industrialization. Typically extravagant lines announce that "[He'll] imprint the earth with [his] soles hanging from the clouds" and "dig through clouds like an elk wheeling away." He had joined the left wing of the Socialist Revolutionary party (a group called the Scythians) in which his first wife was very active, met Ivanov-Razumnik, and under his influence embraced the latter's idea of the revolution, that instinctively was also his own.

The Scythians saw the social upheaval as a revolutionary

uprising of the masses; Esenin who was born and bred in semi-
nomadic central Russia, lawless and vagabond in spirit, believed
that the socialist movement drew its strength and elemental
power from the oldest national tradition of revolt. It was personified for the Scythians by such peasant rebels of folk history as
the sixteenth-century Cossack pirate, Stenka Razin and Pugachev. During this period of revolutionary messianism, Esenin
also wrote a short lyrical drama, *Pugachov* (1922), an exultant
tribute to the daring hero of the peasant masses whom he had
organized into a people's army that challenged the forces of
Catherine the Second. The poet reaches a paroxysm of blasphemy in spitting out of his mouth the body of Christ whom he
presented in another poem, *Comrade*, written in 1918, as a
mystical yet earthly symbol of assistance to the peasant and a
promise of freedom and equality. In this work Christian belief is
mingled with the cosmos against the traditional rural background and earth's yield of fruit and grain is related to cosmic
happenings.

The weight of the contradiction between these illusions and
the de facto Bolshevik action that was ravaging the countryside
to feed the "hated" city proletariat and trampling on the social
and spiritual ties that his pastoral dream held dear, unhinged the
poet's life. In 1924 Esenin wrote a grief-stricken poem, *Soviet
Russia*, which is one of his finest. He describes his return to his
own village, turned actively Communist and Komsomol minded.
The village is now alien to him, and he finds himself in it an
unwanted stranger.

He plunged with the blind, destructive thrust of a primitive
gone berserk into hooliganism that for the next several years
became a kind of self-immolating one-man jacquerie that transformed his private life into public scandal. Rowdyism, brawls,
debauches, and innumerable quarrels with his many mistresses
and wives accompanied him on his incessant round of city taverns. He married the famous American dancer, Isadora Duncan,
who was twice his age. She carried off her beautiful boy husband
to Europe and the United States, where his nocturnal escapades
continued to make headlines in the scandal sheets of two continents. Back home, a feeling of uselessness and isolation over-
whelmed him in the midst of the prevailing Leninism that the

poet, who could not get through even five pages of Marx, was ideologically unable to understand. He flaunted his literary Bohemianism in Moscow basement cafés, sought oblivion in womanizing, narcotics, and alcohol, and, in between fits of depression and wild revelry, he indulged a mounting despair in poems that are self-directed, emotional deflations that vibrate with great lyrical force.

In this last creative period, he returns from the intemperate imagism of the revolution-inspired "hymns" to his former direct, unemphatic melodious verse that is compounded of melancholy and nostalgia for the world of his peasant ancestors. There is a certain central monotony of style and content in such well-known poems as *Return Home* (1924), *A Letter from My Mother* (1924), *Orphaned Russia* (1924), *My Road* (1925). In addition, he expresses dismay and bewilderment at being irrevocably torn away from the beloved "humid earth." These sentiments went straight to the heart of innumerable young Russians who were being evicted from their rural communities. The very simplicity of his utterings won their affection. Esenin remains one of the most popular poets among his countrymen whose earliest national tradition was the vision of the vast Russian steppe, forest, river, land.

The poet himself was finally destroyed on the rack of that memory. He was confined to a mental institution in 1925 and soon after his release, slashed his wrists in a Leningrad hotel room. His last lines, "It is not new to die, but then it is not new to live," were penned in his own blood.

TSVETAEVA (1892-1941), AN INVETERATE ROMANTIC

Another testimonial to the vigorous poetical flowering of the century's first two decades is the dynamic, startlingly original talent of Marina Tsvetaeva. She is Akhmatova's only woman rival as a major Russian poet.

As opposed to Akhmatova's lyrical understatements of private emotional history, Tsvetaeva wrote passionately exclamatory verse. This poetry is less powerful for its abundant show of feeling, than for the torrential undercurrent of the rhythm, now expressed in long, majestic incantations, now jagged and abrupt, edging on hysteria in masculine rhymes of one- or two-word lines that generate a whirlwind of verbal motion.

Less abstruse in choice of vocabulary than Mandelstam, to whom she has been compared for verbal intricacy, and more sparing of metaphor, she adheres to paratactical linkings and juggles syntactical units of stem, prefix, and ending to get at the core meaning of a word and bring out novel sound patterns in the more intimate poems. Her characteristic stanza is self-consciously orchestrated in the modern manner, showily rhythmic, terse and mobile. The stanza is all the more arresting for the infectious beat that is frequently borrowed from folk poetry and simple peasant song. This results in a baroque extravaganza particularly suited to the poet's favorite subject matter: the projection of heroes and heroines from Greek and Christian mythology and Russian folklore in emotional confrontations where the woman in every kind of test of strength remains equal to the man. In such intimate lyrics as *An Attempt at Jealousy* (1924), *The Table* (1933), *I Wrote on a Slate Board* (1920), she expresses grief, passion, and homesickness. They are small marvels of tensile poetic expression, coiled around feeling like a spring.

The poet's personal life was traumatically miscast. Daughter of the curator of the famous Rumiantsev Museum in Moscow, she had been educated abroad. At eighteen, she began publishing poetry *(Evening Album,* 1910, *Magic Lantern,* 1912) that was noticed by Bryusov. In 1921 she emigrated to Paris where severe physical hardships, even penury, pursued her. Despite prolific production throughout the years of exile, only four collections appeared: *Measured Stakes,* Moscow (1921), *The King's Girl,* Moscow (1922), *Craft* and *Psyche,* Berlin (1923). Most of the Russian émigré journals in France refused to publish the "queer" telegraphic poetry that, intransigently "white" in tone, lamented the late Czar, her sheltered childhood, and idealized the counter-revolutionary struggle in the Civil War. *(Camp of the Swans* was written between 1917 and 1921 but only published in Munich in 1957.) Her private life became tragic when her husband, who was a Soviet agent, was involved in the assassination of Trotzky's son and to escape, fled to Russia with his daughter. She was put into a concentration camp while he was executed. Ostracism by the Russian circle became almost total when Tsvetaeva, with typical impetuosity, turned about-face and joined a left-wing Eurasian group in whose magazine she hoped to publish her work. Finally, accepting Communism on patriotic grounds, she returned to Moscow in 1939, but her "bourgeois" poetry was rejected by the State Publishing House. During the 1941 German offensive she was evacuated to a small village on the Volga and, unable to find any but a charwoman's work, she hanged herself.

Tsvetaeva collected her discerning insights into the art of Rilke and Pushkin and vivid personal memories of the poets she knew—Blok, Bely, Khodasevich, and Mandelstam—in a volume titled *Proza* (New York, 1953). Only twenty years after her death a selection of her poems appeared in Russia. Marina Tsvetaeva was the last of the genuine romantics, a "rebel in head and guts," who lived against the grain of her time and in her own words felt to the end that "the world was insane, the only answer to it was rejection." Her poetry was intended, as was that of the early Pasternak, for an educated and poetically sensitive public, and there is no doubt, as Renato Poggioli noted, that her expressionist technique and elliptic imagery bear traces of Pasternak's influence. He was the only poet among her contemporaries whom she considered her peer.

PASTERNAK (1890-1960), A MODERNIST SYNTHESIZER

Even before the publication of the controversial novel *Dr. Zhivago* had drawn the world's attention to its author, Boris Pasternak was considered by serious literary critics outside the Soviet Union as the foremost living Russian poet. He was also recognized as a brilliant synthesizer of the modernist experiments that had rocked Russian literature for the first two decades of the century.

It is difficult to assess the immediate literary impact on Pasternak of the most prominent modernist, Vladimir Mayakovsky. Pasternak met him in 1914, then full of conflict and in conflict. He admitted to an enthusiasm for Mayakovsky's tremendous drive and fierceness that neared idolatry and that dominated him for four years. However, he stopped admiring Mayakovsky after reading the "uncreative" *150,000,000*. He could not understand how a poet of great talent could waste himself on political rhetoric and wondered "what benefit Mayakovsky had derived from the demagnetization of the magnet." Not that Pasternak had been oblivious of the social cataclysm. He had been deeply stirred by the events of 1917, and Tsvetaeva had noted that "he had walked, rapt, alongside of the Revolution." But his poetical expression waited on a personal interpretation of history and a perspective. Only ten years later, he composed some lyrical fragments, *The Year of 1905*, that reconstruct his country's "soul searching" involvement in that political drama. Soon after he took another searing glance into Russia's tumultuous past: the tragic fate of the staunchly patriotic Lieutenant Schmidt (also the title of the long narrative poem) caught in the mutiny on the cruiser *Potemkin*. Pasternak recounted the episode in epic tones and with a starkness and sense of the inevitable that recalls Eisenstein's immortalization of the episode on film.

The social chaos and violent rejection of the past that nourished Mayakovsky and had momentarily exhilarated Esenin, were alien to Pasternak, brought up as he had been in a cultivated Jewish family that adhered to the continuity of humanistic tradition and the universal value of the arts. His father, Leonid Pasternak, was a well-known impressionist painter, remembered for his portraits of Leo Tolstoy and Rainer Maria Rilke (both of whom Boris had known from childhood as guests in his parents' drawing room). His mother, an accomplished concert pianist, had asked one of her friends, the famous composer Scriabin, to give lessons to the musically gifted boy.

Pasternak wrote an impressionistic autobiographical sketch, *Safe Conduct* in 1931, which is striking for its emphasis on the psychic growth of a young consciousness and the absence of cluttering mundane detail. The dilemma of choice is postulated—between a musical career, finally given up because he lacked perfect pitch, and the "intoxicating" world of abstract thought that unfolded in front of him when he became the student of the ardent neo-Kantian, Hermann Cohen, at the

Marburg school in Germany. And suddenly, almost magically, through an unhappy experience in love, young Pasternak became aware that he would be and could be nothing else but a poet. The morning after the emotional exhaustion and the sense of loss, the intensity and absoluteness of a new vision of the world was revealed to him. The need to start recreating his vision in poetry is recorded in the famous *Marburg* (1916).

The awareness of trifles—the autonomous importance of peripheral elements—shocked the poet into a new perception of the familiar landscape of life, as if he were seeing it for the first time. Thus in the *Marburg* poem: "I went out into the square. I could have been considered born anew. Each trifle lived, and setting little store by me, rose in its final significance." So every flower, tree, the wind, light, or any random, inanimate thing appeared to him as possessing its own energy and moving freely in shifting patterns of time, space, and shape in a coincidental and contiguous universe. The leitmotif of all his poetry is this reality, displaced and fluid, as seen in a drop of water under a microscope, in the "montage" of film techniques, in the Cubist painters' preoccupation with mutual relations between things that pull away from centralized representation to the consciousness of an isomorphic phenomenological world that was already sensed by Blok. This seems to posit Pasternak's outlook. Paradoxically, however, it is undercut by the human emotions of suffering, joy, and vulnerability that he ascribes to nonhuman entities, and to which the poet's self, an object in a world of objects, responds "out of a feeling that has displaced reality." This anthropomorphic process is not unlike Mayakovsky's personalization of a city, a street, the machine. But Pasternak is more lyrical and elusive; he is not to be confused with the stylized poetic fallacy or T. S. Eliot's objective correlative to a single human emotion. His is a cosmic experience that, in a return to pantheistic romanticism, the poet creates from within nature. (It should be noted that his third and most representative volume of poetry, *My Sister, Life,* is dedicated to the romantic poet Michael Lermontov.)

Contributor to the Moscow Futurist almanac, *Centrifuga,* and later to the *LEF* magazine, Pasternak published two collections of verse, *The Turn in the Clouds* in 1914 and *Above the*

Barriers in 1917 that received little attention. It was not until his third book, composed in 1917, circulated in manuscript and printed in 1922, that he was recognized as a considerable talent.

The themes of nature, love, and problems of art that prevail in *My Sister, Life* and the succeeding two collections, *Themes and Variations*, written in 1923, and *Second Birth*, written in 1933, treat a limited range of events. Many are related to the weather or to intimate incidents in ordinary settings of a garden, a city square, a country porch, or a room. Following the lead of Khlebnikov, he reacted against the fluidity of the symbolists and Mayakovsky's declamatory free verse. Pasternak produces a poetic word within the verbal structure, not according to Khlebnikov's metonymic principle however, but by breaking up the idiom and piecing it together again into tighter syntactical units for greater compression and sculptured form. This innovation, that did not extend to metrics or rhyme, and which is occasionally broken off in the manner of Mayakovsky, had an important influence on Tsvetaeva, Bryusov, minor Futurists, and later Soviet poets, as did the novelty of his adventurous imagery.

Two factors contribute to a certain difficulty in reading Pasternak and have tended to establish him as a poet's poet, influential but not popular. These are the frequent juxtaposition of words linking together the most dissimilar things and concepts (from strange to familiar, from human to nonhuman). More importantly, Pasternak attempts to express, in a dense style, what in his contracted language is almost inexpressible—the various connections between two emotions, one stemming from an undisclosed personal memory, the other a reflection of it and indicated by seemingly unrelated external phenomena. The effort required to decipher such obscurities is rewarded by an imagery and metaphors that, for dazzling comparative exactness and startling contiguity, are unmatched in modern poetry. They range from complex abstractions to a homely description of love in a gesture of a woman who, standing on a chair, takes the poet's life off a shelf and dusts it, to surreal similies: "the piano licking its foam like a man in an epileptic fit"; a cry "that like a black fork bored into fog up to the haft"; the visual and psychologically multiple sensation of parting in the flash of the last summer thunderstorm at the station that "doffs its cap and takes a hundred blinding snapshots"; the image of a road so polished by cart wheels that at night it reflects the stars and the poet, crossing it, tramples on the universe.

The need to define the function of modern aesthetics and his own art pursues Pasternak in both his poetry and several essays that tend to give to his work a highly studied, self-conscious air and, in some of the poems, a hermetically sealed private vision where intellect wins over emotion. But on the whole, despite the Soviet label of decadence, there is a vibrant feeling of buoyancy and spontaneous excitement of discovery in this poetry that its author has called "a summer with a third class ticket, a suburb, not a refrain." What the phrase means for him are the small, ordinary things in the world of man and nature that his perception has "marvelously" displaced and transfigured. In poem after poem his passionate observation records such fleeting impressions of immortality as two flowers glued together by a raindrop "drunk with thunder" that kiss and drink and do not stop and do not part.

In his self-fulfilling, creative life there was no room for political loyalties or commitments. Pasternak expresses this in a pungent line while looking down from his balcony to the courtyard below and shouting: "What millennium, my dear ones, are you building over there?" In the nineteen thirties, severely calumnied as an "individualist" in the Soviet press, his books printed in miniscule editions, he turned to the translation of Georgian and Armenian poetry, Goethe's *Faust*, Shakespeare's tragedies, selections of poetry from Shelley, Keats, Byron, Verlaine, and Rilke. One volume of his own lyrics, *On Early Trains*, was published in 1943. All the while he was reaching for a more full-bodied, less-personal expression of the fundamental moral issues of the time that culminated in *Dr. Zhivago*, discussed in a later chapter of this book.

ZABOLOTSKY (1903-1958), A SURREALIST-SOVIET STYLE

Recognition of his important poetic gift came late to Nikolay Zabolotsky, the first major poet to have grown up under Soviet rule. When his first collection of poetry, *Scrolls*, was published in 1929 critics attacked Zabolotsky for his pessimism and "outrageous formalist" techniques. The whole edition of the book was soon confiscated by the authorities and never again reprinted in full.

The "Scroll" poems are by far Zabolotsky's most original and significant work and the largest single manifestation of surrealist-inspired poetry to appear in Russia. It vibrates with other literary influences as well. In 1921, young Nikolay, a language and literature student at the Herzen Pedagogical Institute in Leningrad, was already absorbed in writing verse and as one of the most active members of the Society of Real Art was imbibing the radical Futurists trends. Khlebnikov's play on language and the restlessness, the drive and willed brutalities of Mayakovsky's thundering rhythms corresponded to his own perceptions of the cataclysmic urgencies of the age. The post-revolutionary upheaval had affected Zabolotsky's vision of the world. During his late adolescence he had been transplanted from a remote and changeless countryside to urban revolutionary life. The most memorable poems in *Scrolls* such as *At the Market, The Evening Ball, Football, Ivanovy* caricature Leningrad gripped by the fever of materialistic greeds that, in a return to selfish interests, debauchery, and moral squalor, witnessed in restaurants, amusement places, homes of the newly rich bourgeois, becomes an apocalypse of the pseudo. The poems are exciting and strange. They teem with splintered and distorted images of everyday life in motion. Also, the poet's systematic breaking down of the barriers of elements and laws of physics bring to mind the poetry of French surrealists such as André Breton, Philippe Soupault, Jean Arp, and the canvases of Dali and Max Ernst. The surrealist turns away from a rational view of the world. The real and the unreal are mixed and emphasized by recurrent startling metaphors (a fat car taking Piccadilly by the underarms or trees melting and growing fat like grease candles). The poet remains objective throughout, controlling with cleanly rhymed and rapid lines stanzas that at times appear like nonsense verses and then take on the primitive look of a Marc Chagall painting or a child's nonperspective acceptance of the universe. (It should be remembered that Zabolotsky had worked in the children's section of the Leningrad state publishing house in 1927, which may have intesified his flair for fantasy and wit.)

From this tragicomic jumble of philistine overabundance the chaotic view of Leningrad is enlarged to include that of all nature, now predatory, now impassive, beautiful, and haphazard, moving as in a Van Gogh painting in ceaseless and senseless swirls.

Zabolotsky published a long 773-line poem, *The Triumph of Agriculture* in 1932. He composed it in the style of a mock-heroic epic with burlesque overtones. The poet shifts his philosophical position from a belief in almost casual destruction of man in nature to man's gradual ascendancy over natural forces and over his own destiny. Khlebnikov's pantheistic outlook is reflected in stanzas on the liberation of animals and a certain humanization of nature that were castigated by the official press as a satire on agricultural collectivization. At the 1934 Congress of Writers, the proletcult poet, Alexander Bezymensky, specifically charged Zabolotsky with the "sickness" among poets that must be eradicated.

That Zabolotsky conformed in some measure to the social command was made clear in the collection of poetry published in 1936, *The Second Book*. Here he muted his earlier expressionistic stridency. Although the poet remained faithful to his search for harmony between nature and man, the more conventional poems no longer contain naked, "physiological" language, strive for greater musicality, and treat, for the most part, rural elegiac themes in smoother, subdued imagery. He remained, however, on the list of "suspected" writers. During the purges in 1938, he was arrested on a trumped-up charge and exiled to a Siberian concentration camp for eight years. On his return to active life he became a translator of Serbian, German, Italian, and Hungarian literature, and won high praise for his translation of Georgian classical and contemporary poetry and the adaptation of the twelfth-century epic, *Lay of the Host of Igor*, into modern Russian.

In the few poems that were printed in small magazines in 1947 and 1948 and in the later poetry, more widely published in the post Stalinist era—when Ehrenburg acclaimed him as a foremost Soviet poet—Zabolotsky shows a metamorphosis. A new serenity, which may have been attained through private suffering of which there is almost no mention in the poetry, has won over the anger and metaphysical fears that he had expressed earlier. The most successful poems of the fifties are slow paced, neo-classical in manner, sonorous and measured in the eighteenth-century Derzhavin tradition. They celebrate in a fusion of bacchanal and pastoral moods a harmony between the poet's inner feelings and nature.

2 · Dry Run of a Revolution:

Prose Experiments of an Era in Ferment

BLOK'S VISION of Russia as a land about to erupt with the explosive force of an earthquake became reality between 1904 and 1905 when the country was defeated in the humiliating war with Japan and suffered the debacle of Bloody Sunday. Much earlier there had been frequent social and economic upheavals in the form of agrarian riots, workers' strikes, subversive political propaganda, and terrorist acts against prominent government figures and members of the royal family. Meanwhile the class-ridden, caste-ridden autocracy maintained an obdurate and immovable front in the face of changing conditions that called for sweeping social reforms.

Tsarist Russia was losing its feudal look. Industrialization had been on the rise since the late nineteenth century. It had been favored by a government protectionist policy and the adoption of the gold standard in 1897 which attracted foreign loans and foreign investment. This in turn promoted technical innovations in the Russian industrial complex, greatly expanded the network of railroads, and increased the number of factory towns. As a result, the population of industrial workers doubled from 1860 to 1890 and numbered two and a half million by 1900. The towns provided deplorable living conditions; housing consisted of barracks and tenement slums overcrowded with workers who were underfed, underpaid, and exploited. Rural communities were on the decline: a combination of a rapidly increasing

71

birth rate, the paralyzing stricture of communal tenure laid down by the Great Reform laws, and the exporting of grain in order to pay for foreign loans, spelled land hunger. The peasant could not survive on his small land allotment, and he left the village to migrate to Siberia or find subsistence in the factory town.

The political opposition to the regime was composed of liberals—zemstvo leaders, enlightened and impoverished aristocrats, members of the professions—who pressed for representative government and civil rights for all. There also were two leftist parties. The Social Revolutionaries won great popularity among the dissidents for their hot-headed, romantic advocacy of terrorist tactics. They were heirs to the Populist tradition that demanded common ownership of all land (which was to be distributed on "just" principles among the peasants) and to that of federation of all the peoples in Russia in a republican framework. The other group was the Marxists, or the Social Democratic party, that drew its strength from the industrial workers and was guided by Lenin and Plekhanov from abroad. They directed an intensive underground propaganda for a workers' revolution that would be organized by a disciplined vanguard of the industrial proletariat.

At the turn of the century radical action was stepped up. Workers went on strike for shorter work days and more wages (from 17,000 strikes in 1894 to 87,000 in 1903). Peasants increasingly looted and burned private estates during the famine years of 1891 and 1892, 1898, and 1899 to 1901. The usual government reprisals of flogging, imprisonment, torture, and spectacularly staged pogroms of unprecedented ferocity were unable to restore complete order. As a result, the Minister of the Interior, Plehve, proposed the strategy of "a successful little war" that he was convinced would stem the tide of revolution.

The "little" war with Japan, started in January 1904, when the latter without formal declaration attacked the Russian fleet. The war proved to be an unmitigated disaster for Russia. The Russians surrendered Port Arthur after a year-long siege. They suffered the crippling of their 300,000-man army with the loss of 120,000 men killed, captured, or wounded, that showed up the inefficiency and unpreparedness of the Tsarist military command. The public mood was one of embitterment and frustration; the prevailing feeling among all classes of society was that the ruling powers rather than Japan threatened the country's collapse.

All over Russia, protest galvanized against the government with demands for industrial legislation, agrarian reform, an elected national parliament, and an end to the war. The protests were staged with the help of the St. Petersburg Soviet, members of the zemstvo from the provincial cities, and leaders of the intelligentsia. A petition containing these demands was to be delivered to the Tsar on Sunday, January 22, 1905 by Father Gapon. He led a mass of unarmed workers, 150,000 strong, through the streets to the Winter Palace. It was a peaceful march with the crowd intoning hymns and carrying icons and portraits of the sovereign. Nicolas was not in residence, but the imperial guard was ordered to shoot into the mass of the defenseless petitioners. Over a thousand were killed and many thousands wounded. It was one of the greatest political blunders of a regime noted for ineptitude, vacillation, and misrule, and it sparked off a revolution.

For the first time in Russian history a spontaneous revolt spread over the country, arousing the masses to join in the liberation movement. Agrarian agitation produced an All Russian Peasants' Union, which was the first political expression of the peasantry to come from the Russian soil. Half a million workers formed revolutionary unions, and mutiny flared up in the army and navy. The Grand Duke Sergius was murdered. In the ever-increasing flow of humanity that poured out into the streets from the obscurity of slums and workshops, Alexander Blok felt "suddenly and overwhelmingly" the people's will to live and found himself in the streets carrying a red flag at the head of a workers' procession.

During that first "political spring," the opposition parties were united, the propertied classes refused to support the autocracy, and a general strike paralyzed all public functions. The government was unable to quell the countryside. In October, however, a constitutional manifesto, wrung out of the Tsar by his prime minister, Witte, broke the revolution. A legislative duma to be elected by popular franchise was announced, and full civil liberties were granted to all. The liberals, who had become fearful of the continuous brutality of the plundering peasants, accepted the terms of the manifesto. They took no part in the armed December uprising of the workers' Moscow Soviet, and it was suppressed with the most ruthless measures. The enormous unrest within the Russian empire was temporarily calmed, not to be stirred up again until the final cataclysm twelve years later that destroyed the empire itself and put an end to its dynasty.

Meanwhile, an antipolitical reaction had set in and a feeling of frustration and defeat among the avant-garde intelligentsia found expression in purely personal efforts, such as productive capitalistic enterprise or the exploration of the libido. These trends, and reactions to them, were reflected in the esoteric, stylistically ornamental fiction of Remizov and in the works of the most prominent and popular writers of the realist tradition, Korolenko, Kuprin, Andreyev, Bunin, and Gorky.

KOROLENKO (1853-1921), A POPULIST WRITER

Vladimir Korolenko is the foremost representative of imaginative writing in the Populist tradition. He comes nearest to Leo Tolstoy in his love for the common people, faith in man's essential goodness and his right to dignity and happiness. These were humanitarian ideas that he championed indefatigably in editorials of the Populist monthly, *The Wealth of Russia*, and that pervade his short stories. The heroes of the stories are primitive, unlettered, "little men," who are for the most part rootless peasants, turned vagrants, or, by force of circumstance, thieves or murderers. Korolenko treated them with profound sympathy that just escapes the sentimental, with patches of an open kind of unsophisticated humor and highly poetic descriptions of nature that infuse the narrative in a Turgenev manner, with atmosphere and depth.

Northeastern Siberia is evoked in his early stories and particularly the dazzling white wasteland and the subpolar lights of the Yakut region to which young Korolenko, arrested for his activities in the Populist movement, had been exiled for six years. It is the background for *Makar's Dream* (1885), his most famous story about an old semi-Christian, semi-pagan Yakut shrewdly bargaining for salvation. The story contains all the major elements that characterize Korolenko's later stories: the deeply black-and-white Yakut landscape expressing the primeval force of nature at the heart of human conduct, the author's emotional involvement with a savage mind that is finally touched by a divine light, and the delightfully humorous incongruity of the old man's factual interview with God. Korolenko's last work of some length is the largely autobiographical *Story of My Contemporary* (Vol. I, 1909, Vols. II and III, 1921). It is a realistic and vividly presented portrait of Russian society and its radical element from the abolition of serfdom to the assassination of Alexander II.

KUPRIN (1870-1938), A ZESTFUL STORYTELLER

Praised by Gorky, Tolstoy, and Korolenko for his straightforward, vigorous realism, this prolific writer (twelve volumes published by 1917) greatly admired Kipling and Jack London. His work is saturated with action and crowded with a colorful variety of "strongly" situated social types—gamblers, circus wrestlers, prostitutes, horse thieves, master spies, and adventurers.

Kuprin left an army career to wander through Russia, turned singer, dental assistant, actor, fisherman, journalist, carpenter, cook. He became fascinated with humanity, whose talk, habits, and feelings he absorbed in exact detail. Kuprin describes man's spontaneous zestful feel for living; it marks all his characters, even those most damaged by the cruelty and brutishness of their milieu.

Such, in the novel *The Duel* (1905), is the idealistic young officer whose gradual disintegration the author plots against the moral torpor and petty malicious intrigues of the provincial garrison. This powerful indictment of the military, published during the Russo-Japanese war, was received with immediate polemical comment and has become his best known work. Artistically less successful but widely read and translated is another short novel, *The Pit* (1909-1914), that highlights a brothel in a large southern town in sensational close-ups of the women and their clients. To insure the authenticity of his descriptions, Kuprin lived several weeks in such a house and conveys its feverish nocturnal throb with photographic realism. But when he leaves this world for a soul-probing analysis of what has created it, Kuprin lapses into mawkishness. The same loss of aesthetic control flaws the *Bracelet of Garnets* (1911) included in many collections. It is a short story of a minor clerk's passion for a princess that dissolves into a melodramatic ending.

It is in the robust yarn centered around a well-defined plot that avoids moral and social issues or psychic complexity, such as *Staff Captain Rybnikov* (1906), *The Laestrigonies* (1907-1911), *Seasickness* (1908), and *River of Life* (1910), that Kuprin is at his best. His lack of culture and a certain artistic taste are compensated for by a tremendous curiosity and illuminating observations about people and evident enjoyment in building up adventure for its own sake.

After the Revolution, Kuprin emigrated to France but wrote very little, became ill, and in 1937, after ingratiating himself to Soviet authorities, was allowed to return to Russia where he died a year later.

BUNIN (1870-1953), A LAST CLASSIC REALIST

A superb craftsman and the last realist of great talent in the classical tradition of Chekhov, Goncharov, and Turgenev, Ivan Bunin was the first Russian author to receive the Nobel Prize, in 1933.

If it were not for his strong anti-Bolshevik position as an émigré writer, Bunin would appear out of context, so little did the intellectual and political upheavals of the early twentieth century affect his art. Thematically, Bunin's writing was shaped by his personal circumstances of declining gentry life and his inability to afford a university education. His early work consisted of three volumes of orthodox, rather beautiful nature poetry written between 1892 and 1907 that was permeated with melancholy. Although he continued to write verses, it is in his first and only novel, *The Village* (1910) and a long novella, *Sukhodol* (1912), for which he was awarded the coveted Pushkin Prize by the Russian Academy, that his uncompromisingly pessimistic statement was first understood. In a period of the idealization of the moujik it was Bunin's novelty and daring to depict the bestial, barbaric, and poverty-stricken rural life in *The Village* mercilessly, and to lay bare no less harshly in *Sukhodol*, through a servant's recollections, the meanness of spirit and cultural savagery of decaying Russian squiredom.

The numerous short stories are models of Chekhovian economy and compression in which the foreshortened effect of action is dominated by a stagnating existence. The individual, lacking a dynamic society to absorb him, compelled to live by "his own inner light" as it were, is ineluctably driven downward toward death that the occasional brief immersion into love-passion seems only to hasten. This theme obsessively haunts Bunin's best-known stories, such as *The Gentleman from San Francisco* (1916). In this story a wealthy American on a pleasure cruise has a heart attack in Capri and his coffined corpse is shipped back in the hold of the same boat ploughing through an ocean snow storm, while the usual gala festivities throng the upper deck. In *Sunstroke* two strangers meet on a Volga steamer and form a sudden passion which is abruptly broken when she gets off without letting him know her name or address. In *Poor Grass* (1913) an aging and sick factory worker is taken back to his village to die, lingers on, staying approaching death in dreams and fitful memories in a vain attempt to fasten upon some past happiness in his life. In *Dreams of Chang* (1916) a dog watches his master, a down-at-the-heels retired sea captain, drink himself to death because of an unfaithful wife.

Bunin excels in the creation of atmosphere by an almost perfect concordance of word and subject and in the struggle, not always won, of suppressing his feelings just at the moment when he awakens the emotions of the reader. Two later, post-revolutionary pieces are more subjective. They are set in the Russia of the nostalgic exile. *Arsenev's Life* is a semi-autobiographical description of a child from "a nobleman's nest" and his early development. *Mitia's Love*, a banal tragedy of a youth's sexual awakening through jealousy and a crude physical initiation that precipitates his suicide, contains some exquisitely poetic passages such as a beautiful early spring lyrically evoked in poignant contrast to Mitia's growing unhappiness.

To nature in all its forms, from the quiet autumnal sunset over a darkening Russian field to the mast-shattering wildness of an ocean storm, or the density, movement, and heat of the tropical jungle Bunin pays homage with the most precise language. However, his descriptions move us very differently from the way that Tolstoy's openly sensuous love of the earth does, or Turgenev's delicately landscaped correspondences of sound, color, and movement. Between his heroes and their contracted destiny, Bunin places the marvelous externality of the elements, and contemplates them in their mystery and their power, now seemingly familiar participants in the normality of living, now throbbing deeply above and beyond humanity in the splendor and detachment of a cosmic rhythm that reduces man to complete insignificance.

ANDREYEV (1871-1919) and ARTSYBASHEV (1878-1927), SEEKERS OF SENSATIONS

Andreyev's meteoric and ephemeral success is a fascinating footnote to Russian literary history. In dramatic contrast to Bunin's resolute willingness to adapt to his time, Andreyev identified his own neuroses with the psychological depression of the bourgeois avant-garde. He expressed his most intimate wishes and fears in short stories and plays, which are hyperboles of moral horror, nihilism, pathological sex, and madness. Similar to Norman Mailer, he continuously responded to the prevailing intellectual climate and tumultuous current events. They excited and unsettled him and compelled him to project the collective psyche of the Russian intelligentsia in a tormenting and tormented search for a truth that teetered between realistic portrayal and metaphysical abstractions.

Andreyev was influenced by Tolstoy's contempt of culture and insistence on death and sex, Dostoevsky's anti-hero for man's rebellion and withdrawal into an inner loneliness, Schopenhauer's pessimism, Strindberg's obsessions, and Poe's elements of terror. The writer's predilection for shock techniques that in personal life led to an extravagant display of wealth in appearance and habits, also influenced his writing style. The ungoverned rhetoric that aimed to excite and terrify (in Tolstoy's much quoted words "Andreyev wants to scare me, but I am not scared") with spectacular effects is weakened by overemphasis and overabundance.

Still, the melodrama of what appears to us now as escapist best sellers, but what the author developed with great seriousness and sincerity, struck a deep and disquieting chord among his contemporaries. From about 1902 to 1910 each new work increased the writer's popularity, and stories such as *The Abyss* and *The Fog* published in 1902 were lauded by modernist critics.

The hidden power of sexuality and its hold upon idealistic youth that has not learned to recognize it is treated in realistic narrative style. These stories scandalized conservatives who charged Andreyev with pornography and immorality. In the first story a young couple, lyrically in love, is attacked by three drunks who rape the girl and beat her lover into unconsciousness. When he recovers he finds her lying partly clothed beside him. He gives in to passion and rapes her in turn. The second piece deals with the murder of a prostitute by a young student whom she has infected with syphilis and who afterwards kills himself. Waiting for inevitable death is the theme of *The Governor* (1906) based on the assassination of Grand Duke Sergius in 1905. The Duke had ordered a public beating of demonstrators, and in the story the governor of a province who took repressive measures is expecting a terrorist's bullet with an awareness of his end that is strongly colored by the last passages in Tolstoy's *Death of Ivan Ilyich*. Its carefully restrained tone is at odds with the violently antimilitaristic *Red Laugh* (1905), a feverish monologue of an officer who lost both legs in the Russo-Japanese war and, unable to endure the memory of the "horror and madness" of the killings and atrocities, lapses into insanity. Inspiration for Andreyev's finest work and the most widely translated, *The Seven That Were Hanged* (1908), came from the successive death penalties (in Russia imposed only for political crimes) meted out after the 1905 uprisings. The harrowing description of the seven revolutionaries in their solitary cells, who are about to be executed, may have influenced Sartre's play on the same theme. The story may have also affected world history. Its Serbian translator, school teacher Danilo Ilic, was lodging with Gavrilo Princip who was assigned to assassinate the Archduke Franz Ferdinand on June 28, 1914. It was not until Ilic had written an article about the story and had described Andreyev as the greatest contemporary writer that Princip decided to take part in the plot and planned the positions where all the conspirators should stand during the assassination.

From 1905 to 1916, Andreyev wrote twenty full-length plays. They were for the most part symbolical dramas that, in typical Andreyev fashion, insisted on negation of life, its senselessness and vanity, and the haunting presence of death. The originality of the staging illustrated the exciting dramatic techniques of the new movement in the theatre arts. However, Andreyev's theatre was no more alive than a morality play and very much like it in the stilted declamatory prose, the static acting, and the effort to present depersonalized ideas in the form of allegory through cumulative and repetitive devices. This complied precisely with the experiments launched by the brilliant directors Vsevolod Meyerhold and Stanislavsky who were rejecting "outdated" realism in favor of deliberate artifice, stylization, abstract designs, and a concentration in each scene on an idea or a mood.

The earliest play, *To the Stars* (1906), centers on the problem of the unimportance of individual lives in a cosmic context; the astronomer is the symbol of this indifference as he withdraws to his mountain observatory away from revolutionary destruction while a blizzard literally cuts him off from men. The uselessness of all human existence in *The Life of Man* (1907), which was a huge box office success, is stretched to its ultimate allegorical meaning in five acts with Man, His Wife, His Son acting out macabre tableaux to the chronicle of The Man's Life being read near the wings by "Someone in Gray."

A much livelier, expressionistically styled comedy-drama, *He Who Gets Slapped* (1915), exposes the uselessness of the mind itself when an erstwhile intellectual turned clown is bawdily beaten to the delight of a jeering circus crowd. A comic American film is based on this story.

Andreyev's works did in fact reflect the tension between the intellectual inner life of the period and the constant public threat to it. But the writer's powerful insights into this imbalance were too scattered, too spasmodic, and too subjective to create a coherent system of his ideas.

Andreyev is remembered as one of the two leading advo-

cates of the new sensualism that swept over the young generation after 1905. The other, very much less talented proponent of
uninhibited sexual drives was Mikhail Artsybashev (1878-1927)
whose immensely successful novel, *Sanin* (1907), was published
after the final repeal of censorship. It flaunted sexual license in
the teeth of conventional morality that "had outlived its day."
Its message seemed to inversely echo Tolstoy's dictum to reject
the "artifices" of civilization and to espouse natural urges. For
the hero, Sanin, this dictum was realized in the physical union of
man and woman; it contained all the answers to life.

The artless, ploddingly written novel, now deservedly forgotten, is composed of pseudo-philosophical discussions on sexual emancipation along strongly naturalistic seduction scenes.
The admixture of ideological and libidinous elements suited
perfectly the educated Russian public brought up on a serious,
nineteenth-century literature of ideas but now, in its mood of
spiritual and moral depression following the abortive revolution,
avid for powerful escapist diversions. It found them in Sherlock
Holmes thrillers, Jack London adventures, Edgar Allen Poe
gothic tales, in the erotic stimulants of the rediscovered Decadent poets (Bryusov, Balmont, Sologub), and in the fiction of
Artsybashev and Andreyev.

By 1915, Leonid Andreyev's popularity was very much on
the wane. It was to be expected that the work of this most
articulate spokesman for the bourgeois intelligentsia that lived
prior to 1917 would not outlast its own disappearance from the
Russian scene.

REMIZOV (1877-1957), A STYLISTIC ORNAMENTALIST

Alexey Remizov offers a bonanza of grotesque, mischievous,
pathetic, realistic, and fantastic elements in his works. There are
clearly discernible influences. The impressionistic freedom of
structure, a lyrical exuberance, and the lingual novelty of his
prose narratives, with priority given to style rather than content,
recall the novels of Andrei Bely, his early mentor and only friend
among the symbolists. His first two novels are drawn from his
own street experiences as a boy from a poor merchant's family in
Moscow. They outdo Gorky's realism with a pitiless portrayal of
the sordid tenement conditions of the workers' population in

Moscow (*The Pond,* 1908) and in St. Petersburg (*The Sisters of the Cross,* 1911).

Turning to provincial life, Remizov depicts its mental and spiritual barrenness, vulgarity, and vicious pettiness in two episodic narratives (*The Story of Ivan Stratilatov,* 1908, and *Fifth Pestilence,* 1912). Each is centered around the vicissitudes of a civil servant. Remizov chronicles the tangled web of venal meanness and suffering caused by petty desires, or gloats with Gogolian relish over the unlit depths of his hero's mind, and, like the master whom he fully acknowledges, happily brews the trivial and the significant into simmering, humorous grotesque. There are traces of the *Petty Devil* in the compiling of senseless small cruelties. They are treated, however, not with the hatred Sologub expressed, but with pity and resignation. Human beings, it seems, were not equal to the job of controlling nefarious impulses that were, somehow or other, imposed upon them from the outside. In a revealing passage in *Fifth Pestilence* Remizov drops the narrator's pseudo-genial, bantering manner to lament in the dirge-like tones of Russia's oldest oral tradition the "outrages, oppression, destruction, want . . . lawlessness" that is the scourge of the Russian land with its people, "shifting, disunited, sundered by a thousand deliriums, erratic, silent, voiceless."

Remizov also was influenced by folkloric poetry, fairy tales, apocrypha, and ancient legends that he indefatigably unearthed and collected with an obsessive interest. He had come by this interest early. His mother, who had left her husband to return to her family's home of pious observances, would take her children on distant pilgrimages to hallowed monastery shrines and Alexsei's mind, already peopled with fantasy, would drink in the religiously infused popular lore that threaded the constant talk of their fellow pilgrims. This kind of a story of belief in dreams and premonitions was compounded of unbridled fantasy and the most concrete, at times erotic reality. It was laced with pathos or naïve humor. It represented for Remizov an authentic manifestation of native literary genius. His writings before and after his emigration in 1921 contain adaptations and recreations of this earliest evidence of Russian literary imagination (*Russia in Writ,* 1922, *Nicholas Parables,* 1924) and countless fairy tales that featured goblins, gargoyles, witches, weird animals, and evil spirits. Many will remember the gnome-like, hunchbacked, impishly grinning writer receiving his friends in his Paris study surrounded by toy facsimiles of these weird creatures.

Remizov's ornamental prose, that at first glance has a stylistic affinity to elaborate seventeenth-century calligraphy that he favored in his personal correspondence, is in fact a rare example of preponderantly colloquial composition. In the manner of Leskov, another acknowledged master, he creates a "skaz." The individualized intonations for each character constitute a seemingly natural, spontaneous, oral flow. Remizov manages to express in writing the cunningly intricate verbal art of the consummate storyteller. His style was imitated and adopted by many early Soviet writers such as Pilnyak, Katayev, Zoshchenko, Vsevolod-Ivanov. They followed him in his buildup of comic, thrilling, and lyrical effects with teasing digressions, verbal and sound play, sudden changes in structure together with dialectical turns and regional speech inflections that Remizov expressed in the rich idiom of pre-Petrine Russia. His insistence on bringing back Russian to its native lingual sources, when the language had not yet been permeated by German, French, or Latin elements, was no less spectacular than Mayakovsky's depoetization of poetical forms. This constitutes Remizov's great originality.

GORKY (1868-1936), AN EMBATTLED PROLETARIAN

Maxim Gorky is a dramatic example of the involvement of literature with politics that exists in Russia. His early life was full of brutishness and bestiality, physical squalor, callousness, and backwardness typical of the lowest working class into which he was born. He became at the age of ten one of its nomadic laborers. He personified one of the causes of the revolution, in which he, as a writer, was to play a special and world-famous part. During his years as sometime cobbler's boy, icon cleaner, stevedore, servant, and night watchman, he became depressed enough by the senselessness and stagnation of his milieu to attempt clumsy suicide that cost him a pierced lung.

Gorky educated himself with voracious indiscriminate reading and mingled with revolutionary and radical intellectual circles. That gave him an entry into journalism, and he finally had some of his stories published in the regional newspapers of Tiflis,

Astrakhan, and his native city Nizhni-Novgorod. It is significant that in his first creative bid for freedom, he exalted barefoot tramps, thieves, and gypsies as independent lawless outcasts from society, "creatures that once had been men." This young mind, crammed with gothic novels (his first book was the *Mysteries of Otronto*), early Balzac, Pushkin's poems, saints' lives, and reams of pulp fiction, was fascinated by a romantic image of the raw type of Russian vagabond. His adventures were recounted against a detailed background of the immense steppe and rivers of the Volga region that were the path of Gorky's own wanderings. These romantic elements were blended with the tough crude language of his casually cruel, ignorant, bawdy heroes. This was the kind of romanticized and yet vigorous reality that the Russian public, fed on Chekhov's pessimistic understatements, was apparently ready for. Among Gorky's first selection of stories, which came out in two volumes in 1898, was one gem of taut, relentless prose, *Twenty Six Men and a Girl*. The story is set in an airless basement bakery where men knead dough sixteen straight hours at beggar's wages; here, a pretty innocent young girl came to buy some loaves each day. The faith that the men still held in life's beauty despite their wretched existence, is destroyed when a soldier, on a bet with them, succeeds in seducing the girl. Afterwards, they greet her with savage howls of rage and abuse.

It was the merciless realism of this lower world that held the greater appeal for foreign readers, as did the portrayal of the derelict inhabitants of a flop house in the masterful drama *Lower Depths* (1902). (This play may have inspired Eugene O'Neil's *The Iceman Cometh*, so similar is it in structure and theme.) It was produced by the Moscow Art Theatre, with Stanislavsky in Sanin's role, to filled houses and ran for 500 consecutive performances in Berlin. It was not immediately understood among the critics, until Gorky had strengthened Sanin's part, whether he had intended Luka's "brotherly compassion" to dominate the play. That typically Russian beggar-pilgrim, steeped in facile lore and sanctified dogma, dispenses comforting lies to the defeated human beings, and they are momentarily sustained by them. Why not solace the dying Anna with a vision of heavenly bliss, assure the actor, a hopeless alcoholic, that he would be cured at a chimeric sanitorium, and encourage shrivelled Nancy in her identification with a heroine out of a French novel. Why not indeed, until Luke is revealed to be a shady character running away at the first sign of the police and his "sickly" falsehoods are blown apart in Sanin's final speech when in his cups he extols the dignity of man that like Gorky's ex-human hoboes is "large, free and proud unto itself."

In Petersburg, Gorky quickly established a reputation as an embattled proletarian writer. He joined the Social Democratic party. In 1900, he founded his own press, *Znanie*, that attracted the best talents of the neo-realistic school (that included Andreyev, Bunin, Korolenko, and Kuprin). A major purpose of the press was to revive the nineteenth-century notion of the writer's civic responsibility in opposition to the purely aesthetic goals of Decadents and symbolists. As director and editor-in-chief, Gorky encouraged men of letters to treat social and political problems, and with his initiative *Znanie* became the center of revolutionary and democratic literature. Gorky signed, with many others, an outraged letter against the cutting down of students by the Cossacks in a street demonstration. Then, soon after, he penned some allegorical verses titled "The Stormy Petrel," that announced the impending revolution. As a result, a legend began to grow around Alexey Peshkov. He was the son of a Nizjni-Novgorod paper hanger and grandson of a barge hauler. At the age of 24, he had signed his first published short story with the word "gorky," which is Russian for "the bitter one." The bitterness that he recorded against the appalling reality that had been his lot went hand in hand with his faith in man's eventual victory over his own stupidity and enslavement. To the realization of this goal he committed all his extraordinary energy, his intelligence and his writing talent.

The literary production, for sheer bulk, is impressive: nine long novels, seventeen plays, numerous short stories, and three volumes of memoirs. In the best long works, *Foma Gordeyev* (1899) and *The Artamanov Business* (1925), at opposite ends of the creative span, Gorky makes a grippingly realistic exploration of the predatory lower-middle-class capitalist who ruthlessly hacks his moneyed way through the thickets of barbarism and ignorance of which he is a part. But with the dominating imagery once established, the massive structure of the novel begins to cave in for lack of inner development. The problem of opposition to such exploiters dissolves into melodrama (the idealistic Foma unable to endure the festered tangle of his father's injustices and cupidity turns into the village idiot) or remains suspended. Other principal characters fail to grow into vital situations. The same lack of inventiveness and imaginative control flaws two other well-known narratives, *The Small Town of Okurov* (1910) and *The Life of Matvey Zozhemyakin* (1911). The latter is an Okurov resident, like Foma a superfluous man, who fumbles for meanings in the overriding drabness and stagnation of the time that finally overwhelm him.

The Mother (1906) made a great impact on the working class movement and was translated into some twenty languages. It is based on Gorky's contacts in 1902 with the workers of the Sornov region near Nizjni-Novgorod and relates events in the struggle between them and their employers. It is important as the first inside view in Russian literature of the proletarian force in a specific and localized revolutionary action. It is important, as well, for the hero's emotional espousal of the cause and as a piece of fictionalized propaganda that describes the transformation of apathetic, slothful factory hands into effective political activists. Although the novel is steeped in the spirit of socialist evangelism, that is expressed in extravagantly effulgent metaphor, it fails as a work of art. It is piquant to recall that *The Mother* is American born, composed in the Adirondacks where Gorky took refuge from some nasty publicity that had surrounded his would-be triumphant lecture tour in the United States where he hoped to raise substantial money for the revolutionary fund. His welcome to New York was cut short when a rumor was spread, probably by the tsarist embassy, that the actress Andreyeva who accompanied the distinguished visitor was not his wife; all his engagements were cancelled.

None of his plays, among them *The Enemies* (1906), *The Barbarians, Children in the Sun,* and *Summer People* (1905) equals the dramatic mastery of *Lower Depths,* although the "message," that is only stated at the very end of this play, is conveyed in these other dramas. The thematic centrality common to them all is the confrontation of the intelligentsia with

the people. The latter are set as critic of the effete and ineffectual educated class, who, for all its good will, appears incapable
of truly understanding the problems of the masses. The most
powerful play, *Vassa Zheleznova* (1911), is a character study of
another moral despot in Gorky's gallery of strong personalities.
This is a monstrous mother obviously created to refute the
concept of the idealized maternal devotion for the worker-son in
The Mother.

The most-quoted Gorky passages in world literature are
taken from *About Tolstoy,* 1919, an impressionistic recording of
conversations with the great writer whom Gorky met in Yalta in
1910 when he was recovering from a tubercular attack. Tolstoy
comes alive spontaneously and irrepressibly as never before; his
sly irony, huge, guffawing gaiety, flagrant contradictions in
speech and mood, and his immense cleverness are caught by a
master memorialist. It is the same skill of inspired reportage that
shapes another intimate recollection, the first part of Gorky's
Autobiography, Childhood.

With characteristic candor, Gorky noted in 1910 that the
dark and seemingly incredible events that had come from his
own past and that he had tried to express, not too well, in his
fiction, he would now present straightforwardly, as fact. He
averred that his purpose was not to unburden himself of a heavy
past but, to lay it before the reader, in order that its suffocating
reality might motivate an indifferent world to corrective reform.
Unhampered by the imaginative need to invent, associate, and
structure, Gorky gives us the galling reality as it was, with cruel
clarity. The pages are crowded with a great variety of Russian
types, as in his other works. Everything and everyone that he sees
and hears is vivid, instantly there and true. The portrait of his
grandmother who alone protected the small boy from a tyrannical, whip-happy grandfather who threw the ten-year-old boy out
on the street to earn his own living, is a marvel of moral beauty,
affection, and charm. Like Proust's grandmother, like the nurse
in *Eugene Onegin,* she is unaffectedly natural, and her feeling
for oral poetry and sunny religiosity lend hope and courage in
the face of all the sordidness and misery. Still, it is a strangely
externalized personal memoir that eschews inner feelings as if
each individual, including young Alexey, only marginally pres-

ent, were watched and described from the outside, Tolstoy's reflection that Gorky was a phenomenon rather than a writer comes to mind.

Gorky *was* phenomenal in his feral and obsessive conviction that given a decent, just, and economically healthy situation man could be happy and free, and, armed with reason and energy, would become master of nature and the machine. There was something naïve and even touching about his obstinacy in promoting this uncomplicated formula for happiness which he thought could be brought about through revolutionary action. He could not or would not understand a more complex human universe, which explains his impatience with "psychology."

It has been advanced that if Gorky had not been so involved in politics, he would have been a greater artist. However, there is more to be said for the contention of his latest biographer, Irwin Weil, that his revolutionary engagement was generated by his early background that in turn fuelled his creative writing. It was in itself a passionate social protest that gave powerful, if limited, perspective to all his work. The story of his life in between and after the Russian revolutions that he lived actively and dreamed dynamically, and in his personal life as well, he supported the tsar's opponents with pen and substance, often risking his freedom on behalf of the people's cause. He was an active participant in the Bloody Sunday march. In 1905, he was forced to leave Russia to escape imprisonment and settled in Capri. His house teemed with Russian writers, artists, revolutionary émigrés. He met Lenin, who became a close personal friend and who fixed Gorky's course in Marxist ideology. In 1907 he became delegate to the fifth Social Democratic Congress held in London; the following year he taught Russian literature in a school for workers at Capri that he had organized. When a general amnesty was extended to political dissenters in 1913, he returned to Russia. Two years later he founded an antimilitary review, *Letopis*, that attacked nationalism and imperialism in its advocacy for a peaceful Europe without national boundaries.

During the October Days, shaken by the bloody fights, the arrest of old revolutionaries and the loss of freedom, Gorky, no blind follower, attacked Lenin and Trotsky for their "degeneration of socialism." Typically, during the chaos and disorder of the early Civil War, he used his enormous personal prestige and easy accessibility to Lenin to organize a society, *Freedom and Culture*, for the education of the people; remembering his own learning-starved youth he planned to make available scientific and literary matter to all strata of the population. The publishing house, *World Literature*, under his direction, was to make available classics from all over the world. He recruited hundreds of writers as translators, keeping them alive with government rations during the famine years between 1919 and 1921. He saved many valuable minds. In addition, Lenin never refused his friend's plea to save this or that writer from prison or the firing squad and put up with his frequent criticism of dictatorship policy. Lenin, however, did seize the opportunity to urge treatment at a German sanitarium when, exhausted by an excessively busy routine and his constant worry about others, Gorky began to spit blood again.

He went to Germany and then to Sorrento where he kept up a voluminous correspondence with young Soviet writers, corrected their manuscripts, and encouraged their fledgling efforts. In 1928 he returned to Stalin's Russia. Was it a compulsive return? Did he become convinced that Lenin's new order was the wave of the future? Was it simply every émigré's deepest wish to get back home? Or was it the ambition to culminate his long and distinguished service to his country with a seat in the highest cultural councils as the poet laureate of one of the world's mightiest confederations? For whatever reason he decided to go back, his return was met with a nationwide accolade. His native city, streets, monuments, and factories were named after him, and over 800,000 Soviet citizens attended his funeral rites as well as the highest dignitaries of the state.

His allegiance to communism along with his appeal for freedom is one of the many contradictions that marked Gorky. An inner civil war, possibly on an unconscious level, raged within him. He felt alienated from his society, for it was not ordered the way he wished it to be, and yet he was deeply attached to its oldest traditions that his grandmother's folk tales and legends had instilled in him. Gorky also faced another conflict in that he was a fervent altruist who supported the fight for a social upheaval, but he was not prepared to accept its necessarily ruthless realization. He was that contradiction—a conservative revolutionary and in his creative work a romantic realist. He knew and portrayed the bulk of humanity as stupid, mean, cruel, ignorant, and shortsighted. Yet even from the lowest depths of human degradation he had Sanin proclaim that "Man is proud," and in a prose poem called "Man" (1903) he sang a hymn to him. He exposed truthfully the squalor and brutality of the "lumpenproletariat." At the same time he poetized its rejected products, the bums and hoboes, their restless, anarchic spirit that in its lawlessness and independence matched for vigor another breed of lawless men—the money-power merchant tycoons. Out of his sense of moral outrage, Gorky should have abhorred these predatory acquirers who devastated the human landscape with their cupidity and cynicism. It is obvious, however, that implicitly their author was fascinated by them and even admired them.

Maxim Gorky has been acclaimed as the creator of the new "tramp" type and made largely responsible for the invigoration of traditional Russian realism that had declined in the wake of the nineteenth-century masters and was yielding ground to the modernist movement. His main literary contribution is of a documentary nature. He not only wrote unforgettable sketches of Tolstoy, Chekhov, Andreyev, Bunin, and Korolenko but he also gave an authentic picture of prerevolutionary Russian society and its gloomy, external reality. Thus, in his last, longest, and incomplete work, *Klim Samgin* (1925-1930), it was not the new order that he attempted to chronicle but Russia from 1880 to 1917. Although it was a cross section of all the classes, he concentrated on exposing the gradually crumbling intelligentsia that, as Blok had more artistically predicted, was to collapse with the onrush of a new ideological force.

Gorky's influence on Soviet literature, similar to Belinsky's impact, a hundred years earlier, on generations of Russian critics was colossal and disastrous. Formally known as a people's author with a dramatic revolutionary past, Gorky became an idol among the newly educated workers in socialist countries; 42 million copies of his works and translations of them in sixty-six languages were sold between 1917 and 1946.

During his last year in Russia, Gorky became appalled by the decline of realistic literature in the 1920s. He aspired to have it reestablished by means of political directives. The sense of a social mission that he preached and that had flawed much of his own creative writing, was eagerly assimilated in the budding Soviet climate of indoctrination. The worst traits of his writing that projected humorless optimism, earnestness, a restrictive external aspect of the heroes and their situation that eschews universal values, became an approved inspiration for the literature for the masses.

The writer had once respected culture and its freedom above all and he had written that "no socialist society has anything to fear from the unfettered powers of creation." He thought of "creative intelligentsia," even the symbolists, whose "decadence" he detested but whose talent won his praise, as Russia's real leaders. Yet it was Gorky who helped to aesthetically pauperize his country's literature with his own example and impose on the writers who succeeded him formulae that became a creative straightjacket. This was the culminating paradox of his career.

3 · 1917 Revolution:

The Civil War

IT is one of history's many ironies that the collapse of the Romanov empire and seizure of power by the Bolshevik Soviet, perhaps made the greatest political impact on the contemporary world, and that the collapse came about in a most unspectacular way. From March 15, 1917, when the Tsar abdicated, to the overthrow of the Provisional Government on November 7th by Lenin, public disturbances were confined, for the most part, to demonstrations, street meetings, sporadic strikes, and workers' riots. The Red Army's occupation of the Winter Palace, that signalled the victory of the Russian Revolution, did not interrupt Russian life.

Not until the ensuing civil war did the Russian people, transformed practically overnight from subjects of a monarchy into citizens of the largest socialist state, become engulfed in the social upheaval that brought on physical hardships on a scale unprecedented for a modern nation. Two thirds of its territory had been ravaged by White and Red armies that equalled each other in banditry and atrocities. By 1920, the country that had been weakened by a disastrous war was on the verge of economic collapse. Railroads were barely moving for lack of repairs and replacement parts, industry was operating at a very low capacity, and the peasants, whose grain and produce had been forcibly requisitioned by the state, were cultivating just enough of the still arable land for their own needs while the horrors of hunger, epidemics, lack of fuel, and clothing stalked the cities.

State control of all national resources had been further tightened with War Communism measures that conscripted all labor and private wealth, and set up food priorities. Official barter was established after money had lost all value. The result was a huge black-market operation that degraded and perverted human relations. Then, in 1920 Russia suffered famine, with some 13 million peasants lacking even the grain for seed. Unimaginable privation and misery prevailed in Moscow and Petrograd during that terribly cold year.

This was also the most difficult year for writers, artists, or journalists, who for the most part did not collaborate with the new regime and were first and hardest hit by the Revolution. Of their appalling material situation, Victor Shklovsky wrote that "to live at all that winter, was a battle," a ceaseless attempt to keep warm enough to stay alive. Books, furniture, and every scrap that was not food or clothing found its way into what Zamyatin in a surrealist tale *(The Cave,* 1923) wryly called the great God Iron Stove.

During these rough, barren years, the intelligentsia experienced psychological duress as well. Its "bourgeois" concepts of spiritual and moral values, cosmopolitan learning, political idealism, moral refinement, and the cult of beauty were being systematically rejected as irrelevant and without worth to the new social order. This was intolerable to great numbers of writers, among them older representatives of the Silver Age such as Berdyayev, Vyacheslav Ivanov, Merejhkovsky, and Balmont. With scores of journalists, critics, and artists, they chose exile in Paris, Berlin, London, Prague, Riga, Belgrade, Kharbin, and New York. They founded publishing houses, literary magazines and newspapers, and continued to write openly and freely. Some of them, such as Mark Aldanov, a prolific writer of historical novels, and Ivan Bunin, 1933 recipient of the Nobel Prize, earned an international reputation. Although some, among them as Kuprin, Bely, and Tsvetaeva (previously discussed), eventually returned to the Soviet Union, the majority of the dispossessed elite remained in their adopted countries. In the midst of a foreign culture, they kept alive their transplanted language and traditions through persistent contributions to the emigration press despite physical hardships and a necessarily restrained and dwindling reading public. The story of their professional lives has been recorded and illuminatingly assessed in the works of such literary historians and critics as Gleb Struve, Wladimir Weidle, George Ivarsk, and Vladimir Markov, and such memorialists as Nina Berberova and Ilya Ehrenburg.

The Civil War had barely ended in 1920 when the Bolsheviks had to face an even greater inner threat. The peasants began a series of uprisings against grain requisitioning and labor brigades. This was spearheaded by the March 1921 Kronstadt mutiny of sailors, recent draftees from the countryside. They demanded more economic freedom, a breakup of the Bolshevik monopoly, and the right of assembly for trade unions and peasant organizations. Although the revolt was put down by Trotsky's loyal Communist troops after ten fierce days of fighting in blinding snowstorms, it became clear that to save the revolution it was necessary to re-establish an alliance with the peasantry. Lenin proposed to instigate a regular system of taxation and allow the peasant to dispose of his surplus on the open market. Permission was granted to peasants, merchants, and small businessmen to engage in private domestic commerce and trade. This was the basis of the New Economic Policy or NEP that scrapped War Communism measures and helped to revive production of foods and services. Actually these concessions did not prevent the government from retaining a monopoly over all large industry, transport, banking, and foreign trade. Private enterprises only made up 5 percent of the gross national product. The individual businessmen who had done most to stabilize the currency and redress the balance of supply and demand were finally to become the first victims in the era after NEP was instituted.

Nevertheless, the benefits of NEP were immediate and pervasive. Consumer goods began to reappear on an open market. A deliberate and sustained effort was made to improve workers' conditions with social and medical insurance, housing, hospitals, and recreation centers. The government mounted a huge campaign against illiteracy through compulsory elementary education and opened a great number of secondary and graduate schools. These years of the 1920s witnessed a return to normalcy and a renewed vitality in many sectors of national life; most impressively in the world of letters.

Intellectual life revived with the reopening of universities, museums, libraries, and publishing houses. Its pulse quickened with the rapid publication of classics (translated under Gorky's aegis), collections of criticisms, memoirs, poetry, and contemporary Soviet fiction, along with the founding of new literary magazines. The license to travel abroad stimulated a vigorous intellectual exchange between Moscow, Petrograd, and European cities. Officially sanctioned branches of Russian publishing houses were set up in Germany (the only country that had renewed its diplomatic and commercial ties with the Soviet Union) where the works of Soviet writers could be protected by international copyright laws that were inoperative at home. This encouraged some political émigrés to return to Soviet Russia with news of the revival that was taking place after World War I in the theatre, film, literature, and arts in the West. Something of the same exuberance and excitement in novel artistic and literary ventures was reflected in the numerous literary organizations that were now springing up. The party, absorbed in maintaining its hold on political power, was as yet uncertain of its policy in matters of culture. During the NEP period cultural affairs were controlled by the highly cultivated Commissar of Education, Anatoly Lunacharsky. He sanctioned the humanistic tradition of the intelligentsia, an independent aesthetic position toward the arts, Futurist manifestos, and the Proletcult radicals who wanted to sweep out the past completely.

Russian literature had been prophetically announcing the revolution years before its actual advent. Portents of impending social catastrophe underscored the poetry of the symbolists. A religious interpretation as a final struggle between Christ and Anti-Christ by Dmitri Merezhkovsky appeared in his trilogy, entitled "Christ and Anti-Christ," and Andrei Bely, shaken by the human losses in World War I, expressed his fear that the end of the world was coming. The Scythians, among them Bryusov, Blok, Bely, and Esenin, created apocalyptic images of the Russian masses destroying old values in a new barbaric world. The exalted tenor of these "hymns" to the revolution matched the fervor and hyperbole of the Cosmists and Smithy groups of proletarian poets.

Basement bistros, taverns, and clubs had become, with the paper shortage of 1918 to 1920, centers of contact between a poet and his public. These young men, fresh from fighting for the Soviets, caught in the tremendous excitement of what for them were world shaking events, declaimed in overcharged heroic verse the might and magnitude of the workers' revolution. The symbolists' influence persisted in the verbal ornamentation of Cosmist poetry while the glorification of the collective that distinguished the Smithy writers borrowed freely from the Futurist rhetoric to express the "blood and iron" will of the proletariat.

Both groups belonged to the Proletcult (Proletarian Cultural and Educational organization) founded by Alexander Bogdanov in 1917. It was committed to create a true proletarian art inspired by the new social order. It also was to explore the experiences of men who made up the masses. Most of the older writers, members of the Communist party, encouraged provincial literary novices from the heartland of the country to combat "bourgeois" writings, and favored content over form in the style of psychological realism. Creative writing courses for workers were organized throughout the country and well-known literary artists such as Gumilyov, Bryusov, and Bely, participated in the instruction. Unfortunately, they produced little more than politically inspired ideas and rhetoric poorly conveyed by ideological consistency. As a result, the three hundred Proletcult workshops backed by the state, that in 1920 boasted an enrollment of 85,000, were reduced to seven workshops and only five hundred members in 1924.

Among the writers in these workshops Demyan Bedny (1883-1945) and Yuri Libedinsky (1889-1959) should be singled out. Bedny was a witty satirist, who specialized, like Will Rogers, in a humorously folksy style. Bedny was immensely popular among the Soviet masses for his anticapitalistic jingles and songs and a favorite of the party until Stalin rebuked him for lampooning Russian history in one of his comedies. Libedinsky's novels, by contrast, are cast in a framework of great seriousness and purpose. *The Week* (1922) describes means whereby the Reds, with great loss of life, suppress a peasant uprising led by the Whites in a small Ural town. In *Commissars* (1926) an ideological slackening among Red Army political commissars immediately after the Civil War is forcibly tightened. *The Birth of a Hero* (1930) deals with conflicts between parents and children arising from diverging revolutionary attitudes and the deadening effect of conformism and the desire for creature comforts on the vitality of the socialist cause. If it were not for the credibility and variety of his very human characters, these three novels could be considered a kind of aggregate manual with fictional underpinnings of guidelines to Communists for the realization of the hoped-for Communist world.

The author's most engaging trait, that generated great enthusiasm among his many first readers, was the honest approach to the great task of remoulding Russian life. No attempt was made to gloss over the personal sacrifices entailed in the process. They are vividly rendered in flashes of individual resentment, frustration, and anguish, and they lift the story above the political drive to the human dimension of passions. In *The Commissars* the inner operation of the party is observed with the almost naïve directness of a dedicated, pure-minded proletarian who wants to share with his fellow Communists the burdens and risks of the social reconstruction that lies ahead. Particularly persuasive is the portrait of the illiterate Cheka agent in *The Week* whose physical survival is partially due to a psychic insensitivity that allows him to withstand the savage peasant cruelty and inhuman horror of the revolt. The agent's more sophisticated and educated successor, Eidnunen, in *The Birth of a Hero*, is admirably drawn as the efficient, cold-blooded administrator who is rigidly party-minded and does not understand complex human relations. The struggles of the hero Commissar Shorokhov, an aging revolutionary, with the new generation of Communists and with his own libido inclinations, which by the end of the book he has overcome, also came under attack as "weak willed, Hamletic" lingerings of the principal character. Libedinsky was severely criticized for the unflattering depiction of a Soviet official and eventually had to acknowledge his mistake.

Meanwhile, a very young group of writers, of bourgeois origin, dubbed by Trotsky as "fellow travelers" (generally sympathetic to the revolution but unwilling to accept the party line in totality) moved into the center of the literary stage with an *Almanac* (1922) that was acclaimed a vigorous new thrust in Soviet fiction. It included stories by Vsevolod-Ivanov, Zoshchenko, Kaverin, and Fedin. Most of them were newcomers to literature. They had banded with several other fledgling writers in a loose association called the Serapion Brothers (after the hermit, Serapion, a character in one of E. T. A. Hoffmann's tales, who believed in the reality of poetic visions and the freedom to express them).

The original club, frequented later by Katayev, Pilnyak, and Leonov, was formed in 1919, at the Petrograd Translators' Studio of the House of Arts that became a meeting place for discussions of literary problems and goals. What united these young people, most of them recently demobilized from the Red Army, was the urge to recreate the revolutionary experience they had lived through, record the harrowing events in credible images, capture manageably in rapid, episodic form the turmoil, chaos, and fragmentation of a world being destroyed and a world in the making. The content was overwhelmingly there; the question was how to approach it.

When the brilliant Formalist critic and essayist, Victor Shklovsky, was invited to give a course in literary criticism and the writer, Yevgeny Zamyatin, known for his semantically "displaced" narrative language, came to lecture on style, study and discussion naturally focused on problems in literary techniques. For Shklovsky, great admirer of Laurence Sterne, architectonics of narration held first place. He demonstrated the varieties and twists of plot structure that the author could play off against his subject. Traces of his teaching are visible in the broken sequences and digressions in the stories of Pilnyak, Kaverin, and Leonov. Zamyatin concentrated on potentials of language, its rhythm and instrumentalism. He elucidated the continuity of stylistic development in the Gogolian hyperbole, Remizov's ornamental speech in "skaz," and Bely's protean diction and rhyth-mically hypnotic prose. (All are discernible borrowings in Zamyatin's own early stories.)

ZAMYATIN (1884-1937), A PIONEER OF MODERNITY

As an avant-garde writer who broke away from nineteenth-century tradition to create a new portrayal of irrational contem-porary man in his realities of being rather than in his everyday life, Yevgeny Zamyatin impressed upon the Serapions the con-cept of literary modernism. His image of the world that was freed of settled Euclidian assumptions and subject to relative and changing truths was to be expressed by a modern revolution-ary art. Like the new sciences that are based on conditioning, abstraction, and irreality, this art constructs reality through the aesthetics of distortion, displacement, and curvature. Zamyatin's contention that the modern writer must discern the essence of this new reality in his own individual way, through the primacy of subjective impressions, clearly inspired the Serapion manifesto published in 1922. Its final draft had been composed by Lev Luntz (1904-1924) the theoretician of the group. The manifesto protested all ideological coercion and proclaimed the artist's right "to paint his hut to suit himself."

Luntz was the youngest and possibly most brilliant member of the Serapions and had written three swiftly paced and intri-cately plotted plays in the Western romantic style. He equated the current sweep of political events with the writer's creative force and aspired to lift present-day literature out of its dol-drums with organic, living works. Luntz again echoed a govern-ing theme in Zamyatin's well-known essay, *Literature, Revolution and Entropy* (1923), advancing the modernist view that the twentieth century is in a state of permanent revolution.

Zamyatin's own fiction is impregnated with the revolution-ary temper that he inherits from Gogol and Dostoevsky. Like them, he is haunted by the fear of conformity and the mecha-nization of life, and the natural rebelliousness that arose from this fear led him to engage in subversive political action in his student days. Between bouts of arrests, intermittent exile, and training as a marine engineer, he started to write. He early developed a tense internal consistency in satirical exposure of philistinism in a mentally and spiritually stagnant milieu, as in the long short story, *At the World's End* (1914). He defines brutish and vulgar officials of a small garrison in eastern Siberia with Gogolian overtones. It brought an official rebuke that almost brought him to court and did get him sent to England during the First World War to construct ice-breaker ships for the Russian Navy. He stopped publishing until 1917. In the stories, *The North* and *The Miracle* (1918) denigrating effects of spiritual loneliness are emphasized and the better known novella, *Islanders* (1918), stamps Zamyatin's aversion to the conventionally pious, insular, and rigid respectability of the British middle class.

As counterthrusts to the prevailing negation of human values, Zemyatin introduces love as a physiological urge (Katuishka's nymphomania in *Tales of a District*, 1913), idealistic sentiment (Kostia's feeling for Glafina in *Alatyrd*, 1915), romantic interludes *(Summer in the Forest*, 1917), and spontaneous and irrational emotions in *The North*. Even more forcefully, nature and energy wreak revenge on atrophying social and physical existence in *The Womb* (1915) when a healthy peasant girl, craving a child, murders her elderly husband with the help of her young lover. It is made clear that the latter, a political revolutionary, embodies within his revolt against a decaying social class the dynamics of irrational force and individual freedom as well.

By 1918, Zamyatin was considered the most sophisticated, modernist writer of neo-realistic prose. He shed the skaz narrative of his earlier style and began to enrich ornamentation with color symbolism and use a device of Gogolian grotesque in depicting human beings as objects. In *Islanders* the tractor-like Kemble becomes a tractor bogged down in mud, then stalled, then operating with a broken down steering mechanism. (Some of the finest artists of the 1920s attempted to emulate this dynamic device.)

Characteristic of Zamyatin is the integral picture of a principal idea managed with a deft handling of parallel events that flow out of a central metaphor to reinforce each other, as in the stories *What Matters Most* (1924) (a juxtaposition of a kulak revolt ending in fratricide and a similar destruction on another planet where people war for bottles that contain the only available air) and *The Flood* (1929) (the physical disaster of a famine-ridden St. Petersburg reproduced, psychologically, in a murder of passion when the heroine reduced by starvation to a near-barbarous state, is "flooded" with jealousy and kills her husband's mistress).

What Matters Most is startlingly modern. Some thirty years before the "anti-novelists" in France began to advocate the "dehumanization" of literature, Zamyatin announced its salient features: fascination with the relativity of time and space, fulgurations of geometrically repetitive landscape, and depersonalized, unmotivated characters who are observed by the narrator, disconnected pieces of action and dialogue. The most successful "anti-novel" writers, such as Alain Robbe-Grillet (1922-   ), another engineer by profession, and Claude Simon (1913-   ) might claim Zamyatin as their direct predecessor.

A wide scale of spoken forms—colloquial, regional, and Biblically rhetorical—within patterns of rhythmic and musical stylization, adds great vibrancy to the language. Zamyatin never used his methods, however, to express a single arbitrary detail. Every impression, every state of mind is limned with the utmost compression, gathered into a core image that generates derivative images related to each other on several planes of meaning, each segment flashed in a succession of impressionistic scenes.

Most impressive in the virtuoso show of ellipticism is the brilliant caricatural play of object-images as people and artfully interwoven reality with abstraction that is the intellectual matrix of Zamyatin's creative undertaking. What it lacks is a certain human feeling and human warmth. Ideas parade as persons; landscapes, buildings, and colors represent states of mind. Nowhere does the writer do this more dramatically than in *We*, a first modern anti-utopian novel that brought him international fame.

Although *We* has not been published in the Soviet Union, an abridged translation came out abroad in 1920, and in 1952 the complete Russian text was printed in New York. Its significance was not fully recognized until critics noted its great influence on two celebrated satirical fantasies (*Brave New World* by Aldous Huxley, 1930, and *1984* by George Orwell, 1948) at a time when the Western world was beginning to be haunted by the spector of totalitarianism. In this extremely original blend of political satire and science fiction, Zamyatin raises, as Dostoevsky's Underground Man and Ivan Karamazov raised before him, the great issues of the century that deal with freedom and happiness, reason as opposed to irrational will, and the individual's role in an increasingly faceless, mechanized society.

The novel *We* presents a standardized, collectivist One State of the future, ruled by an omnipotent Well-Doer, supervised by an army of trained "guardians," citizens of which live in glass houses, have numbers for names, wear identical uniforms, walk along streets in a four-to-six formation. Work, leisure, and food are communal, and even love-making is rationed to specific, officially sanctioned hours. With uncanny precision, Zamyatin prophesies the climate of a total scientifically geared dictatorship with such features as one-slate, unanimous, computer-recorded elections, electronic listening and seeing devices in public and private areas, gas chambers, brain-washing operations. We learn of this utopia from the diary jottings of D-503, a mathematician assigned to the construction of a gigantic space ship, *Integral*, that is to "integrate the indefinite equation of the Cosmos" by sending the message of "the grateful yoke of reason" to distant planets. Against a background of surrealistic images, the action proper develops when D-503, loyal cog in the machine (although some of his notes are troublingly human, like the strange patch of hair on the back of his hands), conceives a wild passion for a woman, I-330. She is the organizer of a revolutionary movement that propagates the forbidden "uncivilized condition of freedom." His world sunders; increasing attachment to I-330 reveals to him his irrational self that had only been enslaved to official dictates of reason that aimed to correct "the contortions of life." In a typical construct of simultaneous and interrelated parallel planes, Zamyatin proceeds to chart, as on a graph, the mathematician's ascending human curve while real life is beginning to infiltrate through secret channels into the glassed-in and walled-off enclave of the One State. When he is led outside the Green Wall to meet the semibarbarous Memphi—the last survivors of the Two Hundred Years War that resulted in the One State—he is drawn to the primitive urges of this people who are identified by I-330 as "the other half of us." He experiences through his intimacy with her a new, timeless awareness of the universe with his entire being. His restlessness increases even as the "infection" of subversion spreads in the One State; he draws plans with I-330 to sabotage the *Integral* and symbolically restore Self to Nature with the destruction of the Green Wall. The plot is discovered, I-330 is executed, and the space-ship builder docilely submits to a brain operation that removes his nervous Center of Fancy and permanently transforms him into a useful citizen of the One State.

That the ideal of non-freedom as a scientifically established formula for happiness is an illusion, finds point and substance in D-503's tormented diary jottings and his conversations with I-330. She represents, in the novel, Zamyatin's fierce advocacy for man's inner irrational freedom that draws strength from the remnants of an older, more instinctive world. To her lover's conviction that the One State had brought about the last revolution in creating a planned, turmoil-proof society, she answers that "Revolutions never end."

It was generally understood that Zamyatin's *We* originated from his apprehension of tightening party controls over Russian life. The novel, banned in the Soviet Union, was published in Prague in an abridged Russian version in 1929, without the author's consent. He then was systematically vilified by the Moscow press. He was forced to resign from the Writers' Association that issued an injunction against his published and unpublished works. As a result, Zamyatin addressed a personal request to Stalin that was strongly endorsed by Gorky, to leave the country. It was granted. He settled in Paris where his writings were reduced to a trickle, and, after several years of illness, he died in 1937.

YOUNG WRITERS OF THE TWENTIES

In the third decade of the century, the Serapions and other fellow travelers kept bright the reassuring flame of originality, dynamism, and artistic independence in a last phase of uninhibited creativity in Soviet literature.

Soviet society in revolutionary and post-revolutionary process tugged at their imaginative mainsprings and brought about many forms of literary expression. Among them, three major modes of approach to a reality not yet pressed into social and political molds shaped the literary climate of the period: revolutionary romanticism, satire and grotesque, and sociopsychological realism.

REVOLUTIONARY ROMANTICS

From among the revolutionary romantics held in the grip of their experience of the Civil War, Vsevolod Ivanov, Boris Pilnyak, and Isaac Babel came nearest to reproducing its explosive power in a subjective, hyperbolic vision. The vision was created out of the chaos and disorder that was the very fabric of a universe out of tilt, and reflected in stories dipped in brutality, cruelty, and horror. This fiction marks a departure from traditional literary modes. The emphasis is shifted from character to situation. There is neither psychological analysis nor detailed surface realism.

The prose expresses the dynamics of violence that will the disorganization and rupture of common perceptions. It vibrates with Futurist and Formalist accents in its cult of new forms—split narration, sudden transitions, hard images, chiaruscuro contrasts, ellipticism, intersecting surfaces. An atonic harmony is built up between sharply profiled, changing scenes and disjointed composition that moves fast, on several levels, as in Vsevolod Ivanov's stories. Ivanov creates this harmony while shifting constantly in and out of narrative, or lyrical and colloquial dialogue.

VSEVOLOD IVANOV (1895-1963)

He brought into Soviet literature some of the most gruesome episodes of guerrilla warfare that appeared the more exciting and credible to his wide public for being placed in the exotic, little-known Asiatic hinterland, among the Kirghises, Chinese fisherman, Turco-Tartars, and Russian colonists. Like this semi-nomadic population, Vsevolod Ivanov became a rootless drifter early, leaving his impoverished parents' home in a border town between Siberia and Turkestan. He worked at a diversity of jobs (sword swallower, circus clown, laborer, printer) that likens him to the adolescent Gorky. Similarly, he also was attracted to subversive social elements. Politically uninformed but craving political action, he joined the Socialist Revolutionaries and the Social Democrafts, enlisted in the Red Army in 1917, fought with the partisans in the Far East against Kolchak, was severely wounded, and just barely escaped being shot. All his tales from 1922 to 1924 are based on his own harrowing war experiences, including combat at Vladivostok that plotted his first and best-known novel, *The Armoured Train* (1922). It is the story of the capture from the Whites of the seemingly impregnable iron monster, symbol of the capitalistic plague, by partisans only armed with rifles and the voluntary self-sacrifice of one of them who lay across the rails so as to stop the train's momentum.

When his work began to appear in the thick monthly Marxist review, *Red Virgin Soil*, its editor, Alexander Voronsky, wrote glowingly of his primitive partisan fighters. It was a new type of hero, rough, crude, carnal, carelessly cruel, even bestial. He was mindlessly fierce and indifferent to danger and death in combative action. He lived by his instincts and exuded the elemental vitality of the earth from which he seemed to have just emerged. Mutual magnetism of nature and these children of nature vibrated in the exurberant writing about them. Vsevolod Ivanov's bold and striking images that deal with the appetites of the flesh and the uninhibited sensuality of his virile men and women (startling in generally prudish Russian literature) borrow something of the poetry and unexpected shape and color similes of lyrical evocations of the wild Siberian plain, its rivers, the forest, the wind.

The author's "Serapion" training is visible in the "twist" of narrative sequence or its ending that adds "strangeness" to the tale; the stylistic ornamentation and interpolation of the skaz, frequently studded with racy Siberian idiom. His characters lack any ethical principle or regard for larger human values. Instead, the author describes his heroes as being unable to fend against forces that they cannot understand. Like a one-dimensional chapbook character, not yet endowed with moral traits by folklore, each lives in a small space limited by immediate physical urgencies, unaware that outside the action that gives him a function, he is meaningless.

Ivanov unsuccessfully attempted to create an authentic humanly credible Bolshevik leader in Vershanin *(Armoured Train)* and in Vaska Zapus *(Sky-Blue Sands)* that he wrote in 1923. In these loosely linked episodes relating to the capture and recapture of a small Siberian settlement, the two main characters who do not pity, wonder, reflect, or hope and whose purpose is based on ideological banalities, are finally eclipsed by the vortex of "blood and sweat" in which they are caught. The vortex itself fascinates Vsevolod Ivanov; it is the real hero of his shock-charged stories in situations of torture, arbitrary violence, starvation, kill and over-kill. The terse matter-of-factness of the author's tone adds an unreal, gothic dimension to the narrative.

By the late twenties, Vsevolod Ivanov was adapting himself to officially approved trends of psychological character development, deleting from reprints of his first stories some of the "biologism" for which he was being criticized, and writing in a simpler, more direct style. In *Mystery of Mysteries* (1927) Ivanov still portrays the senselessness of man's struggle against overwhelming physical odds, but he does not achieve the earlier sweep and vigor in these somber stories nor in the amusing, fictionalized account of his circus days, *A Fakir's Adventures* (1935), or in *Parkhomenko* (1938), a biographical novel, which is soberly historical, properly "Sovietized" and denuded of the romantic exuberance of his early work.

PILNYAK (1894-1938)

Boris Pilnyak's first novel, *Naked Year* (1921), immediately established him as a foremost Soviet writer. It is, by the least reckoning, a daring attempt to capture the mood of all Russians during the 1919 famine year in the setting of a sluggish provincial town and the countryside around it. It is a startling, difficult, and magnetic book. The immediate effect is of a literary work in process that the author seems to be assembling haphazardly, out of disparate materials—old and recent legal documents, newspaper clippings, citations from the fiction of his own protagonists, refrains from folk epics, snatches of fairy tales, and descriptions of semipagan, semi-Christian fertility rites. He repeats passages at intervals to add to the disorder and sense of incompleteness. He also comments between chapters directly to the reader on the dubious merit of his undertaking. A plotless narrative, less a novel than an elaborately constructed montage of abruptly alternating and disconnected episodes, it breathes, almost palpably, literary influences that infused the sessions of the Serapions.

Bely's impact is most evident in the intricacy of syntactical clusters, hypnotic rhythms, and unfinished allusive phrases. Traces of Zemyatin appear in the ornamented prose and the construction of intersecting and shifting planes. Remizov is recalled in the skaz sequences, paragraphs of pre-Petrine theological writings, and the many archaisms that lard peasant talk. Andrei Bely was reputed to have complained about these wide borrowings, but as critic Robert Maguire perceptually notes, they actually helped the older writers. Pilnyak's own immense popularity as the most exciting chronicler of the Civil War diffused the techniques and devices of his teachers among fledgling authors of the so-called "Pilkyanism" school that was making an important impact on early Soviet literature.

Perhaps unconsciously quoting Balzac, Pilnyak used to say that words for him were like coins to a numismatist. This intoxication with stylistic artifice and verbal forms matched his romantic exuberance in the depiction of the revolutionary whirlwind; the chaos that it wrought fascinated him no less than it did Vsevolod Ivanov. He reveled in "playing," as the Formalists put it, with chunks of the monstrous reality in the same impassive, crudely naturalistic manner. One such famous "chunk" is the course of a southbound freight train through the famine region, packed with starving refugees over whose heads, legs, arms, and human droppings others swarm in an attempt to board the cars at station stops, beating their way in to find a foothold and being beaten off. Unlike Vsevolod Ivanov, however, Pilnyak betrays a passive apprehension of suffering in scenes of wilful atrocities, mental disintegration and decay, bawdiness, degrading daily privations, and the bared thrusts of anguish in the constants of birth, physical survival, sex, fear of annihilation, and death.

Against this darkening landscape of indistinct figures from all levels of the crumbling social order that flit in and out of the text, emerges the only real character in the book, which is Russia herself. It is the semi-Asiatic country that for centuries has lived uneasily between two truths and is now forcing the masses to make their own history by rising up against Western culture. For Pilnyak, as it was for Esenin, this is the meaning of the Russian Revolution. The author welcomes this gigantic revolt as a people's movement, fermented by instinctive, anarchic urges and the need to defend a thousand-year-old, close-to-the-earth existence nourished by superstition, pre-Petrine orthodoxy, and pagan memories. Echoes of the ruthless Stenka Razin and Pugachev mutinies vibrate through the work and seem to invite comparison with the Scythian specter that haunted the symbolists' imagination. But for Pilnyak the major issue at stake within the cataclysm was less the active conflict of East and West than the rejection by the peasantry of Peter's superimposed civilization, in a willed and deliberate return to immemorially traditional life. The author appears to admire the new "leather men in leather jackets" from the city, with their purposeful faces and clever minds, but whose effort to instigate, decree, and direct scientifically planned reforms is savaged by the hostile villagers' reaction to intrusion upon their work and leisure. That the author is actually in sympathy with the peasants is allusively and beautifully stated in lyrical passages following such violent encounters. Pilnyak makes incantory evocations with hallucinatory prose to the "invincible" Russian forest, snow-swept fields, and the heavy blackened river to convey the elemental presence that surrounds and seems to support the huts, inhabited by sheep, pigs, and men. A unique intimacy is created between human beings and nature that Pilnyak acclaims as changeless and timeless.

For his "romantic overreaching" into the sources of historical energies, some critics have called Pilnyak a romantic anarchist, an emotional sociologist. In the preface to a 1927 collection of his works, the writer describes himself as a "naïve romantic vagrant" who happened to be passing through Russia at its fateful hour and expresses the certainty that later generations would justify him. In point of fact, it was not until Freud had popularized for us the clinical approach to psychology that Pilnyak's diagnosis of a political revolution, shorn of national bias, could be understood. In paring the saga of the peasantry down to its primitive bones, he dug deep to the fundamentally regressive tendency in all instinctual life. His originality, of which he probably remained unaware, was to draw the interesting parallel between the Russian ethos and the individual human psyche. His was a creative demonstration of the Freudian principle that an underdeveloped country, under the pressure of hostile external forces, would revert, as a similarly disturbed, semicivilized human being reverts, to an earlier state of things and a kind of inertia native to all organic life.

Pilnyak was an attentive reader of Tolstoy, and he began to develop the theme of the struggle between the gradual mechanization of human beings and the eternal rhythms of nature. In the novel, *Machine and Wolves* (1925), that in accordance with Pilnyak's favored self-plagiarism device, contains whole sections of *Naked Year,* and which it resembles in tone and style, the spirit of city and factory is pitted against somnolent rural Russia. The author's fear of the machine as a destroyer of man's inner peace and personal happiness is the prevailing leitmotif.

Second only to *Naked Year* in astonishing force and resonance, three novelettes, (*Mother Earth* (1926), *Tale of the Unextinguished Moon* (1926), and *Mahogany* (1929), orchestrate variants on Pilnyak's single and obsessive theme. *Mother Earth* is a darkly poetic evocation of perennially changeless peasant life on the steppe and in the forest beyond the Volga, elemental, brutish, self-absorbed. Its resistance to change finally drains meaning out of Bolshevik Nekulyev's reforestation program and brings him to the edge of terror as the witness of the casual atrocities inflicted by the natives on Whites and Reds alike when they make forays into their land. A nostalgic atmosphere pervades *Mahogany*. It is set in a backwater town in the 1930s. The natives still breathe the air of its ancient kremlins, crumbling church towers, beggars, pilgrims, and fools-in-Christ, that survive, like the few remaining pieces of finely carved seventeenth-century mahogany furniture, as collectors items. They are as anachronistic in the NEP period as the hero of the story, a pure Communist who remains faithful to the egalitarian revolutionary ideals. He holds the construction of the new state in abhorrence and chooses to share in a dug-out a poverty-stricken communal life with a few like-minded companions.

Taut, direct, tensely structured, atypically slight in verbal flourishes and detail, *The Tale of the Unextinguished Moon*, constitutes Pilnyak's most savage attack against modern man's violation of the laws of nature. The Tolstoyan ethical imperative of existing in harmony with the physical world is invoked in the "unnatural" death on the operating table of a Red Army commander who was forced by the party machine to undergo surgery that he did not want or need. It was officially ordered "to keep in good repair a valuable worker of the state." The icy, almost unbearably tense climate of the story that moves, like Greek tragedy, toward ineluctable doom, was based on the actual demise of a popular high-ranking military officer, one of Zinovyev's close friends, whom Stalin liquidated in a similar fashion. Ironically enough, a small literary masterpiece and Pilnyak's greatest artistic achievement led to his literary death and eventual physical extinction as well.

Pilnyak was not forgiven *The Tale*, for which both he and the editor of *Novy Mir*, where it was published, had to make extensive public apologies. There was more serious trouble ahead when *Mahogany*, turned down by the Soviet censor, was brought out in Russian by a Berlin publishing house in 1929. A storm of abuse broke over the author's head in the Soviet press. Despite his many abject recantations, the attacks against him continued. Although he held the office of chairman at the Moscow headquarters of the All-Russian Union of Writers to which most of the best-known authors of the period belonged, he was forced to resign from that association. He made an effort to make amends with the novel, *Volga Falls into the Caspian Sea* (1930) that purported to celebrate the inauguration of the First Five Year Plan. He depicted the construction of a hydraulic plant that was to reverse the flow of the Moscow River and make it navigable by ocean steamers. It was characteristic of Pilnyak's emotional and extremely subjective approach to his writing that he felt unable to concentrate on the orthodox glorification of the project in spite of the wealth of technicalities that clutter the book. He plunged instead into the struggle between the recalcitrant villagers and the small army of scientists and engineers. (He made another political mistake, however, by transposing much of *Mahogany* into the novel.) What was not appreciated by the Soviet press, and did him the greatest harm, was the fact that Pilnyak described the confrontation of opposing ideologies in discussions throughout the novel that clearly stated the contradictions and difficulties of the industrialization and forced collectivization that was now underway. His bid for official favor had misfired. He was placed by the powerful RAAP (Association of Proletarian Writers) on the list of authors "out of contact with the times." His next work, an "American novel," *O Kay* (1931) contained little more than scattered impressions of a brief visit to the United States and blended, in the current Soviet fashion, a harsh view of the capitalist system with an admiration for its technological prowess. It was coolly received. By 1936 Boris Pilnyak was no longer mentioned in the press, and his disappearance from public view during the purges was followed by an unconfirmed report that he was executed in 1938.

BABEL (1894-1941)

Gorky reprimanded the "revolutionary romantics" for dwelling on the tumultuous events of the Civil War instead of looking forward and acclaiming the construction of the socialist state. He was specifically referring to Babel's collection of thirty-five highly impressionistic sketches of the 1920 Soviet-Polish campaign, entitled *Red Cavalry* (1924) upon which his international fame as one of the most gifted modern short story writers now rests.

Babel may be linked to Pilnyak and Vsevolod Ivanov for an exotic, hyperbolically romantic treatment of a common theme of havoc and military conflicts. But the revolution, that is considered apolitically as a blindly sweeping force, receives little direct attention in Babel's book. His meditation energized by a governing secret strain in his nature, leads elsewhere. Its essence derives, as in the case of Franz Kafka, Babel's brother in wounded sensibility, from a traumatically conceived Jewish heritage and an early Jewish background that for both writers raises the problem of private identity and conveys a sense of dislocation and loss. It is difficult to gauge how much of the raw material of his personal life and suffering was transmuted through art into *Red Cavalry*. The sketches are set against a crowded and picturesque war scenario and comprise one of the most searing studies of alienation in contemporary literature.

Isaac Babel came from a lower-middle-class Jewish merchant's family in Odessa. At that time, this "Marseilles of Russia" was an exciting place to live in. It was a cosmopolitan, intellectually vigorous city inhabited by Russians, Greeks, Ukranians, and Rumanians. It also had a large Jewish community whose affluent bourgeoisie supported a Zionist center, a burgeoning school of Hebrew poets. The community was located in a bustling, colorful ghetto full of sounds and smells of the port that handled the goods of the world and was rife with criminality. It was the bawdy, lustfully lawless life of this Odessa underworld that the mature Babel was to evoke in the *Odessa Stories* (1921-1924). He looked back nostalgically at his native city. Exuberance and a kind of rough sensuality emanate from the stories that center on the figure of Benya Krik (Benya the Yell), an outsize gangster hero who fleeces the respectably rich with cunning and bravado. His comically prodigious exploits tap the rich vein of popular Jewish humor, a heady mixture of wryness, pathos, sly sexy wit, and the vernacular.

But it is the Odessa of his own childhood that Babel projects in several first-person narratives (*The Story of My Dovecote*, 1925, *In the Basement*, 1930 *The Awakening*, 1931); despite the vividness and charm of certain family scenes, they radiate immense melancholy. The poignancy of these stories resides in their underlying universality. Young Isaac's early social pressures were, on the whole, those of any sensitive lower-class Jewish boy's in Eastern Europe, whose father's driving ambition to inculcate his only son with the virtues of diligence and knowledge forced an over-study of the Bible and the Talmud at home. The lengthy reading sessions of his adolescence resulted, for Isaac, in weak eyesight, nervous disorders, and a puny physique. The barely understood official anti-Semitism that restricted school enrollment to all but a tiny minority of Jewish boys threw young Babel into a cramming frenzy to gain first place in the entrance examination, and shattered the boy's secure world with the reality of a pogrom. The frightening atmosphere of rioting and looting is maximally impressed on the boy's mind in one of Babel's most famous passages. Returning home from the market with the prize purchase of a dovecote—the reward for passing the examination—he is attacked by the street vendor who mistakes his bundle for looted goods. Finding only doves, he hits the boy with them in his rage, their bloody entrails covering his face. Soon afterwards he comes upon his great uncle, Shoyl, murdered by the savage crowd and lying prostrate across the curb with one fish struck in his fly and another in his mouth, still alive and wriggling. At another moment, the boy is witness to his father's humiliation, when he kneels before a Cossack officer, this one politely touching his cap but not preventing a mob from breaking into his father's store. In *The Awakening*, young Babel escapes from the suffocating elements of his family home to the port where athletic Nikita Smolich, proofreader for the *Odessa News*, teaches him how to swim and edits his fledgling attempts at writing fiction that Nikita finds sadly lacking in a feeling for nature. Another kind of freedom is found in the French classes of the Commercial High School with Monsieur Vadon from Britanny who introduces him to Rabelais, Flaubert, Maupassant; by the age of fifteen, Babel spoke fluent French and wrote several stories in that language. Four years later, he went to St. Petersburg, determined to become a writer. To his good fortune he met Gorky, was befriended by him, and had two of his stories accepted for the *Chronicle*. The older writer put him through a tough literary apprenticeship of writing and revising a story a day that he read and corrected but did not publish. He advised Babel, finally, to "go among people" to acquire a writer's experience. History, handily, helped him. Four months of army fighting, for which he had volunteered in October, 1917, may have attracted him to the function of war that he was later to commemorate unforgettably as a crucible for himself and other men. Meanwhile the Revolution engulfed him. For the first time in his life, Babel felt liberated from his racial environment, on equal terms with members of an integrated majority, and he eagerly fulfilled various official missions including a work stint for the Cheka. In 1920, he was appointed political uniformed commissar to the "mounted army" of Cossacks led by the well-known General Budenny that drove the Poles out of the Ukraine back to the borders of their own country, but just missed total victory.

In *Red Cavalry* Babel relives the raids and retreats of this campaign in fragmented two-to-five page episodes of plunder, rape, kill, and overkill that reach an absolute of horror. The destructive ferocity of this world is caught, contrary to Pilnyak's dynamic mass movements or Vsevolod Ivanov's elemental surges, singly: A peasant who has hoodwinked a soldier into letting her on a train is pushed off it and shot; a Red officer fells Polish prisoners as if they were clay pigeons; another slashes an old Jew's throat carefully so as to avoid being splashed with blood; a pregnant woman's belly is split by a retreating Pole; a former master, as told by a young Cossack, is not only murdered by the latter but stamped on for an hour until he becomes a dismembered corpse. A Cossack's letter to his mother describes a double killing—that of his young brother by the father who was fighting the Reds, and his own tracking down and shooting of the latter to avenge his brother's death. Significantly, the most violent incidents take on the form of skaz; secondary characters relate them to the narrator who is the participating "I" in all the stories. Named, ironically, Lyutov (in Russian meaning ferocious, wild), the bespectacled, narrow-chested, undersized narrator is really Babel who fights with the Cossacks, is despised by them for riding badly, and for carrying empty cartridges in his belt to avoid the personal "kill" action. It is his voice that unifies the work. It also infuses it with lyrical undertones that place this slaughtering process into a moral dimension.

Against the immense landscape of sky and plain depicted in Futurist, organically vibrant metaphors ("blue roads flowed past me like jets of milk spurting out of many breasts," "the orange sun rolled down the sky like a chopped head," "the earth lay like a cat's back overgrown with the twinkling fur of wheat"), the mounted regiment moves on "through the smell of yesterday's blood and killed horses" across the trampled land and burned out towns while the narrator searches for meaning in the dazzling contrast between ruthlessness and submission, victors and victims that make up a maddened world. Among the latter he feels drawn to the Galician Jews when on Sabbath eve "the opaque sadness of memories pervades me" and he records the protest against the savage killers in the "unutterable scorn" in the villagers' eyes against the Polish gentry, in the humanism of old Gedali, a shopkeeper, who cannot understand what the Revolution is about but dreams of an "International of Good People." The narrator is moved by "the breath of the invisible order of things" around crumbling churches, the deeper spirituality and creativity of the Judeo-Christian tradition that he finds in the religious art of Pan Apolek who paints his own visions on church walls, and in the total meekness of Christ-like Sashka dispensing comfort to the lonely and the poor.

But the obvious injustices in the unequal struggle are neither clearly stated nor redressed. The main force emanates from the relation of the narrator to the Cossacks who are moulded emblematically and projected in epic relief. Babel seems to have rediscovered the legendary figure of the outsize hero that haunts the Russian literary imagination. His semiliterate, brutish Cossack borrows from the seventeenth-century Taras Bulba of Gogol's fantasy his tremendous physical strength, the magnificent ease of behavior in living and dying that flows out of his own standards of war, and his picturesque appearance in a great black coat thrown over the uniform. The Red Commander, Savitsky, is his modern prototype when he stands up, dazzling Lyutov with "the beauty of his gigantic body" and "the ribbons pinned to his chest that seemed to cut the hut in half, as a banner cleaves the sky." The very violence that hacks nightmarish images throughout the stories seems to epitomize the quality of courage, directness, and a kind of innocence of primitive man to the civilized, timid narrator. He longs to resemble him as Tolstoy's Olenin in *The Cossacks* longed to take on the naturalness and spontaneity of the uninhibited Cossack villagers. The great novelty in Babel's stories is the Jew's fascination for his traditional enemy, the Cossack, who unleashes the pogrom. It leads back to the duality of the writer's psyche torn between the pull of his Jewish past and Jewish character and the effort to become free of it in a bid for another mode of life. Did Babel feel in his heady contacts with these fighting men that his Jewish identity (unknown to the Cossacks who only refer to him as the "four eyed" political commissar, "a nasty little object") stood in the way of a sensuous, vital life, previously denied to him? This was the life "that looked out on May meadows crossed by women and horses" that the narrator claimed he shared with a young Cossack friend. In the miniature stories vivid material imagery sets up the conflict and paradox within an incredible situation when Lyutov submits to the test of proving himself worthy of the savage glory that for him haloed these contemptuous, brutish men. In the frequently cited episode, *My First Goose*, he brutaly kills a goose for his supper. That suggests his capacity to ravish and kill and earns him the momentary respect of the Cossacks who make room for him by the campfire; it is, however, parody of his larger predicament. Finally, their innate hostility to the self-conscious, physical weakling who does not want to make enemies and is even reluctant to inflict death on a mortally wounded friend who begs for release overpowers his constant bids for acceptance among them. The narrator withdraws from other allegiances when he caustically retorts to old Gedali that his idealistic International Brotherhood" is to be eaten with gunpowder and seasoned with the best blood." Finally, he denies his pity and compassion to others—victims like himself of historical inequality. Rejected by the company of men whom he admires, the narrator now stands alone.

The reception of *Red Cavalry* was mixed, particularly owing to Marshal Budenny's conflicting reactions to the work. At the outset, Budenny had praised the stories for their dedication to his revolutionary fighters; later he damned them for what he thought to be a vilification of the Cossacks. Nevertheless, this work and the *Odessa Stories* were reprinted in several editions. Fellow writers and critics immediately saw in Babel a superb stylist, rediscoverer of the modern short story in the tradition of Chekhov and Maupassant (the French author with his concern for form remained for Babel the great master). They praised his infinitely polished art that produced an instant and illuminating communication with the reader through a miracle of taut verbal strategy that is exciting to read.

The illusions that romanticized a historical moment and its participants for the author of *Red Cavalry* indicated that Babel had not yet come to grips with a larger reality that would reveal the final truth about himself. This may account for his relatively meager literary output after the mid-twenties where there was

little room for introspective contemplation. At the First Congress of Soviet Writers in 1934 that promoted socially significant
themes, Babel confessed, not without irony, that he was now
writing in the "genre of silence" so as not to expose readers to
less than first-rate work. Although he survived the worst of the
purges, he was suddenly arrested in 1939, all his unpublished
manuscripts were seized, and in 1941 the military tribunal sentenced him to death. According to James Falen, his latest biographer, a recently unearthed screen play, published in 1939, may
have caused his tragic end. He wrote it in twenty days (an
unprecedented speed for Babel) while gathering material for a
life of Gorky, his constant and loyal mentor. The scenario, titled
Old Square #4, features a sinister character with boundless, unscrupulous ambitions that seem to adumbrate Stalin's decima-
tion of his closest associates. In 1954, Babel was partially
rehabilitated and closely edited collections of his stories were
reprinted.

SATIRISTS

In the aftermath of the revolutionary struggle that had been
exotically relived by some of the younger writers, another kind of
chaos, engendered by the NEP, gave rise to a vigorous literature
of irony, humorous fantasy, and the grotesque. It was a fertile
field for the satirist. The hasty and ill-planned attempt to
strengthen an undeveloped economy with free enterprise under
the panoply of prohibitive bureaucratic pressures resulted in
exploitation, graft, material hardships, and cracked the social
surface with conflicting urges to conform or to retain a measure
of independence. In the works of Bulgakov, Katayev, Ilf and
Petrov, and Zoshchenko, these social evils and confusions are
explored with a malicious skill; the composite picture is that of a
comedy of manners that irreverently treats the more immoderate
elements of the contemporary Soviet scene.

BULGAKOV (1891-1940)

Mikhail Bulgakov was first known for a novel, *The White
Guard*, a straightforward realistic account of the overthrow of
the German-sponsored puppet government in the Kiev of 1918

by the nationalistic leader, Petyara, on the eve of the Bolshevik occupation. Not a single Communist appears in the chronicle. The other unique feature of the novel is the fact that Bulgakov sympathetically portrays the main protagonists, the Turbin brothers, who are White Army officers. They are described as the liberal, generous-minded aristocrats of moral and intellectual integrity that Leo Tolstoy loved to draw. The atmosphere of the Turbin household, culled from the author's recollections of his own Kievan home, is suffused with the mutual trust and affection that recall private moments in *War and Peace;* it is secondary in interest, however, to the panic that spreads through the pillaged city and in its wake brings betrayals, reversed loyalties, murder, arson, death. Bulgakov skillfully constructs a climate of uncertainty and fear that leave blundering fools, cowards, and knaves largely helpless before the onslaught of events. But the nagging impression that remains for the reader is the want of a wider psychological impact of sudden terror on people.

The White Guard had a spectacular sequel. Although it had been banned in mid-serialization in 1924 in the Moscow journal, *Russia,* large and enthusiastic audiences acclaimed its dramatization at the Moscow Art Theatre. The play, cannily stripped by the author of peripheral episodes and mass action, concentrates on the anguish of the morally isolated and heroic Turbin officers, who finally, as patriots, accept Bolshevism. The taut, emotionally charged scenes were brillantly acted by a cast trained in the Chekhov tradition. Nevertheless, Bulgakov was excoriated in the Soviet press, expelled from the Writers' Union, and his play was taken off the boards. Like Zamyatin, he appealed directly to Stalin for a visa or some means of subsistence. Unexpectedly Stalin gave the order to appoint Bulgakov literary counselor to the Moscow Art Company and had the play reinstated. According to unsubstantiated but persistent rumor, Stalin attended the performance some fifteen times.

Bulgakov continued to write plays that showed his gift for exciting theatre full of cannily devised suspense techniques and intensely alive projections of ideas in dramatic form. But of the known thirteen plays that were printed only in early sixties, almost none were staged during his lifetime.

In a collection of stories, best remembered for *Fateful Eggs*

(1924) and *Devilry* (1925), Bulgakov left realism behind and announced himself as a humorous writer.

With a wealth of satirical inventiveness that is clearly inspired by Gogol, Bulgakov attacks the ineptitudes and imbalance of Soviet officialdom in *Devilry* that relates the accidental firing of a clerk and his attempt to recover his job. Fantasy reeling into madness creates the chaos that results from the unhinged bureaucratic process where the hero, not unlike Dostoevsky's Golyadkin, loses his official identity to another. He becomes deranged in a world of absurd dialogue and gestures. Persons are transformed into objects and signs, and naturalistic detail blurs into the unreal. The weakest element of the story is the melodramatic ending. The clerk plunges to his death, for which the reader, caught up in the accruing farcical sequences, is unprepared. Its forte is the author's deft handling of rapidly generating mass confusion and excitement triggered off by a minute, insignificant happening in which a great number of people become extraordinarily involved. This type of situation, that Gogol frequently set up and capitalized on with huge success in his comic grotesque, had become popular among the French "Groupe de l'Abbaye" before World War I. Jules Romains had identified it as a manifestation of supra-individual or collective psychology and had labeled it "Unanimism."

An "exaggerated numbers" humor packs the climax of *Fateful Eggs* in which Bulgakov presses into service H. G. Wells's science-fiction fantasy, *Food of the Gods* to jab maliciously at the state's clumsy interference with pure scientific endeavor. A world-renowned Soviet zoologist had discovered but not yet tested a "red ray" with great reproductive powers. He is forced to apply it on state poultry farms that have been depopulated by an epidemic. Through some muddle of red tape that is never made clear, ostrich, anaconda, and reptile eggs, intended for the zoologist, reach the poultry farm. Of course, there follows a fearful proliferation of these animals. They devour the entire farm personnel, lay thousands of eggs along their path of destruction, put the inhabitants from all the surrounding areas into flight, and defeat the combined efforts of army, navy, and forces of chemical warfare to exterminate them. Finally, an unprecedented frost that grips the entire country puts an end to the plague. These stories, severely censured by the critics, appeared in the twenties only in magazine form.

KATAYEV (1897-   )

A wider bid for obvious jocularity was made in Valentin Katayev's first and most successful humorous novel, *Embezzlers* (1926). It chronicles with relish the ludicrous adventures of two Soviet bureaucrats who get hold of 12,000 rubles from a Moscow state fund less by design than by accident and spend it on a drunken spree while travelling through the provinces. They meet various shady characters including a prostitute down on her luck and a spurious czar who play on their gullibility and unmercifully fleece them. There is humor in these encounters, but the author's satirical intent to expose the two "would be" crooks to ridicule does not quite come off. These dim-witted and credulous characters, eventually brought back to conjugal and official punishment, are clearly lacking in the ability to obtain entry into the high life of elegant women, titled men, and expensive and refined pleasures they dream about. The reader's laughter is nudged by pity when the author describes their pathetic attempt to maintain bureaucratic decorum in keeping a strict account of all their illicit expenses.

ILF (1897-1937), AND PETROV (1902-1942)

Twelve Chairs (1928) and its sequel, *Golden Calf* (1931), jointly authored by Ilf and Petrov, celebrate comedy as a power, Soviet style. The satirical targets for both novels were found in the social climate during the times of the NEP, of unleashed speculation, black-marketeering, and the recrudescence of a money-minded petty bourgeoisie, much as Gogol had sharpened his satire on the conditions of landed gentry life. The great satirist's art is recalled again in the total lack of humanity in all the characters. They use a semi-educated, slangy language, replete with Communist jargon that aspires to "culture" (as difficult to translate as Gogol's ornate style), and the remorseless cult of the picaresque. The plots are strung, as in *Dead Souls*, on a chain of exuberantly comic episodes where the central mission matters less than what happens to the main protagonist, Ostap Bender.

Bender, like *Chichikov*, the main protagonist in *Dead Souls* is an unscrupulous rogue, cynical, nervy, ruthless, the supreme confidence man who courts havoc for his own gains, always keeps his "cool," and is probably the most beloved hero in Soviet fiction. With him, in *Twelve Chairs*, the reader goes off on a breath-stopping ride in search of diamonds sewn into one of a set of twelve chairs that had been sold at an auction and are now scattered over all of Russia. Bender manipulates his friends and allies, who become his victims, as they raise funds for his travels. Once, magnificently, when sorely pressed for railroad fare, he passes himself off as Grand Master and offers to take on one hundred sixty opponents although he only knows one chess move from pawn to king 4. In *Golden Calf*, where satire bites deeply into the problem of personal wealth in a socialist state, Bender practices skillful blackmail on a millionaire while the author mocks Soviet propaganda, Soviet officialdom, Soviet ceremonies, and the incessant official and unofficial fraudulence. In the midst of the buffoonery and numerous slapstick sequences that seem to have been borrowed from the silent Mack Sennet and Harold Lloyd films, Ilf and Petrov create even more satire in one hilarious episode that depicts an accountant's stay in a lunatic asylum where he hid on the eve of an office purge and discovered that other inmates were there for similar reasons.

It may seem surprising that the authorities did not harass the two writers. Ilf died normally of tuberculosis in 1937, and Petrov was killed during the Second World War. Was this relaxed official attitude due to the "happy endings" of the novels in which Bender's operations in the first one lead to his demise, and, when he was resuscitated in the second novel, he comes to a penniless end? Or, more seriously, was the "liberal" climate of the twenties that encouraged self-criticism responsible for the lack of interference with these splendid comic writings that denigrated underhand dealings of the NEP? Despite Malenkov's recognition just before Stalin's death (see p. 000) of the dearth of humor in Soviet letters and his appeal to writers to become Gogols or Saltykov-Shchedrins, none came forth.

ZOSHCHENKO (1895-1958)

Mikhail Zoschenko is the foremost humorist in Soviet fiction, and his prolific output of short stories brought laughter back into Soviet life. Victor Shklovsky tells us that his comic sketches were read everywhere, and often passed off as real incidents and not only in the Soviet Union. Wherever in the world Russian newspapers were printed, there appeared in their columns a Zoshchenko short, short story that would evoke an appreciative chuckle and, momentarily, lighten the hardship of exile.

The formula for his enduring popularity is a seemingly simple one. In its final form, it is a very brief skaz whose narrator is a man in the street, from the lower middle class of artisans, small employees, tradesmen, or clerks who copes or tries to cope with the many discomforts and mishaps that plague the daily life of Soviet citizens in the newly organized society. Part of the comic effect derives from the ludicrous situations that assail the narrator. An altercation with a bus conductor who shortchanges him leads to a fist fight, with the passengers joining in. When a check room stub is washed off his big toe in the bathhouse (where else would a naked man carry it?), he can't get his own coat back. He is attracted to an aristocratic young lady (to judge by her signs of refinement—a saucy hat and a gold front tooth) and invites her to the theatre where she helps herself to four pastry cakes during intermission when he only has money enough for two. Due to the housing shortage, he settles quite cozily with his new wife in a bathroom until the arrival of the mother-in-law who takes over the tub for her sleeping quarters and precipitates a divorce. Persuaded by friends to have a telephone installed in the name of progress, he rushes out obediently when the very first call summons him to meet an unknown person in a distant section of town. When he returns after a two-hour wait on a street corner, he finds his room stripped of all his belongings. He signs in at a new state hospital where he hopes to have a chronic discomfort cured by the "wonders of science"; instead, befuddled by the barrage of forms to fill out and frightened by the contemptuous, bureaucratic personnel, he lets himself be tested and treated for a near-fatal disease.

What may appear to those distant from Soviet reality as absurdity piled on absurdity was at once recognized by the author's compatriots as caricatural take-offs on prevailing living conditions. Although the incidents that shape the stories might have been part of their daily life, Zoshchenko raised them with great comic art to a pitch of exaggeration that kept them at one remove from Soviet readers. Therefore they were able to laugh at the narrator's troubles.

The immediate and most risible impact of a Zoshchenko skaz is the narrator's language. It is studded with picturesque distortions of the spoken idiom that reflect the changes in class structure, mass population shifts from country to city, and the persistent barrage of propagandistic "officialese." It contained a hodge-podge of regionalisms, peasant and factory slang, party slogans, bits of state-sponsored instruction simplified for semi-literate groups. Zoschenko would probably have heard and savored this language during his three years of wandering across Russia between 1918 and 1921. When just out of the army, he drifted through ten cities, working as a telephone operator, gambler, wild-game hunter, policeman, farm manager until he joined the Serapion Brothers in St. Petersburg and settled down to writing. Zoshchenko constructed a masterfully stylized travesty, using *colloquial speech*, that inflates the caricatural shape of the incident with a total realization of diction and tone edging into farce that turns the skaz into comic play.

But there is more to these two- or three-page sketches that reveal the author as a major literary talent. From misadventure to misadventure, the narrator gradually transcends the comical dimension and becomes a real character. He is a semi-educated, half-informed city dweller, of middling intelligence, gullible, a little common and rather cowardly. He is, however, muscled with vitality, resists adversity with vigor, and stubbornly survives small daily defeats through his boneheadedness and a dogged concern for his personal interests. When these do not absorb him, he takes time out to express his faith in the ultimate socialist panacea, although lofty sentiments are not his forte.

Delightfully irreverent and typically down to earth is his comment on the state's ambitious program to electrify all Russia. He conjures up a brightly lit ordinary bedroom where now "a torn slipper, a bedbug racing along, an indescribable rag, a lump of spittle" may be seen that by a kerosene lamp had not been noticed before.

In short, Zoshchenko's narrator is a prototype of the "little man" in the Soviet variant of modern society. He shares with the reader the problem of daily living in a spontaneous and candid dialogue, genuinely funny, believable, and one that defies translation. The difficulty of finding foreign equivalents for the newly minted Soviet terminology is increased by an underlying pattern of pauses, half-sentences, broken-off words, allusions to a charged sub-text that is the mark of high comedy.

Zoschenko's prolific output includes numerous collections of these very brief anecdotal sketches (*Short Stories*, 1923, *Respected Citizens*, 1926, *Nervous People*, 1927). Earlier *Tales Told by Nazar Ilyich Mr. Sinerbryokhov* (1922) are first-person accounts of the war and Civil War by a corporal (when the writer was developing the skaz form from Remizov and Leskov models). He also wrote third-person narratives that treat, as in the later skaz, comically presented characters in absurd situations. These were followed by humorous semi-fiction grafted on the current "gripes" against "minor defects of mechanism," such as lack of consumer goods, inefficiency, red tape, and corruption. All these works are highly charged with malice and banter. The author effortlessly extends a real situation into grotesque and yet the final impression upon coming to the conclusion is not unlike the sense of desolation felt by the reader of Gogol's *Dead Souls* and for much the same reason.

Zoschenko's fictional world is full of people who have nothing to do but exist in his pages. They are nothing but themselves, not registers or conductors of anything. The author shows them limited and driven, part of a process, put in motion for a circumscribed end. What informs this world is a pervasion of vulgarity, pettyness, narrow-mindedness, and selfishness. These traits motivate every action and no room is left for a genuine communication between people or disinterested concern for larger values. The climate testifies to the deep pessimism of the humorous writer.

Popularization of science that was being promoted in the Soviet press offered Zoschenko another target for his satire in a first novel, *Youth Restored* (1930). Introduced as a work meant to divert the reader and yet present a scientific treatise, it is written in the usual chatty manner and divided into brief episodes that favor the writer's penchant for anecdote. It is a cliché-charged story of an aging, married astronomer who rediscovers youth and throws over his past to become the sixth husband of a nineteen-year-old girl. When she deceives him, he has a stroke. However, he recovers and has his youth restored. He then returns to his family but still longs for his young love. This lampooned science fiction is made even more pungent in view of the serious attention that several Soviet critics gave to the garbled expositions on biology and genetics that heighten the mockery in the work. A year later, he composed the longer *Light Blue Book* to include historical and pseudo-historical anecdotes. He pretends that they form part of a study of the history of human relations; activated by money, perfidy and love, they are made to pulsate with steady, pointed irony.

Zoschenko was a moody, restless man, a hypochondriac, addicted to bouts of melancholy, and, in his only serious, and ill-facted, work *Before Sunrise* (1934), he put himself to the task of probing into his past to attempt to discover a reason for his recurrent despondency. The opening chapters are a combination of early childhood memories, minor personal experiences, and sensations brought into a discussion of unconscious drives and pathological behavior patterns. It is difficult to understand why this amateurish attempt at self-analysis, in which Zoschenko was careful to denigrate Freud in favor of Pavlov, produced a fury of critical abuse. It has been suggested that, during the war, when outpourings of patriotic sentiment were called for, it was deemed particularly offensive that a well-known writer should indulge publicly in the revelations of his individual psyche—a psychological process that has no right of place in a collective society.

Zoschenko's introspective search into self was branded socially harmful, pornographic, of a piece with decadent bourgeois psychology. The magazine, *October*, that had printed the first installments of *Before Sunrise* was temporarily suspended. Up to this time the writer had played a winning game with the authorities. Known as the most independent Serapion Brother, he declared that he was close to the Bolsheviks but was not a Communist (or rather a Marxist). In addition, he stated that he did not think he would ever be one. In the liberal early twenties he was not called to account.

Some critics looked askance at his flippant treatment of the Soviet mores, but, in the light of the reigning official approbation of self-criticism that was encouraged to keep Soviet citizens working even harder to produce desired improvement, Zoshchenko was again forgiven. Later he used the brilliant facade of the skaz, dissimulating his personality behind that of the narrator, so that the views expressed could not be attributed to the author. This camouflage was further strengthened in the two prefaces to a work titled *Sentimental Tales* (1929), supposedly written by a certain T. V. Kolenkorov who thanks Michael Zoshchenko in the two prefaces for allowing him to publish these stories. Although in the third preface Zoschenko confesses to the reader that Kolenkorov is but a product of his creative imagination, still he insists that the ideas harbored by this fictive personality do not represent his own.

When the party began to thrust upon writers an official version of Soviet life, Zoshchenko thought it politic to bring out *The Story of the Reforging* (1935) that would seem to have been penned by a party hack. It shows a criminal, sentenced to a labor camp and set to work on the construction of the White Sea Baltic Canal, achieving a regeneration through the morally reforming influence of the forced labor camp management. This tasteless piece, and some stories that sentimentalized Lenin's childhood, were meant to pacify the party after it finally had expressed hostility toward his "frivolous, uncommitted" writings.

During the 1946 Zhdanov purge *Adventures of a Monkey* brought about Zoschenko's downfall. This is a sprightly tale about a monkey that finds itself in a Soviet town, and knows a good deal of mundane "known how" in getting around. Zhdanov singled out the story as a "vulgar denigration of the Soviet people" and violently castigated the writer for his "decadent, empty, fatuous" stuff that for too long had been corrupting literature. He was expelled from the Union of Writers and banned from the press. Partially reinstated after public apologies, he was allowed to publish some new stories in the magazines, but they only feebly reflect the satirical brilliance of his earlier work.

It was perhaps inevitable that when fresh approaches to the experience of the Civil War had been exhausted, writers would turn to new dramatic conflicts. In the comparatively liberal climate of the years between 1923 and 1928 some of the finest writers dealt with the individual and the impact on his sensibilities of the great social upheaval and the difficulty of his adjustment to the ruthless overall reconstruction that followed. This literature was marked by a return to psychological realism and tended to avoid the excesses of fashionable ornamentalism. Its seriousness and detailed study of characters recalled the classic nineteenth-century novel. In subject matter, however, its most gifted spokesmen—Konstantin Fedin, Leonid Leonov, Yurii Olesha, and Veniamin Kaverin—explored the hero's personal predicament in facing a new world, and they came nearest to post-World War I Western writers such as Ernest Hemingway, Jules Romains, and Andre Malraux. All of these writers were bringing into full view the problems that beset modern man with the collapse of moral and social values.

FEDIN (1892-   )

Fedin was one of the oldest of the Serapion Brothers and, although his first collection of stories (*Pastyr*, 1923) reflects the stylistic flamboyance of that group, he was influenced by Chekhov, Gogol, and Dostoevsky in the portrayal of the insignificant little man. Fedin complained to Gorky that he seemed unable to intregate the universals of compassion, self-sacrifice, and love, with the great actuality of events. In his first novel, *Cities and Years* (1924), he succeeds in creating this interrelated image against the background of the pre- and post-revolutionary period. He pioneers the attempt to view the breakdown and transformation of a large segment of Western society in terms of the psychological impact on one individual.

The novel is drawn in part from Fedin's experiences in Germany where he was forced to remain as a civilian prisoner during the First World War. He embroiders on the large canvas of that era in Germany and in the 1918, 1922 years in Russia, episodes from the life of a Russian civilian internee, the student Andrey Startsov. The greatest adventures of the story, based on history, are the dramatic moments of Andrey's attempt to escape and his successful courtship of the financée of a German baron, who ignoring him as a rival, rescues him. Then, at the end of the war, the student now back home and welcomed by the Communists, returns the favor by helping the imprisoned baron to get away. He is shot down by his best friend, Kurt Wahn, a German, now become revolutionary, who placed party loyalty above friendship. The contrast between vacillating, sentimental, and oversensitive Startsov, who is unequivocally on the side of justice and human equality but who fails to retain his spiritual self in the midst of havoc and brutality, and the ruthless man of action, Wahn, resounds with echoes of similar confrontations that are explored in the fiction of Turgenev, Oblomov, and Chekhov. The hero's character is depicted with a great deal of consistency and power, and although he finally becomes the casualty of great events, Fedin has overt sympathy for his fluctuating moods of despair, elation, and doubt that are registered with great artistic tact. There are patches of stark realism throughout the work, as for example, in the return trip of the released Russians to their homeland and the numbed acceptance by the intelligentsia of Trotsky's order to dig trenches outside of Petrograd before the approach of the White Army.

Cities and Years launches anew in Soviet literature the ambitiously heuristic long novels, conceived on a wide scale, that grant full freedom to the interplay of psychological and organic forces. What fascinated Fedin's readers and still elicits comment was the peculiar construction that complicated even further a narrative top-heavy with unrelated incidents. Flashbacks borrowed from film technique (the final denouement opens the work) reverse the normal sequence. The chronological order only reappears in the second part of the work.

The author uses flashbacks also to isolate images and scenes within a bizarre sequence in *Brothers* (1928). This is a tightly knitted shorter novel that again is concerned with the clash of the old world with the new in a restricted family situation. Three brothers of a Cossack family make different alliances with the new order. The realistic but sketchy portrayal of the physician and the active Bolshevik who both merge effortlessly into the mainstream of the Soviet state are less interesting than the dilemma of the third brother, a musician and composer, whose total involvement with his art leaves no room for political or emotional allegiances. Fedin presents him with pungent realism and some bitter irony. For the first time in Soviet writing, music competes with ideology and with some reluctance on the author's part the latter comes out winner.

Fedin's trips to Switzerland, Holland, and the Scandinavian countries in the early thirties, when he was trying to cure a tubercular condition, furnished the background material for the two-volume *Rape of Europe* (1932-1935). The encounter of the West and Russia more forcefully portrayed than in the first novel, is focussed on a business deal between a firm of Amsterdam timber merchants and the Soviets. It falls through when the Russians realize that they have acquired sufficient technical expertise to proceed on their own. It is evident that in writing this long work, crowded with a versatile cast of characters, and where less space is given to psychological probing, Fedin remembered official disapproval of the undue emphasis on the "isolated case" of Andrey Startsov in *Cities and Years*. He manages to "adjust" this novel and his productions that follow to the accepted political category of thought. For example, an arresting kulak personality that dominated in an early story, *Transvaal* (1926), and was disparaged by Soviet critics for his "undue heroic stature," was incorporated into the figure of the Dutch timber dealer in *Rape of Europe* who bears a physical resemblance to the kulak hut he is pictured in very dark colors.

LEONOV (1899-   )

Outside the Soviet Union, Leonid Leonov is best known for his second major novel, *The Thief* (1927). He takes the common postwar theme of displaced man at odds with his universe and, like much Western European fiction, draws heavily on the psychological insights and realism of Dostoevsky.

A versatile and artistically interesting experimenter and assiduous reader of Gogol, Remizov, E. T. A. Hoffman, Leskov, and Blok, young Leonov "practiced" literature in early satirical, humorous, fairy tales. However, when he published *The End of Insignificant Man* (1924), he first disclosed the influence of Dostoevsky and gave promise of an important talent.

In the grim, Civil War setting in Petrograd of Zamyatin's *Cave*, an eminent geologist, weakened by hunger and illness and isolated in the midst of intellectual babblers who are spiritually and intellectually demoralized, gives up the effort to continue research. In an Ivan Karamazov nightmare, his devil visits him during his heart attacks and belittles his work. Leonov develops a situation similar to those Dostoevsky created in which the hero is so absorbed in his writing that he refuses to minister to his dying sister.

In a first novel *The Badgers* (1926) Leonov projected with skill the post-revolutionary social and psychological background against which the private adventures of two brothers and their opposing ambitions allegorize the recurrent and popular theme of conflict between village and town. It is a complicated narrative with numerous lyrical digressions and loosely linked adventurous episodes. They project the divergence between Pashka, who runs away early from an oppressive apprenticeship to join the proletariat movement and reappears in a closing chapter as a dedicated Communist, and his brother Semyon who, yearning in Moscow for his native village, finally returns to it and leads a revolt against Bolshevik rule. Best executed are the opening Chekhov-inspired scenes of the Moscow merchant's shop in tsarist Russia where the bearded owner tyrannizes his family and the two peasant lads apprenticed to him. No less powerful is the sweep of the countryside's anger—deep, dark, wild—that surges even beyond the articulated grievances of forced grain requisition in the final dramatic episode of the "badgers" uprising when its chieftain faces the punitive expedition led by his brother, Pashka, and the revolt is crushed.

The Thief is Leonov's most apolitical work. He claimed to be writing about everyman and what inalienably and unforgettably distinguishes him in his joys, faith, grief, and frustrations. The hero, Mitya Vekshin, former Red Army officer, now leader of a gang of thieves, was to epitomize the exploration of everyman's inner world in a struggle with exterior reality or an outright rejection of it. The main interest of this long, intricately plotted narrative, however, is generated by the "lower depths" atmosphere of the Moscow NEP underworld, crowded with gangsters, circus performers, prostitutes, con men, bar flies, and destitute "has beens" of the pre-revolutionary bourgeoisie. It is a cast of puppets rather than living human beings and the deft author-puppeteer manipulates them within a series of fluid entanglements. He creates a heady climate like that of Dostoevsky consisting of dingy pubs and rooming houses where these shady characters flummox and impress each other, plan subversive exploits, and talk out their passions and discontentment.

Dostoevsky's presence hovers over the entire novel. A former Russian nobleman, Manyukhin, joins the liar-buffoons of the Lebedevs and the Manilovs to act out daily his dissolution with inventive fabrications of his past for anyone of the tavern's customers who will buy him a meal or a drink. Chikilyov, chairman of a House Committee, is spiteful and cowardly in the manner of Dostoevsky's Underground Man, and as incapable of dealing with human beings. Chikilyov comes even closer to the doctrinaire Shigalyov, created by Dostoevsky in *The Devils*, even to his surname, with his plan for a future state of built-in despotic controls and a mutual spying system. The darker side of passion and its sadistic overtones that dominate Masha's attachment to Mitka in *The Thief* is similar to Dostoevsky's portrayal of Nastasya's destructive drives in *The Idiot*. Mitka himself is restless, bored, and unable to reconcile himself to the bureaucratic doldrums of NEP after the Civil War heroics. He has plunged into criminality for the bravura of it and has something of Dmitri Karamazov's agitation in him. When we learn that Mitka's irrational bouts of rage and melancholy issue from a sense of guilt for having killed in cold blood a White Army officer who had destroyed his favorite horse, we recall Raskolnikov's traumatic conflicts. Another page from *Crime and Punishment* seems to be taken for the end of *The Thief* when Mitka is regenerated with a vision of productive community life.

Despite these extensive borrowings from the great nineteenth-century writer, Leonov does not succeed in reaching universals in ideas and feelings or portraying in any one character the whole of man. He can only name crime and unhappiness, whereas Dostoevsky, Tolstoy, and Dickens could write about violence and sorrow in a human context.

In *The Thief*, Leonov makes psychological searchings into human perversity. He illuminates this in yet another way with the device of writing a novel within the novel that immediately brings to mind André Gide's *Counterfeiters*. Tantalizing dialogues between the "inner" novelist, Firsov, and the characters who, Pirandellian fashion, argue with him about his interpretation of their motives and his own discussion of literary problems (to which generous space is allotted) throw significant light on Leonov's limitations as a writer.

Gide, only a year before the publication of *The Thief*, made a case for the counterfeit quality of people who pretend to live fully when in fact they are putting on a fantastic fictional show. Leonov appears to be one of Gide's counterfeit characters. He is incapable of exercising his considerable gift for dramatic plots, artistic verbal and scenic effects, and exciting situations to produce authentic heroes. He seemed to lack the deepest insight that would have endowed Mitka or Pashka or Semyon with a fully integrated personality. Critic Helen Muchnic suggests that Leonov was honestly insecure in his moral and social convictions. His flexible, many-sided, and ideologically unstable art needed an outside purpose to give it strength and persuasion.

It was therefore not surprising that by 1930, Leonov contradicted his own earlier "antisocial" claim for *The Thief* by describing it as an exposure of egotistical bourgeois behavior and was now ready to rally to the "social command." In the two succeeding novels, *Sot* (1929) and *Skutarevsky* (1930-1933), he finds a direction for his art, and their distinct Soviet coloration insured him personal and professional safety.

The later work is more forceful in the psychological analysis of the hero, Skutarevsky. He is an internationally famous physicist who is commissioned by Lenin to work on a secret project that was to bring electrification to the entire country. The story gathers dramatic momentum with a sabotage plot in which Skutarevsky's brother and son participate. The scientist's reluctance to accept the dictator's command, less from political disinclination (he is drawn to Socialist thought) than an ingrained independence of mind, is explored with patience and skill and so is the character of a young Communist, Zhenya, to whom the hero, to his great surprise, is tremendously attracted. The finale that stages rapidly and somewhat artificially Skutarevsky's total inward capitulation to the regime, is less convincing.

In the *Sot* Leonov proceeds to develop the theme of socialist reconstruction that was to be reproduced in scores of properly sovietized novels using the same ready-made formula with a variety of embellishments. The necessary ingredients comprise the carrying out of some industrial project under the direction of one or more resolute, single-minded specialists. They are dedicated servants of the state who face great natural obstacles and subversive elements determined to wreck the undertaking. Leonov enhanced the basic plot with magnificent descriptions of the deep northern forest that is being felled by workers building a dam and a paper mill on the Sot river. The invasion of the ancient land is resisted by the local monastery whose leader Vissarion predicts the coming of Attila to purge Russia of its mechanical civilization. The author adds a typical melodramatic twist by having the sabotage discovered by the Communist heroine whose father is one of the saboteurs and who had saved Vissarion's life during the Civil War. The latter is put to death, the formerly recalcitrant peasants now agree to assist in the construction, guided by the indispensable strong man, chief engineer Uvadyev. Uvadyev is portrayed as tough and capable. He is disliked for his crudity but respected and obviously placed in a superior position to the more intelligent, neurotic Vissarion to maintain the action in correct political perspective.

OLESHA (1899-1960)

Dramatist and author of several short-story collections, Yurii Olesha will be remembered for *Envy* (1927), one of the most original novels in Soviet fiction which lends itself to a number of interpretations. The immediate impact of the work is made by the feverish candor of monologue and conversations that recall the hallucinating psychological analyses of Dostoevsky's Underground Man. Motive, states of mind, and situations are mercilessly exposed in an intricate interweaving of symbol and "dead pan" realism that search for answers to the questions How to live? and What is to be done?

The story contains less of a plot than a confrontation between two opposing ways of life in Soviet Moscow. Andrei Babichev (Russified version of the well-known American surname) is the director of a food trust, who has created a cheap, nourishing sausage and started a huge chain of dime cafeterias. One night he picks up from the gutter an inebriated and insolvent 27-year-old intellectual and poet, Kavalerov. Babichev earns the latter's envy and contempt for succeeding in the new order that has no place for poetic dreams and fantasies. Intelligence without power and desire without means qualify this social outcast who longs to attain personal fame. He tortures himself with a microscopic observation of his benefactor's physical fitness, energy, self-confidence, and indifference to all the intangibles of life's larger reality. The jeering monologues that echo the rancor of Dostoevsky's famous antihero take on purpose when Kavalerov meets Andrei's estranged brother, Ivan, an engineer who has never worked at his profession, a ne'er-do-well, and a pub crawler. The two derelicts form an alliance in their common hatred of the sausage maker and his young protégé, Volodya Makarov who is a champion soccer player and even more computerized than Babichev in his wish to become a human machine. To refute this mechanized society and insulate themselves against its chill, Ivan proposes a "conspiracy of feelings"—tenderness, delicacy, compassion, love—that would woo back magic and imaginativeness into reality. There is something faintly absurd and familiar about the two short, dumpy men in disreputable attire. They might have stepped out of a Beckett play. They repair to a sordid tavern where Ivan beguiles the habitués with his ideal, arising from the "conspiracy of feelings," describes a super machine, Orphelia, a figment of his imagination, that could be worshipped by the new bosses. Orphelia is capable of technical marvels but instead "it will be a searing tongue stuck out by the dying era at the newborn one . . . and it will turn out to be a liar, a sentimental singer of the love songs of the past century." Ivan is an indefatigable dreamer who spins tall stories, myths, incredible inventions. He belongs to that ancient family of fabricators in Russian literature that boasts Gogol's Nozdryov and Leonov's Manyukhin. However, his inventiveness is more fantastic and compelling than theirs. He constructs a scenario for "the most grandiloquent assassination of the century" in which Kavalerov, who has fallen in love with Makarov's financée, the beautiful Valya, suffers because of her indifference. He decides to kill Andrei and leave the world "with a bang." When this does not come off, both friends, defeated and subdued, console themselves with drink and the flabby favors of Kavalerov's landlady.

Even if Olesha had not declared in 1934, at the Congress of Writers, that Kavalerov looked at the world through his eyes, the author's overt sympathy for his weak, emotionally overwrought hero, and as his name suggests, the last surviving romantic cavalier, is evident from Kavalerov's interior monologues that are diffused with a poet's perception of the invisible landscape of the real world. None of the elements—fluidity of spatial and material design, animism of things, mutability of objects, or a vision that draws us to and away from consciousness—are unfamiliar to those acquainted with Bely, Babel, Zamyatin, and the Formalists. Olesha catches unnoticed relationships among ordinary things, such as the "pale blue and pink world of a room that spins around mother-of-pearl objectives of a button," or Andrei's "laughing face swaying through the windows of a car like a pinkish disc."

Olesha primarily articulates *Envy* through Kavalerov's poetically textured perceptions and his friend's fantasies. It thus has been argued that the realism of the novel is but that of a highly subjective and unreal poet's version of the world. Yet the pervading atmosphere is taut, discordant with the anxiety and a sense of crisis and loss that focus the works of other early twentieth-century writers—Hemingway, T. S. Eliot, D. H. Lawrence, and F. Scott Fitzgerald. Olesha is concerned with the very real conflict of living and feeling man in his technological age. Kavalerov calls himself the Russian Babbit's jester and he speaks the Shakespearian fool's truth about the doom of the heart that has been plundered together with personal dignity and individual caprice.

Deeply poignant is Kavalerov's ceaselessly renewed attempt to communicate with his benefactor, to make a dent in his good-humored indifference with the sharpness of a malicious jibe. Even as the monstrously impassive authority of his father devastated Franz Kafka's being and continues to haunt the modern literary mind, so did Kavalerov come up on every side—at a public ceremony where Andrei was presiding and he was thrown out, by Andrei's reading table where the lighted circle of the green lamp kept him an outsider in the shadows—against the prodigious specter of a powerful inarticulate and impregnable presence that fascinated and repulsed him and finally exiled him into a retreat from manhood. But Andrei Babichev is not altogether abhorrent, however, for Olesha is careful to show his kindness. Babichev is genuinely attached to his protégé, Volodya, and pities the destitute Kavalerov.

Within the framework of post-revolutionary Communist Russia, the dominating image of the unimaginative and insensitive Soviet philistine symbolizes the author's apprehension of the emerging ethical pattern that was to shape the typical rank-and-file party member, opaque, regimented, woodenheaded, whose worship of technology will result in a blind adherence to official political dogma. The collapse of traditional emotions and humanity, the mindless arrogance of Soviet youth, and conviction that theirs is the happiest and most privileged way of life is most keenly sensed by the ineffectual, romantic Kavalerov. He yearns for this life which he knows has bypassed him. Is it not possible to infer from this stance of a hero defending the sentiments of an earlier age and of the hero again as an antihero in a society that condemns him to an outsider's role, Olesha's own vacillation in meeting the challenges of the "rising world," as Ivan puts it, and the artist's unacceptable position in it?

These unresolved ambiguities that tease the mind and add yet another dimension to the writer's subtle and complex art were not immediately noticed when *Envy* first appeared and became a popular and critical hit. Pravda praised the novel's contemptuous treatment of the despicable bourgeois remnants vainly pitting sentimental slush against the greatness of national life. When more discerning readers and critics paid more attention to the "low" characters who energized the work, they realized that these were more lively and interesting than the monolithic figure of Soviet avatar. The author was seen to be attacking rather than defending a system that had crushed the flesh and spirit of humanity. Official opinion turned against the author and the highly sophisticated craftsman was accused of

"formalism," and "cosmopolitanism," that is, subversive Western tendencies. His "naturalism" was considered unsuitable reading for the Soviet family, and the delineation of "low" characters
was insufficiently negative. With other short pieces of fiction
that soon followed it, *Envy* was withdrawn from publication
until after Stalin's death.

KAVERIN (1902-   )

At fifteen, Kaverin had penetrated into Moscow avant-
garde poets' groups and had met Mayakovsky, Bryusov, and
Esenin. Three years later he was showing his verses to Mandelstam and Shklovsky who both advised him to try his hand at
prose. Young Kaverin joined the Serapion Brothers. A first collection of stories, *Master and Journeymen* (1931) showed, as in
Leonov's early fiction, the influence of E. T. A. Hoffmann and
Edgar Allen Poe in a preponderance of the fantastic and the
exotic, an addiction to intricate and adventurous plots that were
advocated by Luntz, and experimentation with Formalist techniques. Kaverin became absorbed in problems of inner literary
dynamics and studied the theories of Khlebnikov, Shklovsky,
Eichenbaum, and Tomashevsky.

The young writer seems to have understood more readily
than other Serapions that the discoveries of Formalist and Futurist leaders in literature manifested, as did Stravinsky's asym-
metrical, percussive music, the abstract painting of Malevich and
Kandinsky, the biomechanical expressionism of Meyerhold's theatre, a profound cultural upheaval that placed Russia in the
foreground of all twentieth-century art. This upheaval produced
a new left art no less sweeping and maximalist in its demand for
a radically innovative conception of the world than the imperatives for a socialist order. It was therefore not surprising that left
artists welcomed the revolution as a political and social expression of their search for new forms and their vision of a transformed reality. This utopian ideal was soon crushed by the
Bolsheviks' inate artistic conservatism, their hostility to experimentation, and the ignorance of the masses in regard to most
forms of art. The surrender of painters, stage designers, and
composers in the early twenties to the social command for a
functional "production" art that would create useful objects for

workers marked a critical retreat of Russian artists from their former leading position in the Western avant-garde. A similar dissolution of left art in literature, which was now entering into the socialist realism period, was symbolized in 1930 by Victor Shklovsky's public recantation of his Formalist theories (*A Movement to a Scientific Error*) and Mayakovsky's suicide.

In an astute study of Kaverin's fiction, the American critic and social historian, D. G. Piper, explores this conflict between new masters and pioneering forces in art as it is projected in the writer's most important novel, *Artist Unknown* (1931). The novel describes a confrontation between Shpekhtorov, a Five Year Plan technologist, and his friend, the artist, Arkhimedov, who was obviously named for the Greek mathematician and inventor, who was ahead of his time.

The artist hero appears as a loner and loser whose isolation in a materialistically minded environment is aggravated by personal tragedy. His wife who loves Shpekhtorov and is torn between loyalty to both men commits suicide, and his son is eventually adopted by the real father. But the main theme that derives from clashes in spirit between the two protagonists seems to echo a romantic versus pragmatic attitude toward life not unlike the one that textured *Envy*. In his novel, however, composed with considerably less writing power than Olesha's masterpiece, Kaverin examines at greater length the relation of art to life and the artist's function in a socialist society. Through the arguments of his two disciples, in the creation of his own "pure" theatre where reality is transcended in idealized illusions, in conversations with the obdurately rationalistic Soviet planner, Arkhimedov defends art that for him is qualitatively different from reality. It is nurtured on visions that transform reality by alienating it from the norm, and it offers man a transfigured awareness of the world in the light of new mutations and new relationships. This credo of the adherents to the early left art implies the artist's independence in experimenting with materials, devices, and techniques. According to Kaverin's hero, however, it does not free the artist from serving his society. Contrary to Kavalerov's yearning for a romanticized past, the modern artist remains integrated with the socialist order and supports it by providing Soviet Man, through unfettered art, with the necessary aesthetic and spiritual release from a technologically charged reality that would otherwise dessicate and drain him. The author, who appears only in the opening scenes and as Shpekhtorov's friend, seems to denigrate the artist's quixotic aspiration to enhance Soviet life with visions of the new art. Nevertheless, the reader is haunted by the realization of this aesthetic ideal, embodied as well in the epilogue of the book, in a magnificent painting produced by the artist. It depicts his private suffering and bears witness to his unshackled creative genius.

Kaverin was roundly criticized for his "deviationist" theme and was more prudent in the choice of an ideologically more acceptable subject for his next novel, *Fulfillment of Desires* (1936). Through a complicated plot, centered on the theft of rare manuscripts, he makes several astute psychological studies of the Leningrad university milieu. Particularly effective is the character of the history professor who will serve in Soviet fiction as the prototype of an experienced older man, knowledgeable and wise, acting as mentor to communist youth. In another popular work, *Open Book* (1949) that he later developed into a trilogy with two succeeding novels (*Doctor Vlansekova*, 1954, and *Quests and Hopes*, 1956) Kaverin pursued his bent for adventurous narrative. Vivid depiction of intense rivalry among scientists—for which the author was sharply rebuked—colors the story of a young girl, a medical worker, who inherits an important discovery in the development of an antivirus medicine. She becomes a well-known bacteriologist and comes into conflict with fellow careerists who resort to political informative tactics in a partially successful attempt to impede her research.

4 · Stalinization:

A Soviet Metamorphosis of Literature

In 1928 Stalin launched a huge program of forced collectivization and industrialization with the First Five Year Plan. Russia became subject to an economic and social transformation no less radical and pervasive than the one caused by the Revolution and the upheaval of the Civil War. In its wake came a metamorphosis of literature—its function, meaning, and purpose— that perhaps still remains the most unique intellectual phenomenon of our time.

One had to live in slogan-bristling Moscow or Leningrad during the years when the objectives of the Plan were being carried out or follow day by day the Soviet press flooded with statistics, charts, and urgent and ceaseless appeals for more and more work to realize the entire country's labor effort. It was galvanized by every kind of propaganda and with the intensity and concentration of a nation at war. Indeed, military terms such as "shock brigades, summit operations, battles, and heroic victories" were used. No relaxation or opposition was tolerated during the "push" for increased production on all fronts. Ruthless methods were used to make everyone, intellectuals included, serve in this undertaking. The latter responded for the most part with alacrity and enthusiasm to the immense upsurge of mass energies. They took pride in the spectacular achievements of the Plan and there was as yet no general awareness of the fact that, had they not willingly done so, they would have been coerced by

141

the government to express their opprobrium of Stalin's program. Yet, during the relatively permissive atmosphere of the NEP period, there had been indications that in a socialist state the intellectual superstructure must reflect the socialist economic base.

The Russians began to impose ideological controls in 1923 when articles on the role of literature were published in the party's organ, *The Bolshevik*. It was averred that since imaginative literature had become an important artistic force that was making an impact on the masses of workers, peasants, and youth, some party guidance was required. But this resolution was watered down a year later with an ambiguous pronouncement that the party remained uncommitted as to what direction, if any, guidance in the literary domain should take. This ambiguity seemed to Voronsky clear proof of the party's unwillingness to interfere in the area of literature.

Alexander Voronsky (1884-1943) was a leading Marxist literary critic who had founded the *Red Virgin Soil* magazine on Gorky's and Lenin's suggestion. It was a Soviet variant of an earlier journal that had been published in the twenties to present works of Communists and fellow travelers alike. Voronsky, however, placed creative writing above ideology and vigorously defended an author's right to objective and unhampered creative expression. As a result, he was considered the leader of the Pereval (The Pass) group of writers who were opposed to the narrow definition of proletarian art. He thereby earned the enmity of the RAPP (Russian Association of Proletarian Writers) and that brought about his undoing. When this militant organization of writers, who displayed their proletarian origins like laurels, became, with official encouragement, the most articulate and powerful critical apparatus during the First Five Year Plan, Voronsky realized that his usefulness to the movement was over, but, with characteristic generosity of spirit, he begged his Pereval followers to avoid the danger of defending him in the press. By 1928, he had been expelled from the party and forced to resign from his review.

The RAPP was directed by a Communist fanatic, Leopold Averbakh (1903-1938) who only tolerated fellow travelers for their craftsmanship and as potential recruits to the ranks of the

writers of a truly revolutionary proletarian literature. The principles of this aesthetic were fraught with confusion and contradiction. Writers, on the one hand, were to reflect the new reality of
the class struggle and the expanding proletarian world, and on
the other hand, were urged, in almost Voronsky's terms yet in
blunter language, to uncover the absolute and objective truth
and not compromise their art by reducing to simplification and
idealization the complexity of proletarian man. (For a penetrat-
ing and well documented study of these conflicting views, see
Edward J. Brown's *The Proletarian Episode in Russian Literature, 1928-1932*, New York, 1953.) The extremist elements of
RAPP prevailed, and, as a result, the organization took upon
itself the eradication of subversion from Soviet letters. They
launched a campaign of terror that ended the brief interval of
creative freedom in the twenties. Mayakovsky fell victim to it, as
did Pilnyak and Zamyatin. These two writers were chosen as
scapegoats with the object of intimidating all other "arrogantly
and freakishly individualistic" authors into submission. This was
a foretaste of systematic and public vilification that would develop during the full-fledged Stalinist liquidation program.

In 1932, when the Plan was nearing a triumphant realization that placed Stalin in a position of immense power, the
RAPP was suddenly and somewhat offhandedly dissolved by the
Central Committee. The Committee also announced the creation of a single association, the Union of Soviet Writers, to
which anyone wishing to practice professionally had to belong.
There is general agreement among Western critics, based on the
present knowledge of Stalin's character, that any prominent person or persons were likely to be discarded and frequently annihil-
ated (Averbakh was accused of Trotskyism and later shot)
however loyal he might be to the state, if the loyalty stemmed
from genuine ideological beliefs rather than a personal adulation
of Stalin himself. The head of the state mistrusted any manifestation of principled Communist orthodoxy that, even so,
might be clearsighted enough to discern his political opportunism. Stalin preferred to deal with more pliable, apolitical elements that he could manipulate at will.

The Soviet Writers' Union significantly was to contain one
Communist cell. Fellow travelers or such Communist purists as

the members of RAPP were eliminated because the party no longer found any need for individual factions within a homogeneously organized literary membership. It was assumed that all Soviet writers, properly directed, would gear their production toward socialist goals (a Literary Insitute was set up to form and indoctrinate fledgling writers). What this meant in practice was centralized bureaucratic control of the Union through one board of censorship and a Committee on Art. (These were directly responsible to the government, which administered penalties and awards, set up editorial surveillance of manuscripts for publication, and furnished the agenda for the Union's meetings).

The crux of the 1932 reforms was a provision for a literary method called Socialist Realism that all the members were to follow in their work. Attempts to define exactly what Socialist Realism was has given rise to a plethora of interpretations but, basically, it means that the man of letters must carefully keep within the prescribed ideological spirit of the method and guard against deviating from directives that Soviet critical cannon has (with little success) attempted to make clear through a maze of muddled, self-contradictory, and fatuously rhetorical statements.

The Soviets first tried to define Social Realism in a "gala" presentation of "Literature in the Soviet State," staged at the First Soviet Writers' Congress in 1934. This widely publicized event (all the speeches were immediately reprinted in pamphlet form and disseminated in thousands of copies) was attended by several hundred Soviet delegates and forty foreign authors. They listened to speakers from the highest government echelons and engaged in lively debate in twenty-six sessions that lasted two weeks. Maxim Gorky enhanced the proceedings with his great personal prestige. He took a long backward look, in his address, at bourgeois literature, which he claimed had ignored the underprivileged masses of humanity. He urged the Soviet writer to look for earlier models of the hero in folklore that eulogized the virtues of labor. In an analysis of the contemporary world of letters and "the tasks of proletarian art," the political essayist, Karl Radek expanded on the writings of avant-gardists such as Proust and Joyce. He stated that the Soviets could learn the technique of investigating the soul from these writers but ruled that there was nothing "great" in their novels; the triviality of form matched the intellectually shrivelled, frivolous content. His praise went to André Malraux, Jean-Richard Bloch (these two authors were at the Congress), Romain Rolland, Upton Sinclair, Bernard Shaw, and Theodore Dreiser, who had been drawn to the proletarian movement and had declared themselves friendly to the Soviets. The key speech was delivered by the party spokes-man, Andrei Zhdanov, infamously known for his vilifying be-havior in the 1946 literary purges. His job was to define Soviet literature and Socialist Realism. He named the latter "a hand-maiden of the state," declaring that in an age of class struggle a nontendencious literature could not exist; it was young but richer than all others in ideas, and it must fucntion as "the mighty bulwark of the coming world revolution." Its heroes are the worker, farmer, and engineer who are building the new life and it must express the optimism of this rising proletarian class.

Socialist Realism, according to Zhdanov, takes its meaning and purpose from the pronouncements of the two highest au-thorities. Stalin's definition of the writer as "engineer of human souls" imposes on them the duty "to depict life in revolutionary development" and a truthful and historically accurate portrayal of the "ideological remolding and re-education of the toiling people in the spirit of socialism." His second thessis advanced party-mindedness as being pivotal to that literary doctrine whereby the party could use literature as it sees fit at any given moment with no authorial restrictions. This thesis was drawn from a pamphlet Lenin wrote in 1905, entitled *Party Organiza-tion and Party Literature*. The passage quoted, and since then referred to innumerable times by succeeding generations of So-viet critics, reads: "Down with non-partisan writers! Down with literary supermen! Literature must become part of the common cause of the proletariat, a 'cog and a screw' of the single great social-Democratic mechanism set in motion by the entire work-ing class."

The Marxist literary critic, George Lukacs, attempted to reconcile Lenin's opposition to the freedom of the artist that had been endorsed by Engels, by interpreting these lines as Lenin's admonition to fellow revolutionaries who indulge in "intellectual flights" when writing for Social Democratic journals instead of adhering to the party line. (In a later statement Lenin did say that the writer "must, of course, be given wide scope for personal initiative, individual preferences, range of thought, fantasy form, content.")

Valery Bryusov astutely noted in his response to Lenin's article entitled "Freedom of the World" (published in *Balance* in the spring of 1905) that tolerance for a writer's individual idiosyncrasies did not signify acceptance of uncommitted artistic integrity and the freedom allowed is *in* art but not *of* art. This position was in accord with Lenin's cultural policy, formulated at the First Congress of the Proletcult in 1920 that calls for immediate access of the masses to education, science, literature, and the arts through a critical assimilation of the cultural heritage. Writers necessarily were to participate in the socialization of culture and the prerogatives of absolute art. Neutrality or negation of existing realitieis was to be replaced by political allegiance to the party line.

From the discussions on the floor that followed and the numerous elucidations of Socialist Realism that were made in the Soviet press certain proscriptive features clearly emerged: Modernism that had textured the early twentieth-century literary and artistic renaissance and sparked off experimental stylization in the early twenties was lumped as "Formalism" and harshly denigrated. All avant-garde movements, represented by such international figures as Kafka, Joyce, and Proust, were denounced as bourgeois and decadent. Writers were warned against their "sick" exploration of inner man and a nihilistic view of society.

The language and style of nineteenth-century Russian classics was recommended, and most emphatically so by Gorky, who considered himself the last representative of the great school of realism. However, the abrasively critical spirit in which Tolstoy, Turgenev, and Chekhov had projected their environment was to be avoided. Even the rationalistic, moral Leo Tolstoy of the later period, whom Lenin had acclaimed as the greatest single revolutionary inspiration for the peasantry, was regarded with reservation. Professor Gleb Struve aptly recalls the parallels made by the intransigent Marxist critic, Isaac Nusinov, between Tolstoy and Dostoevsky. Both writers, he insists, were equally dangerous in their projection of human beings as individuals rather than a part of the collective, with Tolstoy defaulting even more than his great peer with his view of man good within himself but becoming evil as a social being. Writers now should underscore the Communist blessings bestowed on the socially functioning Soviet man in his collective society. If realistic present-day evidence was to the contrary, writers were expected to describe a bright Socialist future.

Stalin contributed in no small measure to the narrowly politicized and regimented definition of what Soviet literature should represent. His own taste was atrociously petty bourgois, which may account for the philistine flavor of much popular and, for the most part, second-rate fiction that flooded the market in his day. Besides, he had imbibed from his literary mentor, the radical critic Chernyshevsky of the 1860s, a suspicion of all art without immediate social utility: "Pushkin is of lesser importance than a good pair of boots." He needed a Soviet intelligentsia with technological skills to be used in the construction of the Soviet State. He looked upon the intellectual elite as technicians, whose talents would promote the labor effort needed to consolidate his Soviet empire. When he counseled writers to "speak the truth" he was really enjoining them, as would an American manufacturer his advertising staff, to sell his product with persuasive eloquence, to create consumer demand. In the Soviet instance this meant that writers should maintain the newly literate but still unsophisticated millions of Soviet readers in a state of highly keyed enthusiasm as to the operation of the Soviet state, convince them that the working man was the true repository of hope, and evoke such powerful visions of the beautiful Communist future that the drabness and hardships of actuality would be eclipsed. Writers were allowed to depict conflict, and they were even encouraged to lend excitement and interest to the action of their didactic offerings, which otherwise might lack charm or mystery. But they could only show the struggle against vestigial traces of capitalistic habits or attitudes that at the approach of the inevitably happy ending were overcome.

To understand the triumphant overtones of Soviet criticism that acclaimed the Socialist Realism doctrine as a final victory over "outmoded" traditions, the long-standing quarrel between radicals and liberal writers that lasted almost a hundred years must be recalled. This complicated controversy may seem confusing to the non-Russian reader of the classic nineteenth-century authors whose works, almost to a man, expressed commitment to social and political reform. These writers projected contemporary reality through the prism of their creative imagination. They insisted on celebrating the aesthetic experience and freely exercised their creative right to depict man in all the frailty of his human condition, which at the time was frequently featured as that well-known ineffectual, idealistic hero at odds with himself and his society—the superfluous man. This was the major grievance that political activists harbored against the writers.

In contrast to the literary pluralism of the West that, since the Renaissance, has achieved an increasingly reciprocal relationship between the individual and his environment, in Russia a hero-oriented literature, deeply rooted in the past, continues to prevail. It is in a magnified portrayal of heroes, from the attractive and uncomplicated folklore figures to the immortal personnages of the major novels of the last century, that the Russian people have continued to look for the reflection and confirmation of their own spiritual history.

The Russian revolutionary movement is literally hero-haunted with great codifiers of doctrine, political insurgents, anarchists, and hundreds of nameless terrorists who eagerly accepted probable torture and death in the execution of their assignments. It was of the greatest import to the Socialist underground that, in literature, the single open form of public expression allowed in imperialist Russia, the goals and activities of such heroes be projected in a compelling form. This was of particular concern to the radicals of the sixties who were making subversive forays against the established order. They wanted major literary spokesmen to endorse their active intervention in the country's life by creating credible revolutionary heroes. But these remained elusive. There is not a single political activist of note in the works of Tolstoy; Dostoevsky reduced his only lifesize portrait of the terrorist Nechayev to the grotesque; and the only dedicated revolutionist, Turgenev's Insarov, was summarily dis-

missed by the radical critic, Dobrolyubov, because the protagonist was not a Russian.

Nikolay Chernyshevsky (1828-1889) was for over twenty
years a major spiritual force behind underground action and the
foremost theorist of a new aesthetic realism that strongly influenced radical thought. In opposition to the Hegelian premise
that art was superior to nature, Chernyshevsky advanced the
view that art was a reproduction of reality and that its function
was to judge and explain the external world. This was the core of
the critical realism that the Soviets adapted to their socially and
aesthetically acceptable approach to the arts. The tension between the idealistic and tragic elements in nature and man's
involvement with them is eliminated and replaced by the image
and idea of concrete situations that are humanly solvable in
materialistic and utilitarian terms. Chernyshevsky constructed an
elaborate illustration of this flattening of man in his world in a
piece of fiction, *What Is To Be Done?* (1863) that read more
like a didactic tract than a novel. Its configuration has the same
woodenness of style, a simplistic approach to problems to be
solved in the light of invincible socialist ideals that characterizes
another perennial proletarian favorite, Gorky's *Mother.* Its main
protagonist is an affirmative model of the "New Man," the
fiercely ascetic, self-powered, humorlessly optimistic, irreproacha-
bly doctrinated Rakhmetov. He was to put to shame the "frivolous, sentimental" fiction of the day, and he did inspire several
generations of radical Russian youth. Lenin admitted to having
been "bowled over" by him at the age of nineteen. But it was
upon Lenin himself, the man, his doctrine, and his action, that
post-revolutionary writers attempted to graft the image of the
Soviet hero. The authority and power of their Soviet processed
heroes were often judged in the official Soviet press by the extent
of their mimesis of the beloved national leader.

In the Soviet Union, any biographical comment on Lenin
takes on the fervor of hagiography. Nonetheless, by the most
objective standards he is recognized as an extraordinary human
being. He seemed to have managed to gather into his person all
the qualities needed to attain the immense goals he had set his
mind on: tenacity, intelligence, lucidity, willpower, self-reliance,

leadership, astuteness, memory, self-confidence, endurance, and flexibility. He also lacked to an astonishing degree vanity, temperament, arbitrary caprice, humor, spontaneity, and deep feelings of love and hatred that might have distracted him from the drive of revolutionary action. His entire life's program had been an interlocking series of carefully planned strategies, limited to the specific immediate realization of his goal. All that was irrelevant to his achieving this goal he considered unimportant and boring. This attitude marked him as a special being who moved in a kind of isolation, a man difficult to like and impossible not to respect. His very self-containment, immense purposefulness, and unequalled ability to control and direct all kinds of men, surrounded him while he was building the Soviet state. These characteristics also gave him an aura of infallibility that became yet greater after his death.

With what measure of success were writers able to pattern their heroes in the image of the architect of the revolution and of the Soviet socialist state? How faithful was the adherence to the doctrine of Socialist Realism or to any facet of it? What shape did the mythification of the "desirable and the potential" take on?

In the following section an attempt will he made to answer questions of this nature because they may throw some light on the Soviet writer's creative predicament. The critical review will include the most important works of several outstanding authors who produced writings of permanent value, made peace with their artistic conscience, became well known, successful, and survived.

LITERATURE BY PRESCRIPTION: THREE EARLY MODULES

FURMANOV (1891-1926)

In the mid-twenties, Formalist critic Boris Eikhenbaum acknowledged that literary experimentation was drawing to a close and interest in inner-literary dynamics had capitulated to the demands of a new mass audience for prescriptive realistic fiction. He may have had in mind three immensely successful novels—

harbingers of the new literary mode that was to come of age in the early thirties.

Dmitri Furmanov's *Chapayev* (1923), Fyodor Gladkov's *Cement* (1925), and Alexander Fadeyev's *The Rout* (1927) are filled with the iconography that was to become a constant for writers in search of prescriptive realism. Heroes came from a very modest family background. They had formed an early allegiance to the Bolshevik cause and had zealously participated in the Civil War. In all three novels, the authors highlighted a problem in the transition of Russia into the Soviet Union that has not yet been solved. These men were not mere dispensers of socialist homilies. The interest of each work obtains from the Leninist dynamic slogan "action, pugnacity, partisanship" concretized in their work in a climate of struggle between two orders of Soviet men.

Formally, *Chapayev* is a factual narrative that was very much in vogue in early proletarian circles. It is drawn from notebooks, official directives, newspapers, and the diary of the author who had served in the division of the legendary guerilla fighter, Chapayev, as a political commissar. But the confrontations between the young commissar, named Klychkov, and the picturesque peasant leader are selectively chosen and are supposed to make a definite impression on the reader's "correct" judgment and on his emotions. It would seem difficult not to admire the fierce and fearless anarchistic warrior. He is spontaneous, outspoken, a true friend of the common man whose violence and cruelty, like that of Taras Bulba, derive from an elemental force that sweeps through all the peasant insurrections in Russian history.

It is the disciplined, ruthless, and determined commissar, however, who comes out winner in the unequal struggle between the military genius who at first resists bookish indoctrination. The main point ,of the story, is the patient, methodical, and crafty offensive against the resistance of the peasant, whereby the wild stallion of the steppe is finally broken into a saddle horse, obedient and respectful to his master, that is, the party's will. Particularly memorable in the formless, episodic novel are Klychkov's private reflections about this tremendously appealing, inchoate, raw kind of Russian folk hero. Was it really necessary to domesticate his strength? Finally, yes. Once Chapayev had been placed in command to win partisan campaigns, his usefulness within a more developed technological strategy was over. What Furmanov-Klychkov does not think through, however, is the means by which the Soviets were to subdue or suppress the legends of such guerilla fighters that survive in popular memory as an emblem of peasant needs and peasant aspirations.

FADEYEV (1901-1956)

In Fadeyev's novel *The Rout*, the dedicated Communist is put to a more crucial test. He is the leader of a Siberian Red guerilla band, that desperately fights its way out of an encircle-ment by White and Japanese forces with the loss of all but nineteen men.

Fadeyev prided himself on being Leo Tolstoy's disciple (he had read and re-read *War and Peace* before starting the novel). He visibly emulates the great writer's economy and clarity of language and submits the characters to objective psychological analysis. With no ideological underpinnings Fadeyev presents the main protagonists. They are the miner, Morosko, a daredevil, free-wheeling fighter, his wife, a wanton and kind camp follower, an old workman, Pitka, and Melchik, the idealistic and cowardly student intellectual, who, like Fedin's Startsev, romanticizes the cause but cracks under physical duress.

Levinson, the leader, is Fadeyev's most successful creation and a fascinating study in heroism. He is empowered with the lucidity, based on sensitive understanding of human behavior, that Klychkov lacks. He analyzes throughout the novel the motivations of the men entrusted to him and the predicament in which he finds himself. The situation calls for an involved experi-ence in leadership. Levinson is challenged by the desperate need of the band to rely on his ability to get them out of the trap. He presents a mien that is impervious to the imminent peril that surrounds them and the self-confidence of a resourceful com-mander whose plans to avert that peril are carefully worked out. This display of inner strength and purpose to those who blindly follow him is but a facade behind which Levinson fights for some control over his fears and indecisiveness, which adds a universal dimension to the sorely tried hero. He knows that he must accomplish the job assigned to him by history and that he must do it alone.

Fadeyev emphasizes Levinson's apartness. He appears to have no family; he is a Jew; his hunchbacked, puny appearance distinguishes him from the others, and, although he wields great influence among his subordinates, he is unable to fraternize with them. He lives in isolation and he is sustained by the unbreakable resolve to retain the confidence of his men. This is as powerful an urge in him as his belief in the beautiful good men of the bright Communist future. He feels a kinship with them but is troubled by the present impossibility of making beautiful good men out of them because of their appalling social backwardness. That Levinson allows himself to pose this problem to which no authoritative answer has yet been found makes for the credibility of his portrait. It is further enhanced in a poignant moment when the peaceful forest road is reached by the surviving eighteen guerillas and their leader breaks into tears. Disappointingly, Fadeyev writes a conclusion that flaws the artistic integrity of the earlier passage. The last lines, with unaccountable suddenness, are meant to transform the disparate minded, ragged remnants of the company into a disciplined unit that will now know how to live and "do its duty."

GLADKOV (1883-1958)

Gladkov was abusively reprimanded by the RAPP for artistic imperfections in *Cement* such as excessive stylistic ornamentalism and extremely violent scenes reminiscent of Artsybashev and Andreev. He also was severely criticized by Alexander Fadeyev for the one-dimensional quality of his characters and his lack of penetration into the inner man. This justified criticism in no way invalidates the novel's paramount distinction. It has become the inspiration for a most prolific and enduring form of Soviet fiction that glorifies the industrialization of the Soviet state. For the first time, the glamor of the Civil War is replaced by the heroics of peacetime labor and the machine gun gives way to the tractor, the hammer, the axe. The instant popularity of *Cement* testified to its emotional impact on the restless postrevolutionary population; through the experience of one ordinary working man the author defines what the job is that now has to be done.

Gleb Chumalov is a cement factory worker who returns from three years fighting in the Civil War to his Black Sea hometown where a demoralized population has gone through epidemics, famine, and devastation and the plant where he was employed is closed down and partially demolished. The action starts with his determination to get the factory back into production. He has himself appointed to the Factory Committee and starts to deal with a huge variety and number of obstacles—apathy, ill will, red tape, scarcity of material and tools, and counter-revolutionary activity. He bores through the problems with bullish tenacity and singleminded fervor until the machines are humming again and he is on the job "turning over with a shovel the chalk and clay . . . and there flowed over him in great waves .. the continual pace of the masses about him . . . that were also shouting and striking at the earth with spades and hammers." The momentum of this story, that follows a Horatio Alger pattern, charges, inevitably, toward a happy ending.

Cement also might have served as a manual on personal rehabilitation if it were not for Gladkov's sincere admiration for his hero and the enthusiasm with which he advocates the spirit of collective enterprise. In powerful passages the mediocre, semi-literate Chumalov is shown at his best when he functions with and is surrounded by others infected by the solidarity of mass action. As a private individual he fares less well. He is hopelessly confused and frustrated when he comes home to find his wife transformed into an emancipated and busy party member, unwilling to resume the former role of wife and housewife that he attempts to reimpose on her. She leaves him and the author allows Chumalov's state of emotional bankruptcy to remain suspended, as it were, with no resolution. This is once more a kind of prophecy of the willed separateness between the private and public spheres, with an overwhelming advocacy for the latter, that will characterize most Soviet literature. A Westerner's conjecture, based on elementary concepts of psychology, that Chumalov's ruined family life may account for his involvement in the Factory Committee is not at all valid in the light of the Soviet premise that a man's motives are generated by the ethic of social and political imperative; his private feelings are his own and only infrequently the readers' concern.

Gladkov does not bother to delve very thoroughly or realistically into the personalities of such characters as the miner, Moroska, teetering between amorality and self-discipline, the Cheka representative who is a rake and confirmed Communist, Chumalov's wife whose surge into personal freedom gives promise of other emotional releases stifled by her boorish and inarticulate husband. These people and others like them are barely limned in, considered uninteresting, as Lenin would have it, because of their distance from or incomprehensiion of the Soviet life style.

The three novels enjoyed enormous popular success: *Cement* very quickly sold 500,000 copies; *The Rout* was printed in several editions, and *Chapayev*, received with great enthusiasm, was soon afterwards made into a perenially favorite film. This confirmed the official view of the thirties that the mass reader in the Soviet Union was eager for solemn, instructive, inspirational literature that supposedly reflected his reality and contained a pattern for his behavior in social action.

SHOLOKHOV (1905-), A PARAGON OF SOVIET LETTERS

From the flood of Soviet fiction that has been written on the revolutionary period, *The Quiet Don* by Mikhail Sholokhov is the most likely to survive. The novel has been translated into fifty-four languages and printed in over five million copies, and a grateful country bestowed on the author all existing literary awards. When the fourth and final volume was to appear, Russians stood in long lines through the night waiting for the bookshops to open.

The magnitude of this literary enterprise is impressive. Sholokov recreates the movement of conflicting historical forces that took place between 1912 and 1922, the Revolution, and the Civil War by describing the involvement of the Don Cossacks in these events. He includes innumerable starkly realistic military and peacetime scenes involving a cast of some six hundred characters. It is this Homeric breadth of design and certain external elements that bring to mind *War and Peace*: a return to nineteenth-century realism, the slowly moving narrative rhythms that recall Tolstoy's unhurried pace, the comingling of historical figures with fictive personages in the novel that also borrows for emphasis and dramatic contrast Tolstoy's favorite technique of introducing symmetrical parallels within family, class, and political groupings. But no true comparison can be made between *The Quiet Don* and the profound and densely human Tolstoyan vision of Russian society in crisis and united against a common outside enemey.

Sholokhov's originality lies elsewhere. For the first time rural Russia enters great literature with a most vivid and exhaustive portrayal of a picturesque semi-peasant, semi-warrior people living close to home, saber, and plough. Sholokhov imagines these people as living an uncomplicated action-filled existence as they are shown at work, play, and in all social relations. Regional dialect, rich in archaic forms and language, flows naturally in this primitive setting; other pages are suffused with songs, sayings, superstitions of Cossack folk epic poetry. A major part of the appeal of the novel's first volume for the Russian reader, for whom the Cossack was an embodiment of Tsarist repression, ferocity in war, and pogroms, was the revelation of a self-contained, patriarchial nation within a nation whose remoteness from modern concerns seemed to cast it in a mythic mold. It had been forgotten that fleeing serfs were the ancestors of the lusty steppe brawlers and fighters of Gogolian legend. They had been drafted to guard the outposts of the Russian empire in the southeast steppe and manned cavalry regiments in the tsar's army, for which services they were given almost total economic and social autonomy in their fertile Don region. In the early twentieth century the Cossacks were still on the periphery of national life. They remained semiliterate, extremely conservative, hostile to incursions from the outside, and encrusted in a habit of independence.

With the collapse of the monarchy, the Don Cossacks lost their separate identity in a confrontation with the forces of the new order. This constitutes the main theme of *The Quiet Don*. The author develops the novel through the experiences of the principal protagonist, Grigory Melekhov, a favorite younger son of one of the middle peasant families of the village Tatarsk.

When we meet the impetuous, likable, intelligent young lad he is pursuing an ardent love affair with Aksinya, a neighbor's wife, that his family attempts to break up with a hasty wedding. Barring this defiance of convention that reveals his passionate nature, there is little to distinguish him from other young Cossacks. All are, in the course of the first volume, mobilized into the war against the Germans in 1914. Grigory fights skillfully and bravely, is wounded, and decorated. With the rest of his regiment, he feels the frustration and tedium of the prolonged, defeatist campaigns riddled with the indecision of his superiors and revolutionary rumors from the distant capital. He longs to return home. A turning point in his life, and of the novel, is his encounter with a Ukranian revolutionary whose propaganda holds for him the promise of peace and freedom. From then on Sholokhov's unreflective hero instigates a search for certitudes in a world that is closing in on former possessions, values, and souls. Caught between agonizing alternatives, his allegiance fluctuates between the Reds, who outrage him with arbitrary slaughter, looting, and raping of Cossack villages (that Sholokhov describes with Gorkian naturalism) and the White Army where he is demoted and treated by supercilious officers as a "rough, crude Cossack." Despite his vacillations and precipitous reactions to events, he instinctively preserves intact his only true faith, which is a belief in the former Cossack freedom that motivates all his actions. In his opposition to history, he is clearly marked as a victim of it. The ill-fated Don uprising, that united all the Cossacks with the aim of restoration of Cossack autonomy, and in which Grigory participated as division commander, was crushed in 1919; it symbolizes the fall of a people and the fall of the hero.

A last-ditch attempt to regain Soviet favor with a show of bravery in Red Marshal Budenny's campaign against the Poles is thwarted by the denunciation of Misha Koshevoi, a former boyhood chum and now Soviet Chairman in Tatarsk. Grigory's only remaining wish is to go back to his land, his children, and to Aksinya for whom he had deserted his bride and whose memory continued to stir his blood in and out of his numerous military adventures and in his sleep, beside other women.

The love between Grigory and Aksinya recurrently highlights the entire novel and informs its most beautifully lyrical passages. It is a simple passion only possible for simple people, elemental and irrational, that survived all the terrors and disasters surrounding the two young people and which required, for its justification, nothing but fulfillment of itself. When Grigory was with her, he realized the senselessness of war and counterwar; for her, a primitive, free, instinctive being, there was no other reason for living but their love for which she happily renounced respectability, family, and material welfare.

Aksinya is the prototype in history and fiction of the woman who follows her man everywhere, lives by her needs of him and his occasional need of her; she is utterly submissive to her love destiny. The other two women in Grigory's life are also timeless, spiritually stronger configurations. The primitive mother is drawn in epic style as the pillar of the household, with immense resources of fortitude and forbearance, who accepts uncomplainingly injustice, brutality, the anguish of separation from her sons, and their illness and death, and even the son-in-law who has killed Grigory's brother. Pretty, innocent Natalya symbolizes the tragedy of the unwanted wife in a society that allows no solace save caring for the children of the neglectful husband. She has no means of retribution, only pity and derision from her familiars, or suicide. She attempts to kill herself with a scythe; this curbs the passionate rebellion that is gradually transformed into a deep attachment for the family and her children. Grigory's continued unawareness, however, of his wife's increasing spiritual and emotional maturity and his indifference to her shy caresses, bring on a frenzy of anger. She aborts the child and dies according to her wish cleansed of her husband's impurity in her body.

Toward the novel's closing the hero finds himself completely alone. He had come out of hiding from the Soviet control commission to find Aksinya and while escaping together on horseback, a Soviet patrol bullet fatally wounds her. When he presses the damp clay over her body and eyes staring into the black disc of the sun in a black sky Grigory knows that his life has been permanently darkened, that everything is finished. He throws his gun and cartridges into the Don and walks back to his native village.

Sholokhov cannily leaves the novel unfinished. A happy

ending, Soviet style, with Grigory's conversion to Communism, would have been artistically vitiating; to give over a popular hero to be executed by the Soviet authorities would not have passed the censor, although it is implied from the entire downward pull of the hero's pilgrimage toward freedom and truth that there was no other fate for him but the Cheka. Besides, did it matter? There remained only an empty hulk of a man who had relinquished his Cossack pride and manhood in offering his weapons to the Don.

Mikhail Sholokhov was born in 1905 in the Don Cossack region to an illiterate Cossack peasant woman and a young merchant from Ryazan which caused him to forfeit full Cossack status. Growing up in an increasingly unsettled world that was soon to lapse into savagery, he did not complete high school, was frequently displaced with his family as villages and towns were occupied by Reds and Whites during the Civil War, worked at fifteen for the Revolutionary Committee, and was sent on grain-requisitioning brigades to the village. At nineteen, he married and started to write. The *Don Tales* (1925) attracted the attention of A. S. Serafimovich, writer and prominent literary personality in Moscow, also from the Cossack lands, who acclaimed his fellow countryman as a promising young talent. The tales include twenty-four fictional sketches and two longer stories of adventures in a Civil War setting whose main protagonists were Komsomols, young grain-requisitioning Communists and Cossacks. They are written in a choppy, crudely realistic manner. In 1925 he conceived *The Quiet Don* and completed the first three volumes by 1930. There were serious setbacks. The magazine *October* rejected the first part of the *Don* for its "political irrelevance" and it was only through Serafimovich's intervention that publication was permitted in 1928. At the same time rumors began to circulate that the Don manuscript had been stolen from a dead White Army officer. Affluent RAPP members (Averkamp, Serafimovich, Fadeyev, and Stavsky) defended the young author, but no tangible evidence that he actually had written *The Quiet Don,* such as rough drafts, sources, or notes, were forthcoming to prove their assertions, and the rumors did not completely die down.

The first volume of *The Quiet Don* was dubbed by a number of critics as "kulak literature" until it became known that Stalin had found merit in the work, although he pointed out certain falsifications in regard to prominent Communist generals. The basic value of "comrade" Sholokhov's work was then affirmed in the official press and with minor deletions publication of the third volume in 1933 and the fourth volume in 1940 was approved.

Meanwhile, Sholokhov had written the first volume of *Virgin Soil Upturned* that began to appear serially in 1932. (It has been suggested that the full party membership he had been soliciting for two years was the commission paid for the second novel. Its theme of rural collectivization was suffusing the Soviet political air and sections of it were sent to Party members for correction and advice while they were still being composed.

The genesis of the work and its ideological edifice shape a classical conformist piece of fiction. The plot pattern is simple: imposition of forced agricultural collectivization on kulaks and peasants of a small Cossack village and their reactions to it. They are threatened throughout with counter-revolutionary reprisal that does explode into melodrama at the end. The enforcement officer, Davidov, is chosen from the 25,000 trusted members of the party who are sent on these missions. For all his flexibility and reasonableness, he is a robot Communist who doggedly pursues his job of human devastation and dreams of no larger reward than to have the kolkhoz named after him. The plot of the first volume is occasionally enlivened by eccentric farmer types caught with trenchant realism in conversations and incidents.

Stalin was pleased with this tedious and oppressive contribution to his rural program from the famous writer. The faithful portrayal of the calamities and privations that faced a recalcitrant peasantry made excellent propaganda for voluntary participation in the kolkhoz.

The second volume, that in English has been erroneously given an independent title, *Harvest on the Don*, follows on directly as a victorious culmination of the collectivization effort. All the villagers are now working cooperatively and Davidov, with his assistant, is somewhat unaccountably killed by an anti-Communist group. Yet, in the Soviet logic of things it is not surprising that the enforcement officers, having completed their work, would become expendable. The second volume is excessively long, suffers from loose episodic construction, lacks humorous relief, and is distinctly inferior in sustained interest to the first part of the novel. Despite diminished writing energies and a scarcity of production, following *The Quiet Don*, Mikhail Sholokhov became known as the author of one monumental work, for which he received the Nobel Prize in 1965.

The lasting popularity of *The Quiet Don* among Soviet readers is not difficult to understand. For the first time the country's great upheaval was portrayed to them through the ordinary existence of people like themselves who had experienced displacement, homelessness, and changing political allegiance. Scene after scene depicts mass movements, family intimacy, and casually splintered talk, so faithful to reality that it seemed as if the author had caught them with a tape recorder and camera rather than through the prism of his imagination. As the novel unfolded, revolutionary and counter revolutionary conflicts were shown objectively, not didactically and Grigory remained a complete individualist. The more discerning readers were astonished at the freedom that Sholokhov took in his arrangement of credible and real situations that not only made fiction out of history but also revealed the fiction out of which history is made.

Sholokhov describes the Cossack ethos in the first volume in a manner that falls somewhere between ethnography and a folk epic. In all of the four volumes, he relates the spontaneous play of appetites and instincts that exalt the natural grandeur and dignity of man existing in harmony with the rhythms of nature.

In situations where ideological dogma regulates conduct and the uneducated hero is forced to face the complexity of historical forces beyond his understanding, the writer comes to lose some of his creative force. He seems incapable of bringing in imaginative elements to enlarge the hero's inner world, and the continued use of exteriorized reality, even to the conveying of inward agony through body movements, leads to a central monotony in the narration. There is also a sense of strain in the portrayal of non-Cossack protagonists—White Army officers, the Bolsheviks Abramson, Bunchuk, and others. Sholokhov did not exercise the necessary inventiveness to develop them fully. They remain one-dimensional figures, emblems of politicized partisanship. That Sholokhov seems to falter in his art when it is not directly concerned with a projection of the Cossack people indicates his ambiguous involvement with his novel. Does he, as a Communist writer, press forward the belief which Grigory's odyssey seems to imply that the Don Cossacks were at last ready, in view of the vulnerability and impermanence of their earlier position, to be absorbed into the new social order, or is this novel, considered a masterpiece in the Soviet Union, fundamentally a celebration of a simpler, primitive life?

The troublesome question of *The Quiet Don* authorship was reactivated in 1974 with the appearance of a 140-page booklet, *The Current of The Quiet Don*, published in Paris and written under a protective alias "D" by a Soviet literary scholar with a preface by Alexander Solzhenitsyn. The fragmentary study was based on a detailed scrutiny of the text and attempts to prove that the more wooden, less poetic passages were "co-authored" by Sholokhov. Many of his insertions, according to "D," distorted the original meaning of the work and perhaps, most plausibly, were written by Feodor D. Kryukov (whose biography concludes "D's" exposition).

As writer, populist, and White Army officer, Kryukov, son of a Cossack ataman, was associated all his life with the Don. By 1892 he was writing historical tales culled from Cossack legend, and for twenty-five years stories about his people appeared in *Russian Wealth*, a monthly review. Its editor, Korolenko, spoke of him as the writer from the Don in whom the Don lived. Elected Cossack deputy to the First Duma, he signed, in the cause of labor, the well known "Vyborg Appeal," was imprisoned for it, and forbidden to return to the Don region. He continued to write in St. Petersburg, became a high-school teacher, and started a long novel on Cossack life. Conscripted into the First World War army, he returned home in 1917. He then was chosen secretary of the Independent Union of Cossacks and when the White Cossack troops began to retreat from the Don, Kryukov accompanied them southward, like Grigory Melekhov, not quite comprehending the significance of that event. In 1918 and 1919 he directed the staff of the *Novocherkask Don News* that included Piotr Gromoslavsky, young Mikhail Sholokhov's father in law. When the Red Army was approaching Novocherkask all the White functionaries were evacuated and Kryukov, in the company of Gromoslavsky, left taking only a metal box with him that contained all his manuscripts. While traveling, he caught typhus and succumbed to it with Granosvky at his side. The latter returned home, and in 1924 the young Sholokhov couple joined him in the Cossack community of Viochenskaya where Sholokhov started his intense literary activity.

The various arguments advanced by "D" as to the destructive impact of the fledgling writer on the novel, which led to incoherence, broken up sequences, and imposition of ideology on poetic images, have been refuted point by point in a lengthy review of the *Current* by Herman Ermolayev in the Fall, 1974 issue of the *Slavic Eastern European Journal*. Professor Ermolayev tries to explain that many inconsistencies throughout the novel resulted from the censorship of many passages and Sholokhov's own compliance in making necessary corrections to clear each volume for publication. Ermolayev then brings up examples to demonstrate Sholokhov's genius and originality. However, the main issue becomes blurred in a parrying match between the two scholars. The near impossibility of rendering an accurate assessment on the basis of inner textual evidence without the original manuscripts becomes apparent as other instances of illogicality, mistakes, and borrowings from other sources began to emerge.

A year later, the dissident historian, Roy Medvedev released *Who Wrote the Quiet Don?* for publication in Paris. He had collaborated with a Cossack historian, Serge Starikov, in a reconstruction of the Civil War in the Don region based on documents in the Rostov archives that Starikov had been examining until these sources were closed in the early twenties. The documents confirmed the historical accuracy of the novel in the precision of military details and true-to-life portraits and conversations of the military staff with whom Kryukov had served. This tended to support Alexander Solzhenitsyn's and "D's" conjecture as to the probable identity of the novel's author. Medvedev questions, as others have before him, the "miraculously" swift and brilliant completion of the first three volumes in a little under three years by a beginning writer whose subsequent trickling production never attained the same literary quality. He focuses on two outside factors that had hitherto escaped notice. One deals with the seeming conspiracy on the part of the authorities to relegate Kryukov's works to undeserved obscurity: His works are omitted from the most exhaustive literary histories of Russian literature of the period. His name is likewise absent from biographies of his close friends and professional associates such as Korolenko and Serafimovich. In the other instance, Medvedev brings out the wide cleavage between Sholokhov's *Don Tales* and the Cossack epic. The early stories reflect Mikhail Sholokhov's own background in the cast of young Communists, grain requisitioners, junior party memmbers. The occasional Cossack appears in a harsh light as "the bad man" stalking peasants who covet his land or that of the landed gentry. It is a typical pogrom figure. The steppe itself is presented as depressing, dirty, arid, not unlike the uncultivated terrain of an impoverished farm. Medvedev finds it difficult to reconcile this attitude with the deep attachment to Cossack traditions that throbs through the novel, the Cossack's determination to keep his dignity and privileges and the magnificently lyrical evocations of the beauty of the steppe in complicated, ornamental metaphor that give additional power to the first two volumes of the work.

Medvedev's analysis circulated in typed copy from hand to hand in the Soviet Union early in 1975 at the time when officials were preparing a new edition of Sholokhov's work and conferences to honor the author's seventy-fifth birthday in May. The stubbornly persistent charge of plagiarism, whether veracious or not, is a heavy burden to bear for the famous writer whose reputation as a genius in his own country may have been a huge embarrassment to his own lesser talent and meager imagination. Despite the "riddles" of *The Quiet Don*, however, Michael Sholokhov will be remembered for having introduced a great regional novel into world literature.

TWO CONFORMISTS

The ability to gauge astutely political change in Moscow may partially explain the long and successful careers of Alexei Tolstoy (1883-1945) and Ilya Ehrenburg (1891-1967). Both possessed to a high degree the poet laureate's writing temperament that is easily inspired by directives from above and skillfully knows how to develop, with suppleness and vigor, the expression of officially sanctioned sentiments.

This quality came in good stead when the two writers returned to the Soviet Union after a prolonged sojourn abroad—one as a repentant emigré-nobleman, the other a restless cosmopolitan Jew with a cloudy past of literary bohemia and shifting political allegiances.

ALEXEI TOLSTOY (1883-1945)

By 1917, Count Alexei Tolstoy had already written several novels, a number of plays, and some extremely popular short stories about the declining landed gentry to which he belonged. Composed in the neo-realistic style that writers were resorting to in reaction to symbolist mysticism and its excessive refinements, Tolstoy favored the objectively described anecdote and zestful, vividly concretized detail. He made monstrously self-indulgent, erotic, ignorant, squires come alive without attempting psychological studies or resorting to the distortion of satire. His most successful tale was *The Lame Landowner* about a despotic and grotesque eccentric who brings his own wheat to market. When he does not get his own price for it, he dumps all the seventy carts of wheat into the river.

For this apolitical nobleman, the revolution and exile abroad were less a disaster than a personal disturbance. Tolstoy chafed under the material privations of émigré life and hungered after the physical "Russianness" of the native landscape of smells, sights and sounds. So, during the propitious NEP period he returned to the Soviet Union. He brought with him, like an amulet against harm, his open Russian charm, an immense flexibility of behavior and the reputation of a talented writer.

During the time of the revival of nationalism, which crested with the Five Year Plans, Count Tolstoy was welcomed as Comrade Tolstoy. He immediately understood that acceptance and reconciliation depended on the "regenerated patriot's" creative effort to project the strength and achievements of the Communist state. Trying to find the "correct" outlet for his great writing energies, Tolstoy composed a prodigious number of scenarios, plays, anti-émigré pamphlets. He also attracted a large public with a spectacular succession of science fiction, very much in vogue in the twenties. He wrote these stories with verve and earthy realism; as a result they were accessible even to the newly literate reader and sufficiently flavored with official ideology to satisfy the censor. That the ideas were obviously borrowed from the current press and the intricacy of plot and subplots padded with melodramatic happenings that strained the verisimilitude of seemingly direct and concretized narrative mattered little to the thousands of Tolstoy fans. They feasted on such social fantasies as *Aelita*, 1922 (a Soviet expedition to Mars that results in a love affair between the Russian engineer and a Martian woman and the attempt to foment a social revolution), *Garin the Dictator*, 1925 (the fascist-minded inventor of a death ray surrounded by a moral underworld of criminals, con men, international profiteers, and beautiful prostitutes plans to remake Europe into a slave state), *Seven Days in Which the World Was Bled*, 1926 (the defeat, by a worldwide revolt of several Wall Street speculators who had succeeded in bombing and splintering the moon and were about to subjugate the entire planet Earth).

With the income from his publications, Tolstoy became one of the country's wealthiest men and in socialist Russia resumed an aristocrat's way of life. He was a lover of good food, good wines, and a good story. He entertained lavishly at his Tsarskoye Selo villa near Leningrad where he settled with his third beautiful young wife, at his house in Crimea, or at the largest hotels of the capital where he was an expansive and witty host at munificent dinner parties attended by the higher echelons of the Soviet bureaucracy. He continued to enjoy an agreeable and comfortable existence to the very end, when a sudden and easy death spared him the illness and old age that he dreaded and considered an indignity, and which he never imposed on his heroes.

The voluminous *Road to Calvary* (1919-1941) comprises three distinct novels, *Sisters, Nineteen-Eighteen,* and *Bleak Morning*. Four upper-class Russians (two sisters and their fiancés and eventually husbands, the engineer Teleghin and the officer Roshchin) are introduced in the first and best novel. Tolstoy wrote this in exile, and it conveys the intimacy and ease of a memoir. The main protagonists, who might have been the author's relatives or friends, are masterfully drawn in the setting of untroubled, leisurely pre-World War I St. Petersburg.

In *Nineteen-Eighteen*, the rhythm of events is accelerated to near violence. Some of the most gripping pages produce, unforgettably, the emergence of the Soviet state out of chaos in the symbol of a former Cossack officer and adventurer who defects to the Reds. During the war years and the revolution, the heroes undergo great hardships. Gradually, however, the hatred of the new order that destroyed their security and traditions is transformed into a recognition of the "tremendous forces emerging in the land," in the words of Teleghin who, at the end of the work, sees Communism as the inevitable national movement forward. A vast panorama of the country in movement during the social upheaval thronging with Russian types from every class marks the trilogy as the most ambitious historical novel in Soviet literature.

Its artistic merit is less certain. The careful and sure character delineation in the first part is reduced in the last novel to a portrayal of one-dimensional personalities. Tolstoy brings in a number of pungent scenes and sharply etched small happenings, but they are not brought into focus as a main theme and so fail to give a central meaning to the work. Tolstoy may have conceived the novel as an aggrandizement of his personal experience. He may have wanted to establish a continuity between pre-revolutionary and post-revolutionary Russia in the survival of his heroes whose personal fate, like his own, was linked to the nation's destiny. However, the general drift of the discursive passages he resorts to to achieve these objectives frequently weaken the narrative with rambling and simplistic statements concerning Marxist philosophy. Nowhere in the long novel does the writer equal the delicacy and freshness of the autobiographical fragment, *Nikita's Childhood* that preludes it. Like a Proustian memory, plotless and unattached, it evokes in the author's racy, pungent Russian, a small boy's happy life on a country estate.

Did the celebrated writer find it necessary during the Great Purges to safeguard his Kremlin privileges with a personal offering to the Stalin cult? Perhaps so, for in 1938 he composed

Bread, a flagrantly falsified account of the Bolshevik capture of the Volga port, Tsaritsyn (later renamed Stalingrad). At the expense of the Trotskyites, the book glorifies the military skill and valor of commander Joseph Stalin in the civil war. Soon after the publication of *Bread*, Tolstoy was decorated with the Order of Lenin and made a member of the Academy of Sciences. Then, when his third, unfinished volume of the historical novel, *Peter the First* was being serialized, he received the Stalin Prize for Literature.

In a 1917 play and story, both titled *Peter's Day*, Tolstoy had sketched the monarch as an inhumanly cruel, crude, and ignorant despot. His interpretation was derived from liberal, late nineteenth-century historians. Intensive research led him to make a wider and more objective assessment when he set to work on Peter's fictionalized biography in 1929. The statesman and great reformer replaces the tyrant proper and the barbaric methods used to modernize Russia are mitigated by emphasis on the need for them in the struggle with arrogant and recalcitrant boyars. This view of Peter, to the author's good fortune, coincided with a resurging sentiment of nationalism in the Soviet Union in the thirties and the apotheosis of historical Russian heroes such as Alexander Nevsky, General Kutuzov, and Peter the Great. Whether Tolstoy intended to convey a resemblance between Peter's sweeping program of reforms and Stalin's ruthless methods of sovietization remains unclear, but Tolstoy's political patron reacted most favorably to the novel.

Tolstoy continued to write *Peter the First*, happily and steadily, until 1945. Then, six chapters were published posthumously (which brought the events up to 1701). The task was suited to his talent and nature. Even as he had admitted that the October Revolution had given him everything in subject matter that he needed, so did the dynamic action of his hero. His own exuberance, love of instinctual, spontaneous, earthy manifestations responded to the blend of anarchy, organic forces, aggression, and endurance that agitated the age and its fabulous leading figure. Tolstoy mingles historical characters with fictional ones in scrupulously restored settings of the epoch. The tsar and his entourage are presented in a rapid succession of scenes, in the splendor of their circumstance but they do not attain the level of thinking and feeling that we expect from these well-known historical persons. What is absent from all of Tolstoy's imaginative writing is the awareness of higher human consciousness that takes in the world of ideas, wisdom, moral pathos, and spiritual mutations. An obvious disinterest in these matters reduces his fictional world to singular flatness, condemns it to psychological shallowness and exteriorization, and may account for the cardboard quality of most of his plays.

EHRENBURG (1891-1967)

The vitality emanating from Alexey Tolstoy's fictional resurrection of his country's past, to which he was passionately attached, greatly overshadowed his own individuality. In contrast, Ilya Ehrenburg, the most European of all Soviet writers, is a man who is fully as interesting as his writings which are relentlessly involved with the present and have kept the writer in the foreground of the Soviet scene for the last forty years.

Was Ehrenburg, according to his own boast "a loyal Soviet citizen of Jewish origins," or a subversive rebel turned rebellious conformist. Or was he a pamphleteer who breathed with relish the agitated air of his time, ferreting out topically important material and tailoring it into the "good story" that would accord with the reigning political sensibilities?

His father was a brewery owner, the first of the family, as his son put it, "to break away from the Jewish faith and the ghetto" but not enough for young Ilya to escape the persecutions of Russian boys in the Moscow high school—an experience that may have incited him to rebel against the tsarist regime. He became a student agitator in the 1905 revolution and was imprisoned at sixteen. He was soon released, however, and made his way to the Paris of the Left Bank, where, from 1909 to 1917, he lived in heroic and happy poverty rubbing elbows with Russian radicals, French symbolist poets, and avant-garde painters Picasso, Modigliani, Ribera, and Leger. He became enamoured of the Middle Ages and started to write mystical poetry. He considered converting to Catholicism and entering the Benedictine order. Then, to escape from the "bourgeois infected" environment, he tried to enlist in the Foreign Legion but failed the physical test. He returned home in 1917, barely managed to remain alive during the Civil War between the pogroms and the Bolshevik secret police, and finally received a foreign assignment from a Moscow newspaper, only to be captured by the French police as a suspect Bolshevik. He went off to Brussels where he wrote a picaresque novel, *The Extraordinary Adventures of Julio Jurento and His Disciples* in 1921.

The principal characters of the novel include a loquacious Italian tramp who models and collects cigarette stubs, a zealous German organizer who worships Marx, Kant, and the Kaiser, the sad-eyed, intelligent and cowardly Paris café habitué, Ehrenburg, an American missionary intent on improving the world and its brothels with Bibles and dollars, a lachrymose Russian intellectual, a Berlin restaurant owner, a French undertaker with a taste for pretty women, Calvados, and logic, a Senegalese Negro with three carved charms and their Mexican teacher, Julio, anarchist and "agent provocateur" by profession. They travel through all the European countries which to their delight are caught in an orgy of stupidity, hollowness, and hypocrisy. They witness the disintegration of Western civilization as it loses its positive ideals, love, faith, and art. There is much talk in the nihilist fantasy of freedom or of the revolution, blessed by Julio as "the first day of an epidemic that will either regenerate mankind or do away with it, clearing the earth for another race of curs." On landing in the Soviet Union the band is at first welcomed and then locked up. With deadly cynicism, the Master acclaims the "comrades" for instigating the "harshest and sweatiest purgatory . . . that will create a new mystique for a new slavery" and train men to adore their yoke of sturdy well made iron. The teacher's utterances appear to echo the chilly paradoxes of Dostoevsky's *Legend of the Grand Inquisitor*. For the teacher-prophet who is concerned for the world only in terms of its future, the time has not yet come and on a walk through a lonely park he is murdered for his new boots. Where does mockery begin or end in this savage castigation of Europe? As in an eighteenth-century philosophical novel, such as Voltaire's *Zadig* or *Micromegas*, Ehrenburg diagnoses the social ills by means of parodistic happenings, hoaxes, and deliberately planted absurdities. He makes, in the process, startlingly accurate prophecies on the collapse of colonial empires, the worsening situation of the Jews, and the encroachment of dictatorships. It is Ehrenburg's best, most revealing book. He himself regarded it, decades later, as his most sincere. Nevertheless, it was summarily dismissed by the Soviet press for its negations and soon banned. For over forty years it remained a collector's item. Recently it was reprinted in a first volume of the writer's collected works, available by subscription only.

Back in the Soviet Union by 1923, Ilya Ehrenburg embarked on a versatile and extremely prolific production. He wrote poems, numberless articles, travelogues, movie scripts, short stories, and novels. A large number of the novels were reprinted by Russian publishers abroad and translated into several languages. He seemed to have quickly developed a literary formula that insured lasting popularity. For the mass Soviet reader, the appearance of a new Ehrenburg piece was an entertaining and exciting event. He produced about two a year. They were clever and touched upon important topical ideas in lucid reflections and dialogue and contained a sensational plot with stereotyped, black-and-white characters. The lack of complex, living personalities in his fiction disqualified Ehrenburg, in the opinion of many Western critics, from a claim to being a serious artist. That Ehrenburg was aware of his inability to create characters and a tendency in all his writings to speak in his own voice comes out in a comment he made in 1962 on his novels that "left off the old notion of building up a character to become humanized chronicles of our time." The arresting fact about this talented chronicler was his extraordinary chameleon-like agility to alter the color of his commitment when there were shifts in the official party line and his power to respond to political changes before others had even become aware of them. The skillful maneuvering, as well as Stalin's friendship, may account for the unbroken success of his career.

In the twenties Ehrenburg explored the fashionable themes of the capitalistic influence on Hollywood (*Factory of Dreams*, 1924), the European car industry (*10HP*, 1925), and Europe taken over by American finance (*Trust DE*, 1925) that in his works exposed souless and corrupt materialism dominated by the sounds of the ticker tape machine and the pen scratching on a checkbook with the simplistic imagery of a Mayakovsky poster. Attacked by Soviet critics for excessive sarcasm in the portrayal of NEP men in *Grabber* (1925), Ehrenburg turned to the historical novel that was becoming popular at the time. In *Conspiracy of Equals* (1928), he showed his familiarity with French history with his portrait of the eighteenth century revolutionary, Babeuf.

In order to comply with Stalinist aesthetics Ehrenburg wrote *Out of Chaos* in 1935 and *Without Pausing for Breath* in 1937. They deal with industrial construction but reflect the monotony and bleakness of "glorified labor." The perspective of *Out of Chaos* is widened by the juxtaposition of Volodya Safinov, a maladjusted, introspective student with the positive shock-worker hero that brings to mind the conflict between Kurt Wahn and Startsov in Fedin's *Cities and Years*. The anger directed at the ant-hill existence of the settlement, recorded in the student's diary, could have been written by one of Julio's disciples or directly expressed by Dostoevsky's Underground Man.

Upon returning to the Soviet Union from the coverage of the Spanish civil war to which he had been fortunately assigned during the great purges and from a visit to France on the eve of the German invasion, Ehrenburg wrote the Stalin Prize-winning work, *The Fall of Paris*, in 1940. This is less a novel than a chronicle; Ehrenburg focuses on the tensions in political, intellectual, and social circles that are pressing the country toward the debacle, against a daily background of love making, eating, and petty parliamentary tactics. The writer demonstrates a sense of history, which, although strongly leftist, in no way interferes with his conveying the charm of the French scene nor obscures his deep attachment to the city of Paris itself.

When Hitler launched his attack against Russia, the author made haste to transform, in the parts of the novel that had not yet been serialized, French Communists, up to then indifferent to the Germans, into fervent anti-Nazi patriots. Similarly, in *The Storm* (1947), when Stalin renewed his hostility toward the West, Ehrenburg lays emphasis on the honorable behavior of Russian soldiers and the many differences that (to Soviet advantage) separate Russia from Western Europe. He reached the summit of his popularity with the widely publicized war articles that he wrote between 1941 and 1943. They were written daily, with unflagging intensity, and were violent anti-German diatribes. Partisans swapped precious packages of tobacco for a bundle of Ehrenburg clippings that Stalin said were worth more than 20 to 30 divisions. Early in the post-Stalin era Ehrenburg skillfully identified with the changed cultural defrosting of the Soviet hierarchy. He wrote *The Thaw* in 1954 that, for the first time in three decades of Soviet fiction, rated private feeling higher than public action. In a community built around a large factory, a doctor, an engineer, a woman teacher, and a girl student attempt to find ways out of emotional misunderstandings, to come closer in communicating their feelings for each other. The plight of an officially recognized painter, Pukhov, forms the main theme. He realizes that he has betrayed his artistic integrity when he paints uniformly cheerful pictures of peasants and workers. He envies a fellow artist who prefers obscurity and indigence to the forfeiture of his talent and taste. The writer seems to be genuinely, even passionately involved in the portrayal of Pukhov who "has missed out on love, life, art."

In an earlier work, *The Stormy Life of Razek Roytshvanetz* (1929), Ehrenburg also had allowed himself the luxury of sincerity, however. A meek, pure-minded Jewish tailor from Gomel wants to live for the human rights and justice that he finds trampled on in his many humiliating experiences in many countries until he finally dies of exposure to life's immoral maw near Rachel's tomb in Jerusalem. The pitiful and absurd saga recalls Julio's adventures in a minor and more poignant key. The work, that was only published abroad, conveys Ehrenburg's anger and personal anguish, tempered by light-weighted irony.

In his memoirs, *People, Life, Years* (1918-1921; 1921-1941; 1941-1945; 1945-1954) Ilya Ehrenburg gathers in fragmentary reminiscences the richly varied and multiple facets of his professional life. He also ruefully acknowledges the rule of covertness and silence that he was frequently forced to follow in order to survive. For all the convenient lapses in memory, lack of candor, and some apologia for Stalin's dictatorship, the memoirs were of immense interest to Soviet readers. The artistic and literary world that existed beyond the Iron Curtain is disclosed for his readers and presents them with the "exotic" setting of the Western bourgeoisie. The fact that he narrowed the cultural cleavage between his country and the West does him honor as do the efforts of his later years, already manifest in *The Thaw*, to bring a measure of aesthetic freedom and humanism into Soviet art. But these achievements do not entirely contain Ilya Ehrenburg. He is uniquely interesting in yet another way.

Intelligent, vastly inquisitive, erudite, observant, Ehrenburg was a man upon whom the century started ringing alarms early with contradictory ideologies and revolutionary cataclysms. He was a witness to and observer of fascism, revolutionary action, nationalism, totalitarianism, multi-national capitalism, and nuclear warfare that have kept the continent in perpetual sociopolitical turmoil. His lyrical writing, imaginary and real, reflected the issues, afflictions, elations, hopes, and problems of which he, as individual and writer, was an integral part.

One of his most poignant identifications with his age was his sense of permanent displacement. Not only as a Jew whose rootlessness he shared with millions, but as a cosmopolitan and cultured European he sought shelter from the mass uniformity and physical ugliness of the Soviet life style in his Moscow apartment where autographed canvases by Picasso, Chagall, Modigliani, and Leger hung above bookshelves crammed with banned Western European works. But, as a declared Communist, he was not at ease either in the bourgeois environment of Western European cities. To believe with Buffon that "style makes the man" is to realize Ehrenburg's tremendously eclectic quality. As a result, he wrote in a multifaceted, synthetic, and extremely modern fashion that fused bits of Voltairean irony, Dickensian sentimentality, and French nineteenth-century melodrama into a rapid cinematographic image and produced a kind of unreflective idiom which had an immediate emotional impact that has come into its own in the mass media today.

PASTORAL AND EXOTIC ESCAPES

Against the relentless policy that enlisted literature to persuade the proletariat to transform a vast agricultural land into an industrial state, three gifted, resolutely apolitical writers managed to indulge solely in an exploration of fanciful and exotic modes of existence. Because of Mikhail Prishvin (1873-1954), Alexander Grin (1880-1932), and Konstantin Paustovsky (1892-1968), a certain psychic balance was restored for millions of Soviet citizens. They were offered an escape from the drabness, tedium, and toughness of their reality into worlds that fulfilled their yearning for beauty, for adventure, and the plenitude and mystery of nature.

PRISHVIN (1873-1954)

Agriculturalist and ethnographer by profession, amateur folklorist and passionate hunter, Mikhail Prishvin jotted down miniature landscape sketches of animals, plants, the sound and movement of water. He recorded talks with semi-primitive people living in out-of-the-way places that he came upon in his solitary meanderings through the Russian countryside with gun, dog, and notebook. The many skaz episodes that he later developed from these sketches are suffused with the joyousness that can be derived from the constant discoveries of natural phenomena. They convey the sense of man's important place in the cosmos that links him, his beliefs, superstitions and traditions to all living things. The writer's prevalent themes, of a pagan love of life and all its vital instincts and the certitude that man's primordial fears disappear when he attains harmony with nature, are contained in his longest novel, *The Chain of Koshchey*, written in 1924. It is a fairy tale based on the experiences of his own childhood and youth. The diabolical force of the monster Koshchey in Russian folklore is here presented as the symbol of slavery, injustice, and poverty that the hero tried to overcome. Although he does not succeed, he constantly renews his efforts and with increasing inner strength, which gives an optimistic flavor to the narrative. In *Nature's Calendar* (1923) and *The First Forest Thaw* (1945) Prishvin gives precise and delicate descriptions of nature through a lyrically contemplative tone.

GRIN (1880-1932)

For thousands of his readers and fellow writers the name of Alexander Grin immediately evokes the beautiful nonexistent country of Grinlandiya that the author never left. Its exotic islands, white-walled cities and hospitable harbors were inhabited by lovely women, audacious heroes, derring-do scoundrels, and bandits. In tale after tale, some of these characters would set sail on the ship *Felicity*, manned by a stalwart captain and a responsibly brave, intelligent crew on endless sea voyages to perform deeds of valor and engage in fantastic escapades and adventures of high adrenalin content. It mattered little to this inveterate daydreamer that life had allotted him just enough to get by as a one-time sailor, woodcutter, stevedore, miner, beggar, and hobo—occupations that finally undermined his uncertain health. Ever since he had run away from home at fifteen to Odessa, lured by the Black Sea, he had lived with his friends Robert L. Stevenson, Jules Verne, Conan Doyle, Jack London, Merimée, Kipling, Rider Haggard, Edgar Allen Poe, and James Fenimore Cooper. He had been nourished by their literature, which was exotic, startling and adventurous. From it, he built a happily romantic world of his own out of the richness of his imagination. His stories, like himself, were unique in their total detachment from Soviet reality. When they appeared in various popular magazines from 1906 to 1930, they were ignored by critics and passed the censor because they did not contain any current themes. It was not until one of his most gossamerlike fairy tales, *Scarlet Sails*, about a girl waiting for the prince promised to her by a sorcerer, was adopted for a successful ballet during the Second World War, that he became nationally known. In Crimea, where Grin lived for the last ten years of his life, he was regarded by the southern school of writers Babel, Bagritsky, Ilf, Shengali as something of a legend. Upon meeting the "austere poet" at that time, Paustovsky wrote a splendid essay about the spell that his tirelessly inventive yarns cast upon his readers. Grin seemed to have brought back into a hurried modern world the ancient and leisurely craft of the story-teller where something is vitally alive at every moment of the telling and slowly draws the audience onward with the delicious anticipation of more excitement ahead.

PAUSTOVKSY (1892-1968)

One of Konstantin Paustovksy's most persistent preoccupations was to experience all life so as "to learn, feel and understand everything." He combined with this catholic desire a rapturous attention to the minutiae in nature, human gestures and speech, and eccentricities of behavior and a great curiosity about all kinds of persons—soldiers, priests, teachers, children, beggars, chance passengers on trains and tramways, artists, fishermen, doctors, peasants—whom he met in his many travels around Russia. It is difficult to say whether it was his ability to construct absorbing plots from his experiences that made him one of the most beloved writers in the USSR from the thirties through the fifties or whether it was the unfailing serenity and unshakable belief in the value of each separate man and woman that emanated from everything he wrote.

A prolific output of plays, travel books, and biographies of great men for adolescent readers provided enough inner space in his short and longer pieces of fiction for what was peerlessly alive and entertaining. It included straightforward sea adventures, colorful stories about exotic lands inspired by the Caucasus and Crimea. In two of his most-read works, *Kara Bugaz* (1932) and *Kolchida* (1934), he wrote about the near miraculous transformation of the inaccessible Caspian Bay, Kara Bugaz, rich with sodium sulfate, into a thriving center. In the second novel he describes the equally stirring success of converting a subtropical Caucasian region into fertile terrain. There is romance in these science fiction tales in the endless and endlessly repeated discoveries of the interior of nature and in the thrilling episodes filled with danger for the explorers.

Not a thinker or ideologist, Paustovsky takes his reader into places where exciting things happen. He is not interested in intellectual or emotive concerns. Through a sequence of demonstrations he tries to show "what is" and "how it is" not "why it is" which brings about for him, as it does for Grin and Prishvin, an instant estrangement from politicized Soviet life.

Paustovsky became known outside of the Soviet Union in the fifties for his autobiography, *Story of a Life* (1964). This is almost his only translated work. In it, the engagingly unassuming narrator follows the continuum of Russia's first two decades of the twentieth century in a series of private encounters with the great events and those involved in them. To readers unfamiliar with the Soviet Union it is a splendid unbiased introduction to the diversity of its population in all walks of life. The very long work is not unlike an old-fashioned nineteenth-century novel with its large cast, fateful and variegated action, and vividly described locales. The steady beam that illuminates it is the character of the writer himself—a noble and gentle human being always open to the claim of beauty, sentiment and an incorruptible conscience.

SOCIALIST REALISM IN ACTION

A vast amount of mediocre fiction, inspired by the "great offensive" of the First Five Year Plans, was published during the decade before the Second World War. Fortunately, from among the numbers of facile and submissive practitioners there emerged certain more able and prolific writers who may serve as illustrations of unimpaired socialist realism in action.

In the first two volumes of *And Then the Harvest* (1930) F. Panfyorov narrates the experiences of a demobilized peasant who is first lured by kulak speculations and then employed in factory work in a town, only to find contentment at last when he joins the village commune. In *Driving Axle* (1933) V. Ilyenkov animates the descriptions of a factory in construction with the sabotage by engineers from the "bourgeois" class that is discovered and fails. A cult for the purposefulness and technological tempo activates V. Katayev's *Forward, O Time* (1933), in the depiction of one day in a big coke-chemical plant operation at which a number of foremen and workers are involved in a record-breaking Stakhanovite race. The only ironic twist left over from the author's earlier *Embezzlers* comes through a denigrating portrait of a God-fearing and God-loving American magnate. A tremendously popular novel, *How Steel Was Tempered* (1935) draws on A. Ostrovsky's own life experience qualified by the author as "a small raindrop reflecting the sun of the Party." It is the story of a poor boy, an instinctive revolutionary, steeled by his participation in the great events to overcome all kinds of obstacles. He renounces personal life for party work without caring for his health that has been shattered by war wounds. *Loneliness* (1936) by N. Virta centers on a real counter-revolutionary uprising that took place in 1921 in the Tambov region. It was led by a powerful and ambitious kulak who finally loses his hold on the villagers and is socially ostracized. *Our Friends* (1936) by Y. Herman features an average Soviet woman, twice married to NEP businessmen who are absorbed in their money-making schemes. Both leave her alone to fritter her days away in romantic "Prince Charming" reveries. She is socially and politically rehabilitated by the director of a construction project when he places her in a responsible job. Y. Krymov sets the significant part of the action in his novel, *Tanker Derbent* (1938), on board an oil tanker. An inventive but surly and uncooperative engineer who has been in trouble with the bureaucracy redeems himself by instilling a laggard crew with Stakhanovite enthusiasm and rescuing the men from another boat that has caught fire.

The most popular and officially approved examples of socialist drama would include *Fear* (1931) by A. Afinogenov. An old professor is influenced by anti-Communist elements and made to believe that Soviet citizens' actions are motivated by fear of the regime. He realizes in the last act that this situation only existed during the Tsarist epoch. N. Pogodin's *Aristocrats* (1935) is set against the background of the construction of a canal from the White Sea to the Baltic, carried out with forced labor. The rehabilitation of the thieves and bandits from among the prisoners into socially constructive Communists is enacted in scene after scene by Cheka men. In V. Pletnyov's comedy, *The Hat* (1935), an efficiency manager is sent to restore production in a failing enterprise. He brings back order and sobriety to the young cadres of workers who had degenerated under the influence of old individualistic traditions and aging factory hands. The younger workers then gradually learn to respect the reforms.

This party-minded production is no longer dominated by the portrayal of masses in action as were the Civil War stories. This is frequently replaced by the study of individual Communists in relation to the group. In addition, the satirical exposure of illicit speculation, philistinism, and Kafkaesque bureaucratic machinery that emanated from the stories of Bulgakov, Ilf-Petrov, and the early poetry of Zabolotsky disappears. The bourgeois is still drawn in dark colors but now he is portrayed as less than perfect and as a vacillating intellectual, or a dreamer, an inflexible bureaucrat, or stubborn individualist. He is subject, however, to re-education and, through party pressure or the services of a noble-minded Soviet citizen, is transformed into a usefully functioning member of socialist society.

Usefulness is defined in story after story as a joyous, unstinting participation in the work of the collective and now becomes idealized as the supreme fulfillment of the new Soviet man. To this end all fictional enterprise moves. Despite a great variety of settings and imagined situations the writer must bring out or develop positive heroes who may go through any number of intermediate struggles brought on by character flaws, personal emotion, or adverse circumstance but who finally achieve victorious self-realization. It is epitomized in this period by the images of Stakhavonite workers, collective farmers rewarded by the state for bumper crops, disinterested and flexible officials, and zealous factory managers. Average men and women, turned into heroic personalities through their love of labor and staunch optimism in the Soviet future, become familiar prototypes, locked, as in a puppet theatre, into fixed, predictable, one-dimensional roles.

The exteriorized reality of this fiction eschews the imponderables of existence and the inner world of subjective complexities that are common to all mankind. It concentrates on materialistic and purely national concerns. It is the preoccupation with these concerns exploited continually and at length in pictures of industrialization or agricultural collectivization at work bolstered with abundant factual and technological data describing various aspects of this process that gives the literature of this decade a singularly parochial character. It is steeped in the national ethos, which is aimed, in language and content, at the mass of the Soviet working population and remains for the most part indifferent to matters outside immediate Soviet problems.

WAR LITERATURE

The artistic decline of Soviet fiction during the decade preceding the Second World War could readily have been predicted at that time. The feverish period of the early thirties when the Soviet work force across the nation was straining to fulfill and overfulfill production quotas and writers were called upon to glorify its labor ended with the successful completion of the first two Five Year Plans. They brought greater economic stability, improved living conditions and on the cultural front, the elimination of illiteracy, the construction of some 20,000 additional rural schools and over six hundred new institutions of higher learning. The socialist state, under the dictatorial rule of one man, was assuming an inner coherence—"Life, comrades, is now joyous," in Stalin's words—and literature, conditioned since 1934 to serve the interests of Communist destiny, continued to execute the party's will in projecting progress made in all fields of material endeavor in its steady ascent toward the socialistic ideal.

It produced a kind of meiotic literary art that is like no other and that nothing in our modern habit cultivates. Opposed to Western pluralism, it embraced unanimity of views, and studied man only in terms of his function within a collective unit. The imbalance between inner life and society's public threat that haunts writers in the West today has no place in the Soviet awareness. Of great documentary value to the sociologist and unavailable to him elsewhere, is the care and space given to factual information on the daily lives of innumerable types of Soviet citizens (factory and kolkhoz managers, trade union leaders, miners, school teachers, scientists, engineers, oil drillers, and political commissars) placed against their job backgrounds. These men and women, for the most part, are quite ordinary, and it is in relation to their work, its process, difficulties, and rewards that they acquire a certain vividness and become active and important participants in the plot.

Not all writers conformed to the gnawing simplicity of such narrative patterns that insured a falling off in risk and inspiration. Many talented artists, among them Pilnyak, Babel, and Olesha, were reduced to silence and during the purges between 1936 and 1938, numbers were persecuted, imprisoned, or killed. Others rode out to official approbation and popular success with historical narratives on the wave of nationalism that was sweeping Russia in reaction to the increasing Nazi threat. The best known works of the genre included Alexey Tolstoy's *Peter the First* (Part II, 1933), Sergei Borodin's *Dmitri Donskoy* (1937) (the heroic struggle of Russian princes with the Mongols), Vasily Yoncheventsky's *Genghis Khan* (1938) (portrayal of the Tartar empire in the Middle Ages), and Sergei Sergeyev-Tsensky's *The Ordeal of Sebastopol* (1937) (gallant feats of the Russian Army in the Crimean War).

Another form of nationalistic writing conveyed a pride in the very real technological victories that the country had won against incalculable odds within a very brief period and with no outside assistance. It was not difficult for these writers, sincere Communists, to believe that the fundamental bases of Soviet society were steadied and expanded by Stalin's authority. Whatever injustice or lamentable disregard of the common goals existed then did not blur their appreciation of the salutary changes in living conditions. The cautionary fable of the menace of controls to the effect that the longer they last the more dangerous they become was not for them. As Arthur Miller astutely observed after his many conversations with the Soviet literati, writers gained a feeling of solidarity with others. The Soviet writer shared the same reality, and it identified him as a "worker" (the most honorable Soviet appellation) in the art of literature and a part of the collective society "that is."

Besides, large numbers of literary men of proletarian origin had early developed conservative attitudes that distinguish an isolated, mass community. Like Stalin, they were imbued with a bourgeois morality expressed in their works with emphasis on the family and distrust of the individualistic vanguard. They lacked the sophistication to question their leader's limited artistic taste, or consider grotesque such a gesture as Stalin's angry departure from a performance of Shostakovich's *Lady Macbeth of Mtensk District* (which caused a decree from the Kremlin that henceforth all Soviet opera should have happy endings.

Nevertheless, when Russian territory was invaded by an outside enemy, liberating winds surged through literature. It was now exclusively concerned with the German-Russian war, shared the country's deep anxiety as to the outcome, and like a reserve force being rushed into action, became thematically committed to victory over the enemy. The intensity of life that was released in spontaneous, uninhibited images of anguish, bravery, stoicism, and martyrdom, with authentic heroism on all sides, replaced the ideologically colored positive figures, and showed that creative writing in the Soviet Union still possessed vitality and moral force. The huge quantity of war novels, stories, plays, poetry run off government presses between 1941 and 1945 was written by authors who with few exceptions had been assigned to the front as military correspondents. Much of this vigorous and factually authentic writing was composed in haste, under the impact of immediate impressions. It lacked the necessary psychological depth and did not survive.

Among the most representative, artistically viable war novels, Konstantin Simonov's *Days and Nights* (1944), Leonid Leonov's *Taking of Velikoshumsk* (1944), Victor Nekrasov's *In the Trenches of Stalingrad* (1945), and Alexander Fadeyev's *Young Guard* (1945) received the greatest critical attention. Nekrasov and Simonov, relative newcomers to literature, both born in 1915, treat the heroic struggle at Stalingrad. The latter shifts his story back and forth, impressionistically, between the besieged inhabitants and the deadly fighting of the troops while Nekrasov's straightforward account in the first person describing routine of the battle is textured with individualized sketches of Russian officers and soldiers. In a dramatic thrust, Leonov's short novel symbolizes the entire conflict in a single tank battle west of Kiev, with the action focused on the five man crew of a tank attempting to repel the enemy. It is enhanced with overtones of Russian and Ukranian epic poetry and its heroic leitmotifs heighten the tension of the incident. The theme of the *Young Guard*, as Fadeyev calls the teen-age underground in a German-occupied town, stresses the martyrdom of the young Communists, and their unswerving loyalty to the cause even during the civilian evacuation and the Red Army retreat.

As happens in times of military tension everywhere, drama also was enjoying great popularity. Audiences crowded theatres to relieve vicariously the war communiqués and be heartened by examples of courage and resourcefulness on military and civilian fronts. Such a play by Simonov was the very popular *Russians* (1942). It brought out with pungent realism the unselfishness, fortitude, and readiness for personal sacrifice of ordinary Russian people in a town seized by the Germans. An issue that ignited controversy in the Soviet high command was effectively dramatized in *The Front* (1942) by the Ukranian playwright, Alexander Korneychuk, where the conflict is poised between an older officer clinging to civil war methods that stake victory on hand weapons and bravery and the technocrats of modern warfare. More successful in the construction of taut, tense dialogue drama were the two Stalin Prize-winning plays, *Invasion* (1942) and *Lyonushka* (1943) by Leonov, where individualized personalities move through a complicated and exciting plot. The later play develops dual situations of treason among partisans behind German lines and a love affair between a girl partisan and an officer who is burned alive when his plane is shot down. *Invasion* is a more thoughtful psychological study that juxtaposes the unquestioning patriotism of the parents and their neurotic, one time criminal, son, who is jolted out of his cynical poses by German brutality and accepts torture to save a partisan leader and his men.

Rivaling in popularity Leo Tolstoy's *War and Peace* that brought consolation to hundreds of thousands during the darkest days of the war, was the avalanche of poetry, inspired by the national disaster. It registered more openly than fiction or drama the reality of the perilously fragile new order and the uncertainty of the promised happy life. Hundreds of poems that vibrated (to the Western ear) with old-fashioned simple rhythms returned to the celebration of the Russian hinterland, the earth, and the people of the earth, as in Simonov's *Villages* where the Russian and not the Soviet countryside is evoked and the endurance and unassuming courage of the inhabitants make up the substance and weight of the poem. There was hardly a poet, including Pasternak and Anna Akhmatova, who did not pay a lyrical tribute to the unwavering and ubiquitous patriotism of their compatriots. The young talent of Olga Bergholtz and Vera Inber matured through the rendering of personal experience, for the former in verses, now subjective, now classical, of the Leningrad siege, and for the latter, in a long romanticized reflection of what it is to be a woman in a time of war. With the exception of Alexey Surkov's tradition-haunted verses comemmorating Russia's heroic past, the themes of the best known poems, memorized, sung, or recited at public gatherings, were directed inward, small lyrical explosions of grief at parting, at the trial of separation, of anxiety for the loved ones left behind, and, in the last year, the soldier's yearning to return home. One of the most distinctive longer poems was *Vasily Tyorkin* by Alexander Tvardovsky (1910-1971) that strikes a genial picaresque note similar to his earlier humorous epic, *The Land of Muravia* (1936). This earlier work animated in folk rhythms the travels of a peasant. He is hostile to collectivization, tries to find land for himself in other countries, and finally joins a kolkhoz. Tyorkin, in the later work, is invariably optimistic and resourceful. He recalls Tolstoy's Platon Karateyev, and his exploits, serious and amusing, are vividly rendered in zestful, engagingly rhymed language.

The party encouraged literary effort calling for sacrifice and continued endurance in the face of the enemy. It should be noted, however, that millions of Soviet officers and soldiers were captured and joined the Germans in the first months of the military action. They were branded traitors by the Kremlin and deprived of International Red Cross aid. Further, the outright defection of many Russian communities to the Germans were not touched upon in the war literature. Similarly, the fact that the Soviet high command had been severely weakened by the purges of its most brilliant military men in the middle thirties and whose expertise may have reversed the course of the war received no mention until 1962 in the story by Admiral I. Isakov, *The Gage of the Flying Dutchman* that appeared in the *New World* review.

ZHDANOVISM: THE DARKEST CHAPTER

The hopes expressed in Russia that the many contacts made with Westerners during the war would result in a relaxation of ideological controls did not materialize. For Stalin was still at war in 1945 and he continued to wage it on two fronts throughout the last eight years of his life. At the end of hostilities international friction was sparked off when Russian divisions that had been brought into the very heart of Europe to check the German advance, remained in eastern territory. By lowering the Iron Curtain over a ring of satellite Communist states, Stalin, fearing future imperialistic attacks, repulsed the initial gratitude and good will of the allies. He restored Russia's isolated position and instigated the cold war. At home, the battle was launched to overcome the huge devastation of war with a reconstruction of over two thirds of European Russia that had been inhabited by 70 million people (17,000 towns, 70,000 villages, 31,000 factories, 84,000 schools, 40,000 miles of railway track and 45 million horses, cattle, and pigs had been destroyed). Once the war damage was repaired, the population that had suffered 20 million war dead, as many wounded, and another 20 million dead of starvation or disease was to maintain economic austerity for the next ten years in the interest of the development of heavy industry and the production of armaments.

On February 9, 1946 Stalin made a speech that spelled out the double aspect of the country's militant program. The necessity for foreign policy to be dictated by the concept of unassailable cleavage between two ideologies was made clear by the emphasis on victory over Hitler in the Great Patriotic War, a "decisive event in world history," that was won by the superior forces of the great socialist state. On the domestic front, a campaign was to be launched with the next three Five Year Plans for increased industrial production that would "guarantee the USSR against all possible accidents." Russia would emerge as an international super power and bring even greater prosperity and happiness to the Soviet people.

As in time of war, all the Russians were made to collaborate in the program. Among them the writers were mobilized to "drum in" the idea of Russian supremacy in every field and promote feelings of hostility and derision toward all phenomena originating outside the Soviet Union. This in turn precluded, on the part of the writer, any individualized language or "esoteric" experimentation with style that were infallibly branded as "formalistic, cosmopolitan," a deviation from the mandatory style of socialist realism that was simple in form and readily accessible to the masses. According to this literary policy, the party became the only intermediary between the writer and his public and dictated to him not only what to write but how to write it. This was obliquely announced when the Central Committee of the party censured two Leningrad monthlies, *Zvezda* and *Leningrad* for lack of correct ideological direction and their espousal of bourgeois culture. Two contributors, Anna Akhmatova and Mikhail Zoshchenko, were singled out. The first was reprimanded for her vacuous unprincipled poetry, the other for ridiculing Soviet behavior. They were expelled from the Union of Writers and banished from the magazines. *Zvezda* was editorially reorganized and *Leningrad* suspended.

A week later, Andrei Zhdanov, member of the Politbureau, Stalin's cultural commissar and heir apparent, labelled Anna Akhmatova "half-nun and half whore" whose moods of loneliness and hopelessness were "alien" to Soviet literature. He berated Zoshchenko for his undermining mockery of Soviet customs, most recently in *The Adventures of a Monkey,* that equated a monkey to respectable Soviet citizens. He restated the Central Committee resolutions that urged writers to help the state bring up youth correctly, in the spirit of cheerfulness and faith in the country's cause and to be the first to show Soviet people the road to their development. Writers who failed in these tasks should be expelled from literature.

Zhdanov's lengthy report inaugurated an era of the most intransigent ideological dictatorship. His policy throttled creativity from 1946 to 1953 and is popularly known as "Zhdanovism," although Zhdanov himself, who died in 1948, was but an ambitious and cynical bureaucrat who had acted on orders from the Kremlin.

The official ferreting out of "servility to the West" that, not without reason, began in Western-oriented Leningrad, increased at an alarming rate. "Adulators" of the West, "cosmopolites without kith or kin," and those who failed to extol invincible Russian superiority in all endeavors were exposed. They had publication of their works suspended until they recanted and had them revised. Critic Lev Subotsky, possibly envious of Fadeyev's political prestige, detected in the latter's acclaimed novel, *The Young Guard,* a "false" emphasis on the partisans' independent action that did not reveal the party's guidance behind it. Fadeyev abjectly apologized and immediately revised his story, undercutting the original ideas that had inspired it.

In the surge of Great Russianism latent anti-Semitic attitudes began to be expressed against critics of Jewish origin particularly. They were obliged to append their surname to the frequently used pseudonym when signing articles and reviews that were carefully scrutinized by the party watchdogs. Any sign of reluctance in stamping out literary heresy or what appeared to be Western favoritism resulted in public exposure of the "crime," dismissal from the post, exile.

How to account for the subordination on the part of writers and artists to the tragically successful campaign against intellectual and artistic integrity? No one rose in protest to defend the rights of the creative imagination. Konstantin Simonov said at a meeting of theatre workers and dramatists that "art was an arsenal meant for war." Mikhail Sholokhov declared that "each one of us writes according to the dictates of his heart but our hearts belong to the party and to the people whom we serve with our art." Alexander Fadeyev attacked a critical study of Pushkin's role in world literature by a votive Marxist, Isaac Nusinov, for the nefarious, anti-Marxist exposition on the European aspects of the poet. Did these talented and well known writers speak out of sincerely held beliefs?

All three men had spent most of their adult life in a closed society. (Sholokhov, who came to London in the late fifties and accompanied Premier Khrushchev to the United States, returned home as adamantly anti-Western in his views.) They rose in their profession under dictatorial rule that tolerated no public expression of life that did not emanate from party doctrine. This, together with a national cult of the dictator, was pounded into their consciousness by every available means. The dictatorial presence dominated Soviet existence and after the war in thousands of printed daily evocations Stalin was hailed as the Great Teacher, the Great Leader, and the Savior of the Russian nation. Under such psychological pressure, a sense of perspective was lost, and, once the Stalinist myth was accepted, all the rest of the myths fell into logical place. It was not difficult to become convinced of the need for an inhumanly accelerated industrialization as a first weapon against capitalistic aggression or to enter into a kind of conspiracy with the authorities to extol the "potential" native resources and strength.

A case in point is Alexander Fadeyev. He had been a young

Red Army commissar, a dedicated Communist, and author of a brilliant first novel. He had neglected nevertheless the promise of a successful writing career to devote his energies to politicized posts and rose steadily in the political hierarchy through his ability, intelligence, and total loyalty to Stalin who made him the party monitor of the Writers' Union in 1946. An extremist, Fadeyev managed to make for himself a fully successful life by entrusting his very identity, within a dense social and political space, to the leader he idolized.

At the Twentieth Party Congress in 1956, however, Fadeyev was forced to listen as Khrushchev disclosed Stalin's crimes and abuses, in some of which, as Stalin's trusted lieutenant, Fadeyev must have been implicated. He also had to bear the brunt of Mikhail Sholokhov's cutting remarks about the potentially fine writer who had degenerated in fifteen years of "useless administrative activity" into a power-hungry bureaucrat, and had run the Writers' Union like a penal colony. Fadeyev returned home from the Congress, stayed drunk for two weeks, then sent his small son into the garden, and put a bullet through his head.

Older writers and more independent-minded ones who may have privately wondered whether Stalinism was not to industrialization what cannibalism is to the attainment of a high protein diet, had to conform. Their personal survival and that of all their collaborators in the process of book production was at stake since the government held each one personally responsible for ideological deviations in the published fiction.

Artistic quality almost ceased to matter in what passed for literature in hundreds of stereotyped stories. They dealt primarily with the reconstruction of villages and towns, ably planned and heroically executed by resourceful and industrious Soviet workers who finally overcame all psychological and material difficulties. Great emphasis was placed on the interweaving of public and personal activities, which resulted, not without certain struggles provided by the author for plot interest, in harmonizing all human relations. Such, for example, is the theme of V. Kochetov's widely acclaimed novel, *The Zhurbins* (1952). The story is placed in a family of dock workers whose home life is made happy through their work in the dockyards.

This fiction created a climate of fairytale irreality, as if mental maturity were being intentionally rolled back for grown-up readers.

Dramatic works of the period were even more visibly bleak. Another 1946 Central Committee resolution had harshly reprimanded Soviet producers for the dearth of Soviet plays on contemporary themes. Of 142 stage productions in Moscow and Leningrad theatres, only twenty-five were concerned with current Soviet subjects. Control over theatre administration was tightened with the replacement of the artistic manager by a chief producer. Although he was second in command to the administrative director of theatres, he was a political commissar little versed in dramatic production. He was held responsible for the repertoire to the People's Commissariat of Education that stipulated the staging of at least two Soviet plays a year. These plays were to reflect the best aspects of Soviet Man's character, show him in constant movement toward national goals that are in striking contrast with the repellent war-mongering bourgeois culture. In his book, *Russian Theatre* (1961), critic Marc Slonim writes a spirited page on the playwright's obedient response to this command. Dozens of anti-Western plays featured corrupt Americans and pure-hearted Soviet protagonists along with "uplifted" presentations of the home scene. They present social, romantic, and economic obstacles that are invariably overcome in such collective efforts as drilling yet another oil well, meeting a superhuman agricultural quota, or finding new methods of growing potatoes.

Literary devastation reached the level of the absurd when the presentation of such dramatic fare in near-empty theatres jolted ·the control apparatus into recognition that something to combat spectator apathy had to be done. A leading *Pravda* article discerned a "deplorable state" of "nonconflictness" in Soviet drama, urged a deeper coloration of reality, and fuller characterizations. The article berated dramatic critics for their favorable reviews of dull, unlife-like plays. In 1952, on the occasion of Gogol's centennial, numerous discussions of his satirical art in the Soviet press culminated with a call to writers for the satire and grotesque of a Gogol or a Saltykov-Shchedrin to enliven and invigorate contemporary letters. As in the story of the emperor's clothes, the self-evident truth of Stalin's gross miscalculation of the effectiveness of art as a purely educative and propaganda instrument was passed over in silence. The dismal postwar creative sterility was brightened by works from the pen of the established Konstantin Fedin and of a newcomer, Vera Panova.

With the first two novels of a trilogy *(Early Joys*, 1946, and *Extraordinary Summer*, 1947), models of nineteenth-century realistic tradition, the talent of the author of *Cities and Years* reached its maturity. Fedin's earlier concern with a reciprocally informing analogy between Western Europe and his own country shifts to a concentration on Russian affairs between 1910 and 1941. *Early Joys* and *Extraordinary Summer*, respectively centered on the years 1910 and 1919, project the historical events of the period. The third novel, *Bonfire*, serialized in the *New World* in 1949, centers on the crucial days of June 21, 22, and 23 during Hitler's invasion.

Although Fedin limits geographical space in both of the first two novels to his native Volga town, Saratov, what impresses at first reading is the total recall of Russian society through its numerous representatives—merchants, tsarist officials, intellectuals, tradesmen, peasants, children, artists, and captains of industry. They come wonderfully alive in a generous profusion of talk, amusing genre incidents, and domestic scenes interspersed with discussions on philosophy, politics, and the arts. Fedin constructs a lively chronicle of closely woven relationships by which he manages to sort out masses of information on the idiosyncrasies of principal characters and the socio-political atmosphere of the time.

With the practiced skill of a realist and a warm attachment to boyhood memories, Fedin evokes in some of the more memorable passages the leisurely mindless pace of small-town living spent at neighborhood gatherings, on fishing trips and at carnival fairs, as well as the quiet beauty of the river and meadow landscape of an evening walk into the countryside. Against this prerevolutionary background, the image of a new Russia emerges, in the less-than-original story of Kiril Izvekov. He is a strong and intelligent eighteen-year-old-high school student, who, foreseeably, is drawn into underground revolutionary activity by a proletarian worker and is imprisoned. In *Extraordinary Summer* Izvekov returns to Saratov and becomes a member of the local Soviet. More led than leader, the fresh-cheeked, straightforward young Communist resembles hundreds of other forgettable positive heroes in Soviet fiction. Fedin attempts to individualize him by giving importance to the young man's very human emotions as we watch him fume, embittered at being jilted by his fiancée for a wealthy man when he was in Siberia, and later wholly transfixed in a state of love. The idyll between Kiril and Annochka, his future wife, is handled with an intensity of lyrical power that recalls Grigory Melekhov's affair with Aksinya. Kiril, however, is a far less interesting figure than Sholokhov's Cossack hero, and he lacks the neural drive and complexity of Fedin's own Andrei Startsev in *Cities and Years*.

There are shows of great writing strength that electrify the narrative from time to time. The description in *Bonfire* of an air raid in Brest is powerful. Fedin's purpose of tracing, as does Alexey Tolstoy in *Road to Calvary*, the link between past and present that forges Russian life, is superbly executed in the inner unity of the first two novels. The ably envisioned characters of the opening part that are scattered are gathered together again in the second novel. The immediate perception of the turnabout in the class situation, the humiliations and misery of the former privileged ones, is invoked to serve the work's larger design in an implication that the revolutionary upheaval has not fundamentally affected human character.

Leo Tolstoy was an influence on the entire work. There is no doubt that the writer's great novel inspired the size, depth, and historical distillations of Fedin. In 1910, when the first novel opens, Russian's moral landscape had darkened with the passing of Tolstoy. Fedin seems to predict the inevitability of change in the hearts of men. This change is symbolized by the disturbed reactions to news of the great moralist's flight from his home and his death at a railway station. No one is more deeply shocked than the playwright, Pastukhov, who is probably Fedin's alter ego and the most successful creation in the work.

Worldly, cerebral, apolitical, disinterested in problems that do not touch on art, Pastukhov is forced, to his bewilderment and rage, to take sides between the Reds and the Whites to the detriment of his artistic freedom. The marvelously analytical worryings and probings to which his tortured consciousness submits in his dilemma, and which are recorded by Fedin with magnificent objectivity, pose the major problem. It is the incompatibility of an individual's way of life with the historical determinism of his time, familiar to readers of *Cities and Years*. Pastukhov's characterization is flawed by his ultimate espousal of the Revolution that he comes to view, implausibly, in Tolstoy's light as "the new life for man on this earth."

Other criticism that could be made against Fedin's imposing opus would include the uninspiring "arm chair" accounts of military engagements, the falsification of history in transforming Trotsky, commander-in-chief of the Red Armies, into a traitor, and Stalin into the valorous savior of Tsarytsin that was probably inserted to win official approval for the work. There is a tendency to overextend realistic description and give us more of the diurnal existence of the author's subjects than we need to know. Albeit the trilogy is an outstanding work in Soviet fiction, its very size and labor command respect. But a Soviet "War and Peace" remains to be written.

At the high noon of socialist realism there appeared a refreshing new talent who sidestepped standard literary formulae with a successful return to the exploration of emotional sensibilities. Vera Panova's first novel, *Travelling Companions* (1946), that received a Stalin award, immediately attracted a large reading public by the grippingly human quality of the main protagonists—ordinary people—caught in the holocaust of war. Drawing on her own experience as a correspondent assigned to a military hospital train, Panova situates the entire action in an ambulance train that reproduces in microcosm the totality of war in the suffering and scurrilousness of the wounded who are being evacuated from the front, and the patient, skillful care and compassion that is offered to them by the ambulance personnel. The author's main concern is to present these dedicated workers (the doctor, surgical nurse, nurse, attendant, and the official hero, a political commissar who is in charge of the unit) in their full human dimension. By means of brief and broken dialogue the author gradually reconstructs their prewar personal lives. They are shown to be fraught with broken dreams, love and love's failure, sentiments of personal duty and honor, and the tragedy of the loss of family, casualties of the military conflict. Panova probes with great psychological tact into these ravages of an intensely private nature that are simply, almost laconically, described, where nothing calls for abstract reasoning, and which like life itself seemed bound to happen. The author's objective tone that is maintained throughout insures against lapses into sentimentality.

The work achieves within limited means the effect of a complete human experience. Introspective flashbacks into poignantly relived private memories cut into the gathering momentum of the ambulance in action. They reflect, as in a moving mirror, momentary fusion of intimate and public domain and create an interchangeable movement between peacetime and wartime existence.

In her second novel, *Kruzhilikha* (1947), Panova was less successful in maintaining the intensity of personal feelings. They are generated here by a conflict between the hard-driving manager of the factory, Kruzhilikha, and its trade unions' steward, a plodding party cog-in-the-wheel who hates the resourceful, more highly placed executive. A sensitized probe into the characters of both men reveals their temperamental polarity upon which all communication between them must sunder. It culminates in a gripping scene that recalls Dostoevsky's *Eternal Husband* in forceful projection of human incompatibility. The manager, in a moment of sudden and deep emotional fulfillment, spontaneously offers to make amends to the other and is rejected. Power drains out of the author's psychological study with recourse to the stereotyped "re-education" formula that is meant to resolve the conflict. Party leadership is called in; it condemns the manager's "unprincipled" and independent behavior, mired in unacceptable private relations, and enjoins him to cooperate in the collective enterprise with the trades unions' official who is praised for selfless dedication to his work.

Another extremely popular work that was well written, with vigor and drive, was Pyotr Pavlenko's novel, *Happiness,* which he wrote in 1947. In contrast to *Travelling Companions* and *Kruzhilikha*, it fully embraced Stalinist aesthetics. It is centered around the theme of demobilized soldiers and their resettlement into civilian life. This became a prevalent problem during the postwar period and was called "voropaevshchina" after the hero's name in *Happiness*.

After his discharge from the army, the partially disabled Colonel Alexei Voropaev goes to the Crimea where he hopes to restore his health in the beneficent climate and live to the end of his days in peaceful retirement. His plans go awry when, at the Yalta conference, he happens to see Stalin who makes him feel "a 1,000 years younger"; through contacts with agricultural leaders of the district, he becomes interested in local affairs and throws in his lot as an active participant in the working community. The official "happy ending" imperative is summed up in Voropaev's understanding, toward the close of the story, that happiness derives from an active life within a collective. Pavlenko fulfills yet another party-inspired stipulation when the English-speaking Colonel expresses strongly anti-Western views in his conversation with an American journalist.

Happiness won the Stalin Prize. So did S. Babayevsky's *Knight of the Golden Star* (1948) where a similar theme of return home from the front is developed in the story of a former war hero. He modernizes his village with the construction of an electric power station and is given a top job in the local Party committee when he puts the plant into operation. Another prize winning novel, *The Harvest* (1950), by G. Nikolaeva involves a plot based on a marital triangle with personal feelings played off against woman's status in the socialist society and her newly acquired civic pride. The peasant heroine, Avdotya, is forced to renounce her second husband whom she loves and who treats her as an equal when her first husband, Vasily, believed dead, returns from the war. Unable to endure Vasily's treatment of her as a servant-wife, she leaves him to work on a collective farm that he directs. The dilemma of their relationship in human terms blurs and finally dissolves in the stereotyped "re-education" finale. Avdotya is encouraged by the party secretary to help her husband with some kolkhoz problems that brings them together and makes him appreciate in his wife an emancipated and progressive Soviet citizen.

Although these three novels by Pavlenko, Babayevsky, and Nikolaeva create a more sustained interest through more skillful plots and individualization of characters than the majority of prize-winning novels of the period (forty-nine were chosen for the award between 1948 and 1952) they fit as snugly into the literature of socialist realism and were therefore eligible for the highest distinction in the land.

Beyond the practice of awarding annual prizes, officials expressed their approbation of "good Communist" writers in other ways. Tangibly, the government provided material advantages: financial security, comfortable living quarters, enviable social status, and encouragement from state publishing houses to submit manuscripts to their editors. A more intangible and, in modern times, unique form of support was extended to the "favored" members of the writing community in eulogistic press comments on their work, radically different in tone from the most enthusiastic critical reviews that appear in the West. They are addressed directly by name and locality to the happy "achiever" and reflect sentiments of paternalism and subjective expressions of encouragement. Through and beyond professional criticism, flow assurances that the author's production is of vital importance to his fellow citizens, that his progress is sympathetically observed, that he is cared for, and "belongs."

5 · Post-Stalin Era

IMMEDIATE CONSEQUENCES:
THE FIRST AND SECOND THAW

Stalin's death in March, 1953 lifted Zhdanovist terrorism, and a resurgence of hope swept through the Soviet literary world. The years 1953 through 1956 are known as the time of the "thaw" (taken from the title of Ilya Ehrenburg's novel) that marked a melting away of the constraint and restrictions of Stalinist literary policy. Censorship became less strict, former rigid Central Committee decrees were replaced by more relaxed confrontations between high state officials and writers, who were now emboldened to protest against conformism in articles, speeches, and creative writings. Suddenly, for the first time in twenty years, it became possible to engage in open debate on theories of literature without fears of official reprisal. It was soon evident, however, that such freedom would not be permitted to continue. The party's right of final arbiter in literary matters remained inviolate and periodically political opposition was expressed against what appeared to be dangerous demands for greater individual expression of emotions and ideas. A rapid chronological account of the advances and setbacks in the liberalizing process may be helpful in gauging the absolute gains made by writers in the struggle for creative freedom and the limits set upon that freedom during the vacillating "thaw" years.

Just a month after Stalin's funeral, the poetess Olga Bergholtz voiced a plea in *Literary Gazette* (April, 1953) for the restoration of subjectivity in poetry. She reported that in reading

197

over a hundred recent lyrics, she did not find a single theme that related to the poet's inner self and declared that, in the absence of the expression of personal feelings of love, sorrow, and suffering, poetry ceased to exist. In June, Alexander Tvardovsky, editor of the prestigious *New World* magazine (a forum for more progressive authors) published the fifth and sixth chapters of his poetic *Horizon Beyond the Horizon* cycle. He castigated in it what was routinely approved by ideologically minded editors as "indigestible work," that made one "want to scream," and questioned their ability to discern the poet's truth.

Toward the end of 1953, Ehrenburg's article in the magazine, *Znamia*, "On the Work of a Writer," and that of a new critic, V. Pomerantsev in the *New World* attacked bureaucratic regimentation and argued for the writer's privilege to choose his materials and depict what is available to him and in the light of his own writer's experience. Both wrote against the simplification of personality into accepted stereotypes, deploring the inauthentic or evasive portrayal of private, emotion-charged life that Ehrenburg was to bring out into the open in his novel, *The Thaw*. The reasonable tone of Ehrenburg's essay was studded with scholarly references to Russian classics and Western authors such as Joyce, Hemingway, and Upton Sinclair that served to blunt the underlying heresy of a return to humanism. It was outmatched for immediate effect by the manifesto-like stridency of Pomerantsev's "On Sincerity in Literature." He urged his fellow literati to abandon "production line" plots with their "conveyor belts" and "tractor nerves" and treat honestly varied and complex features of Soviet society that for its moral well-being and strength of character does not depend on material benefits alone.

It is not surprising that a first creative manifestation of the change in the literary climate came from the pen of Vera Panova who had managed to maintain in the Zhdanovist era the prerogative of endowing her characters with emotional urges that intensified their reality and impinged upon the collective.

In *Seasons of the Year* (1953), the "production line" pattern is abandoned for the private story of two prominent Communist families living through a crisis. One household consists of the railroad worker, Kuprisnov, and his intelligent wife, a peasant girl who has risen to party membership and is a leading figure in town affairs. The seed of disaster is planted in the behavior of the mother's adored eldest son, Gennady, a weak-willed "stiliaga" who shuns work, neglects his young wife, and finally joins a gang of thieves to satisfy his craving for cars and easy living. It is perhaps significant that the son and daughter of the other family of nonproletarian origin are disciplined, upright young people, although their father, Stepan Bortashevich, director of the City Trade office, turns out to be an embezzler. The formerly conscientious citizen divorced his wife to marry his secretary, a calculating and luxury-loving woman. To support her opulent style of life, he began to dip into state funds. When the law blows open his elaborate cover up, which caused innocent people to be sent to prison, he commits suicide.

The novel was immediately successful, but it was censured by *Pravda* for the inconclusive ending that does not draw a lesson from the wrongdoings of the main protagonists. In fact, Panova leads from artistic strength in the unfolding of this overt human drama where everyone in turn is at least partially involved. She presents the study, rare in Soviet fiction, of the multiple behavior patterns of personality that are subject to indecisive, elusive, and opposing influences. There are no villains; the wrongs are mixed. Lucidity edged with compassion marks the author's attitude to Dorothea and her son, both victims of her overindulgence. It is implied that Stepan, made desperate by financial pressures, is not altogether to blame for his profiteering crimes in the upper levels of the Communist world that is riddled with venality and corruption.

A more direct and concentrated attack on the moral decline of highly placed Communists is the subject of Leonid Zorin's play, *The Guests*, staged in February, 1954. Building the plot on an ideologically charged conflict between generations, Zorin conceived his drama in the spirit of a courtroom trial with the audience acting as jury to the declarations of the main protagonists who defend their position and views. Aleksei Kirpichev is a Supreme Soviet deputy, one of the famous revolutionary architects of the Soviet state. He is imbued with 1917 socialist ideals that his youngest grandson, Tyoma, considers quaintly old fashioned and straight out of the textbook on War Communism that he had studied in school. Tyoma's father, Peter Kirpichev, Minister of Justice, is a ruthless, cynical bureaucrat. He is good-naturedly contemptuous of his father's loyalties and heroic past that are as remote from his careerist concerns as is the fate of ordinary citizens who have suffered a miscarriage of justice and are refused a hearing by his order to protect the Ministry's reputation. The play centers around such an incident—the illegal disbarring of a provincial lawyer whose case is taken up by a local journalist. It appears likely that the Minister's unsavory involvement in this case will be exposed. Peter is superbly drawn as a typical representative of the new elite class. He is solidly entrenched in the prerequisite of privilege and has acquired the speech and manner of arbitrary power. Zorin highlights his vulgarity and obsession with creature comforts in an effective scene with Tyoma and his wife. They are shown gloating over a piece of newly acquired property and one of the bystanders calls him "a filthy little bourgeois." The sequence, at times hurried and confused, comes to a dramatic climax in the final confrontation between Peter and his father who befriends the injured lawyer. He turns against the younger man for betraying socialist ideals but not without condemning himself for the permissiveness of his son's upbringing and making use of his own high position in the party to promote Peter's rapid advancement to the seat of power.

Ehrenburg's novelette *The Thaw* was published in May, 1954 in *Znamia*. It would have become famous for its name alone if the author had not also touched on the currently emerging themes already explored by Panova and Zorin—the deteriorating impact of environment on character and the inhumanity of the high-ranking managerial class. When the conservatives attacked *The Thaw* the author agreed with them that the work was defective but only because "it had not gone far enough." This exchange took place at the Second Writers' Congress in December, 1954 (it had originally been scheduled to meet in 1937). During the preceding seven months the party-dominated presidium had organized writers' symposia in the provinces for the discussion of literary issues and the election of delegates to the All-Union Congress. It was planned as a massive public retaliation to the "Young Turks" (of the 720 present, 522 were party members). The congress opened with a clarion call for strict adherence to socialist realism supported by heavy Stalinist rhetoric from the Union secretary, A. Surkov, and his second-in-command, F. Gladkov. A spirited riposte was made by such prominent figures as Ehrenburg, Bergholtz, Kaverin, and the famous children's writer, K. Chukovsky. It called for an art without false embellishments, genuine aesthetic criticism, and pointed out the writer's need to follow his creative bent. This was received with distrust nearing hostility from the assembly. Further, when Sholokhov denounced, in a tone half humorous, half obscene, "recent literary miscarriages" flooding the bookstalls (381 million pieces of fiction were printed in 1954), he was reprimanded for his "non-party" criticism. Nonetheless, fissures did appear in the obdurate refusal of the Union to sanction wider liberties. At the congress, Anna Akhmatova was readmitted into the Union, and Tvardovsky, who had been dismissed as chief editor of the *New World* for publishing Pomeranstev's article, was elected to the Union's executive board. More indicative still of increased tolerance on the part of the authorities was the rehabilitation during 1955 of writers such as Babel, Bunin, and Pilnyak, who had been purged during the thirties and forties. Unobtrusive notices announced limited editions of their writings. Bulgakov's plays were reprinted and Feodor Dostoevsky was reinstated as a great Russian writer with a commemoration of the seventy-fifth anniversary of his death and the publication of his collected works.

In the following year, the famous "secret session" of the Twentieth Century Congress touched off resistance to literary orthodoxy. Writers who attended the session were forbidden to refer in their works to Nikita Krushchev's disclosure of Stalin's crimes and the Premier's condemnation of the Stalin cult. The writers opposed this and soon made the crimes and the condemnation well known. They shook the Communist world, and the monolithic facade that Stalin and his followers had imposed on political life was shattered. Liberal-minded writers then began to bring out works that broke away even more decisively from the official mold. Among them, *Day of Poetry, Literary Moscow, II* and *Not by Bread Alone* by Vladimir Dudintsev made the most sensational literary news.

VLADIMIR DUDINTSEV (1918-   )

Following Ehrenburg's lead of denigrating the conventional Soviet novel, Dudintsev strikes with greater frankness and intensity at one of its most hallowed entities—that of the successful positive hero. His disarming strategy in *Not by Bread Alone* was to endow his main protagonist, Dmitri Lopatkin, a former physics teacher turned inventor, with traits that ensure official favor. Lopatkin is a loyal Communist and a hard worker who is proud of having discovered a centrifugal machine design that would revolutionize a whole segment of Soviet industry. When he submits the project to Drozdov, the head of the local combine, the Soviet reader expects the young inventor, who may encounter some difficulties (introduced by the author to create several interesting subplots), to be publicly rewarded for his service to the state.

Instead, the entire action revolves around the hero's eight-year struggle to win recognition for his invention in a conflict between two opposing forces, as the Biblical title implies. It is a tug-of-war between individual talent, intellectual and moral integrity, and a despotic, narrow-minded bureaucracy engaged in the safeguarding of hierarchy and personal advantages rather than in furthering the interests of the Russian people. Like Peter Kirpichev in *Guests*, the status-haunted, bootlicking, morally callous Drozdov represents the bureaucratic elite. He is the most fully developed character in the novel. He is also Lopatkin's chief antagonist. He vilifies Lopatkin's "individual" genius as being "unnecessary" to "our collective genius" and fails to forward the inventor's plans to the minister because he fears to offend a superior whose protegé had submitted a similar but inferior design for a water pipe. In his private life we find him at odds with his sensitive young wife who wants to establish a deeper personal relationship with him and whom he rebuffs with the boast that, as a brilliant economic planner building socialism on a material base, he has no time for personal feelings. Behind him is felt the presence of the formidable power elite and its innumerable careerists and opportunists. They emerge briefly in slight but joltingly real detail as a minister, a well-known scientist, Lopatkin's rival research workers, and engineers. Their clandestine intrigues conspire to discredit and humiliate the young hero, who, deprived of important political connections, ends up being exiled to Siberia on a trumped-up charge. Finally Lopatkin is found innocent, and his machine, to which he adds further refinements while in prison, is approved. The question that Dudintsev poses as to the nugatory effects of the monopoly of power in Soviet society, however, remains unanswered. No "evildoers" are found. Officials who had ruthlessly attempted to destroy the inventor when he refused to give up his independence in return for a lucrative post, remain entrenched in positions of privilege. Drozdov is promoted to the rank of deputy minister.

The novel became a "cause célèbre" overnight, both at home and abroad. In the West it was considered as a portrayal of the angry young man pitted against the establishment. Attention was drawn to the work's inherent weaknesses that have characterized conformist Soviet literature since the forties: didacticism. The unconvincing delineation of the hero, who is indeed little more than a wooden emblem of his obsessive purpose. Also, he is almost totally unaware of his small but supportive cast, such as the barely outlined figures of his co-workers and the provocative glimpse of an embittered older inventor who serves as the spokesman for the individual's superiority within a collective. The delicately hued delineation of Nadya Drozdov, who is in love with Lopatkin and leaves her husband to become the latter's companion, is disappointingly allowed little place in the narrative.

The artistic flaws and the heavy verbosity of the writing itself was less noticed by the Soviet commentators. What impressed them was the author's daring themes that exposed degenerate leaders not as occasionally defective parts of a young governing apparatus but as typical and prevailing members of the New Class. The moral right to tenure of the entire party system was placed in doubt. A furious controversy followed. *Pravda* accused Dudintsev of falsifying reality and distorting Soviet life. In *Izvestia* he was castigated for "excessive individualism and a non-comprehension of the significance of the collective." An attempt was made in the first reviews to narrow the importance of the author's challenge to a personal experience with no ideological meaning. In a much-quoted defense of the work, Konstantin Paustovsky, speaking at the Moscow Union of Writers, acclaimed the author for bringing out into the open for the first time "the merciless truth about Drozdovshchina against which Soviet literature must wage war until it is crushed."

THE DAY OF POETRY; LITERARY MOSCOW, VOL. II

The appearance of a thick anthology, *The Day of Poetry*, was further evidence of the swiftly spreading liberalism on the literary scene. In a spirit of daring and enthusiasm the publication invited over a hundred poets (some of whom had fallen into disfavor) to contribute poetry with no regard for conformist views. The selections ranged from intensely subjective pieces to rollicking satire that asserted the poet's right to express in his own way his vision of the world. Several of Marina Tsvetaeva's lyrical poems that had been suppressed since her suicide in 1941, prefaced by her statement of nonacceptance and noncomprehension of the October Revolution, were included as well as essays on the writing of poetry that fearlessly dealt with "seditious" modernist experimental techniques.

The second volume of *Literary Moscow*, a miscellany of fiction, criticism, and verse, was published by Moscow editors and writers with the collaboration of such outstanding figures as Akhmatova, Fedin, Ehrenburg, Shklovsky, Zabolotsky, Kaverin, and Aliger. It advanced an ambitious two-fold program of emancipation from the inartistic doldrums of Socialist realism.

On the one hand, open revolt against party abuses was declared in a table of contents that included the following pieces: Ehrenburg's sensitive appraisal of Tsvetaeva's art that was to preface a projected one-volume edition of her poetry; the rehabilitation of another forbidden author, Yuri Olesha, silenced since 1934, with extracts from his recent *Notes of a Diary* which testified that he was still alive and writing; Veniamin Kaverin's novel, *Quests and Hopes;* an allegorical fable by the playwright, Sergei Mikhailov, on the skill of certain Soviet men of letters to follow the prevailing political mood; the most trenchant and bluntly worded analysis of the Stalinist cult and its crippling effect on the entire body politic that had as yet appeared in print by the dramatic critic, Alexander Kron.

On the other hand, in three very short stories (*The Light in the Window* by Yuri Nagibin, *The Levers* by Alexander Yashin, *The Trip Back Home* by Nikolay Zhdanov) relative newcomers to literature struck a note of hope for the future.

It is difficult, in the case of these writers, to disassociate style from content. As in the works of Chekhov who is obviously their foremost teacher, idea is closely linked with subtlety, obliqueness, economy of means, and the idea is expressed in low-keyed language. Their common theme that echoes Dudintsev's revelation of the dehumanized bureaucrat and his estrangement from ordinary Soviet citizens eschews the didactic finality of his accusations. They reach back to nineteenth-century humanism and a concern, so characteristically Chekhovian, with the vulnerability and many-sidedness of the spiritually impoverished man. What is sought for in all the stories is the possibility of human fulfillment which regimentation of the system had been methodically wiping out. Zhdanov's story is also impressionistically constructed of slight but telling detail. The good cut of a plaid coat, a pile of cables on Varygin's office desk, and the luxurious train compartment that identify him as a high official are contrasted with the broken samovar, the wooden knot of the table in his childhood home, and his mother's ragged old clothing that spell out the squalor and poverty of his native village when he visits it for a day to attend his mother's funeral. He hears the just complaints of the collective farmers who have been mistreated by the central authorities with mingled sensations of unpleasantness, depression, and guilt. They are not entirely mitigated by his attempt to escape from their grim reality by a hurried return to the reassuring safety of administrative routine at the capital.

In *The Light in the Window* an even more palpable awareness of a nefarious hierarchy assails the director of a rest home who is forced to keep a suite of rooms with a TV set and a billiard table in readiness for the possible visit of a highly placed Ministry member despite the pressing need to lodge other vacationers. His resentment is spearheaded by the revolt of the maid who has been cleaning the suite for over a year and finally moves in with her family. In ordering her out he is filled with self-loathing. In the magnificently targeted six page story, *The Le-*

vers, the image of the party as wise counsellor and friend of the people is toppled. Yashin shows within the same men the split between party indoctrination and the natural way of life. Four party members of a collective farm are criticizing the arrogance and callousness of the district office that pays little attention to their local problems. With the arrival of the school teacher the party meeting begins, and the author pumps the scene full of irony in an immediate turnabout of roles as the farmers in their official attitudes take the roles of their superiors. They become haughty to the other peasants and treat the regional secretary with obsequious respect. The art of this story, filled with conversation, lies in the triumph of tone. Yashin handles the verbal patterns and shifts in speech with authority, making us hear the duplicity and fear of dangerous commitment in the bureaucratic patter, while he infuses the casual colloquial dialogue with a sense of ease, openness, and mutual trust. There is no doubt of the author's belief in men's faculty to resist, however mutely, the degradation of artifice in personal relationships. After the meeting, the atmosphere becomes relaxed, the friends resume their casual talk about life and their own interests. The author steps into the narrative for the first and only time in the concluding sentence: "And once more, they were warm, cordial, straightforward people—not levers."

These slight stories are of a high artistic order. The cultivation of understatement by their authors marked a welcome departure from the overwritten and overemphatic style of socialist realism. It was a release for cramped artistic energies. It was equally significant for their future work that during the protest in 1956 young Nagibin, Yashin, and Zhdanov were showing signs of dropping simplistic anti-Stalinist situations, conflicts, and characters and attempting to explore the larger reality of contradictions and ambiguities in man.

The *Literary Moscow* almanac, ready for the press in 1956, was not printed until after the Hungarian and Polish revolts that had been stimulated by the intellectuals of these countries. The party went into action. The relative permissiveness that had prevailed was suddenly cut off and a vigorous attempt to crash all literary opposition was instigated by the regime. The editorial staff of *Literary Moscow* with other "offending" writers were targeted for the first, major barrage of attacks. Khrushchev threatened them with corrective measures and reaffirmed the supremacy of party rule over literature. He restated the tenets of orthodox Socialist Realism in two speeches that were summarized in various newspapers and journals and took on the air of a national campaign. Kaverin, Ehrenburg, and Kron, who had defended the almanac's policy, took refuge in silence at the Writers' Union meetings where administrative officers virulently denounced "deviationist" writings, exhorted the dissidents to give up their erroneous views, and called for unanimous votes of confidence in the "beneficial" party spirit. Many writers, among them Margarita Aliger, E. Kazakevich, and Dudintsev, recanted.

The advent of the first Sputnik that filled all Russians with deep national pride brought further disarray into the formerly articulate ranks of the nonconformists. In the face of the great scientific achievement in space, there was reason to believe that the "Drozdovs" were not entirely mistaken in their glorification of "collective" genius. Besides, some progress had been made. The heady expectations of the "thaw" period had not been realized, but apparently the hateful punitive measures of the thirties and forties were to remain part of the past. Some fiction was being published of a more human coloration whose subject matter was less concerned with technology than with the private lives of Soviet men and women. Soviet critics were less likely to reprimand writers for treating a darker side of reality if it was later redeemed by an optimistic ending.

BORIS PASTERNAK: *DR. ZHIVAGO*

During this moment of compromise, a scandal with international repercussions erupted in the Soviet world of letters. In 1957 a novel by the greatest living Soviet poet, Boris Pasternak, was published in the West, and the following year its author was awarded the Nobel Prize.

The novel, *Dr. Zhivago*, had a long gestation. The poet had been writing it for about twenty years, during a period of personal obscurity, when, one by one, the major talents of his generation (Mayakovsky, Esenin, Mandelstam, Babel, and Tsvetaeva) were forcibly extinguished. He felt the need, as a last survivor, to record in a creative meditation the experience and thought that the last forty tragic years had bequeathed to Russian history. In this work which he considered "the most difficult and important" that he had ever undertaken, he decided to put away the "earlier excesses" of his "hermetic" poetry and turn to prose. He believed that prose would be more suitable for the expression of the "immensity" of our experience and a way of life which had become "too crowded and complicated" for the possibilities of verse.

In 1956 the manuscript was submitted to *New World* magazine. It was returned to the author by the editorial board that included Fedin and Konstantin Simonov, erstwhile admirers of Pasternak's poetry, with a thirty page rejection letter couched in courteous and reasonable terms. The editors claimed that the novel was "anti-democratic," historically inaccurate in its depiction of the Revolution, contained no positive revolutionary figures, was alien to the interests of the Russian people, and partial to the self-indulgent main protagonist who attempts to pursue in the midst of "great events" a life of personal well-being and tranquility. Pasternak had also sent a copy of *Dr. Zhivago* to the Communist publisher, Feltrinelli, in Milan, and, certain that his novel would be published in Russia, had granted the latter all the foreign rights.

In fact, the Soviet publishing house of Goslitizdat did offer to bring out the work with the deletion of some politically charged passages, to which the poet had agreed. He asked Feltrinelli to delay the Italian publication, but the translation was already under way. Feltrinelli also had rightly guessed that Pasternak was being pressured at home, and as a result was asking to have his manuscript returned for corrections. He accordingly published the original version in 1957. When its author was awarded the Nobel Prize it was translated into eighteen languages and received immediate world acclaim. This occurred at the peak of the Cold War, and it was probably inevitable that this book of considerable literary magnitude from a Soviet writer, with its denunciation of Communism, would generate international excitement and become something of a political issue.

Boris Pasternak cabled his joyous acceptance to the Stockholm committee but was forced to refuse the honor a week later when the party chose to regard the prize as a political ploy invented by the enemies of the Soviet Union. This succeeded in making the writer a "cause célèbre" in the West and poisoned the last years of his life. *Pravda* dubbed him a "malevolent Philistine"; the *Moscow Literary Gazette* excoriated the Nobel Board for recognizing "an artistically squalid, malicious work replete with the hatred of socialism" although three Soviet scientists who had just been similarly honored went to Stockholm with official blessing to receive their prizes. The Writers' Union deprived Pasternak of his membership, the Komsomol leader, Vladimir Semuchatsky, called the poet at a public meeting "a pig who dirties the place where he sleeps and eats." An assembly of some eight hundred Moscow intellectuals unanimously demanded that Pasternak be exiled abroad. This brought on Pasternak's partial recantation of some "errors" in his novel. He made a formal statement to Nikita Khrushchev in which he begged the head of the state to allow him to remain in Russia to which "he was bound by birth, life and work" and wrote that for him to leave his motherland would be tantamount to death. Russian dictatorship, infamously known for its persecution of scores of writers, philosophers, and thinkers was again at work and Pasternak's name may now be added to the classic roster of Russian writers (Turgenev, Tolstoy, Dostoevsky) who asserted the independence of literature and its role as the conscience of the nation and were persecuted by the authorities.

In *Dr. Zhivago*, Pasternak bypasses Soviet literature, to which he remains a stranger, to make a full statement about the situation of modern man. Pasternak was deeply disturbed by social and political conflicts in the years when he was composing his novel. There is to be found in this long work something of the apprehension in Thomas Mann's *Magic Mountain*. He reflects T. S. Eliot's visitation of the wasteland wracked by manmade violence. To do so, he relies on a central treatment, as in Joyce's *Ulysses*, to portay uprooted man looking for certainties. He expressed his vision in exhaustively rich and plastic but nonpoetic language that has the vigor but not the Joycean verbal effusion and play. The development of these universal themes and others of a metaphysical nature is charged with moral passion. Pasternak seems to draw on the great national heritage of Dostoevsky's spiritual dilemmas and the thought of Tolstoy. But finally, this work, that in Frank Kermode's words "belongs to that small group by which all other novels will ultimately be judged," eludes literary geneology or a classical definition.

The main action is concerned with Yuri Zhivago, the only fully developed character, whose life from 1903 to 1929 is traced against the backdrop of a dissolving society during the First World War, the 1917 Revolution, and the Civil War.

The orphaned boy of formerly wealthy parents is taken in by an upper middle-class intellectual Moscow family, marries, becomes a doctor, and serves in World War I. During the early period of the social upheaval, he leaves starving, epidemic-riddled Moscow and sets out with his wife and children across the lurid landscape of devastated cities and villages to find a refuge from want in Varykino, a hamlet in the Urals that has been part of the family estate. Of the sixty schematized figures appearing in the book, a number of them are memorably caught in gestures of pain or despair in the packed freight train on the endless journey through Russia. The description of that trip with its realistic poignancy and pitch constitutes a small classic in the "displaced persons" saga of twentieth-century fiction. At Varykino, Yuri finds a measure of peace and eventually happiness in his passion for Lara Antipova, whom he met previously as a war nurse. This is shattered when a red guerilla band in need of a doctor abducts him to their camp. Zhivago finally manages to escape from the forest brotherhood camp whose members had forced him to join in the shooting of White Army cadets. He returns to Yuriatin (the town adjoining Varykino) where he learns from Lara that his family has been exiled abroad. Another brief idyll with Lara at Varykino proves to be short when, to the nightly danger of approaching wolves and the scarcity of food, is added the possibility of her capture by the Cheka who is on the hunt for her husband, Pasha Antipov, a former Bolshevik commander. After Lara's departure, the doctor makes his way back to Moscow, lives in great poverty, first alone and then with the daughter of his former janitor, disappears for a time from view, and finally dies of a heart attack on the street.

Through the life of his utterly credible and vulnerable hero, Pasternak recreates his own inward journey in search of truths with which to combat the madness and bloodshed of his age.

The autobiographical imprint is clear in Yuri's portrait. A member of Pasternak's liberal bourgeois class, he was attracted to ancient legends and literature early and attempted to write. In medicine he became known for the uncanny precision of his diagnosis, a sort of intuitive second sight in discerning illness through a particular symptom even as a poet captures the world's natural beauty in the shape and color of one flower. Dr. Zhivago is receptive to everything around him. He is also endowed with a poet's radical innocence that looks for affirmations of joy in the multiple, mobile, and mysteriously interrelated universe. The result is a poetical portrayal of actual events and their consequence expressed in a symbolically diffused and expanded vision of reality.

Pasternak constructs his novel while depicting reality by almost the only narrator, Yuri Zhivago, in nature scenes where "man is silent and images speak," in heady philosophical talk, in the grimness of war incidents, and in moments of spiritual tranquillity. The dynamism of abrupt transitions, erratic chronology, and, most startling to the conventional reader, an overabundance of coincidences, achieve an almost surrealistic effect. How elated Pasternak must have been to break through traditional realism with manifestations of extraordinary, inexplicable existence that "had struck [him] from [his] earliest years" and which denies the laws of causality and logic. It is the rejection of unpredictability that Pasternak considers to have flawed Lenin's genius. He looked for support for his own belief in the prevalence of chance and hazard. In turn, he turned to modern science, which in Bronowsky's statement declares randomness as the actuality and sees the factor of chance not as a related but an inherent trait of phenomenology.

In another instance, Pasternak describes a room in Moscow which contains, as in some of Joseph Brodsky's most haunting verses, echoes and re-echoes of fateful moments where the lives of the characters touch, pull away, and are brought together again in the image of a lighted candle on the window sill of that room. It had been Pasha Antipov's room in his student days. Lara, who had intermittently been engaged to him, came there one winter night on her way to a Christmas party where she planned to shoot her seducer, Komarovsky. She had asked to have only one candle lighted and in the semi-darmness told Pasha that they must marry. At that moment eighteen-year-old Yuri was driving past with his future wife to the same party. He saw the candle making a black patch on the frosted window pane.

It seemed to him that it was casting glances down the street as if waiting for someone, he felt something mysterious beckoning to him and involuntarily whispered "A candle burned." It is to this room that toward the end of his life the doctor is brought by his half-brother, Evgraf. Here he finds the necessary isolation in which to write and where Lara, by chance in Moscow, comes to keep vigil over his body and remembers that far-off Christmas time when the candle burned. A centrally realized metaphor such as the lighted candle radiates premonitions, prophetic clues, corresponding sensations that bring into focus the indivisibility of all experience and a fairytale feeling of a spiritually and spatially limited world.

What is Communism in Russia, asks Dr. Zhivago from the depths of his thinking and observation and how has it met the demands of the age? It had soon become obvious to him that the purity of revolutionary faith articulated by the early Bolshevik rulers quickly degenerated into an amalgam of textbook formulae, poster slogans, and rules that shaped the official ideology. This hollow ideology imposed by the Communists on Russian life was espoused mistakenly and tragically by Pasha Antipov, a high-principled revolutionary who was consumed by the Revolution. Son of a railway worker, brought up in a factory slum, Pasha had graduated from the university with science and mathematics degrees, and accompanied by his young wife, Lara, took a teaching post in an Ural town. He was puritanically minded, courageous, and yearning to accomplish some extraordinary mission. Yet he was lacking an inner staying center and was easily influenced by someone such as Lara who was stronger than himself. The boredom of provincial life and a possible flaw in his marital relations decided him to volunteer for the army. At the front, exposed to Marxism, he imbibed socialist dogma uncritically and single mindedly with all the obsessive ardor of his nature. He plunged into the Revolution. Zhivago, on his way to the Urals, was accidentally arrested by a Red commander known as Strelnikov (the Shooter) who was none other than Antipov living under a suitable revolutionary name. He had been entrusted with the destruction of recalcitrant village settlements and seemed to the doctor to be a depersonalized human being. "He needs a heart in addition to his principles," said Yuri later, "if he is to do good." The two men met again at Varykino after Lara had left and Strelnikov, who had been denounced by the Bolsheviks as a traitor, came to the doctor's house where a night was spent in talking about the woman they both loved; the passage recalls another great and similar dialogue between Myshkin and Rogozhin in Dostoevsky's *Idiot*. In the morning, Strelnikov shot himself. There is little doubt that Antipov is meant to symbolize the destructive effect of the Communist system on human beings. This is not to say that the historical reality of the Revolution is denigrated. Zhivago speaks of it as "splendid surgery" and "the first step toward the new order that will be all around us and familiar as the woods on the horizon or the clouds above our heads." What he fears, speaking to another Red guerrilla chieftain, and where he echoes Dostoevsky's *Underground Man*, is the idea of social betterment that in a manipulated bureaucracy feeds "vulgar common-places" and opts for mandatory collective action and thought that transforms Russians into robots. When the doctor hears his former friend, Misha Gordon, just released from a concentration camp, speaking gratefully of his prison experiences and all that the interrogator had taught him, Zhivago witheringly likens him to "a circus horse describing how it broke itself in."

What Pasternak defends with vehemence and consistency in his abrogation of the socialist state and by implication the technological society of the West is the individual's right to live life as he will, unhampered by importunate and partial prescriptions for happiness. The celebration of personal fulfillment is one of the major themes of the novel and Yuri finds it in his love affair with Lara. The meaning of love is brought back from exile but it was probably the author's indifference to the externals of the world as against the importance of men's absorption in the life of personal emotion and creativity that the Soviets could not ultimately forgive him.

The image of Lara who has been called the most poeticized

woman in Russian literature lies at the very heart of the novel. Restless, intelligent, given to moods of self-scrutiny and repentance, she had been sensually attracted in her teens to her mother's lover, the rich, handsome corrupt lawyer, Komarovsky. The seduction would have been just another pleasurable episode for him if she had not aroused his guilt by her candor and innocence. She married Pasha Antipov to whom she appeared as beneficent as fire in a hearth but with whom, because of some inner weakness, he was not completely at ease. It was only Yuri who felt totally and happily himself with her. To him she represented a life-giving force. Her presence evokes images of flowing water—torrential waterfalls, drenching rain, a rushing stream. The doctor compares her beauty to that of the Russian landscape, now gentle, now fierce. He loves her as he loves Russia which, like Lara, is open to suffering and humiliation and yet remains alive and whole in the midst of the social and political nightmare. Among the many symbols that Lara inhabits throughout the book, her identification with Pasternak's-Zhivago's native land is the most recurrent and in the final chapters significantly binding. It may be surmised that Lara's recapture by her evil genius, Komarovsky, who forces her to leave the Varykin retreat and her lover through a lie, is a reflection of the predicament of Mother Russia, turned over to her destroyers. Lara's eventual death in a concentration camp hints at the fate of the Russian people sold into bondage.

Across numerous pages sparse and masterly descriptions of the Russian landscape are scattered. Dynamic natural changes gain in power and density when they are suggestively compared to human states of being and human moods. Everywhere natural phenomena are humanized, and reversely, in his proximity to nature, the poet returns to his sources of being and creative mainsprings. Instances of the underlying continuity of nature living in man and man within nature inform the most beautiful passages and resound again in Dr. Zhivago's poems.

It is a consensus of the critical forum that Dr. Zhivago's twenty-five appended poems constitute the novel's symbolic substructure that in a fusion of pagan and Christian leitmotivs offers a poetical interpretation of the hero's experience. Not the least interesting aspect of the work is this eaves-dropping by means of one form of art on the creation of another whereby the poet does from within what the novelist does from without. We are shown how the alchemy of the poet's perceptions and imagination works on existence, tells the truth about it but tells it "subjectively and slant."

The startling similes and hermetic obscurity of Pasternak's earlier poetry have largely disappeared from this poem sequence. These poems roughly follow the cycle of seasons, although scrambled physical and abstract images with elliptic referrals to other associations persist. Certain stanzas remain mysterious or like a silent film without subtitles, imperfectly understood.

Personal lyrics packed with images from nature celebrate, as does the novel, the love of a man for a woman where rupture, loss, and foreboding of loss are suffused with the sense of beauty that the understanding of such suffering brings. The intimate involvement of the natural order in human affairs is again heard in expressions of pure epiphany as in "March," for example, in the reeling abundance of spring that pushes through all the doors. There is a sudden shock of recognition as to the nature of his art when the poet, who had mourned "blurred with weeping" the departure of his beloved, yearns to be removed from her presence so as to keep her image intact in his creative consciousness. One of the seminal themes in the prose narrative of the poet's role and the meaning of his creativity in relation to values in art and in life is brought to its ultimate culmination in two major poems, *Hamlet* and *The Garden of Gethesmane*. (They are, respectively, the first and last poems of the sequence.)

The "I" of the first line in *Hamlet* stands for the actor playing Hamlet, for the Shakespearean tragic hero himself, for Christ who consents to execute "Thy rigorous conception" and for the poet. The part that the "I" must play is to be understood in Pasternak's interpretation of Hamlet's drama which is "all duty and abnegation . . . he is chosen as the judge of his time and the servant of a more distant time." The analogy with Christ's martyrdom is clear, but it is not until the beautifully worded evocation of Christ's Passion in *The Garden of Gethsemane* that the full meaning of the poet's mission is revealed. He must suffer, as Yuri has suffered, endure losses, personal humiliation, and death, and propagate with the power of his art the dignity of individual man and his independent conscience. The poem moves solemnly as do the several devotional lyrics preceding it that commemorate the ritual of the divine pre-Easter drama, and the air holds the promise of the living presence after death. It seems to reach out to a distant Moscow evening, after the war, as described in the epilogue to *Dr. Zhivago*. Two of his oldest friends, many years after his death, are reading and re-reading the doctor's poems. They are suddenly enveloped in a feeling of peace and happiness as if a very near future of which they are a part will contain a renewed lease on freedom. Was this not a manifestation of the personal resurrection that the poet had attained through his art?

The theme of immortality surges through the entire work. It is announced in the opening scene, a symbol of rebirth arising from death, of the burial of Yuri's mother, Maria Zhivago. The hero's surname conveys the idea of "livingness," renewed life; in the Russian translation of the New Testament the angels' words to the women who approach Christ's open tomb are: "Why do ye seek the living *(zhivago)* among the dead?" The concept still associated with Christ is developed by Yuri's uncle, Vedenyapin. For him, the gospels in which Christ used parables taken from ordinary life, that remained in the consciousness of men for centuries, were the confirmation of immortal communion among all mortals. Yuri is made to speak of the perpetuity of human life in another way. When he is asked by his adopted mother to help her master anxiety in the face of approaching death, he assures her that she would continue to live in others, that her soul would remain in the consciousness of all those who had known her. Thus she would enter the future and become a part of it.

This belief that Pasternak instills in his hero is reinforced by yet another vision of the renewal of man in his post-mortal union with the life of nature. After the mother's death young Yuri sees her in the sky that seems to come close to him and hears her voice again through the melodies of the birds in the meadow. Here, the presence of the Prague poet, Rainer Maria Rilke, whom Pasternak had admired since early youth, and whose influence he freely acknowledges, is almost palpable; it merges with that of the late nineteenth-century Russian scholar, Nikolay Fedorov. The latter enthralled several generations of writers from Tolstoy to Blok with his sweeping conviction of continuous and eternal individual existence. He claimed that men could rule the world in an absolute, divine sense, banish the causes of death from earth, call back the dead to the living and insure thereby the fusion of men and every man with the self perpetuating movement of the cosmos. (Fedorov's work is reminiscent, in turn, of German romantic mysticism, the wisdom of the Upanishads, and primitive magic.) Pasternak also was influenced by his study of eastern religions and the history of primitive man. In the novel, the most decisive statement regarding modern man's equivalent to earlier animistic beliefs, as Vedenyapin explains it, is rooted in history that he thinks did not begin until the advent of Christ. Individual man then stepped into history and made it what it is, that is "centuries of systematic exploration of the riddle of death, with a view of overcoming death."

The importance of *Dr. Zhivago* cannot be overestimated. As a novel it has impressed a disbelieving age with the depth and sincerity of its Christian humanism and denounces the materialism of both East and West. It reaffirms the primacy of the individual and the independence of the creative artist. The tantalizing question remains as to the possible response of Pasternak's countrymen to this wide, free, and powerful work, still inaccessible to a vast majority although it was written for them.

NEW LYRICAL VOICES FROM THE SOVIET UNION

Poetry, like water in the Russian earth, never flows far underground. From the turn of the century, when the symbolists initiated new forms of art in Russian literature, almost every decade has witnessed a revival of poetic utterance. In Russia poetry commands a wider and more receptive audience than anywhere else in the world. Pushkin had made his countrymen aware of their national greatness in a language whose musicality and verbal power had been forged by his own genius. From then on Russian poetry had come closest to recording the heart beat of the country, its ideals, suffering, affirmations, and discontent. By the late fifties new lyrical voices were heard in the Soviet Union that became spokesmen for the post-Stalin generation. The poetry of newcomers such as Evgeny Evtushenko, Andrei

Voznesensky, Bella Akhmadullina, and Joseph Brodsky expressed the restlessness of young men and women who had grown up at the end of the last world war. They were better educated than their fathers and had matured in the comparative relaxation of political control. They now were yearning for wider intellectual horizons, emotional realization and a way of life beyond stereotyped collective images and the bleakness of a world they had not made.

Evgeny Evtushenko (born in Irkutsk in 1933) seemed to embody these aspirations. He began to write poetry at sixteen, made an immediate hit with the long autobiographical *Winter Station* (1956). He intermingles patriotic overtones with the pride of living boldly and freely. In *Prologue* (1957) he expresses the poet's right to rub elbows with everything and everyone in all corners of the world and drink in the various forms of art to which his consciousness was creatively attuned. But to live from direct experience, in the mode of Hemingway, to whom Evtushenko dedicates several poems, to invoke the immediate taste, smell, feel of existence through the sharpness of concrete detail in lyrics now ironic, now tender did not suffice this energetic and exuberant talent. The world excited Evtushenko, not only with its diversity that he conveyed in beguiling images of markets in Paris, London Streets, and plantations in Libya, but also with its political and social conflicts. His was a temperament that was affected by current happenings and it resembled Mayakovsky's civic bent. He eagerly espoused the cause of justice and the vindication of past wrongs in his most famous poem, *Babi Yar* (1961). He puts to shame the invectors of anti-Semitism in the Soviet Union by pointing out that no commemoration has been made to the martyrdom of 34,000 Jews buried alive by the Germans in the Babi Yar ravine near Kiev in 1941. (A simple stone slab was placed there five years later to mark the site of the massacre; in 1976 it was replaced by a bronze monument of eleven figures that include a young mother with her child and a Communist member of the anti-Nazi underground). The poet warns against inhuman bureaucracy in *Stalin's Heirs* (1962) and excoriates fascism in *Snickering Fascism* (1963). He satirizes imperialist American aggression and eulogizes Fidel Castro in *Poems about Abroad* (1963). He became the idol of Soviet youth. The rhetorical style of these poems relied on reiteration, facile versifying, versatile cadences, and powerful but uncomplicated metaphors for effect. They were meant to be declaimed out loud and they integrated admirably with the public image of the poet—bearer of new and important tidings of moral and emotional fulfillment for young Russia. Wherever the tall, handsome, lean limbed, and superbly confident Siberian read his poetry in the West he made headlines and was dubbed the "angry young man from USSR." At home he was looked upon as the leader of the poetic renaissance. This movement proliferated and hundreds of poetry clubs were started across the country. Monthly magazines invited contributions from the new poets (*Youth* with a 160,000 circulation devoted over ten pages to poetry in every issue). The young poets' individual works were being published in first printings of 50,000 to 100,000 copies.

The rise of Andrei Voznesensky (b. 1933) was no less spectacular than that of Evtushenko. His first collection, *The Masters* (1959), won instant acclaim and in subsequent crowded public readings in the Soviet Union and in the West he became known for the mobile, nonconformist candor of his verse. As was Evtushenko, he was considered by the young Soviets an innovator who moved poetry into a range of subjects never explored before. If Evtushenko attracted the Westerners with his physical charisma and provocative political rhetoric, Voznesensky was recognized as a serious modernist, a virtuoso of form whose themes lyricized the reciprocity of cosmic reality and human existence. He represented a return to the creative freedom of the great innovators of the early twentieth century. He is clearly inspired by his mentor Pasternak, and by Mandelstam, for he exhaustively explores the meaning of language by creating assonances, alliterations, manipulated verb roots, word play, and paradoxical metaphors that withhold straight meaning. Where Voznesensky is most original is in the startlingly contracted naked image as in that of the globe, "a watermelon with peel removed," that is not explained or amplified. For thematic content the most interesting poems that give him a prominent place in the contemporary era are to be found in the volumes *Mosaic* (1960), *The Triangular Pear* (1962), and *Anti-Worlds* (1964) that deal with anti-matter, worlds and anti-worlds, reversibility of time, the mystery of outer space. They recall the paintings of Joan Miro, Malevich, Kandinsky, and Paul Klee. These best-known pieces have made Voznesensky a favorite among the Soviet scientific intelligentsia.

A former student of architecture and son of a scientist, young Voznesensky tries to define the role of the lyric poet in the atomic age. He accordingly sets up in *Oza* (1964) a debate between a physicist and a poet in which automation and nuclear fission are discussed in the light of human values. As in all of his work, problems raised are refracted into speculative conjecture that leaves the mind free to withdraw into a private world or take on, as does the author, the challenges of technologically oriented life.

It is perhaps surprising that in a society where science and scientific training have primacy and its specialists are the privileged citizens of the state, Voznesensky alone has imaginatively integrated the sound, shape, and color of technological objects into everyday functions. He is fascinated with the "god damned" machine that spews out artificial fabrics, cliff-clinging motorcycles, rockets, electric trains, and airports. He projects them in complicated imagery that is meant to reflect the complex laboratory process of their initial production.

Second in popularity to Evtushenko and Voznesensky, who seem to complement each other in poetic action was Bella Akhmadulina (b. 1937). She was regarded by numbers of the Soviet literati as the most genuine poet. A native Muscovite of Turkish and Italian origins, she had studied at the Gorky Institute where she met her future husband, Evgeny Evtushenko. She has since been divorced and was married to Yuri Nagibin. Her present husband is a Soviet stage designer, Boris Nesserer. She was first distinguished, in an unprecedented way in the Soviet Union, by Evtushenko's celebration of her glamour and beauty in his early love poems. Since 1955 her work has been published in all the leading magazines. A selection of her brief lyrics in *Struna* (1962) and the longer poem, *My Genealogy* (1964), characterize her writing.

Although the poetry has the look of traditionally rhymed stanzas it is no less modern than Voznesensky's in the inventiveness of alliterations, broken rhythms, and the sophisticated subtlety of metaphor. In contrast to Evtushenko's bombastic manner and Voznesensky's violence, this resolutely feminist poet conveys the excitement of the seemingly ordinary through the prism of delicacy and understatement. Seasons of the year, ordinary objects and common place events, such as a village wedding or a meeting on a street, are made dramatic by the undercurrent of feeling, gentle or perverse, that races through the poem and LOCKS IT IN. She is set apart from others in the poetic use of things. A soft-drink machine, an icicle, a thermometer or a waxed floor establish communication between the inner being of the human self and perceived reality in a code of stammered passwords that touch the core of existence and mute discordant notes into a single vibrant tone. Akhmadulina has been severely criticized in the conservative press for her preoccupation with personal emotions that suffuse her poetry. Since 1964 she has published little and rarely.

Two other outstanding older poets of the avant-garde, Boris Slutsky (b. 1919) and Evgeny Vinokurov (b. 1925) also stress the importance of individual feelings. Both composed within a conservative metrical and rhyming structure, but each offered lyrical and philosophical interpretations of his world that bypassed politbureau injunctions. "The more they tried to shape my mind, the more I wanted to be myself" is one of Vinokurov's typical statements in a poem from his major collection of verse, *World, Music, Characters* (1961-1966), where the embodiment of ideas concretely is less striking than the poet's exuberant exploration of spontaneous verbal utterance. Slutsky wanted to "create out of verse truth and happiness." He wrote more tersely, at times roughly, about the average man's emotions and thoughts about nature, animals, war experiences, and social progress in a representative selection of poems *Today and Yesterday* (1961). His rather formal exposition, possibly due to his legal training, just escapes ideological commonplace by the openness and sincerity of his approach.

It is ironical that Joseph Brodsky, the most apolitical of all the young poets, became internationally known as the victim of a miscarriage of Soviet justice. Born in Leningrad, of a middle-class Jewish family, he left school at fifteen. Then he perfected his knowledge of English, learned Serbian and Spanish, joined the translation staff of the Writers' Union and began to write poetry. A retired secret service policeman denounced young Brodsky (who did not smoke or drink and was rather prudish in his personal behavior) as a "corrupting" influence on the city's hip youth who listened to his poems at drunken orgies. This accusation was supported by some members of the Writers' Union who resented the poet's independence in writing as he pleased and making no effort to have his work published. He was brought to trial at a civil court in March, 1963, convicted for social parasitism, and sentenced to five years' labor on a kolkhoz in the Arctic region where he was assigned to load and transport manure.

Petitions for his release from such luminaries as the famous children's writer, Kornei Chukovsky, critic and writer Samuel Marshak, and Dmitri Shostakovich, affidavits from his employers vouching for the superior quality of his translations and a transcript of the Kafkaesque court sessions were smuggled abroad where they sparked off indignant protest among Western intellectuals. Twenty months later, Brodsky was allowed to return to Leningrad. His poems began to circulate in Samizdat and were published in Russian and other languages abroad where critics recognized his unusual talent. In 1972, the thirty-two-year-old writer, acclaimed by Anna Akhmatova as the "greatest living Russian lyricist," was officially served notice of expulsion from the USSR. He left for the United States where he is now teaching Russian literature at American universities.

It was probably less the alleged offense of refusing "to fulfill his citizen's duty of working for the building of Communism" and maintaining his right to live simply as a poet that scandalized officialdom than the content of his "decadent" poetry that is alien to the Soviet ethos and therefore considered intolerable. Brodsky's early and astonishingly mature work described the inevitability of loss, life's many horrors, emotional ambiguity and the isolation of self that he approaches, as Blok put it, from within a poet's creative tranquility and in "secret freedom." He seems to be writing for no one but himself and he dares the reader to follow him across the flamboyance of baroque constructions, extravagant exercises in assonance and alliterations in a variety of meters and rhymes, hypnotically repetitive sound

effects that suddenly break into "dead pan" lines, and to share
with him musings on the human condition. Sadness emanates
from the many poems, some of which are ironic, some lyrical,
some mundane in tone. They reveal the small private deaths,
which Brodsky detects in antique and Biblical myth *(Aeneas and
Dido, Isaac and Abraham)*, the metaphysics of English seventeenth-century poets *(Elegy to John Donne)*, his own fruitless
youth *(Love)*, in empty furnished houses *(The Tenant)*, along
the nerves of memory *(The Funeral of Bobo)*. The sadness is
interrupted, however, with exultant affirmations of the poet's
survival. He who does need to be loved, is chosen to "place the
clear word" at the end, as the Maker had uttered it in the
beginning, or, as in the well-known "Verses on the Death of T. S.
Eliot," the creative artist is only shorn of his mortal envelope by
time but lives on forever in his works.

In exile, Brodsky completed *Gorbunov* and *Gorchakov*
(The Cripple and the *Bitter One)*, an ambitious fourteen cantos
of one hundred lines each speculating on the nature of existence.
As in his earlier religiously colored poems, the influence of Berdyayev, Solovyov, and the Russian existentialist thinker, Leo
Shestov, is clearly felt. From a conversation between two patients in a mental hospital about all their experiences and
dreams a totality is achieved when long suffering Gorbunov
emerges as a Christ figure while his companion is likened to
Judas. The poet's most recent verse has been more restrained in
tone, less aggressively picturesque in the profusion of verbal
techniques. It has also been enriched with the touches of comic
grotesque that seem to derive from the theatre of the absurd.
According to one of his most sensitive critics, George Kline,
Brodsky's present poetic achievement may be compared with
that of his famous predecessors, Akhmatova, Pasternak,
Tsvetaeva, and Mandelstam when they were writing in their
mid-thirties.

The rehumanizing movement of the new poetry that resisted official cant, developed modernist techniques, and turned
to the language of symbol and fantasy to express universal truths
was brought to a halt by 1963. The forces of the opposition
composed of orthodox critics perturbed by Voznesensky's "formalism," less-successful writers jealous of the young poets' astro-

nomical sales, and party watchdogs fearful of the spontaneous and spreading enthusiasm that took over at the poetry readings were waiting for a signal from above to launch a campaign against the liberalizing poetic trends. The signal was given by Khrushchev who released a torrent of scurrilous denunciation against modern painters at the Manege exhibition of art in March, 1963. Days later young writers were subjected to a similar treatment. For seven months the "starry boys," the "beatniks" were vilified in officially organized literary meetings across the country and in the press for the mediocrity of their "overpraised, unrealistic" verses. Evtushenko, who had just published in Paris, without Soviet permission, a part of his "Precocious Autobiography" that disclosed some difficult conditions in Russia but also opted for international coexistence in the arts, was severely reprimanded for his dangerously unpatriotic behavior and summoned home. Deprived of foreign travel privileges he was "invited" to spend some time in his native Siberian region. Voznesensky was sent to an industrial plant in Vladimir and forced to print a recantation of his "past errors" in *Pravda*. Poetic recitals, in number and size of attendance, were severely curtailed.

Still, the avant-garde poets continued to publish. *Stolen Apples* by Evtushenko (1968) contains powerful love lyrics; in *Glance* (1972) Voznesensky's disclosures of his emotional world are no less effective in the use of audacious comparisons and exciting auditive effects. But the heady creativity and sense of freedom lost fire. Evtushenko has been downgraded by the progressives as a mouthpiece of the regime for his publicist verses against China and the Chilean junta. He has antagonized university circles in the West by siding with the Kremlin in the Sinyavsky and Daniel trials.

At a 1972 recital of his verses in Moscow, Andrei Voznesensky was still magnetizing a carefully selected intellectual and official elite with his powerful actor's voice. He teased meaning out of cunningly inverted metaphors and kept the audience bedazzled while playing the dangerous game of complying with censorship and fulfilling his talent with his satirical thrusts at the vicissitudes of daily Soviet living. But the muffled and cautious protests had lost the brashness and youthfulness of the earlier poems and Voznesensky now admits that in the Russia of the seventies there is no place for the liberal-minded poet.

REHUMANIZED IMAGES OF SOVIET SOCIETY

During the 1960s there was a movement toward a freer authentic prose literature. Debate and discussion between liberal and party aligned opinion, instigated by the "thaw," continued to favor ideological manoeuverability that did not exist in other areas of Soviet life. Official vigilance was still in force but reprimands to recalcitrant writers were rarely followed by a suspension of publishing rights. Numbers of highly placed progressive critics in the Writers' Union, on editorial boards of *The Literary Gazette, Youth,* the powerful *New World* where Alexander Tvardovsky had been reinstated as editor-in-chief, imparted a sense of independence and flexibility to the antiestablishment literary minority. Among them such talented writers as V. Nekrasov (b. 1910), Y. Nagibin, V. Bykov (b. 1924), V. Tendryakov (b. 1923), Y. Bondarev (b. 1924), V. Aksyonov (b. 1932), and Y. Kazakov (b. 1927) were rebelling against prescriptive rules with an aesthetic that intended not to change the image of Soviet society but to humanize it. They wanted to restore to literature its normal function of exploring the human condition in the sphere of personal feelings and inclinations. They were, generally speaking, wary of the public domain and emphasized personal primacy. A dominating theme was the search for truth, an intensely subjective truth that sustains or destroys the individual within his inner world. In the most representative and best known writings this truth is revealed when the hero is drawn into a struggle with the vicissitudes of his destiny.

In *Kira Georgievna* (1961), Nekrasov created a new type of Soviet heroine. She is a somewhat scatterbrained and emotionally unstable sculptress who finds time for amorous dalliance with her young boy model between the obligations of a solid marriage with an older man and her work. At eighteen, she had fallen in love with a young student, Vadim, who was falsely arrested a year later. He was released after Stalin's death from prison camp and renews his intimacy with Kira that is soon broken off when she becomes bored with his seriousness and concern for his own wife and child. Western critics were quick to single out Vadim as the first innocent victim of Stalinist terror depicted in fiction, who retained throughout the twenty-year ordeal of his imprisonment, his integrity and will to live. The burden of the story, however, rests on Kira's own analysis of her loves and lost loves that is recorded by the author with detachment and consummate irony. It reveals an "Emma Bovary" oblivion to all but her own sensuous longings, reflected, as in Flaubert's novel, in the illusory images that Kira builds of the three men around her.

Aksyonov's *Starry Ticket* (1963) voiced the protest of Soviet adolescents against their parents' conformist, boring lives. Exciting experiences, similar to those in Salinger's *Catcher in the Rye*(published in the Soviet Union in 1960), are developed in the fast-paced activities of four seventeen-year-old Moscow dropouts (three boys and a girl) who go off to the Baltic coast where they lead a hobo-like existence working on fishing boats. The short novel was castigated by conservative critics who were shocked by the runaways' crude, outlandish language, peppered with profanity, American slang, and technological terms, that encoded rejection of establishment cant. They also professed dismayed concern for the misguided youth looking for an "impossible" self-realization when their leaders offered them "heroic" adventures building communism at construction centers. The teenagers' break for freedom is led by Dimka. His restlessness reflects that of his twenty-eight-year-old brother, Victor, a successful scientist, and a major narrator of the story. The fact that his brother who is about to become a party member is tormented by the lack of opportunity for individual research and, like Dimka, longs for a fuller intellectual life is only brought to the boy's awareness in a concluding metaphor which explains the title of the work. After Victor's death in an airplane crash, Dimka looks at a segment of night sky framed by his brother's window that is pierced with a star as a railroad ticket is punched with a star-shaped hole by the conductor's clipper.

Bondarev tackled the demobilization problem of his own

generation in *Silence* (1962), a somber and terse account of a decorated young officer's attempts to regain a civilian foothold in postwar Moscow. It is presented entirely through Sergei Vokhmintsev's personal perceptions. The story takes on additional power and intensity when it becomes clear that the impetuous, straightforward, morally courageous hero is bound, by his very qualities, to lose out to the cynical indifference and shabby ambitions of his milieu. The drama of his situation resembles that of Dostoevsky's Raskolnikov in its isolation and spiritual suffocation. In the Western view, the story verges on melodrama when certain confused and unaccountable incidents lead to Sergei's dishonorable dismissal from the Institute of Mines where he is enrolled, and to his father's iniquitous arrest. But according to Paustovsky, who commended *Silence* as "an act of high civic courage," Bondarev was only exposing Stalinist terror. Sergei was forced to become a common laborer in the provinces and the last impression of him, his head bent in the "silence" of defeat and solitude, is that of the tragic waste of human potential.

Tendryakov is haunted by the presence of evil in man that he sees made up of self-deceptions, ambiguities, cowardice, and rationalization. He creates situations, as in one of his most popular stories, *The Trial* (1961), where the main protagonist is given the latitude of a moral choice that would cut through conventional wisdom and compromise to the truth. A veteran peasant hunter, Semen Teterin, his friend, an army surgeon, and Dudyrev, head of the local forest industry are bear hunting when a young bystander is accidentally shot. It is up to Semen, who did not fire but found the fatal bullet, to name the guilty man. Semen destroys the evidence that would have exonerated his friend and perjures himself. He fears reprisal from above if he were to tell the truth, and he is convinced that the examining magistrate would not sentence the highly placed bureaucrat. Ironically enough, it is the ruthless and aggressive Dudyrev, in his insistence on sharing responsibility for the murder with his fellow hunter, who shows the moral integrity that the old peasant, in his agony of soul-searching, was unable to summon. The case is dismissed for lack of conclusive proof but, in the understated manner which is Tendryakov's forte, the timid, muddleheaded peasant who thinks that "all people are bad and violate the truth" is made to feel the deepest guilt. In *The Trial* the author searches for moral purity by means of serious, implicitly didactic writing where the sense of humanity remains obstinate and strong.

Y. Trifonov (b. 1927) was first known as a twenty three-year-old Stalin Prize winner for his novel, *The Students* published in 1950). (The plot is centered on the hero's morally difficult decision to criticize his professor publicly for cosmopolitan attitudes.) For twenty years, Trifonov has gradually strengthened his gift for objective and authentic realism in stories that portray psychological and emotional difficulties in the mores of the professional class in Moscow. He gained popularity with a short novel, *The House on the Embankment* (1976), that openly espouses a cynically passive accommodation to the system. The hero willfully remains "a nobody" to advance safely in his career without feelings of responsibility or guilt. The radically subversive theme that unaccountably eluded the censor, must have touched a living Soviet nerve. The issue of the journal, *Friendship of Peoples*, where the novel appeared was sold out within hours and could only be obtained at fabulous black market prices.

There was a new wave of war novels, among them Bondarev's *Last Salvos* (1960), *Alive and Dead* by K. Simonov (1963), and Baklanov's *July, 1941* (1965). They were distinguished less for artistic merit than the forceful depiction of the horrors of war and found perhaps their most compelling spokesman in V. Bykov. He was preoccupied exclusively with the phenomenon of military combat as a monstrous assault on the human psyche and instills something of Tolstoy's wonder and apprehension in his study of various forms of cruelty (*The Dead Do Not Suffer*, 1966). In another novel, *Krugliany Bridge* (1969), man is reduced to his former state of savagery under pressures of modern warfare and the inhumanity of the Stalinist regime. Is a human being redeemable in the light of absolute values under these circumstances is the question posed in Bykov's starkly graphic novella, *Sotnikov* (1969). As in *The Trial*, Bykov suggests that man is offered the latitude of a moral choice and, therefore, is redeemable.

Rybak and Sotnikov are White Russian partisans sent out

to get food in a German-occupied village. They are caught, interrogated, and about to be executed when the offer is made to save their lives if they join the military police force. Sotnikov refuses. Rybak yields, and his first job is to hang his fellow partisan. After the hanging he attempts suicide and fails. He is then forced to become a collaborator. Rybak is a career officer who has been trained in the strategy of foiling the enemy by all available means. The act of treason, for him, spells immediate survival that presages the resumption of combat later on. It is the urge to go on fighting that provokes his anger at the severely wounded Sotnikov who caused their capture. In another disclosure of his inner self, he hopes for the death of his comrade, the only witness to his betrayal.

For Sotnikov, a teacher and a civilian, these equivocalities do not exist. He feels that any compromise with the enemy is a crime that cannot be justified by the extremity of the situation. He knows that his conviction stems from a personal moral code and he wonders, when the other asks for the pardon that is not given, whether he has the right "to demand of others what he demands of himself." Despite great physical pain, Sotnikov experiences, in the last harrowing moments, a joyous existential affirmation of his life in the presence of death through his freely made choice.

Some of the long-suppressed short stories by Andrei Platonov (1899-1951) were reprinted in *The Fierce and Beautiful World* (1966). They established the writer's reputation for stylistic originality and humanitarian concerns. A railwayman's son and Red Army soldier in the Civil War, he began to write in 1922 and joined the idealistically Communist Pereval group. He wrote stories describing the rhythm of obscure lives, with a variety and richness of colloquial idiom, that did not harmonize with officially propagated Soviet reality. A caricatural picture of the dismal effects of collectivization on rural inhabitants *(For Future Use*, 1931) brought on Fadeyev's savage denunciation of "this agent of the kulaks." His works were almost completely banished from print and it was not until he had become a war correspondent that he was able to publish a postwar-theme story, *The Homecoming* (1946). One of its readers, Joseph Stalin, called it "scum" and his name disappeared again. Platonov left a considerable legacy of unpublished short fiction and one long novel. He died poor and ill as the custodian of the Moscow Literary Institute Building which for many years constituted his only contact with his fellow writers. This is the kind of irony that pervades his best pieces.

In *Homecoming*, for example, the conventional exultation of a soldier's return to his wife and children after the long war, is ironically undercut by the fact that both have been unfaithful. Even more subtly flavored with irony is his best-known story, *Fro* (1943). It shatters another Soviet piety when a Soviet citizen's zeal to serve the state and further his professional ambition cannot withstand the deeper private imperative of physical longing and love.

A fresh regional voice was sounded in the minor talent of V. Solukhin (b. 1924) who was enamoured of the countryside in the deep interior of central Russia. He describes the landscape and peasant life with no apparent bias, in a somewhat old-fashioned lyrical idiom. His way of writing recalls that of Prishvin. He expresses a sense of being in deep relation with the tangible world. Woods, the river, a tree in the field, and the unpretentious village inns where he stops for the night elicit unhurried, meandering sketches of his journey as in *Lyrical Stories* (1962). The more poetized passages celebrate nature's beauty and quotidian human routine but at the center there remains a disconcerting emptiness of human tensions.

Vladimir Kaverin whose timely response to contemporary Soviet problems has been frequently reflected in his fiction produced three smoothly written, engagingly plotted novellas in 1966—*A Piece of Glass*, *The Double Portrait* and *Slanting Rain*. The latter is perhaps best known and is of particular thematic relevance to the liberalizing fiction trends of the sixties. It is a psychological study in which Kaverin introduces a mature, politically active, and sensitive Soviet woman who has lived and suffered and is now beset by emotional conflicts with her mentally inflexible adolescent son. What appeared as an unbridgeable parent-children gap in *Starry Ticket*, Kaverin now explores from the older generation's side that has preserved, in Alexander Kron's words, "an emotional literacy." In this story, it is a stronger emotional force that combats external adversities rather than the adamantly negative attitude of the young who remain "cool" to the world of feelings in the modern scientific age. Kaverin suggests that young people become emotionally blighted in every technologically developed society, not only in totalitarian Russia.

Both Nagibin and Kazakov, the most apolitical and non-didactic writers of the decade, have been acknowledged as present masters of the small short story. They have reinstated Chekhov's formula of projecting the seemingly trivial, brief, intensely private emotional happening that in a sudden seizure of awareness illuminates and transforms the commonplace.

Their sketchily depicted characters are drawn for the most part from marginal areas of society. In some stories an outcast, or an off-beat personality, is flooded with fear. A typical example of Nagibin's creative maturity is contained in *Before the Holiday* (1961) that analyzes the psychological upheaval of a very young girl who has just reached puberty and is caught in a tangle of physical and psychic sensations. However, the effect of a magnificently pungent last line when she is overcome by a new and fearful feeling that "her whole being may become a burden to her" is blunted by some excessive descriptive padding of setting and people. This is Nagibin's persistent weakness. He frequently insists on burdening the narrative with superfluous background material until the action seems to have spun out from under him.

Kazakov, in contrast, is economical in the precisely plotted movement of the story and by far the more persuasive verbal artist. He is extremely deft in creating a subtle accord of poetic images with the surrounding landscape that produces a mood now poignantly lyrical, now instilled with gentle melancholy. An occasional rapture in tone recalls Paustovsky to whom Kazanov has dedicated one of his books. *On the Island* (1966), that has been called a minor Soviet classic, explores a spontaneous love between a man and woman. In a routine visit to an island in the North Sea, a thirty five-year-old married inspector is attracted to the young woman director of the meteorological station. In the description of one day and one night that these two rather ordinary and bored people spend together, Kazakov suggests a rich complexity of erotic experience that taps at elusive sources of emotional being. As in Bunin's masterpiece, *The Sunstroke*, whose similar plot may have inspired the Soviet author, the reentry into reality is sudden and sure. A typical ending that avoids the sense of loss with an unexpected deflection, the hero, the next morning, in the cabin of a ship taking him back to Arkhangelsk, recalls to the lulling sound of the waves, the brief adventure that has already taken on the remoteness of a dream.

Avant-garde writers, in the 1960s, concerned with the individual's subjective response to social and moral pressures, became emancipated from the simplistic anti-Stalinist patterns of the previous decade. For the first time since the 1920s, a disengagement from state dictated portrayals of collective life allowed writers to record the complexities and ambiguity of the human situation.

This literature, however, dependent almost entirely on native sources, must be considered on its own terms. The serious and honest approach to man's emotional and spiritual needs, with a hankering after old fashioned virtues, was clearly inspired by the Russian classics. In their manner of writing however, Tendryakov, Aksyonov, Kazakov and others adhered to the principles of nineteenth-century realism that had been adopted by Socialist Realism. They took a "realistic" view of the world as an external phenomenon governed by rational and logical concepts of time and space. As a result, concepts of character, plot, psychological analysis were unilinear. These writers remained isolated from their own native early modernist movement and the experimentation in techniques, form, modes of thought in twentieth century art outside the Soviet Union. There seemed to exist a relatively imperfect awareness in the Soviet writing community of the breakthrough that the great writers of contemporary literature had made in the exploration of the worlds of self on multiple levels of being.

INSTANCES OF MODERNISTIC WRITING

The discovery of new forms of reality and its pluralism was not entirely absent from the Russian literary scene. The Western reader brought up on the modern symbolism of Thomas Mann,

Kafka, Joyce, Virginia Woolf, Musil, and Sartre would feel at home with the singularly un-Soviet approach to modern man that marks the short pieces of A. Bitov (b. 1937), a late fictional extravaganza by Valentin Katayev, and Mikhail Bulgakov's two posthumous novels.

In two stories from *Druggist's Island* (1968), Bitov deals with alienation. In one an adolescent is placed on trial for his shiftless work habits *(The Lodger)*. In the other, a widower is unable to "take in" his wife's death *(Infantiev)*. In the boy's harrowing tram rides across a city he perceives windows opened on other people' lives and sees objects dissolving and changing into human shapes; through Infantiev's other world visions in the cemetery, Bitov traces a gradual loss of contact with external reality. The final experience on the split level of consciousness in both stories that culminates in the whirling confusion of an inner world is described with Kafka's objectivity and his taste for low-keyed, concrete language.

Katayev is a writer whose career, like that of Ilya Ehrenburg, for example, has reflected shifting political moods. The exuberant satire of the relatively tolerant twenties (*Embezzlers*, 1926, and *Squaring of the Circle*, 1928 (a hilarious comedy in vaudeville key on Soviet housing conditions) was followed by a long novel, *Time Onward* (1932), an apparently sincere, glowing account of a construction project. In 1948, the author was obliged to rewrite a war novel on underground resistance that in the party's view did not sufficiently acknowledge the partisans' debt to Stalin's leadership. After a long silence, Katayev may have decided, in the comparatively liberal climate of the sixties, to redeem his artistic independence with *The Holy Well* (1966). It is less novel than autobiography, and the first impact on the reader is of the enjoyment the author had in writing it. The initial "take-off" for this zestful adventure of the mind is made by a hospital patient who is put to sleep by the nurse and wakes up with his wife in paradise. This is followed by Proustian penetration into memory. It is a surrealist mosaic of travelogues, dreams, satirical sketches, and an occasional love story. From Soviet paradise, the narrator makes a pilgrimage to the United States to visit a woman he had loved as a seventeen year old. With a certain naïve insistence (but not for the Soviet reader) on

modern metaphysics, Katayev cuts the flow of immediate perceptions back and forth between object-subject transformations
when he feels the analogy between himself and a car, a hotel, a
department store, or discovers while looking at an artificial duck
in a Houston hotel lobby pond that "man has the magical ability
to become for an instant what he is looking at." The poetic and
philosophical exploration into consciousness is occasionally interrupted with satirical barbs directed at the United States, and
artfully merged with Soviet reality in living metaphors, designated by Katayev as a "new system of signals," These metaphors
such as the absurd TV antics of a "world famous Russian eccentric" (Krushchev) or the talking cat trained to speak at banquets
(as writers were forced unnaturally to write to order) obliquely
reflect the apprehensions for the future of an enlightened intellectual in Russia.

A vastly more powerful satirist and one of the most unorthodox Soviet writers was rediscovered at the peak of destalinization in 1962 when a rehabilitation committee was appointed to
study and edit the unpublished manuscripts of Mikhail Bulgakov who died in 1940. This led to the publication three years
later of *The Theatrical Novel* (translated as *Black Snow*), a
magnificently vitriolic take-off on the sacrosanct Moscow Art
Theatre and its world-famous director. Konstantin Stanislavsky
is shown as a vain old tyrant feeding on the adulation of his
fawning, intellectually pretentious, hypocritical votaries. It is a
short semi-autobiographical novel that hinges on the attempts of
a fledgling writer who has fallen in love with the theatre, to have
his first novel adapted for the stage. Bulgakov had a similar
experience having his play, Molière, produced. The creative torment in the constant rewriting of the PLAY at the bidding of the
"great man" reflects the author's four year running feud with
Stanislavsky while *Molière* was being prudently cleansed of any
possible likeness between Stalin and Louis XIV. *Black Snow* is
undoubtedly a form of revenge, that Bulgakov realized could not
be published, for the failure of *Molière* that was closed at the
end of a week's run. Whatever pathos was first generated by the
young writer's near despair and thoughts of suicide is dispelled
by the rampant satirical spirit of the novel. No one is spared.
Absurdities such as Stanislavsky's self-protective devices against

germs, the ossifying effect of the famous "method" on acting, and the backstage in-fighting for power and prestige are staked out in scenes of subtle irony or rolling burlesque.

The second, more-substantial novel, *Master and Margarita*, that Bulgakov had been writing during the last twelve years of his life was serialized in two issues of the liberal magazine, *Moskva*, in 1966 and 1967. This work, that placed Michael Bulgakov alongside Boris Pasternak among "the greats" in Soviet literature, was immediately translated into English by Harper and Row who had successfully bid for the unexpurgated text. The Grove Press editors used the censored *Moskva* version that was cut down from the original by some 23,000 words. Some of the deletions point rather comically to the sexual prudishness of the censor; others affirm the contemporaneousness of a text that at a twenty-six-year remove contains subject matter in a subversive framework that was still considered too inflammatory to handle. To wit: currency speculation, jewelry hoarding, shops stocked with imported goods that can only be purchased with foreign money, the fear of arbitrary arrest.

The action starts when Satan, here known by his medieval name, Woland, arrives in the Moscow of the thirties with two demonic companions in humanoid form, a naked red-haired vampire with decaying breasts, and Behemoth, a huge black talking tomcat who smokes cigars, sports a white bow tie, and a deadly Browning revolver. In the mild, Turgenev-like, opening scene, Berlioz, senior editor of a highbrow literary magazine is seated on a park bench talking to his tame poet, Ivan Homeless, about Christ. He is admonishing Ivan for having written a poem about the mythical figure as if he had existed when he is interrupted by the elegantly dressed Woland. Woland proceeds to affirm the existence of Christ (and therefore his own) in a foreign accent. To give proof of his powers to the two respectable atheists, he predicts that Berlioz would not attend a scheduled meeting that evening because his head would shortly be cut off by a woman. Within the hour, the editor is decapitated when he is struck down by a tram driven by a woman.

For the next four days, Satan and his minions indulge in a necromantic spree of Gogolian exuberance and overabundance that transforms the city into pandemonium. Disarray escalating into hysteria reigns among bureaucrats, administrators, restaurant keepers, and the police as disembodied suits of clothing continue to conduct their owners' administrative affairs. Banknotes change into champagne labels. Tenants are burned out of flats by a cat holding a primus stove. One citizen is instantly removed to a great distance; another seeks the refuge of an insane asylum. Finally, magically oiled naked women are transformed into broom-wielding witches. They fly through the moonlit air to a full-dress Satan's ball that is a dazzling display of medieval diabolics drenched in violence and gore. Bulgakov distills the thickly supernatural brew with a comingling of blandishing and shocking devil's antics that sets his satirical machinery in motion. Soviet citizens shaken out of their assigned social roles reveal core traits of selfishness, greed, meanness, and an endemic fear of the authorities. These traits also are caught in such singeing comic lines as the description of a secretary "whose eyes are permanently screwed up from lying" or an official's vociferous protest to "attend an illegal meeting" when he is being carried off to the Satan's ball. The sharpest lashes are reserved for the rank and file of the world of letters that has barricaded itself away from genuine talent in the enclave of mediocrity and material privileges.

We are alerted to the more serious meaning of the richly satirical and immensely entertaining novel by four interpolated chapters that tell the story of the Passion in a pungent realistic style saturated with sensuous images that recall the prose of two other creative rediscoverers of antiquity—Robert Graves and Marguerite Yourcenar. They are chapters presumably are taken from the manuscript of the Master (he has no other name). The Master is a Faustian figure who has withdrawn from the world to grapple with the problem of evil inherent in Pilate's treatment of Christ. Pilate and Jesus confront each other on Pilate's terrace in Judea. The Roman governor is drawn to the modest philosopher from Galilee with no popular following, who has just been physically tortured. During their talk, Jesus succeeds in striking at the root of the Roman's spiritual malaise with the simply stated belief in people's goodness and the eventual disappearance of all coercive power. Pilate's tormented brooding over the justice of the crucifixion, his hallucinations, insomnia, psychosomatic headaches, and the author's invention to have Judas assassinated to expiate his guilt, cast the Procurator's image into a tragic mold. Bulgakov describes Pilate's struggle with his conscience (which refutes the historical charge of political cowardice associated with Pilate's name). A politically ambitious man yet with considerable purity of intellect, the Procurator is perceived by the author as a man of his time, but mature within the conditions of that time. He believes in a man's innocence, but the infallibility of Roman law makes him abide by the decision of the man's own religious community that declares the Galilean philosopher guilty.

The concentric circle of themes widens with the personal story of the Master and beautiful young Margarita who lives in a happy illicit union with him and—what is surely every writer's dream—worships his creative endeavor. She is conceived in the Russian literary tradition of a strong-willed heroine, stranger to all fear. Woland summons her to preside, in the form of a witch, at his ball. She easily and gracefully enters into the Saturnalia with no loss of self-confidence or human compassion. And Woland is impressed by her unswerving loyalty and belief in the Master who had burned the manuscript and become mentally deranged when his novel was rejected for "dragging Christ in." Woland, accordingly, has the unhappy author released from the psychiatric clinic, restores the manuscript for posterity, and unites the couple in "unconditional" peace after death. The novel ends on a romantically Gothic chord. The demonic cavalcade soars out of Moscow and mortal life into moonlit eternity. The two happy lovers and the Prince of Darkness are followed by his retinue, now transformed into splendidly inhuman apparitions of the nether world.

Bulgakov creates relationships between disparate elements that give order and consistency to the seemingly unbridled lunatic whimsy. The pervasive presence of Woland gives the novel a central focus, but the effectiveness of his action is partially defused by the ambiguous function of his sinister powers. Thus, his wicked deeds in Moscow seem to be drained of evil when he treats his victims tolerantly, making the comment that "all people after all are just ordinary people." In addition, Woland awards happiness to the Master and Margarita for creative independence, compassion, and love. In another dramatic moment he obeys Christ's order to free Pilate from the purgatory of repentance by destroying in his mind the very memory of the crucifixion.

It would appear that Bulgakov fails to come to grips in his philosophical meditation with the enigma of coexisting good and evil that haunted Dostoevsky in all his novels. Nevertheless, man's easy surrender to the devils within himself, which is a major theme of this complex work, elicits the author's muffled panic and despair in the final chapter with the outcry: "How sad the evening earth is!" It is a willful echo of Gogol, the master spirit of Bulgakov's satire.

"COUNTRY PROSE" WRITERS

In the introductory article of the *New World* Jubilee issue (1965), Tvardovsky drew attention to the so-called "Country Prose" writers who were strengthening a "denunciatory role" in the hitherto forbidden area of the "tragic" collectivization process. For the first time, they wrote about the immense problems of kolkhoz economy. They dwelled on the depopulation of the villages, the gross mismanagement, the callousness of quota-obsessed district officials, the lack of proper tools and equipment, and the recurring famines. Among these writers are F. Abramov (b. 1920), V. Shukshin (1925-1974), V. Belov (b. 1933), and S. Zalygin (b. 1913). Many had a rural background and were little known in the West. By means of frightening realism, they show the individual "kolkhoznik" as beleaguered, no less than the pre-revolutionary serf, by coercion from above. Abramov writes about his plight in *About and Around* (1963); it is shown during the round of visits to local farmers by the kolkhoz chairman. During one visit, the chairman finds only one well-fed inhabitant, an old man on a pension who cultivates his own plot.

In exhaustive, unembellished narratives that bring an authentic flow of daily rural life but barely qualify as artistic work, main protagonists are picked from the peasant mass. Their difficulties in adjusting to the collectivization process are shown, for example, by the outward acceptance but hidden anger, of a prodigiously able and industrious farmer that Abramov wrote about in *Two Winters and Three Summers* (1968). Outright revolt against collectivization by hoarding grain to feed his own household and the fatherless children of a neighboring family shapes the plot of Zalygin's story *At Irtych* (1964). Belov describes the persistent theft of government property in *Carpenter's Stories.*

Shukshin's stories imply the demoralizing effect of collectivization on human beings. In *Stepka* (1964) a mortally homesick young farmer escapes from the labor camp three months before his term is up and is made well again by the native sounds and smells of the countryside. He then returns to prison willingly for a new sentence. What emerges from these forays into the peasant's mind is the tenacity of the rural traditions of tilling of the earth and bearing and bringing up children. In the Soviet twentieth-century world, the peasant desires most of all to preserve continuity and his own being surrounded by familiar props of family, village, landscape, and his habitual modes of food and work. Despite official assertions to the contrary, the average kolkhoznik, as he is depicted by the "Country Prose" authors, is not infused with Socialist ideology. The sources of his spiritual and moral sustenance, however, remain unclear.

A more fully developed portrait of the Soviet rural inhabitant was treated with equal sympathy and greater insight by a far superior artistic talent. Two short works by Alexander Solzhenitsyn, *One Day in the Life of Ivan Denisovich* (1962) and *Matrena's Home* (1963), illuminated and widened the scope of Kolkhoz literature. Alexander Solzhenitsyn was born in 1918 in Kislovodsk, a summer resort in the Northern Caucasus. Brought up in great poverty by his widowed mother, he graduated with a physics and mathematics diploma from the University of Rostov-on-Don. He served as an artillery officer in World War II and was twice decorated for bravery in action. In February 1945 the secret police intercepted one of his letters to a school friend that criticized Stalin's weakness in the first phase of the war. Solzhenitsyn was arrested, stripped of rank and medals, and sentenced to eight years of hard labor. He was released from the concentration camp in 1953 and was ordered to remain in perpetual exile in Central Asia. When a malignant tumor, developed in the camp, brought him near death, he was admitted to the Tashkent cancer clinic and was cured. In 1956, the Military Section of the Superior Court annulled the original criminal charge in his case and he was allowed to return to European Russia. All the while he had been secretly writing. *One Day* was completed in 1958. But it was not until the public arraignment of Stalin's crimes at the 22nd Communist Party Congress in 1962 and Tvardovsky's declaration at that meeting of the need to recruit literary forces for the formation of anti-Stalinist sentiments, that Solzhenitsyn ventured to send the manuscript to the *New World*. He could not have chosen a more propitious moment. The editor knew that official permission was necessary to have this controversial work published. He therefore sent the manuscript to Krushchev, who was in the midst of his destalinization program, with the canny suggestion that more political gain would be accrued by printing the novel in *New World* than risking its appearance abroad. Also, because Solzhenitsyn expressed his anti-Stalinism, the work appealed to Krushchev, who desired support against Stalin as well. He personally authorized the publication with no deletions.

The great originality in this almost documentary record of eighteen hours between reveille and lights-out in a Siberian prison camp is the presentation of the story exclusively from the point of view of Ivan Denisovitch Shukhov. We live with him and through him the dreadful ordeals that he and the other prisoners experience daily in a struggle for sheer physical survival. His unemphatic realistic account of them ends on the thought that he had had "a pretty lucky day." He did not freeze to death on the job in the 28-below-zero weather. He had not been thrown into a solitary cell in which most inmates died. He had not been arbitrarily beaten by a guard. He was afforded a moment of exquisite joy from three puffs on a cigaret butt. And the boss surprisingly gave him an extra piece of bread for building a wall that stayed his usual feelings of hunger. He does not question the injustice of his sentence, the stupid cruelty of the jailers, or the squalor and misery of the camp's subhuman existence anymore than his fellow peasants "outside" reflected on the validity of the kolkhoz system. Ivan submits to his imprisonment as the Russian peasant has always accepted the hardships of existence. He is canny and observant enough, however, to take advantage of any lapses in official surveillance to help himself or another even more bereft member of his work brigade.

The innate generosity and sensitivity to others and the sense of moral preservation and dignity that keep Ivan from the temptation of bribing or being bribed to obtain another bit of food or a smoke, seems to endow him with superior individual traits. Despite the camp's endemic indifference to a work ethic, Ivan, in addition, continues to feel obligated to do a job well, even under the most adverse conditions; he takes pride in the skillful work of his hands. When he learns from his wife's letter of new, well-paid jobs in carpet painting that lure the men away from the impoverished kolkhoz, he is bewildered. He cannot understand why men would switch from honest hard work to what he suspects is a fraudulent "too easy way" of earning a living. On the other hand, Solzhenitsyn also emphasizes his peasant illiteracy, a certain condescension to reason, that eludes his practicality and the evidence of his senses. (In common with all his village neighbors he believes that God breaks up the old moon into stars and makes another one every month, or else where does the moon go?)

Soviet critics acclaimed Solzhenitsyn's artistic gift and agreed with Tvardovsky that the effect of the novel "is to unburden our minds of things thus far unspoken, but which had to be said, thereby strengthening and ennobling us."

In 1963, however, Khrushchev's agricultural reforms had failed, and he was falling into disfavor. The publication of Solzhenitsyn's *Matrena's Home* this time provoked a severe rebuke in the Soviet press for the author's "lack of understanding of the life of the people" and the un-Soviet characterization of the main protagonist. In contrast to the earlier story it was an explosive treatment of an extremely touchy theme. A description of concentration camp horrors in *One Day* that avoided generalized polemic could be safely shelved by Soviet official opinion as a tragic but temporary aberration of the recent past. The story that followed is an overt indictment of the wretchedness of village life that bred vicious acquisition and brutality. Against it, the old peasant woman, Matrena, observed by a young physics and math teacher living in a corner of her hut, emerges as an embodiment of individualism and spiritual strength. She has been denied a pension or a piece of land large enough to grow food on. Neverthless, the selfless, pure-hearted heroine endures physical privation and poor health with serenity and is always willing to help even those neighbors who contrive to rob her of her last belongings. She lacks the more ordinary peasant attributes of shrewdness, adaptability, and guile that enable Ivan to cope with his environment. She does, however, realize the moral certitudes that constituted the ethos of peasant Russia. That this moral force is still to be reckoned with in Soviet society which is almost evenly divided between an urban and peasant population, Solzhenitsyn unequivocally states in the story's last line:

> We had all lived side by side with her and had never understood that she was the righteous one without whom, as the proverb says, no village can stand.
> Nor any city.
> Nor our whole land.

6 · Literature of Dissent

SAMIZDAT

Human freedom is a precarious enterprise in autocratic and totalitarian countries, and the role of the dissenter who fights for it, has always been an ennobling one. During the last twenty years, a small but vigorous cultural elite has expressed its opposition to the ossified ideology of the state and its coercive prevention of normal intellectual and spiritual development.

By 1966, the Sinyavsky-Daniel court case, followed by other rigged trials of dissident intellectuals, left no doubt that under post-Khrushchev leadership, the halcyon period of liberalization had come to an end. As one result Solzhenitsyn's manuscript for *The First Circle* was seized by the KGB (it was later returned to him) and another novel, *Cancer Ward*, already set in type for publication in the *New World* was dismantled by the order of Konstantin Fedin who was then First Secretary of the Writers' Union. The editor of *New World* refused to endorse all the tenets of Socialist Realism, and he was dismissed in 1969. After his death from illness and chagrin two years later, his magazine was liquidated. In a repressive move that recalled former terrorist tactics, some two hundred persons from academic, literary, and publishing circles were arrested in Leningrad in 1967. They were charged with possession of arms to be used in a revolt against the State. This was followed by a purge of liberal elements in Czechoslovakia in 1968. There were other signs of re-Stalinization. In 1974, the popular writer, Victor Nekrasov, Stalin Prize winner for the wartime novel, *In the Trenches of Leningrad* (a required high-school text), was deprived of publishing rights when he refused to denounce Solzhenitsyn. In a stepped up campaign to do away with ideological troublemakers, new procedures were devised by the Brezhnev-Kosygin regime. Historian Andrei Amalrik, author of a political essay, *Will the Soviet Union Survive in 1984?* (1969) that dooms the Soviet system to eventual disintegration, was sentenced in a pretense of a trial to three years' imprisonment. At the end of his term he was arbitrarily reconvicted and awarded another three years' corrective labor. Enforced exile became another way of felling opposition, as in the case of the physicist, Valery Chalidze, a dissident "zakonnik" (zakon is the Russian word for law) who propagated the thesis that if the government were made to abide by the democratic principles set forth in the Soviet constitution, the party's vitiation of individual rights would disappear. During a lecture tour in the United States, Chalidze's passport was seized by Soviet Embassy officials, his citizenship revoked, and he was refused a return visa.

The brutal repression, however, only served to stimulate and intensify liberal opposition shown, for example, in the changing position of the most headlined dissenter, academician Andrei Sakharov, The father of the Russian H bomb and 1975 Nobel Peace Prize winner caught the attention of the world with his manifesto, *Progress, Coexistence and Intellectual Freedom* (1968). He stressed the need for worldwide cooperation to preserve civilization, and recommended reforms both to Western and Soviet systems in a judicious and objective manner. But four years later, Sakharov exposed in strong, concrete language the Kremlin's social crimes. He pleaded for political prisoners and victims of psychiatric mistreatment. He called for the immediate restoration of intellectual freedom in Communist Russia by the abolition of Glavlit, the omnipotent censorship board of 70,000 full time censors that controls all writing printed in the USSR.

It is almost as difficult to pinpoint all the aspects of Soviet literary censorship as it is to overestimate its power. Reactions to a creative work in the Soviet press that may range from a mild rebuke to a systematic vilification campaign is but the last publicly visible sign of the built-in censorial process. Once the manuscript has been sent to a publishing house or a literary magazine, it is carefully screened, beyond its validity as an interesting and artistic piece of work, for politically controversial or deviationist elements. It is then returned to the editor, more often than not with numerous deletions, mutilations of text or the order for outright rejection. Of course, the Glavlit's stamp of approval also depends on the censor's own personal interpretation of style, mood, dialogue, descriptions. The inner tension of writing in ways acceptable to this kind of vigilance is heightened by the fluidity of the current taboos placed on content. Although the central commitment to Party ideology is constant, recently approved topics may suddenly become prohibited. If the writer does not conform to such changes in the process of his writing, the road to publication will be blocked. It is impossible to determine how much talent was snuffed out or disfigured by Soviet censorship.

Nevertheless, a number of independent literary artists did preserve their creative freedom during the past forty-five years. There was for Mayakovsky, Esenin, Marina Tsvetaeva, the irreversible way of suicide. Others, like Andrei Platonov, Bulgakov, and Anna Akhmatova chose to continue writing but only "for the desk drawer." (Akhmatova's magnificent *Requiem* continues to circulate in typed copies among her admirers in Moscow and Leningrad.) Still others defected and continued to write. Most often, they became "non-returners," who were sent on Soviet mission abroad and asked for political asylum in a foreign country, as did Mikhail Dyomin (b. 1927) and Anatoly Kuznetsov (b. 1931).

Kuznetsov became internationally known for his documentary novel, *Babi Yar* (1966). It seared Russian nerves once more (and more effectively than Evtushenko's famous poem) with the story of the Jewish massacre by the Nazis in the Kiev ravine, and the author's implication that many Russians were secretly in accord with the liquidation of the Jews. In a London interview, in 1969, Kuznetsov referred happily to his voluntary exile that allowed him to speak the truth. He disowned all his previous works, which he claimed had been ruthlessly distorted by the censor. He also described what had been for him, and for most Soviet writers who had achieved some prominence, a common and intolerable collaboration with the secret police. There was hardly anyone among his colleagues, he averred, who was not asked, at one time, to report on "anti-Soviet" activities among his friends.

Some writers even managed to have their manuscripts published, but overseas. They wrote as they pleased and then smuggled the manuscript abroad through foreign correspondents and students, diplomats, sailors, or ordinary tourists. The work might be published either in the émigré press or translated into other languages for production by Western publishing houses.

In 1959 a long essay, *What is Socialist Realism?*, written under an assumed name, Abram Tertz, appeared in the French monthly, *Esprit,* and in the American quarterly, *Dissent;* it provoked wide critical repercussions. In tones of wry Voltairean irony and with the confidence of a specialist in Russian and Soviet literature, the author analyzes the contradictions inherent to the official literary dogma that has dominated Soviet creative writing since the 1930s. The basic Socialist Realism formula contains the concept of an all-embracing ideal goal in the direction of which Soviet life is, unerringly, advancing. The writers are prescribed to fulfill the impossible task of depicting this goal in terms of nineteenth-century realism, that is portraying a "should be" or "will be" future as if it already existed and creating from ideal Communist types, positive heroes who are supposed to represent actual Soviet Man. With more imaginative boldness and wit, Tertz shows up what had already been described by Ehrenburg, Pomerantz, Bergholtz, and other progressive writers. He exposes the artistic improbability and authorial hypocrisy in the creation of hagiographic images of heroes.

Tertz proposed that all attempts at realism in Soviet literature be abandoned in favor of a new phantasmagoric art. The author claims that by doing so writers could project the inner realism of truth. Such an art would correspond best "to the spirit of our time." He suggests that works of E. T. A. Hoffman, Dostoevsky, Goya, Chagall, and Mayakovsky be used as models of the absurd, the fantastic, the bizarre as well as Bulgakov's novel, *Master and Margarita,* which captures "the spirit of our time." It is the spirit of the "Dark and magical night of Stalin's dictatorship" in a world of dramatic hyperbole where the incredible reality of purges, persecutions, assassinations, pervasive fear, death, attains the supernatural level of "miracles, sorcery, perfidy, artifice."

Tertz illustrated the character of phantasmagoric art in a very brief novel, *The Trial Begins* (1960), in *Fantastic Tales* (1961) and in a longer novella, entitled *Lyubimov (Makepeace Experiment* in English) that was published in 1964. Immediately after the Sinyavsky-Daniel trial, *Encounter* brought out the last story, *Pkhentz*, that soon appeared in all the major languages and achieved a *succès de scandale.*

The title of the first work, refers to the "arraignment" of Russia's privileged class by the Socialist émigré writer, Alexander Herzen in 1855. It is a trenchant satire of the Soviet elite at the moment of the so-called "doctors trial" in the last years of Stalin's life. The episodic narration juxtaposes, in Andrei Bely's cinematic style, the feelings and gestures of the Public Prosecutor, his wife, and her lover in a marital triangle. It emanates the decadence, lack of communication and pulverization of human concerns that saturated T. S. Eliot's brilliant *Cocktail Party.* That comedy, however, seems like an urbane exercise in social manners compared to the vicious interplay of grabs for power through physical beauty, sex, or political manipulation that motivates the main characters. In the author's somber view, independent action, whether morally debased or pure, such as an adolescent's open defiance of Marxist dogma, is bound to fail in the Soviet climate of suspicion, hypocrisy and fear. (Man will only find personal freedom in resorting to the fantastic and the magical that invade the familiar with other irreal orders and transform subjective reality.

In *The Icicle*, a story haunted by the fear of arrest, the hero steps out of reality when he is endowed, in a somewhat clumsy imitation of E. T. A. Hoffman's device, with the gift of clairvoyance. He also has visions of himself in many guises and many lives and is frightened by the recurring prophetic image of his beloved Natasha killed by an icicle dropping off a Moscow roof. He participates, as does the hero in Dostoevsky's *Dream of a Ridiculous Man*, at his own funeral. The sense of doom that emanates from these revelations is lifted when he is restored to a normal state after Natasha's death. In *At the Circus* Konstantine learns the art of a circus magician that releases him from a stifling mundane life. Turning to crime for additional excitement, he accidentally kills his teacher, thereby losing his magical skills, and dies in a spectacular attempt to escape from prison. Tertz's sensational, anti-science-fiction tale, *Pkhentz*, symbolizes man's profound alienation from time and space. It seems to have been grafted on Kafka's great story, *Metamorphosis*, for a similarly startling treatment of the theme. A creature from another planet, marooned on earth a long time ago who has a treelike body branching off into multiple hands and feet, survives in utter loneliness in the guise of a Moscow accountant. He is nourished by the hope of rediscovering his landing place on this planet that will enable him to return to his native universe. In a harrowing scene that allows the author to exaggerate his own rather crude and frequent emphasis on the sexual act (possibly meant as a prodding of reigning puritanism in Soviet fiction), the hero is cornered by a woman who is attracted to him. He is repulsed beyond measure by the naked human body that he finds so hideously different from his own, and he finally rejects her.

Release from burdensome individual freedom, is the theme of *Makepeace Experiment*. Men readily submit to governance by authority, mystery, and miracles. This utopia is created when the hero, Lenny Makepeace, former bicycle mechanic, is hit on the head with a magical book (another E. T. A. Hoffman touch) and acquires the power of thought control over all the inhabitants of a provincial Soviet town. He makes them believe, without coercion, in a mythical reality conceived in his own dreams. They imbibe his aspiration for world peace that will emanate from the town of Lyubimov (renamed Makepeace) under his benevolent rule, partake wholeheartedly in the make-believe, that recalls Gogol's magnificent hoaxes in *The Nose*, of feasting on caviar and champagne that is really toothpaste and water, and allowing themselves to be divested of their hard-earned rubles to be used to paper the walls in the houses of the town elite. The novella may be read as a political fable similar to Voltaire's *Candide*, as a savage take-off on the human condition that recalls Orwell's *Animal Farm*, as a monstrous lampoon on the Stalin-

Krushchev era, or as a philosophical reflection on the frailty of personal perceptions and the illusory quality of power.

Like the rest of Tertz's fiction, *Makepeace Experiment* exposes the imbalance between inner life and the constant world of the public threat which is not clearly defined. There are many exciting passages in his extravagantly nonrealistic form of writing. But it is flawed by an overabundance of surrealist images, protracted macabre or grotesque fantasy, recourse to supernatural devices and an uncomfortably insistent echo of the author's famous fictional forebearers such as Gogol, Dostoevsky, Zoshchenko, Kafka, Poe, and Borgès. The bookish scholar tends to eclipse the artist.

In the early sixties there appeared in France and in the United States, four stories under the pseudonym, Nikolay Arzhak (like Abram Tertz, a slang name for "bandit"). The author's heroes are middle-class Soviet intellectuals haunted by the Stalinist nightmare. In the story, *Hands,* a former Cheka officer is afflicted with uncontrollably trembling hands for serving on an execution squad that used to kill dissident priests. Tertz makes a more subtle treatment of individual and collective guilt in *Atonement.* A man has been falsely accused by his friend, just released from ten years hard labor, of denouncing him. The man is, accordingly, unanimously ostracized, even by his fiancée who turns against him because she cannot endure his ordeal. He realizes that his real guilt is in accepting a system in which ". . . the prisons and the cages are still operating. . . . the prison is within us and we are in it, all of us locked up."

Arzhak's best-known story, *This Is Moscow Speaking,* is a magnificent, full blown satire, perhaps only equalled by Swift in its coiled-in savagery and universal applications of the theme. A Kremlin proclamation sets aside a day when, between six A.M. and midnight, Soviet citizens are allowed to murder each other with impunity. The author's grotesque asides during the shocking actions that follow emphasize the implication that years of legalized state murders have dulled the Soviet public to the moral enormity of arbitrary killings. Is this not also, the author seems to ask, the basic principle of all wars? He concludes with the statement that most citizens renounce the "One Day" privilege not for ethical reasons but because "the State will liquidate those who deserve it."

There was much speculation in the West as to the identity of the two daring, non-comformist authors. Tertz's open break with Socialist Realism, his assumption of the artist's immemorial role of sorcerer and myth-maker and his familiarity with the most sophisticated contemporary writers seemed to place him, for many European critics as a defector or a Russian emigré. Finally, nine years after he had smuggled his first manuscript abroad, the KGB determined that Abram Tertz was the 39-year old Andrei Sinyavsky. He was an established literary critic who wrote sensitive, but wholly acceptable, reviews for *The New World*. Also, he was a member of the Gorky Institute of World Literature and had published scholarly studies on Russian revolutionary writers. Of the thirty critical pieces composed between 1959 and 1965 only two articles were related to his clandestine creative endeavor. One was written about fantasy and reality in science fiction and the other was written in collaboration with the art historian, Igor Golomstock, on the fantastic art of Picasso.

Sinyavsky had been exposed to disillusionment with the Soviet system when he was attending Moscow University. Hundreds of university students had protested against a reign of terror that unleashed an anti-Semitism and anti-national minorities campaign. They joined a movement that according to Brigitte Gerland's account in her memoirs of life at the Vorkuta camp *(Vorkuta (1950-53): Oppositional Currents and the Mine Strikes, 1956)* had generated from a discussion by four Moscow University students in 1948. They were reading Pasternak's long banished poetry that contained the idea that "spiritual freedom is incompatible with social justice" and decided to "make it possible for this kind of freedom to exist in a collective society." Boris Pasternak had held out against compromises with the State and considered it his right to dispose of his manuscripts as he pleased. When Andrei Sinyavsky and Daniel (both had been pallbearers at the poet's funeral) were looking for channels to disseminate their heretical fiction, they may have been inspired by Pasternak's example. Four days after Sinyavsky had been arrested for "spreading anti-Soviet propaganda abroad," Yuri

Daniel, a former teacher, translator of poetry and a children's writer was imprisoned for committing the same "social" crime under the name of Nikolai Arzhak. It was learned at the trial that their writings had been taken to the West by Helen Pelletier Zamoyskaya, daughter of a French naval attaché.

At the three-day trial that was conducted in February 1966 the party served notice on the international community that its hard line dominated the Soviet literary establishment. (Accordingly, members of the Writers' Union, that appointed two novelists to act as junior prosecutors, made vilifying attacks against the two.) Neither writer recanted or confessed and both pleaded guilty. Sinyavsky and Daniel were sentenced, respectively, to seven and five years of hard labor. At the end of his term, Sinyavsky obtained permission to emigrate and is now teaching at the Sorbonne in Paris. He has returned to the field of literary criticism with two extraordinarily perceptive and interesting studies *(Strolling with Pushkin, In the Shadow of Gogol,* (1975). His most recent publication, *A Voice from the Chorus* (1976) composed of some 15,000 entries from bi-monthly letters to his wife from the camp deserves high rank in the annals of Russian prison literature together with Dostoevsky's *House of the Dead* and Solzhenitsyn's *Gulag Archipelago*. Against the chorus of camp voices that break in like concrete fragments of human drama on the author's meditation, he puts to the test the flexibility and convolutions of the human mind, his own mind, as the ebb and flow of multirealities is perceived on the landscape of art, literature, metaphysics. Yuri Daniel remained in the Soviet Union and no longer writes.

The Daniel-Sinyavsky trial and the revived Stalinist tactic of imprisoning writers for their work sparked off a more intensified resistence and consolidated the struggle for a socialist democracy, centered around Samizdat. The Soviet term "Samizdat" that means self-publishers is an ironic take-off on the official acronym Gosizdat—the State Publishing House. During the relatively relaxed censorship of the Khrushchev "thaw" a few anti-Socialist Realism writings were read and circulated privately among trusted friends. A broader, more systematic, and organized literary uncensored press developed during the Brezhnev-Kosygin regime. By the mid-1970s, Samizdat was no longer mentioned in quotation marks. It had produced an impressive output of forbidden literature and documentary material written as Osip Mandelstam puts it, "without permission, out of stolen air." (A small portion of the entire Samizdat production since 1972 has been reproduced in Munich and Ohio State University.) These writings had been typed in numerous carbon copies by successive readers or reproduced in makeshift photocopies and circulated by means of a wide, private network. They compromise creative literature, memoirs, manifestoes, lampoons and epigrams, transcripts of secret trials, treatises on religious and political tolerance and on human rights, open letters, reprints from the Soviet Criminal Code, and reportage from prisons, camps, asylums. As can be seen, this unofficial press concentrates on protests against state abuses and state injustice against artists and proposals for reform. It provides a forum of free opinion in an unfree world for the critically minded, educated Russians who speak of themselves as a corpus of resistance or as "the enlightened one percenters of the population."

The need to keep this public informed about the dissidents' cause, was evidently recognized by Samizdat editors. They published several periodicals, of which only *The Chronicle of Current Events* survived from 1968 until 1972. Then, the editor-in-chief, Peter Yakira, was seized, broke under interrogation and was forced to falsely confess the *Chronicle*'s ties with anti-Soviet émigrés abroad. The periodical was suppressed. The purpose of this bulletin was to secure for the Soviet people the basic democratic rights guaranteed in the Soviet Constitution of 1936 upon which, officially, all Soviet law is based. While *The Chronicle* lasted, its correspondents managed to gain entry to sensitive, maximum security areas from concentration camps to nuclear research laboratories and send in terse, factual reports on prison conditions, racial persecutions, illicit trials, exclusions from the Party, unwarranted arrests that reached opposition circles in major cities, punctually and with speed.

In the last decade, the musical Samizdat—recording the ancient oral tradition of song with the tape recorder—has produced the underground ballad. The seemingly artless rhymed quatrains, sung to the accompaniment of a guitar, are slyly witty, humorous, folksy, sharply satirical. They range from village folk songs to cabaret ditties and songs on daringly subversive themes of anti-bureaucracy, the senseless cruelty of war, concentration camp life, and the daily privations of the ordinary citizen. It is rough masculine poetry that meshes street jargon with concentration camp slang. One of the most gifted balladeers, Alexander Galich (1919-1977) articulated for ordinary people their bewilderment or mute despair at the basic inadequacy and spiritual vacuum of their days. Some of his most acerbic barbs are directed at those who "wash their hands" and remain silent. Like Galich who seemed secure as an established playwright of dull and frequently produced comedies (he was finally exiled in 1974) another even more popular balladeer, Vladimir Vysotsky, is a famous movie star in his official life. Less philosophical than Galich, he appeals to the mass listener with seemingly light banter and broadside humor to disparage the luxurious lifestyle of the Soviet "nobility" and their low grade culture. Bulat Okudzhava published several volumes of poetry, among them *Islands* (1959), *The Jolly Dawn* (1964), and *The Magnanimous Month of March* (1967) that were melodic, and "romanced" in the gypsy song style. He is one of the most musically talented poets and his songs—harsh indictments of Stalinism, chauvinism and war—are nonetheless intimate in tone and confiding. For him there is no private poetry, "all my songs belong to my generation." This may be said of all the outlaw troubadours.

The upsurge of tourism and cultural exchange programs has made it possible for Russians to read Western fiction, articles from Western newspapers and international journals. They can be brought in and translated and are distributed through Samizdat. Conversely, a certain number of Samizdat writings are published outside of the Soviet Union. These printed books often reappear in the Soviet Union and are privately circulated in dissident circles. There exists, however, a certain uneasiness, called "fear of abroad," in handling and reading printed matter "tainted" with a foreign trademark. In case of a house search, as likely as not, it would constitute evidence of a link with "Western Intelligence" and lead to a legal arrest under article 38 (anti-Soviet propaganda) of the Soviet Criminal Code.

The confiscation of home-typed Samizdat material by the authorities, on the other hand, as every well-informed dissident knows, is illegal, since a self-publishing action does not constitute an infraction of Soviet law. Although in point of fact, the Samizdat writer who supports himself with non-literary work in order to compose uncensored and uncompensated literature finds himself in the beleaguered position of a man who lives in a crime-infested neighborhood and takes a calculated risk in venturing outdoors. Nonetheless he does so if only to test his lawful freedom of movement even as it is the habit of the Samizdat author, who does not consider himself an outlaw, to sign his work.

What is the quality and character of this freely creative literary enterprise that for the first time in over forty years has become emancipated from "other directed" controls? An attempt will be made to judge it and to distinguish it from standard Soviet fiction by evaluating two recent, better-known Samizdat novels or novellas that have reached the West.

Two powerful studies of irreversible alienation have elicited critical attention abroad. One is entitled *A No One* (1973) by (Nicolay Bokov); the other is *Faithful Ruslan* (1975), from the pen of the young and talented George Vladimov.

A No One may be summed up as a lonely cry of despair that remains unanswered and unassuaged in the winter of post-Stalin Soviet life. The hallucinations of the only distinct protagonist who has converted himself into a "No One," recall in tone, pitch, and urgency the monologues of Dostoevsky' Underground Man and the Ridiculous Man but lack their lucid articulation. The hero is haunted by the moral evil that stalks his world. He attempts to rupture all commitment with it by divesting himself gradually of external attachments—a wife, a home, friends—only to find that in the isolation of a hole-in-the-wall room he is still pursued by the spector of tyranny, injustice, and pervasive falsehood in his semi delirious dreams. He cannot forget his own practiced and lying compliance with authorities when as a professor of philology he used to offer distorted instruction in his classes. In his endless wanderings along freezing, crowd-driven Moscow streets he has chance encounters with people as indelibly marked as himself. One vivid example is the fawning bureaucrat whose palms are hardened from applauding party bosses; another is the newspaper man who resorts to collecting matchbox covers in order to forget the indignity of writing to command. For the hero, there is no escape. In a series of surreal dreams, he has visions of God, with whom he holds long conversations. When he awakens from them he is convinced that even Jesus has retreated before the inhumanity that holds Soviet society in its grip and that happiness and justice will never again be accessible to him or his countrymen.

No less accusatory than the author of *A No One*, Vladimov describes the life and death of a wolfhound in a swiftly paced narration that has surely not been matched for sensitivity to the mental and emotional states of dogs since Bunin's story, *The Dreams of Chang* (1915). Faithful Ruslan is one of the watchdogs on a construction site in the far north. He keeps the rows of conscripted workers moving in a straight line as they march to the plant from the barracks and back again and overpowers anyone attempting to escape from the compound into the wilderness beyond. The smells, sights, and sounds of the forested winter landscape are evoked with extraordinary acuity through the dog's consciousness. His awareness of an inner world is enlarged to a near human and yet credible dimension in his recurring dreams of a happy existence by the side of an exacting but trustworthy master and in the conflict that rages within him. Ruslan is torn between atavistic instincts to become all wolf again in the freedom of the surrounding taiga and a tenacious devotion to the job that has to be done and in which he exultingly shows his strength, skill, and indefatigability. This highly intelligent animal is made wretched by the consistent human disregard of what he considers a "sacred call to service" that in the world of men, to his bewilderment and confusion, is disregarded for self-indulgence, self-interests, negligence, and drink. His master abandons him, but Ruslan carries on, with no urging or encouragement, until one day he is wounded in the head by a sadistic and bungling guard. He goes off to die alone, away from men, in the solitude of the great forest. The parable of this wise and deeply moving tale refers, as clearly as the talking cat anecdote in Katayev's *Holy Well*, to the difficult if not impossible situation of talented writers in the Soviet Union who have to struggle against incalculable odds to achieve their creative fulfillment.

Satire has been used as an aggressive weapon to curb the intemperance of conservatism and intellectual backwardness ever since Gogol's time and for the most part with sparkling literary effect. Vsevolod Kochetov (1912-1973), editor of the *October* and who conformed to the party ideology in several artistically valueless novels, was the target of a scathingly satirical long short story, *Troubles of Recent Times* or *The Amazing Adventures of Vanya Chmotanov*, signed with a tongue-in-the-cheek flourish by the anonymous author, with the name of the "reborn" Kochetov. The cleverly contrived, fast and hilarious comedy sequence bites deeply into sacrosanct Communist domain.

In the story, reverence for the embalmed Great Leader who is viewed daily by thousands of awed citizens, turns into spirited mockery. An inventive thief, Vanya Chmotanov, blessed in his face and body with an exact replica of Lenin's physique, manages to steal the hallowed Leader's head which he hopes to sell abroad as a collector's item. But the scheme misfires; he discovers, to his chagrin, that the precious loot, made of crumbling cork, disintegrates in his hands. No matter. He is immediately plunged into a more spectacular escapade when the brief closing down of the mausoleum to allow for the substitution of the mummy by an actor generates rumors of Lenin's resurrection from the dead. Vanya rises superbly to the occasion by impersonating the Great Man. For several exhilarating days (until he is caught) he issues wildly unorthodox directives to the credulous Soviet populace.

The Life and Adventures of Private Ivan Chonkin (1975) by Vladimir Voinovich is another satirical enterprise of greater richness and complexity that bristles with malicious jibes at petty bureaucracy of small-town vintage and at the Red Army operation. Disenchanted with his earlier popular, "approved" fiction, Voinovich decided, like many typical samizdat writers, to ignore ideology. As a result, he was expelled from the Moscow Writers' branch of the Writers' Union at the end of the 1960s. Since then, he has been fearlessly perfecting his humorist's gift in a Zoshchenko manner, gleefully exposing pretentiousness and ineptitude on various levels of Soviet hierarchy of which the

Ivan Chomkin tale is the latest and most successful example. The scabrous, somewhat overlong, but exceedingly funny novel is concerned with a simple-minded young soldier who is sent off to guard an old plane that broke down and landed in a field of the Krasnoye village. Niura is the village postal clerk, near whose garden Ivan is sentry. She takes him into her cottage where the young couple share all the domestic chores and the pleasures—albeit somewhat too emphatically—of physical love. His unit seems to have forgotten all about Ivan. He makes friends around and about and the inoffensive idyll would have continued but for the inconvenient event of Hitler's invasion at that particular moment and an overzealous district policeman's suspicion of Ivan's identity. The hero is denounced to the local military headquarters as a White General or possibly a Nazi spy. The situation explodes into farce when a faulty telephone communication is distorted; Ivan is described as holing up with his gang rather than his "girl." A detail of masked and armed men is sent by the authorities to Krasnoye with kerosene bottles that they neglect to ignite, to be thrown at the plane. As they creep up to Niura's cottage, they are disarmed, one by one, by the young couple and locked in the cellar. Voinovich achieves his most comic effects through the dim-witted dialogue between the lower officials in fear of higher authority but still retaining vestiges of imperturbability and pomposity that the protocol of their offices demands. Against the pandemonium of orders and counterorders where everyone from the general down loses his head, the slow but straight-thinking Ivan emerges, surprisingly, as a rather lovable and trustworthy individual.

Arkady Strugatsky reflects somberly on the situation of the writer in a dictatorship in *Ugly Swan* (1967). Arkady Strugatsky, an astronomer, (b. 1925) and his brother Boris, a linguist, (b. 1933) have been collaborating for over twenty years on creating fantastic situations in distant and unknown countries that, following Zamyatin, contain satirical analogies to Soviet reality. Their fiction has reached millions of readers through the black market and hand to hand dissemination. It also appeared, for the most part, in little-known provincial magazines, some of which were closed for publishing the "incorrectly slanted"

Strugatsky writings. This may have impelled the brothers to project in the *Ugly Swans* the hopelessness of genuine creative effort.

The hero of *Ugly Swan* is Victor Banev, a fashionable and entertaining writer. He returns to his home town and lives in a lavish style at the main hotel until several happenings jolt him into a new political awareness. In this nameless city where it has been steadily raining for the last few years, Banev is beaten up by the secret police for interfering with the kidnapping of a leper from a colony just outside the city walls that is supposed to contain insurgent elements. Then, at what seems to be a harmlessly flattering reception at the local high school, the well-known author is assailed by the young audience for wasting his talent on outworn platitudes issuing from a decaying world. After all the children in the city have left their homes to join the lepers, he is charged by the mayor to write an article condemning their behavior. The peremptory order goads Banev into denouncing the sanitation inspector, his constant drinking companion, to his superiors in a malicious outburst of "let them all cut each other's throats." To his disgust, he is awarded the second highest medal. Meanwhile, the insurgent colony takes over the city and on the morning of its victory, the sun begins to shine again, magically destroying the mildewed buildings and rotting pavements that give way to greening grass upon which stride the local children, builders of the new social order. The writer walks toward them, alongside his beloved Diana whom he had never before seen looking so happy. But Banev is beset by inner torment and doubt. He finds it difficult to believe in a new world constructed on the pyre of the old one. Is it possible, he asks himself, to end coercion and violence with still other forms of violence? And would his writer's role be less prescriptive in the burgeoning utopia than under the old system where his cynicism and adaptability have served him well? The last lines are fraught with ambiguity. The hero is caught admiring the shape of new things to come and is at the same time reminding himself of his own former life.

Although Varlan Shalamov entered literature as a poet, he will be remembered for *The Stories of Kolyma* (1969), a semific-tional, semidocumentary work based on his prison camp experiences. He was arrested on the eve of the purges in 1937 and sent to the Kolyma hard labor camp, situated in the farthest northeastern section of Siberia where gold ore had been discovered in 1925.

Shalamov was incarcerated in that frozen wasteland for seventeen years. Upon his release in 1954, he began to piece together the recollections of his imprisonment, which he probably survived only because he became, by chance, part of the camp administration as medical orderly. The somber realism of the narrative does not make for relaxed reading. A more-resourceful writer or one aiming at popularity would have placed his stories into wider fictional space and spared the reader some of the more unbearable close-ups of brutality rendered for greater effect in somewhat dry and factual prose. But the twenty-seven episodes bring out various aspects of the camp life that are to Shalamov the sacred drama of lived experience. Unforgettable is the opening epitaph in which the author commemorates the untimely death of his fellow prisoners. It is followed by a vivid sketch of their attributes and antecedents of arbitrarily cruel incidents or systematic draining away of their physical endurance until they are put beside countless other corpses in the snowbound ditches around the mining site.

Beyond the recurring individual atrocities in brutishness, malice, sadism committed by convict to convict and by jailers to convicts, the most lasting impression that emerges is of the inhuman hardship of the mining job itself. The work quota is imposed on the entire camp community from above, with orders to starve and finally shoot down recalcitrant workers. The occasional friendly snatch of dialogue or the gesture of sympathy or trust that lightens one or another passage in the stories only reinforce the reigning bestiality of behavior in that closed and forgotten world of men who become less than men. As the author writes at the conclusion of this testimonial to an inferno, "every man who has lived in it inevitably becomes worse than he was before."

Anti-Leninist sentiments, risibly treated in Vanya Chmotanov's adventures, resound with the verdict of history in Grossman's last, deeply thoughtful work, *Forever Flowing* (1964). Vasily Grossman (1905-1964) had been one of Gorky's protegés and considered a gifted novelist until his 1946 play, *If You Believe in the Pythagorians*, was attacked by party critics for "cosmopolitanism" and since then he had difficulty being published in Russia. The most interesting pages in *Forever Flowing* deal with Lenin as a true predecessor to Stalinism. According to Shalamov, Lenin imposed on Russia a policy based on economic progress and a denial of freedom that was nothing less than the continuing Tsarist policy of developing the country on a base of serfdom that had keyed the "modern" reforms of Peter the Great. This is not new to a Western historian. It is startling to find in Soviet fiction, however, a systematic breaking down of the myth of a constructive and humane Lenin. Shalamov does this clearly and lucidly through the hero, Ivan Grigoryevich, who has just returned to Moscow from thirty years of hard labor in the Arctic north. He had been imprisoned as a university student, during the doctors' trial, when he had spoken out in a lecture hall against dictatorship. He learns that freedom is more important than life itself.

Forever Flowing is the story of the hero's life, or what is left of it, after he is released. Ivan settles for a marginal existence at the edge of the Philistine flow of activities that engulfs his former self-centered associates. His own bitter thoughts in regard to the bankruptcy of revolutionary ideals are interspersed with two lacerating personal accounts. One is that of a wife of an arrested man, who in turn perished in prison, and the other is that of his landlady, a former party activist who describes to him the deliberate starving of the Ukranian peasantry during the collectivization campaign in the 1930s.

There is a disconcerting emptiness at the center of this plotless novel, as if the author, pressured by an analysis of the immense social and political problems of his country, could not keep his mind on a coherent fictional sequence and structure. It is an important work, nevertheless, if only for the questions that Grossman poses with trenchancy and fervor: "Who were the new people who survived the Revolution? . . . Were they not the children, not of the Revolution, but of the new state that did not even require servants but just clerks? . . . Is there any hope for Russia who has made clear throughout her history her acquiescence to the institution of slavery?"

Some of the answers to Grossman's disturbing questions emerge in an ambitious saga of a proletarian family, *Seven Days of Creation* written by Vladimir Maksimov in 1971. He is one of the most stubbornly liberal writers, who had attracted Paustovsky's attention with a daringly subversive short story in the anti-dogmatic almanach Tarusa Pages (1961). He also offended Krushchev's successors with a long running play that castigated the early Stalin era. Maksimov was "invited" by the government in 1974 to leave the country and settled, somewhat unhappily, in Paris. He misses the country of his native language, his native landscape, and his associates and friends. He remains one of the most active exiles in maintaining contact with dissident Moscow circles by telephone and underground communication.

Seven Days of Creation is a reminiscence, overladen with a bewildering profusion of flashbacks, of the fortunes of the three Lashkov brothers in a style of gritty, plebian realism. Externally, the economic status of these "new" proletarians (a retired railroad conductor, a Moscow tenement janitor, and a forest ranger) has not been altered by the Revolution. But what is made abundantly clear, and of which these ordinary, little-educated Russians are inchoately aware, is the psychological undermining of their lives by the pressures and control of the new regime. They express their doubts during bouts of alcoholic savagery, in revealing emotional outbursts, and through endless thoughtless conversations concerning the sense of shared failure that grips all the members of the family. Stolid Vasily's spirit is broken "behind the dark chaotic jumble of corrugated tenement roofs" that breed hostility and fear in the midst of arrests, fights, and denunciations. Although Andrei finds a measure of peace in the forest, he is haunted by the image of his world composed of "the drivers and the driven" and the knowledge that he belongs to the latter group. The former revolutionary commissar, Peter Lashkov, asks himself, "What happened, why did everything turn out this way?" when he returns feeling helpless and disillusioned from a trip to the city's bureaucratic stronghold. He concluded, "you couldn't get anywhere against people with power." Perhaps the most somber and forceful response to the speculations in *Forever Flowing* is made by one of the few positive and thoughtful characters in Maksimov's novel; he tells Peter's grandson who has been incarcerated in a criminal asylum and is now "gutted of life" that "the world should bless Russia from now until doomsday because with her own experience of Hell, she has shown the rest what not to do."

Daughter of the beloved children's writer, poet, and essayist, Kornei Chukovsky (1882-1969), Lidia Chukovskaya (b. 1907) has been a famous dissenter. She has protested against illicit trials. She wrote an open letter castigating Sholokhov for his statement that Sinyavsky and Daniel should be shot. She defended Solzhenitsyn in 1968, which was circulated in *Samizdat*. This doomed her official activities as editor and translator in the high councils of the Union of Writers and she was expelled from membership in 1974.

Her two brief novels (*The Deserted House*, 1965, and *Going Under*, 1972) are minor masterpieces of delicately toned writing and low keyed control in the handling of intensely emotional and poignant content. In the earlier work, Olga Petrovna is an ordinary, middle-class doctor's widow and successful manager of the typists' pool in a Leningrad publishing house. She also is the proud mother of a dedicated young Communist who has been mentioned in *Pravda* for distinguished technological achievement. The year is 1937. Suddenly her world begins to crumble. The director and some of his associates are taken away by the KGB. She is herself placed under suspicion and forced to resign when her son is arrested. She is certain that in his case, it is all "an absurd mistake," and it is only after long suffering that she perceives that the state has unjustly imprisoned her son.

Going Under is a first-person narrative of the heroine's stay at a writers' resort house near Moscow where she worked as a translator. She is an educated and sensitive woman whose husband, innocent of any misdoings, was arrested without charges or trial some years ago and has not been heard of since. Both women gradually descend into despair and estrangement from normal reality through the same three stages: disbelief in the happening during the first shock of the arrest, as the two men, in both cases glancing back with a reassuring smile, walk down the stairs between soldiers to a waiting car; the endless daily queuing at the prison gates for information (never given) as to the interrogation and its result; waiting for a letter that in the writer's case does not come since the sentence of "ten years without correspondence" is a euphemism, as she learns during her vacation, for an early execution, used apparently to prevent the howling and crying of the women in the prison corridors.

The central theme of *Going Under* takes place in 1948. The plot is widened to include the heroine's abortive love affair with an ex-convict writer whom she meets at the resort. She repulses him upon reading his just completed short story where his deportation experience is used to celebrate the system, and after she meets another Jewish writer and the caretaker who are, like herself, victims of the terrorist campaigns. The main thrust of *Going Under* is revealed in the urgent, indeed overwhelming need of this woman to "go under" the surface of her outward life into the collective memories of the incredible happening that is "impossible to understand," to resist the daily brainwashing by the powerful state apparatus with the haunting questions as to the why and the how of the horror that descended upon her and countless others and the speculative when of a possible release from it. The secret session with her diary in the solitude of the resthome room produces the *Going Under* novel that constitutes a form of liberation and a search across the wide Russian land "for brothers, if not now, then in the future."

The situation of the samizdat writer is unique in contemporary letters. Beyond the worry and anxiety concerning his physical and professional safety, he is handicapped by the absence of an objective audience of critics that in other countries functions to sustain, modify, and assess the writer's output. He also suffers from the lack of editorial blue-penciling; this is evident in the occasional roughness of style, a sense of incompletion, overflowing content, immoderate ideological emphasis that make for the uneven quality of many works. However, as a member of an embattled minority engaged in a risky and forbidden enterprise, he leads a heady, adventurous life sustained by the honorable commitment to speak out the truth, a commitment that is deeply imbedded in the Russian literary tradition. It is immediately apparent from the several works just reviewed that the creative underground writer, passionately concerned in recording his protest against existing moral and social falsehoods, must write out of the experience of collective suffering of which he is a product, as a man and as an artist. This is at the core of literary dissent in Russia and has been most pungently expressed by the greatest Soviet dissenting writer of our time. Alexander Solzhenitsyn wrote to Tvardovsky: "My ways are those of a convict, of a prisoner at hard labor. I will say plainly that I belong as much to the camps as I do to Russian literature and that I owe them as much. This is where I was formed and for all time."

ALEXANDER SOLZHENITSYN (1918-   )

Alexander Solzhenitsyn became widely known after the publication of One Day in the Life of Ivan Denisovich and Matrena's Home as a political polemicist, a critic of contemporary society, the most famous Soviet dissenter, a universal moral force, and the only Soviet writer whose international reputation may be compared to that of his compatriot, Leo Tolstoy. A chronology of his professional life following the appearance of the two early stories, with brief introductions to his minor writings and a discussion of his major works, will facilitate the understanding of his literature.

His career formally ended in his own country with the publication of Zakhar-Kalit, in 1965. This had been preceded two years earlier by two other short stories, For the Good of the Cause and An Incident at the Krechetovka Station, where for the first time the author's personal experience did not obtrude on the contemporary Soviet scene. In the first story, the students in a technical secondary school have enlarged and modernized their building out of a collective enthusiasm. This enthusiasm is dashed, however, by callous regional bureaucrats who appropriate the premises for a Research Institute that will increase both their personal prestige and that of the town. The Incident is a more complex study of a young railroad depot manager, Lieutenant Zotov. He is an instinctively pure and honorable man, brought up, however, with all the correct attitudes and thoughts of a dedicated Komsomolist. He has the responsibility for transporting soldiers who had barely escaped the German encirclement in the first dreadful months of World War II. He meets one of them, a gentle-mannered and cultivated actor from Moscow to whom he is instantly attracted. However, the actor speaks of Stalingrad by its former Tsarist name, and Zotov's conditioned mind bristles with suspicion. He suppresses his spontaneous feelings and turns the actor over to the authorities as a spy.

In 1965, his first long novel, *The First Circle,* was rejected for publication and seized by the KGB with other unpublished manuscripts in a friend's house in Moscow. Two years later, Solzhenitsyn wrote an open letter to the Writers' Union that branded the Glavlit as illegal and urged the abolition of censorship. He deplored the current inferiority of a previously brilliant national literature and called on the Union to defend and protect its members rather than act as a repressive instrument of the party. In 1968, Solzhenitsyn's second long novel, *Cancer Ward,* was refused publication in the Soviet Union and appeared in the West in an unedited and possibly incomplete version. The author wrote a letter to the Soviet press accusing the secret police of selling the manuscript and having it published abroad without his permission. The following year, Solzhenitsyn was expelled from the Soviet Writers' Union. Two plays, *The Love Girl and the Innocent* and *Candle in the Wind* were published at the same time in the United States. *The Love Girl* takes place in a Stalinist concentration-camp setting and makes somber and intense theatre in the action of total enslavement of the convicts. They are portrayed as the victims of fear, hatreds, cheating, mendacity, and pandering—everyday factors of the camp routine. The heroine, who despite all the vicissitudes of her lot, remains like Matrena, selfless and compassionate, is the most fully developed female character in Solzhenitsyn's fiction.

Candle in the Wind is a rather static and windy play, placed in an unspecified country of the future. A mathematician projects his apprehension of misused scientific techniques in a stepped-up technological society during a neuro-stabilizing operation of a psychically insecure young woman. The postoperative result—submission and passivity on the part of the patient—alerts the hero-scientist to the danger of technological dehumanization and the need to preserve the total human being who is "the flickering candle of our time."

Solzhenitsyn was awarded the 1970 Nobel Prize for literature and accepted it in absentia. In 1972, the lecture prepared for the Nobel ceremony was published in the West. The writer used it as a platform to decry the increasing materialistic pursuits of both East and West and propagate the traditional Russian attitude toward the character and role of art which is serious, outward looking, and apostolic. The artist, in the modern world of relative moral values, must dedicate himself to the interpretation of ethical absolutes as they appear in the experience of one man, of one people and one generation to another. He must represent the indivisibility of truth and freedom everywhere and act as the conscience of his nation and of mankind.

The manuscript of a new novel, *August 1914*, that presents the first part of a projected three-volume historical narrative, was sent out to seven different Soviet editors and returned with rejection slips from all of them. He consequently forwarded it to his Swiss lawyer with permission to publish, and it appeared abroad in 1971.

In September, 1973, the KGB found a copy of the *Gulag Archipelago* in Leningrad after its hiding place was revealed to the police by the author's former typist during a five-day interrogation, at the end of which she hanged herself. Solzhenitsyn, who had been withholding the work in fear of reprisals against people mentioned in it, now immediately permitted the first two parts, that had previously been sent to the West on microfilm, to be published. Seven months later he was arrested in his wife's Moscow apartment and the next day forcibly exiled to West Germany. While he was airborne, accompanied by a guard, he felt triumphant, "like a calf who butts against the oak tree" (that is the Soviet system) and remains unharmed.

In a memoir, *The Calf Butted the Oak* (1975), Solzhenitsyn sets down his life as an underground writer in a dangerous game of hide-and-seek with the secret police, the difficulties of making professional contacts from within his official isolation, and maintaining creative and personal independence in a sixteen-hour working day. One of the most rewarding portraits and no more charitable than one would expect from a distrustful, grimly alert former *zek* (camp slang for prisoner) in a hostile milieu, is that of Alexander Tvardovsky. Solzhenitsyn does not minimize the vacillations and frequent alcoholic bouts of this generous and charming man; on the other side, the editor's high intellectual integrity and the inestimable value of his sensitive and astute critique of the author's work is fully acknowledged. Disappointingly, little is revealed of the author's actual work process, problems of method, literary approach, composition. In 1975, Part III of *Gulag Archipelago* was brought out in Russian and other languages outside of the Soviet Union.

Solzhenitsyn next published *Lenin in Zurich*, a semi-fictional, semi-historical account of Lenin's stay in Switzerland from 1914 to April 1917 when Lenin returned to Russia in a sealed train. It was based on materials that Solzhenitsyn found in the Zurich archives. With boldness and evident political intent, he reconstructs the image, absent from the portraits made by Marxist historians, of the "great leader" in a helplessly isolated position. Lenin is deserted by all but a few squabbling and distrusted followers, without an underground organization or contacts with Russia. He vacillates between the strong sense of his destiny and the imminent collapse of all his plans. The polemic argument, however, is by far too obtrusive and lengthy.

Solzhenitsyn relies upon the stream of consciousness technique to reveal Lenin's inner world. It is the author's most successful, imaginative recreation to date of a famous historical figure in human terms. Lenin, thoroughly demythified, is depicted in his tensions, calculations, anxieties, feelings. Solzhenitsyn presents him as a shrewd and selfish man, given to emotion and mental over-exertion, inherently suspicious of minds as powerful as his own, and inclined to blame others for his mistake. Startlingly interesting is the author's disclosure that the "Architect of the Russian Revolution" who had been preparing during years of exile for the take-over of his country as the agent of history, was caught unawares by the collapse of the Russian empire. He was inclined to discredit the momentous news, too preoccupied by the continuing silence from his absent mistress, and the local Swiss proletarian agitation. The book represents one of three omitted chapters from *August 1914* that is the first knot or fascicle as the author names the different volumes of his historical narrative; the other two chapters will be included in knots II and III (*October 1916* and *March 1917*). These "knots," for Solzhenitsyn, are the key moments when "everything mysteriously merges together" in one space and is vitalized by one set of energies. On a smaller scale, he had already used that device in *Cancer Ward* and *The First Circle*.

THE FIRST CIRCLE

From the imprisonment in a concentration camp described by a single peasant spokesman in *One Day*, Solzhenitsyn turns to another form of imprisonment in the *sharashka* (camp slang for a fraudulent facade). It takes place in the Mavrino Scientific Research Institute near Moscow. It is staffed by elite convicts—scientists, technologists, mathematicians—whose many voices express the more refined torture which is their lot. Transported from the lower circles of the hell of labor camps, these outstanding specialists, like the philosophers in Dante's *Inferno*, are placed in the "first circle" of a clean, well-lighted prison (the author, a mathematician, spent four years at Mavrino). The prisoners are given plentiful nourishment, warm clothing, and even sheets and blankets. They are put to work on secret electronic and cybernetic devices for Stalin's private purposes and for the KGB. The project is skillfully used to build the novel and to interrelate the closed world of the *sharashka* with a wide diversity of Soviet lives on the outside.

In the opening scene, dated Christmas eve, 1949, Innokenty Volodin, a successful thirty-year-old diplomat, is grappling with his conscience, and finally decides to warn his old family physician, from a public telephone booth, of his possible arrest. The call is intercepted and a tape recording is sent to the Mavrino laboratory. Four days later, (the duration of the novel) Volodin, with a plane ticket to Paris in his pocket, is taken to the dreaded Lubianka prison. Solzhenitsyn projects through "key moment" episodes an immense and frightening scenario of Soviet society.

The social structure of the Institute is pyramidal. The highest political echelons and top ranking administrators are members of the secret police who direct the Institute. They keep their posts with grovelling subservience to the slightest caprice of the dictator whom the author scathingly portrays as a grotesque victim of obsessive hatreds and paranoia. Volodin's colleagues are overpaid state functionaries who reap the reward of material privilege for total servility to the system. They include university students who are forced to spy on one another to retain their scholarships, wives of the Mavrino inmates who are condemned to a marginal social and civic existence for their loyalty to "the enemies of the people" and all these lives are marked by suspicion, pervasive insecurity, and fear. No one is free with the exception of the prisoners themselves. Having little left to lose, they alone defy their jailers, and their defiance constitutes the major theme of the work. Their argument for inner freedom and moral independence is set back, however, when Rubin, an erudite Marxist who is sympathetic to the harassed Volodin, nevertheless sacrifices him out of his party loyalty and support of the "positive forces of history". He identifies the diplomat's voice on the tape.

Solzhenitsyn discusses the ideals of freedom and independence in a more abstract form in the countless polemics between Rubin and the prisoner-mathematician, Gleb Nerzhin, the main protagonist in *The First Circle*. Nerzhin is unbought and unbossed, caught, in the same manner as his creator, in the mounting wave of terrorism, and since late adolescence he has been pondering the reasons for the mutilation of his society. Absorbed in his need to understand, he builds within himself a shelter for his reflections and remains extraordinarily whole.

The strength to resist corruption is tested further, when Nerzhin and another fellow convict, Gerasimovich, an electronics engineer, are ordered to work on sophisticated eavesdropping methods to entrap Soviet citizens into the secret police net. The importance that Solzhenitsyn attached to publishing the description of a concentration camp day *before The First Circle* is made clear in the choice faced by the two men: an early release from prison if they comply with the odious command, the immediate return to a hard-labor camp if they do not. Gerasimovich cannot bring himself to become an instrument for the entrapment of innocent people who will, like himself, become victims of the system. Nerzhin's refusal is more complex, in tune with an avid desire to remain alone with his thought. He actually prefers the camp to Mavrino, where nothing will interfere with his inner freedom, nor the stifling material possessions that he honestly despises, nor the imposition on his time spent in spurious scientific research, nor even the emotional demands made upon him by his wife, Nadya, whom he loves.

CANCER WARD

Solzhenitsyn asks how man can preserve self in the face of imminent death in his second novel *Cancer Ward*. It is situated almost entirely in a cancer ward of a Tashkent hospital in 1955 and is concerned with morality, guilt, and repossession of free self. Against a grimly realistic description of medical treatment, the author gradually reveals, in the semidirect monologues, characteristic of his style, and in brusque, brief discharges of dialogue among the patients, a transposition of values as intimacy with pain loosens the hold on the nonessentials of former healthy lives.

A growing awareness of the little time left to live in, kindles rage in the former KGB agent, Podduev, a tough, wenching, and drinking operator, ill equipped to endure immobility and physical suffering. Upon reading Tolstoy's stories, *What Men Live By*, he realizes the meaninglessness of his bungled and loveless life. For the old academician Shulubin, the incurable illness is a blessed release from the torture of guilt that has racked his years of cowardly, compliant participation in the conspiracy of silence during the Stalinist terror. Free at last to condemn the system, he damns it with a proposal of governance for Russia that would replace existing state dictatorship with ethical socialism—the matrix of Solzhenitsyn's most cherished political reforms. Shulubin explains to the eagerly attentive Oleg Kostoglotov that under ethical socialism all of society's relationships and its institutions would be based solely on moral principles and concerns.

Kostoglotov and Rusanov present antipodes, as did Rubin and Nerzhin in *The First Circle*, but they are more powerfully and sharply drawn. Their language to each other across the ward is that of perpetual abuse and scorn. Kostoglotov is the most fully developed hero in Solzhenitsyn's fiction; Rusanov is the petty bureaucrat, par excellence, brother to the bribe-taking Gogolian official and in the state of his illness, an inevitable reminder of Ivan Illitch. But he lacks the capacity for the spiritual growth inherent in Tolstoy's superb creation. He remains impervious to simple humaneness, absorbed in the selfish, material pursuits that exemplify his limited mind, snobbery, status consciousness, and complacency. It is significant that during his four months' stay in the ward (likewise the duration of the novel), his attitudes, alone among the rest of the patients, undergo no change. It may be assumed that his fatal illness symbolizes the social cancer of Stalinism that, two years after the dictator's death, seemed to have reached a terminal stage. Rusanov emerges as a typical creature of Stalin. He is perfect totalitarian fodder in the unquestioning acceptance of orders from his superiors. Further, he is proud of his rapid ascent up the state ladder due to carefully planned denunciations of his friends and colleagues and personally devised spying techniques.

Oleg Kostoglotov is another artistic success. The writer endows him with his own crippling legacy of a long experience in a labor camp, permanent exile, and the seemingly incurable disease, that again, as in Solzhenitsyn's case, is arrested by a remarkable tolerance of x-ray treatments. He comes fully alive in the conflict between his destiny and his intractable, free-thinking spirit, which, rebellious of all restrictions, has sustained him, as it does Nerzhin through all the indignities of prison. We cannot but admire the thirty-year-old, self-educated, intelligent, and resolutely forward-looking ex-convict for his intensely human contacts with fellow patients and the doctors, his capacity to feel the value of life in the midst of death and his fierce hunger for some measure of happiness even if it be only "a few months of living without guards and without pain." The pathos of Kostoglotov's outcry against his fate, denied by history the normal development of being, is further weighted by the assault on Oleg's virility caused by the hormone injections needed to prevent a recurrence of the cancer. The choice of refusing the treatment, now that he has regained the measure of health that ignites a yearning for sexual intimacy, is complicated by the fact that the injections are administered by a young woman doctor, Vega, with whom Oleg falls in love. To the author's admiration and pity for his hero is added another dimension when Oleg, on the first day out of the hospital, comes into a greedy repossession of the world. It in turn intoxicates his senses, repels him with its arbitrary cruelty and materialistic obsessions and yet fills him with the strength and patience to endure. The novel ends on this day, a symbolic enactment of a last act in the drama of survival when the ex-convict returns to his former life.

AUGUST 1914

August 1914 is Solzhenitsyn's first major work that does not flow out of the author's own experiences. To begin with the obvious, all but one fifth of the long novel deals with the Battle of Tannenburg in East Prussia in August 1914 that ended with the defeat of the Second Russian Army and the suicide of its commander-in-chief, General Samsonov.

Solzhenitsyn started writing this tri-volume in 1936 that he believes may take another twenty years to complete. His goal is to reconstruct Russia's recent past, falsified and simplified by Soviet historians as a reactionary chaos that could only be swept away by the liberating forces of the revolution. He wants to relate yesterday's reality to that of today with an imaginative rediscovery of the early years of the twentieth century. Solzhenitsyn tries to demonstrate that prewar Russian society was not necessarily doomed, that gradual moral and social reforms were making headway, and the potential of great economic productivity was encouraging the newly emerging task force of technological specialists. These ideas, and the characters who utter them, however, are barely sketched in the initial chapters. The real ballast of the work lies in forty-eight chapters treating the war itself. The general reader will find the dense thicket of military action overdocumented and overdetailed. He might be compensated, however, by other, more lyrical passages that recall similar descriptions in Sholokhov's *The Quiet Don* celebrating comradeship among men, officers and soldiers, starry nights, backdrops of conversations by the bivouac fire, and the stillness just before combat. Solzhenitsyn especially extols the behavior of the Russian soldier, whom he presents as brave, pious, intensely attached to his motherland, and uncomprehendingly submissive to his officers despite the inferiority of his equipment and the contradictory, confusing commands that augur his personal destruction rather than the country's victory. The same qualities distinguish General Samsonov, a historical personage and the only completely realized character in the novel. A deeply religious man of simple and abiding faith in his country and the tsar, he has been trained in a long career to the execution of commands from above. Here he is shown as the victim of a hastily planned and foolhardy campaign that has been brought about through the ineptitude and petty jealousies of the General Staff. The orders and counterorders from the General Staff abetted by faulty reconnaissance and poor communications, seal the destruction of his army and eventually the Russian defeat in the First World War. The tragedy of Samsonov reaches a Shakespearean dimension in the author's depiction of the commander's acceptance of the disaster for which he feels personally responsible and which, in the absoluteness of his moral ethic, must be atoned for with his own death.

Nonetheless, Solzhenitsyn does not minimize Samsonov's lack of leadership that played a decisive role in the critical deployment of his troops and resulted in a German encirclement. His inability to act independently is adversely contrasted with Vorotynstev's lucid, enterprising intelligence, self-reliance, and eagerness to assume initiative when occasion demands.

In *August 1914*, Solzhenitsyn engages in a moral and intellectual investigation of the many layers of the nation's social structure but of the many characters introduced from the upper middle classes, the peasantry, the military, or radical students' circles, none is allowed sufficient fictional space. Until they are developed in the following volumes, it is difficult to assess the integral art of Solzhenitsyn's ambitious and historically important fictional narrative.

GULAG ARCHIPELAGO

Solzhenitsyn recounts the totality of Soviet terror under Lenin and Stalin in the *Gulag Archipelago*, and the way it has affected millions of human beings. The author calls the work a "literary" investigation and with cause. Despite the scrupulous documentation based on hundreds of prisoners' accounts and letters, and his own eight years in a prison camp, his will is to testify issues from a still deeper level of communication that transmits the suffering of one man into the experience of another. With the telling detail of a word, a scream, or a repressed gesture, the prisoner's external life story is transformed into a universal happening.

Solzhenitsyn thinks of the G. U. LAG. (Central Correction Labor Camp Administration) as an archipelago, the islands of which (some 220 labor camps) are scattered across the Russian continent. The camps receive perpetual shipments of convicts. There, some 15 to 20 million zeks make up a mobile, easily replenished, and unpaid labor force that needs no housing conveniences, schools, or hospitals. Working in substandard conditions, they constituted a significant economic factor. Between 1940 and 1953, nine cities, several large canals, and eight heavy industrial centers were constructed with slave labor, although productivity was uniformly defective and low.

The long work contains three sections. *Gulag I* (1973) deals with the history of political repression since 1917, with descriptions of political trials in the 1920s and 1930s, various methods of arrest, and different means of transferring the deportees to the archipelago, and these special prisons. In this section, Solzhenitsyn makes clear that the punitive Gulag apparatus was originated during the time of Lenin's rule, when only a negligible percentage of the prisoners were actively opposed to the regime. Most of them were innocent victims, swept into prison because they belonged to suspect groups. The people in these groups may have been kulaks, Old Bolsheviks, relatives of émigrés, White Army soldiers, or POW's from World War II who automatically were imprisoned for their "contact with Germans" and all of whom might be likely to commit crimes against the state.

Gulag II (1974) is centered on camp life itself. It embraces all aspects of work routine, daily existence in the cells, the systematic brutality of the guards, officially encouraged tyrannization of the "politicals" by the common criminals, and a precise analysis of the psychological effect of the camps on the various prisoners.

Gulag III (1976) gives the story of mutiny within the camps that, like other peasant uprisings in Russian history, is a revolt against unendurable hardship. It is unarmed, spontaneous, and briefly united in a heady repossession of freedom but ends in death. This is an account of the Vorkuta prison revolt in 1953, which followed several unsuccessful hunger strikes and that counted sixty-six prisoners shot and left to rot in the prison yard.

He also relates the more sensational mutiny at the Konguir camp a year later when the prisoners, demanding more food and clothing, controlled the camp for forty days. A large military unit finally was sent out to restore order and crushed the rebellion with the massacre of 600 convicts. This second part of the book is the more moving section. It reverberates with the many prisoners' voices and the author's invective, indignation, remorse, and occasional exhaltation. From the innumerable prisoners' experiences Solzhenitsyn recreates Ivan's world. For example, Alesha, the Baptist, tells Ivan that he finds happiness in prison where "there is time to think about your soul." This happiness is intellectually deepened in Solzhenitsyn's conversations with his cell companions, "real, open, human beings," who help him shed the slogans and clichés of his Marxist convictions and understand that "good and evil does not run between states, classes or parties. It runs through every human heart."

J'accuse! is the major message of the *Gulag* and those standing trial are not only the obvious evil doers—the Soviet state and its secret police underlings. Ordinary Soviet citizens are in their company for their compliance and fear of official reprisals and those weakling prisoners who accept soft "trusty" jobs without which the camp operation would break down. Strongest is Solzhenitsyn's self-accusation of cowardly nonresistance during his own arrest and acceptance of an informer's assignment, which he never fulfilled and which was only terminated because of his illness. The real criminal, however, and the perpetrator of the Gulag horror is Communist ideology that sanctifies certain abstract and absolute notions of a desirable socialist society and decrees that only by exterminating individuals and classes inimical to it will this society come into being. It is the absolute value attached to the ideology, as George Kennan proposes, that justified and continues to justify the uninhibited malevolence of party leaders to anyone who is not blindly loyal to the regime. They are considered as enemies of the state and therefore treated as less than human beings.

Solzhenitsyn wrote *Gulag Archipelago* to commemorate the martyrdom of millions of fellow convicts who did not survive the camp ordeal. He also wanted to record the Soviet horror in the living memory of the nation so that it would not pass, unknown and forgotten, into oblivion. Up to the present time, it is the writer's most important achievement.

From where does this tenacious, fearless, mentally and physically durable man derive his sources of strength? One answer would be Solzhenitsyn's immutable belief in his writer's destiny which—similar to that of former titans, Tolstoy, Dostoevsky, Belinsky, and Gorky—is inseparable from the fate of Russian literature and of Russia itself. He considers it his responsibility to speak as the moral conscience of the nation, recreating the whole truth, as he understands it, regarding Soviet society, all the while cherishing Russia's ancient mystical and religious reality and its continuity. To read the sixteen Solzhenitsyn prose poems, none more than a few pages long, is to understand the spiritual sustenance derived by the author from a nostalgic glimpse of the lake and river country (*Lake Segden*), from Russian religious life of yore in the peacefulness emanating from half-ruined churches across the countryside, from the memory of heroic history (*Zakhar Kalita*) that Solzhenitsyn depicts in extraordinarily compelling language.

The originality of his verbal art eludes translation, for, among other things, he returns to Remizov's lingual reforms. He introduces old forgotten words, a tantalizing dialectical variety of standard words and phrases and "purifies" Russian by freeing the native language of Western European borrowings. Slavic consonant clusters and strongly accented vowels are favored and they have an effective aural appeal and seem particularly resonant in passages savaged with irony.

Irony is a pervasive presence in Solzhenitsyn's writings and nowhere is it more flagrantly evident than in the concept of freedom: Only prisoners are really free (Ivan, Nerzhin, Alesha the Baptist) while in the police state all the rest are shackled by fear for their jobs and their lives. The author's overall indictment of his government may be summed up in the ironical statement that a classless society pledged to the extermination of privilege contains the largest slave population in the world.

There is a further ironic reflection to be made on the writer's own position in his country's literary canon. As the critic Alexander Schemann justly remarks in accordance with official pronouncements, his works are the epitome of Socialist Realism. They deal with typical features of contemporary Soviet life and are addressed to the mass of the Russian people in the familiar style of old-fashioned realism. His novels contain positive heroes, an optimistic ending, and the vision of a great and good society in the Soviet future.

Solzhenitsyn expresses his belief that Russia now is ready to abandon the materialistic improvements of the collective with its oppressive power apparatus and set out on the path of "repentance and self limitation" in the pursuit of individual spiritual regeneration. To accomplish this, Russia must renounce its present political ideology and the morally degrading complex modernisms of the West. It must withdraw into its own northeastern and Siberian lands, under the guidance of a church-connected authority that would harmonize with the personal directives of ethical socialism.

Solzhenitsyn has been greatly influenced by Nikolay Berdyayev and such former Marxists as Peter Struve and S. Frank, who have been propagators of spiritual priority over external forces. There is nothing quixotic in this historical solution for his country. It is consistent with the moral coloration of all the human concerns that vibrate through his work that were forged from within by his knowledge of the world in freedom and in slavery and his conversion to Orthodoxy during his prison term. It is perhaps the greatest irony of all that these dynamically expressed and sincere persuasions of a great contemporary specifically addressed to Russians in Russia, will not be heard by most of them.

7 · A Glance at the Present-day Literary Scene

THIS STUDY concludes with a brief summary of recent literary events in Russia. A large number of writers, their translators, critics, and editors have been allotted spacious co-op apartments in a large residential block of buildings on Red Army Square. They have formed the center of Russian letters, and in the early years of the 1970s, Solzhenitsyn's disclosures in *Gulag Archipelago* made a shattering impact on this writing world where, among progressive intellectuals a mood of discouragement had already set in. It was brought about by increasing numbers of emigrating or forcibly exiled dissident authors, a systematic levelling-down of artistic quality in the monthly magazines, and tightened censorship. They have seen the fate of such talented writers as Vasily Aksyonov and the avant-garde poets of the sixties who were still writing, but were rarely published and received little mention in the official press.

There were signs of health as well. With Tvardovsky's demise, the spirit of artistic independence and receptivity to new talent that had distinguished his review, reappeared in a more subdued form, in a monthly periodical, *Our Contemporary*, published by the Union of Writers of the RSFSR. By 1974, it had grown to a circulation of 100,000 and in that year marked its tenth anniversary with a volume of prose works that had first appeared in that magazine.

Among the contributors were Belov, Yashin, Shukshin, and

Trifonov, and Kazakov and Nagibin, possibly the most prolific and successful writers of the previous decade who were now no longer published or written about. The furious theology of the immediate post-Stalin era, generated by a search for moral certainties, was conspicuously absent from these prose selections. But other distances marked the relationship between political authorities and literature as well. None of the stories contains allusions to the Marxist-Leninist articles of faith, which seemed to imply that the Soviet writer was no longer fearful to aver, if only by omission, the irrelevance of Communist dogma in an imaginative piece of work. Even more glaringly lacking were the formal tenets of Socialist Realism. Glowing images of socialism at work in the portraits of stakhanovite heroes and avuncular directors of political consciousness had disappeared. The avant-garde of the sixties rediscovered nineteenth-century Russian humanism, which has nowhere more forcefully been expressed than in the stories by Astafyev and Nosov, who had emerged with Rasputin as "ruralist" writers.

Victor Astafyev (b. 1924) and Valentin Rasputin (b. 1937) rank among the most talented and successful Soviet literary practitioners today. Both are Siberians, born in the rural remoteness of the north. The landscape of their novels and stories is that of the small village settlement surrounded by the formidable Siberian taiga. There man, both threatened and supported by the forces of nature, achieves a reciprocal and profoundly fulfilling relationship with the organic world. These authors search for meanings in the vastness of the Russian forest and the deep endless rivers and they believe they have something of importance to say to their countrymen. In contrast to the dominating concern of other "Country Prose" writers with the collectivization syndrome and its effects on the life of the peasants, this fiction takes the kolkhoz structure for granted. The two writers focus on the individual and the problems of private existence. Placed against the background of rigorous natural environment, the main protagonist is shown grappling with difficult personal situations that test the strength and vitality of his inner resources.

Two studies of character memorably illustrate this major theme. In one of Astafyev's best-known short novels, *The Last*

Greeting (1975), the narrator evokes from boyhood memories, scenes of village life in northern Siberia centered around his grandmother who brought him up. Her portrait is skillfully pieced together with colorful, yet sharply realistic incidents and bits of remembered conversations. She is seen coping successfully with want, illness, malice, and the loneliness of old age. Her being is packed with energies of generosity, hard, constructive work, and an insatiable zest for living. She seems to embody, for the narrator, the abundance and vigor of the sweeping seasonal renewal of the majestic natural universe which towers over her native village. The hard edges of daily reality are occasionally blurred with nostalgia, less acceptable perhaps to the Western reader than to more sentimentally inclined Russians who are also drawn to the author by the singular purity of his language. Like the ecologically untouched wilderness in Astafyev's stories, the idiom in which they are written has remained free of urban slang, bureaucratese, American hip, and acronyms, and it supports the writer's claim that the Russian of his prose is not heard in Moscow.

Another peasant woman is delineated in Rasputin's starkly somber novella, *Live and Remember* (1976). The insoluble dilemma in which Andrei and Nastena Guskov are caught had not been previously explored in Soviet fiction. Andrei has been thrice wounded in the four years of frontline fighting and is gripped by the fear that he may not survive the war. He deserts in the last year of it, returning to his Siberian village and a deserter's perilous existence. Hiding in the frozen forest that grants him a reprieve during the winter span, he is totally dependent on his young wife, who manages to supply him, undetected, with daily provender and attempts to assuage the tensions building up in him with the comfort of her body. Nastena's courage and endurance are further tested when the deep longing for a child from Andrei which she harbored before he was sent off to war is now, when she may no longer acknowledge a legitimate pregnancy, finally granted. In emotionally charged conversations between husband and wife, Nastena's inner monologues and the dissimulation in public of her envy and bitterness when victory is celebrated with the men back from the front, Rasputin projects the strength of his heroine. Although no social resolution is possible for the couple, the author conceives an artistically plausible ending, in harmony with the lyrical laws espoused by the "ruralists" that symbolizes the impress of natural forces on human destiny. Nastena drowns, which presages the discovery of her husband's forest hideout and a deserter's sentence.

Subject matter only second to the theme of rural Soviet life that continues to preoccupy writers in a country where peasants constitute 50 percent of the population, is a persevering interest in the Second World War. The memory of the shattering national experience that personally involved almost every Soviet citizen who is over forty today, haunts the creative imagination in the works of such gifted literary figures as Grigory Baklanov (b. 1923) and Vladimir Bogomolov (b. 1919).

Baklanov wrote several novellas in the 1950s that featured scenes of violent combat. He contrasts the bravery and will for self-sacrifice on the part of ambushed Russian soldiers with the inhumanly murderous enemy. These melodramatic effects were discarded for a wider vision of the war in a more serious and sober novel, *July 1941* (1965). The purpose of this work was to denounce the weakness of Stalin's leadership at the outset of the war and extol the fortitude and moral stamina of the common soldier.

Emphasis on moral and political issues and the somewhat slick didacticism that emanated from Baklanov's novel, is no longer representative, however, of current war literature. Younger writers are building new myths to convey the bloody battlefield through the individual's reactions to the collective horror of modern combat. They offer in descriptions of a man alone facing daily death or mutilation objects for contemplation rather than arguments. Such is the case of the deserter in *Live and Remember*. Andrei's tormented monologue reveals to us his psychic inability to go on with the "terrifying soldier's business" to kill or to be killed.

In the vanguard of this trend may be placed the talented writer, Bogomolov, whose recent collection of war stories, *The Pain Around My Heart* (1976), became an immediate success. Among the shorter stories, *Ivan* and *Zosia* were singled out by the more perceptive critics for the author's skill in developing a totally realized personality in a flashback to a moment in the narrator's life at the front. The tale of Ivan is stark, violent, and simple. It is that of a frail, undersized, fourteen-year-old boy, who becomes a casualty in the invading German Army. He had become, when we meet him in an active war zone, a crack reconnaissance scout who has bested older and more experienced men. Even among battle-scarred officers to whom courage was commonplace, the boy's dauntless penetration of German-patroled territory and his fearlessness and skill in executing the most difficult missions aroused admiration and a concern for his survival. All efforts on the part of Soviet High Command to send him to school failed. Until he was finally caught by the Germans and executed, he did not leave his job. It was not the excitement or patriotism that motivated him but an obsessively personal hatred of the Germans who had massacred his family and demolished his home. In his reconnaissance work, he was waging a relentless private war. Ivan's personal urgencies are brilliantly projected through change in narrative pace which accelerates when the boy appears on the scene. His impatience to be sent back into enemy territory is contrasted with the slower "stand-by for orders" behavior of the second lieutenant who is telling the story.

In *Zosia*, Bogomolov gives central fictional space to another private moment in the midst of the general holocaust when the narrator's regiment is stationed for a few days' rest in a semi-abandoned Polish village. The situation is conventional enough. The hero's euphoric sense of peace away from the guns is expressed by his exact sensuous description of such simple things as a swept garden path, a bed of flowers, and a carefully prepared family dinner in a clean kitchen. His consciousness unfolds to encompass other, friendly human beings and these feelings turn into a special miracle when he is smitten by the delicate young beauty of Zosia, the daughter of the house. Overcome with timidity and unable to communicate in her own language with the Polish girl who seems to be flirting with another Soviet officer he passes the night on the rack of mingled exaltation and despair. This is made doubly moving by the events of the next day when his company is suddenly recalled into combat. Zosia gives him his first and last kiss when he is leaving and makes him realize that she has preferred him to all the rest. Years later, the narrator continues to relive in his mind the bitter-sweet moment of unavowed emotion and the possibility of happiness that had glanced his way and which remains his most vivid memory.

The compelling image or metaphor by which upwardly mobile Soviet writers seek to understand and organize their age, may be identified, at the risk of using a term applied to a variety of perceptions, as a "new romanticism." It is based on the conviction that certain inner rhythms inherent in man, that part of a human being that Joseph Conrad has called "a spontaneous gift, not an acquisition," cannot be quelled by other, external priorities. This theme with its many variants has prevailed in recent dramatic literature that since 1956 has been showing signs of healthy revival.

The Russian stage, a source of dazzling, world known experimentation and achievement from the beginning of the century until the 1930s, had become practically moribund during the Stalin era. The reasons for the theatre's decline during that period have been cogently summarized by the English critic, Michael Glenny in his article, "Soviet Theatre—Two Views" (*Tulane Drama Review*, Vol. XI, No. 3, Spring, 1967).

Before the Second World War, Stanislavsky was able to impose his method of acting and the naturalism of the Moscow Art Theatre, for Stalin felt comfortable with it. Stanislavsky guaranteed the staging of Russian classics and financial support for actors through the fixed repertory he had established. However, it restricted young talent from entering into the nation wide organization bound by tenure, seniority, and artistic rigidity.

There was a resurgence of creative writing for the stage during the war years, when plays reflected the national mood and its hopes. During the depressed postwar period, however, the Soviet theatre reached its nadir. Government subsidies were removed, demolished playhouses were not rebuilt and the 200 working theatres (about a fourth of their prewar number) had to finance their productions with box-office receipts. Disastrously, their economic autonomy did not extend to an independent choice of repertory or technical experimentation. The arts were restricted by Zhdanov, and no artistic medium was more immediately and visibly affected by it than the theatre. Producers and directors were forced to present grindingly dull conformist fare that kept the spectators away in droves.

The protest that novelists and poets made against Socialist Realism that was fueled by the denunciation of Stalin's crimes at the Twentieth Century Party Congress, provoked vigorous repercussions in the world of Theatre Arts as well. As a result, a number of provincial were reopened. Two brilliant, avant-garde directors, Georgii Tovstonogorov and Oleg Yefremov, were appointed, the first to the Leningrad Gorky Theatre and the second to the Contemporary Theatre in Moscow, respectively. They instituted modern acting styles and excitingly original stage designs. They launched imaginative productions of the old masters, ventured into contemporary European drama, presenting the works of Brecht, Osborne, Ionesco, and others. They also enriched the repertory with plays by gifted contemporary writers (Panova, Zorin, Shvarts, and Pogodin) who have brought to both theatres financial and artistic success.

What has perhaps contributed most to the powerful renewal of life in the theatre is the deep and abiding love of the Russian people for this form of art. They expect from a seriously constructed stage production, whether drama or comedy, not only entertainment but spiritual and emotional nourishment. This may explain why television, which in the West is threatening legitimate theatre with extinction, cannot replace the attraction of the stage in the Soviet Union (where state-controlled television offers only standard, propaganda-saturated programs). Due to the fact that the group of active playwrights is relatively small and many of them are film scenario writers as well, some of their most successful vehicles are returned to national repertory year after year. In this way the recognized talent and popularity of such playwrights as Alexander Volodin (b. 1919), Eduard Radzinsky (b. 1936) and Victor Rozov (b. 1913) have been animating and continue to animate Soviet dramaturgy during the past fifteen years.

Their most representative plays (Volodin's *Five Evenings*, 1959, Radzinsky's *104 Pages About Love*, 1964) are known to every Soviet theatre-goer today, and are revived every two or three years on the stage. Rozov's earliest drama, *Alive Forever*, was performed for the first time at the Contemporary in 1956 and has initiated each winter season at that theatre ever since. In all three works the "new romanticism" trend prevails with the larger social consciousness giving way to the cult of personal emotions and relationships. Tensions are conveyed in brief scenes of straightforward dialogue that are innocent of any comic device. They are generated by love's lost illusions and the imprecise, unacknowledged yearning for its fulfillment. Against the urban, white-collar background of physicists, doctors, university students, and factory executives, who are barely limned in as individual characters, the love story plot moves in linear fashion, simple in structure and sensually discreet. Nothing in these plays could offend the touchy puritanism of the Soviet officialdom.

In *Five Evenings* a love affair, interrupted by the war, is renewed when the hero and heroine meet seventeen years later. Each boasts to the other of professional advancement which in the case of each is a lie. He pretends to be chief engineer of a large factory, although he is only a chauffeur and a mechanic. His dismay at her pride in his supposed status leads to a temporary estrangement until she seeks him out and convinces him of their need for each other. *104 Pages About Love* treats acceptance and rejection game of mutual attraction between a clever young physicist and a beautiful air hostess who seem to be easily pulled away from each other by the exciting demands of their jobs. In the last act, the girl dies saving passengers in an airplane crash, and the young man who had been playing it "cool," is now seen stripped of pretenses and vanity and overcome by the realization of his great loss. *Alive Forever* involves an even more conventional wartime theme. For Rozov's student heroine, Veronica, life becomes emptied of meaning when her young fiancé, Boris, volunteers for military service during the war and she makes a hasty, loveless marriage that is bound to end in divorce. It is not until Boris's courageous death in action is confirmed and Veronica and his family succeed in finding, after the war, the spot where he was shot down that the memory of his purposeful, hard-working life assails her and her love for him is articulated again. It inspires her to bring order and constructive action into her own existence.

It has been noted that there are no villains in these plays

nor a sense of some unendurable condition (palpably intolerable condition) that kept the nineteenth-century romantic hero in perpetual rebellion against his society. On the contrary, people who are misguided and emotionally overwrought are always being "set straight" by their friends and family. Advice and assistance are freely given, and everyone exhumes energy, friendliness, and a great desire to learn. The chauffeur-mechanic explains to the heroine's nephew the value of studying chemistry. The air hostess frequents modern poetry readings to enlarge her literary awareness. Veronica banks on a two-year course in a construction institute to provide her with some form of a happy adjustment to life.

The emphasis on private emotional concerns and the intimate events of ordinary existence, that charts a course away from the shoals of ideological cant, is artistically, at a great remove from the Utopia-building potboilers that passed for literature in the Stalin era. Nevertheless, these writers express a fundamental optimism in the face of personal adversity that is alarmingly reminiscent of Socialist Realism dogma. Most really believe that everything is unalterably right with the Soviet world for all Soviet citizens in terms of attractive employment, recreation, professional opportunity, and education. Finally, those writers who explore the mirky, confused, and contradictory inner world of emotions remain willing accomplices of a conformist society. That is, they are, more often than not, willing to turn away, in a moment invaded by a larger social truth, from the problematics of inner directed self and find surcease for their public in a head-on affair with bright, external reality.

Victor Rozov was the editor of *Youth* magazine, artistic director of the resolutely avant-garde, anti-establishment Contemporary Theatre, and an active recruiter of young talent from provincial theatrical enterprises. Rozov is considered in his own country as an authority on the changing attitudes of young Russian men and women. In a recent interview for the Lithuanian magazine, *Niamunas* (December, 1976) he voiced his concern for the present restlessness of the young who are beginning to re-examine their parents' values and are impatient with educational norms that have been set up for them. "The twenty-year-olds think that they already know everything there is to be learned about life" and this issue has dramatically highlighted several of Rozov's best known plays. *Before Dinner* (1963) he explores the sensibilities of a very young group of Soviets and advocates an understanding of their demands. In *Search for Happiness* (1957) and *Reunion* (1965) he examines problems and feelings of high-school and university students, as well as in what progressive critics consider Rozov's finest play, *In Good Time*, first staged in 1958. The author catches late adolescents who have just completed their first ten years of schooling and are at the crucial moment of taking entrance examinations to institutes and colleges that will determine their careers. Those who fail, and those whose fathers do not have the proper contacts to have them admitted to the institution of their choice, or rebel against this underhanded procedure, face the alternative of an unalluring profession or being drafted into the blue-collar work force. Rozov's hero is eighteen-year-old Andrei, a spoiled and gifted boy whose nimble mind and sense of humor make everyone look stuffy. However, he has made no serious effort to prepare for the examinations and rejects the "personal pull" that would help get him admitted to college. What quickens the Western reader's interest in him is Andrei's own solution to his problem which haunts the modern writer's awareness of self to self and of self to others. He is determined to find his own identity (within the Soviet framework). He therefore leaves the comforting environment of friends and family who have been letting him get by on his cleverness and charm and turning him into a "stunted parasite." The play ends with his departure from Moscow to a remote rural area where he hopes to realize "the best of himself" by dint of hard work and find "the right place for him alone."

The most creative Soviet writers are now examining problems that arise in the mainstream of Russian life that less than two decades ago would have been unutterable, and the avidity of the Soviet public for their works indicates the relevance of their material to the daily reality of the Russian people and to their aspirations and ideals. It is a very straightforward, serious kind of literature for the most part, that vibrates with immense purposefulness, a belief in the realization of man's potential through work and in a certain undefined goodness that marks it with moral intensity.

It fulfills a function for a people, regimented and isolated under dictatorship, and indeed provides spiritual succor in familiar, human terms that is analagous to the effect that was made on millions of Soviet citizens when they read and reread Tolstoy's *War and Peace* while the German Army was invading their country. But the nature of the function Soviet literature fulfills for the West, whose writers are largely apprehensive of fundamental truths, and feel them to be illusory or intolerable and therefore to be evaded or by some means imaginatively transformed, remains open to question.

Conclusion

THE ACHIEVEMENT of Russian writers during the first twenty-five years of the twentieth century seems infinitely superior to Soviet literature of the later period. With the withdrawal of Russian writers from the scene of international avant-garde art where, for the first time in her cultural history, Russia had been a full participant, and with the curbing of free creativity by Socialist Realism, literary horizons gradually closed around a depiction of public national concerns. The art of the previous era that had been created by educated men for members of their own class, became distinguished by literary fare directed "downwards" for wide readership among the masses, and that was accessible to them in content and style, related to their interests and uplifting. Writers were enjoined to make field trips to industrial construction projects in far-flung areas of the Soviet Union so that they could make the factually detailed descriptions in their novels of daily life in the factories, executive offices, and recreation centers. (These novels also were of particular interest to the Westerner for whom such documentation was otherwise difficult to come by.) A variant of this theme appeared when a measure of abundance was attained on the consumer level. Soviet readers were inspired when they saw that deserving workers could raise their standard of living by hard work. Special emphasis was given to their acquisition and enjoyment of hitherto unknown material goods.

But on the whole, standard Russian fiction from the middle thirties on, was considered by American and European critics who applied Western criteria, as didactic and bleak. This kind of writing affirmed the heroism of labor, the value of collective enterprise, belief in the Communist millennium, and the need to fight for socialist progress against reactionary capitalism that might imperil the Promethean program of the State. It also provoked doubts in the West whether the bureaucratic world of the Soviet Union was one in which the writer could truly survive. Alberto Moravia equated Christianity with Communism as the two most powerful forces of indoctrination in the Western world. He also queried the compliance to coercion on the part of the Soviet writer, able to live personally and creatively outside the political dogma, as compared to Italian Primitives who produced Christian art because they were of necessity Christians and "nothing else."

While the drama of the 1917 upheaval has been draining away from world memory, its result—the transformation of a primitive agricultural country into an industrialized superpower within fifty years—is a pervasively present fact. No less astonishing and comparatively impressive has been the creation of a national literature within the same time span that now produces a quarter of all the books globally printed and numbers over 5,000 writers. To judge from the mass output, it would appear that the majority of Soviet men of letters, during their process of ideological formation and due to a historical circumstance, have committed themselves to the creation of a propagandistic form of literary expression and have become Soviet Communists and "nothing else." A parallel could be drawn between the American hack grinding out commercially successful pulp to popular appeal formulae and the Soviet writer who is imperturbably guided by socialist directives. The major difference stems from the latter's socio-political situation which has molded him into an unprecedented type of writer. In contrast to his fellow literary practitioners in other cultures who maintain a distance from the establishment and are commonly its severe critics, this compliant Communist writer is a loyal supporter for its policies (and, in return, is rewarded with material privileges and the status of a high-ranking civil service functionary). However, this "assembly line" literary production under the party aegis is really only partially representative of the literary climate in the Soviet

Union. Throughout the period, since the inception of dictatorial leadership, a determined minority of progressive writers have struggled to preserve a measure of creative autonomy and produce works of indisputable artistic value. Some of them have maintained the continuity of the Russian classical tradition, as have Zoshchenko and Bulgakov, inspired by Gogol; Fedin who was influenced by the psychological realism of Tolstoy; and Paustovsky who was indebted to Turgenev for the fusion of landscape and introspection. Short-story authors who have written after the thaw have drawn on the spiritual strength of the great masters. They emphasize humanitarian sentiments and basic moral values that are meant to mitigate the fear and distrust that alienate individuals under totalitarian rule. Thus, Sholokhov shows his nostalgia for a dying civilization with Tolstoyan breadth in *The Quiet Don*. Pasternak makes a plea for a fully realized personal life in *Dr. Zhivago*.

Western critics had expressed the hope that during the Khrushchev thaw writers would find a release for their pent-up creative energies and try to express a more complex view of life and human behavior than had been tolerated by the Stalinist dictum. This did not occur. Writers tended to continue to conform to the tenets of Socialist Realism. Those who did protest did so for having to write in such a manner as to conform to the officially glossed-over reality or against bureaucratic indecencies. They did not complain about the bureaucratic structure itself, and they were not, to any large measure, vitally concerned with the individual's private emotional world. There was as yet little evidence of interest in stylistic innovation or Western existential thought that was to fascinate Andrei Sinyavsky.

The galling bonds of the establishment had been loosened but the pervasive pressure of the collective on the personal and professional life of the writer, an integrated member of a closed society, remained strong. What was needed to give pitch, tune and a shaping power to the fitful signs of rebellion among the progressively minded Soviet literati was the possibility of the total emancipation of the writer's work from state strictures. This became a fact in samizdat literature that took upon itself the role of the only outspoken critic of the regime from within Soviet society. Although, with the exception of Solzhenitsyn, no writers have as yet proposed an overthrow of Soviet dictatorship, their works are witness to the horror of that world.

It is still too early to speak conclusively of this very young Soviet literature that is in the process of growth. The major question that contemporary writers face is whether the Kremlin authorities who have been intensifying a neo-Stalinist repression of dissenters will succeed in crushing all literary expression that does not conform to the strictures of the regime as it proceeds toward the technological age. It remains to be seen whether Soviet writers, bolstered from within by a successful culmination of the dissenting action, will finally obtain their right to untrammeled creativity and consequent reentry into the world community of letters.

Bibliography

SOCIAL AND POLITICAL BACKGROUND

Amalrik, Andrei, *Will the Soviet Union Survive in 1984?* New York: Harper & Row, 1970.

Barghoorn, F. C., *The Soviet Cultural Offensive.* Princeton: Princeton University Press, 1960.

Billington, James, *The Icon and the Axe.* New York: Vintage, 1970.

Brumberg, Abraham, ed. *In Quest of Justice: Protest and Dissent in the Soviet Union Today.* New York: Praeger, 1970.

Brzezinski, Z. K., *The Permanent Purge.* Cambridge: Harvard niversity Press, 1962.

Crankshaw, Edward, *Russia Without Stalin.* New York: Viking Press, 1956.

Dunham, Vera S., *In Stalin's Time.* Cambridge, England: Cambridge University Press, 1976.

Fischer, Louis, *Fifty Years of Soviet Communism.* New York: Popular Library, 1968.

James, Caradog Vaughan, *Soviet Socialist Realism.* New York: St. Martin's Press, 1973.

Jaworskii, M., ed. *Soviet Political Thought: An Anthology.* Baltimore: John Hopkins Press, 1968.

Kolakowski, Leszek, *Toward a Marxist Humanism,* tr. by Jane Peel. New York: Grove Press, 1968.

Mandel, William M., *Soviet Women.* New York: Doubleday, 1975.

295

Marcuse, H. A., *Soviet Marxism: A Critical Analysis*. New York: Columbia University Press, 1957.

Maynard, Sir J., *Russia in Flux*, ed. and abridg. by S. H. Guest from *Russia in Flux and the Russian Peasants and Other Studies*. New York: Macmillan, 1948.

Nettle, J. P., *The Soviet Achievement*. New York: Harcourt, Brace and World, 1967.

Randall, Francis B., *Stalin's Russia*. New York: The Free Press, 1965.

Riha, Thomas, ed. Readings in Russian Civilization, Vol. III. *Soviet Russia 1917-1963*. Chicago: University of Chicago Press, 1964.

Rothberg, Abraham, *The Heirs of Stalin: Dissidence and the Soviet Regime, 1953-1970*. Ithaca: Cornell University Press, 1972.

Saunders, George, ed. *Samizdat, Voices of the Soviet Opposition*. New York: Monad Press, 1974.

Sinyavsky, Andrei (defendant), *On Trial; the Soviet State versus "Abram Tertz" and "Nikolai Arzhak,"* tr. and ed. by Max Hayward. New York: Harper & Row, 1967. (This is based on the trial before the Supreme Court of the R.S.F.S. held in Moscow Oblast Court in February, 1966.)

Smith, Hedrick, *The Russians*. New York: Quadrangle-The New York Times Book Co., 1976.

Sorlin, Pierre, *The Soviet People and Their Society*, tr. by Daniel Westbort. New York: Praeger, 1969.

Swayze, Harold, *Political Control of Literature in the USSR, 1946-1959*. Cambridge: Harvard University Press, 1962.

Treadgold, D. W., *Twentieth Century Russia.* Chicago: Rand McNally, 1959.

Trotsky, Leon, *Literature and Revolution*, tr. by R. Strunsky. Ann Arbor: University of Michigan Press, 1960.

CRITICISM

Beaujour, Elizabeth Klosty, *The Invisible Land: A Study of the Artistic Imagination of Iurii Olesha*. New York: Columbia University Press, 1970.

Brown, Clarence, *Mandelstam*. Cambridge: Cambridge University Press, 1973.

Brown, Edward J., *Mayakovsky: A Poet in the Revolution.* Princeton: Princeton University Press, 1973.

Driver, Sam N., *Anna Akhmatova.* New York: Twayne Publishers, 1972.

Dunlop, John B., Richard Haugh, and Alexis Klimoff, eds. *Alexander Solzhenitsyn: Critical Essays and Documentary Materials.* Belmont, Mass.: Nordland Publishing Co., 1973.

Dyck, J.W., *Boris Pasternak.* New York: Twayne Publishers, 1972.

Falen, James E., *Isaac Babel.* Knoxville: University of Tennessee Press, 1974.

Hughes, Olga R., *The Poetic World of Boris Pasternak.* Princeton: Princeton University Press, 1974.

Karlinsky, Simon, *Marina Cvetaeva.* Berkeley: University of California Press, 1966.

McVay, Gordon, *Esenin, a Life.* Ann Arbor: Ardis Press, 1976.

Mochulsky, Konstantin, *Andrei Bely,* tr. by Norm Szalavitz. Ann Arbor: Ardis Press, 1977.

Moody, Christopher, *Solzhenitsyn.* New York: Harper & Row, 1975.

Piper, D. G., *V. A. Kaverin.* Pittsburgh: Duquesne University Press, 1970.

Poggioli, Renato, *The Poets of Russia, 1890-1930.* Cambridge: Harvard University Press, 1960.

Reeve, F. D., *Blok, Between Image and Idea.* New York: Columbia University Press, 1962.

Rice, Martin P., *Valery Briusov and the Rise of Russian Symbolism.* Ann Arbor: Ardis Press, 1975.

Rothberg, Abraham, *Alexander Solzhenitsyn—The Major Novels.* Ithaca: Cornell University Press, 1971.

Shane, A. M., *The Life and Works of Evgenii Zamyatin.* Berkeley and Los Angeles: University of California Press, 1968.

Stewart, D. H., *Mikhail Sholokhov: A Critical Introduction.* Ann Arbor: University of Michigan Press, 1967.

Weil, Irwin, *Gorky: His Literary Development and Influence on Soviet Intellectual Life.* New York: Random House, 1966.

Woodward, James B., *Leonid Andreyev: A Study.* Oxford: Clarendon Press, 1969.

Zelinsky, K. A., A. A. *Fadeyev: A Critical-Biographical Study.*
    Moscow, 1956.

ANTHOLOGIES

Blake, Patricia, and Max Hayward, eds. *Dissonant Voices in
    Soviet Literature.* New York: Pantheon, 1962. (Pasternak,
    Zamyatin, Shklovsky, Esenin, Paustovsky, Babel, Grin, Pil-
    nyak, Zoshchenko, Kazakov, Ehrenburg, Evtushenko,
    Arzhak, and others.)
Guerney, Bernard Gilbert, ed. *New Russian Stories.* Norfolk: J.
    Laughlin, 1953. (Grin, Gorky, Zoshchenko, A. Tolstoy, Pas-
    ternak, Zamyatin, Babel, Pilnyak, and others.)
–––––. *An Anthology of Russian Literature in the Soviet Period
    from Gorky to Pasternak.* New York: Random House, 1960.
    (Gorky, Blok, Esenin, A. Tolstoy, Fadeyev, Zamyatin, Ka-
    tayev, Ehrenburg, Olesha, Ilf and Petrov, Pasternak, and
    others.)
Kern, Gary, and Christopher Collins, eds. *The Serapion Broth-
    ers: A Critical Anthology.* Ann Arbor: Ardis Press, 1975.
    (Kaverin, Luntz, Shklovsky, Vsevolod Ivanov, Fedin,
    Zoshchenko and others.)
Kunitz, Joshua, ed. *Russian Literature Since the Revolution.*
    New York: Boni and Gaer, 1948. (Bely, Blok, Mayakovsky,
    Vsevolod Ivanov, Babel, Fadeyev, Libedinsky, Gladkov,
    Zoshchenko, Katayev, Esenin, Gorky, Sholokhov, Ehren-
    burg, Leonov, Ilf and Petrov, Aliger, Simonov, Akhmatova,
    Surkov, Tvardovsky, Kaverin, Nagibin, Paustovsky, and
    others.)
Langland, Joseph, ed. and tr. *Poetry from the Russian Under-
    ground: A Bilingual Anthology.* New York: Harper & Row,
    1973.
Markov, Vladimir, and Merrill Sparks, eds. *Modern Russian
    Poetry.* London: MacGibbon & Kee, 1966.
Pomorska, Krystyna, ed. *Fifty Years of Russian Prose from Pas-
    ternak to Solzhenitsyn.* Cambridge: MIT Press, 1971, Vol.
    I. (Pasternak, Tsvetaeva, Zamyatin, Babel, Pilnyak,
    Vsevolod Ivanov, Platonov, Grin, Paustovsky, Nekrasov and

others.) Vol. II. (Yashin, Nagibin, Solzhenitsyn, Okudzhava, Kazakov, Panova, Zhdanov and others.)

Proffer, Carl, and Ellendea Proffer, eds. *The Ardis Anthology of Recent Russian Literature.* Ann Arbor: Ardis Press, 1975. (Poems by Akhmatova, Mandelstam, Pasternak, Mayakovsky, Tsvetaeva, Brodsky, Akhamadulina, Evtushenko, Slutsky, Tvardovsky, and others. Stories by Aksyonov, Belov, Voinovich, Maksimov, Yashin, Bitov and others.)

Reeve, F. D., ed. *Contemporary Russian Drama.* New York: Pegasus, 1967. (Rozov, Panova, Zorin, and others.)

Reavey, George, ed. and tr. *The New Russian Poets, 1953-1968.* London: Calder and Boyars, 1968.

Scammel, Michael (comp.). *Russia's Other Writers.* London: Longman, 1970. (Maksimov, Rostopchin, Mandelstam, Shalamov, Bukovsky, Goryushkov, Ktorova, and Velsky.)

Yarmolinsky, Avrahm, ed. *Soviet Short Stories.* Garden City: Doubleday Anchor Books, 1960. (Zamyatin, Pasternak, Zoshchenko, Olesha, Katayev, Paustovsky, Yashin, and others.)

RECOMMENDED TRANSLATIONS OF INDIVIDUAL WORKS

Abramov, Feodor, *One Day in the "New Life,"* tr. by David Floyd. New York: Praeger, 1963.

Akhmadulina, Bella, *Fever and Other New Poems,* tr. by Geoffrey Dutton and Igor Mezhakoff-Koriakin. New York: Morrow, 1969.

Akhmatova, Anna, *Selected Poems,* ed. and tr. by Walter Arendt. Ann Arbor: Ardis Press, 1976.

Akayonov, Vasily, *A Starry Ticket,* tr. by Alec Brown. London: Putnam, 1962.

Andreyev, Leonid, *The Seven Who Were Hanged,* tr. by H. Berstein. New York: Boni and Liveright, 1920.

———. *He Who Gets Slapped,* tr. by G. Zilboorg. Westport, Conn.: Greenwood Press, 1975.

Arzhak, Nikolai, *This is Moscow Speaking,* tr. by John Richardson in *Dissonant Voices in Soviet Literature,* ed. by Patricia

Blake and Max Hayward. New York: Pantheon, 1962, pp. 262-306.

Babel, Isaac, *Collected Stories*, tr. by Walter Morison. New York: Meridian, 1960.

Bely, Andrei, *Petersburg*, tr. by John Cournos. New York: Grove Press, 1959.

———, *Kotik Letaev*, tr. by G. Janecek. Ann Arbor: Ardis Press, 1971.

Blok, Alexander, *The Twelve*, tr. by B. Deutsch and A. Yarmolinsky. New York: Rudge, 1931.

Bondarev, Yurii, *Silence*, tr. by Elisaveta Fen. London: Chapman and Hale, 1965.

Brodsky, Joseph, *Selected Poems*, tr. by G. Kline. New York: Harper & Row, 1974.

Bulgakov, Mikhail, *The White Guard*, tr. by Michael Glenny. London: Collins and Harvell, 1971.

———, *Black Snow*, tr. by Michael Glenny. New York: Simon & Schuster, 1967.

———, *The Master and Margarita*, tr. by Mirra Ginsburg. New York: Grove, 1967.

Bunin, Ivan, *The Gentleman from San Francisco and Other Stories*, tr. by Bernard Guilbert Guerney. New York: Knopf, 1933.

Bykov, Vasily, *The Ordeal*, translation of *Sotnikov* by Gordon Clough. London: Bodley Head, 1972.

Chukovskaia, Lidia, *The Deserted House*, tr. by Aline B. Werth. New York: Dutton, 1967.

———, *Going Under*, tr. by Peter M. Weston. London: Barrie and Jenkins, 1972.

Dudintsev, Vladimir, *Not By Bread Alone*, tr. by E. Bone. New York: E. P. Dutton, 1957.

Ehrenburg, Ilya, *Julio Jurenito*, tr. by Anna Bostock and Yvonne Kapp. London: MacGibbon, 1958.

———, *Out of Chaos*, tr. by Alexander Bakshy. New York: Holt, 1934.

———, *People and Life: Memoirs of 1891-1917*, tr. by Anna Bostock and Yvonne Kapp. London: MacGibbon, 1961.

———, *Memoirs: 1921-1941*, tr. by Tatiana Shebunina and

Yvonne Kapp. Cleveland: World Publishing Co., 1964.

———, *The Thaw*, tr. by Manya Harari. London: MacGibbon, 1961.

Esenin, Sergei, *Confessions of a Hooligan: Fifty Poems*, tr. by Geoffrey Thurley. Hulme, England: Carcanet Press, 1973.

Evtushenko, Evgeny, *The Poetry of Evgeny Evtushenko*, tr. by George Reavey. New York: October House, Inc., 1965.

Fedin, Konstantin, *Cities and Years*, tr. by Michael Scannell. New York: Greenwood Press, 1962.

Furmanov, Dmitry, *Chapayev*, tr. by George and J. Kittell. Moscow: Foreign Languages Publications, 1959.

Gladkov, Feodor, *Cement*, tr. by A. S. Arthur and C. Ashleigh. New York: Ungar, 1960.

Gorky, Maxim, *The Lower Depths and Other Plays*, tr. by Alexander Bakshy. New Haven: Yale University Press, 1945.

———, *Mother*, tr. by Margaret Wettlin. New York: Collier, 1961.

———, *The Artamanov Business*, tr. by Alec Brown. New York: Pantheon, 1948.

———, *Selected Short Stories*. New York: Ungar, 1959.

Brossman, Vasily, *Forever Flowing*, tr. by Thomas P. Whitney. New York: Harper & Row, 1972.

Gumilyov, Nikolay, *Selected Works of Nikolay S. Gumilyov*, tr. by Burton Raffel and Alla Burago. Albany: State University of New York Press, 1972.

Ilf, Ilya, and Evgeny Petrov, *Twelve Chairs*, tr. by John H. C. Richardson. New York: Random House, 1961.

———, *Little Golden Calf*, tr. by Charles Malamuth. New York: Ungar, 1961.

Ivanov, Vsevolod, *Armoured Train*, tr. by Gibson-Cowan and A. T. K. Grant. New York: International Publishers, 1933.

———, *The Adventures of A Fakir*. New York: Vanguard, 1935.

Katayev, Valentin, *The Embezzlers*, tr. by L. Zarine. Conn.: Hyperion Press, 1929.

———, *Squaring the Circle*, tr. by N. Goold-Verschogle. London: Wishart & Co., 1934.

———, *The Holy Well*, tr. by Max Hayward and Harold Shukman. New York: Walker, 1967.

Kaverin, Veniamin, *The Unknown Artist*, tr. by P. Ross. Westport, Conn.: Hyperion Press, 1947.

Korolenko, Vladimir, *Maker's Dream and Other Stories*, tr. by Marian Fell. New York: Duffield, 1916.

Krymov, Yurii, *Tanker Derbent*, tr. by B. Kagan. Kuibeshav, USSR: Mezhdunarodnaya Kniga, 1940.

Kuprin, Alexander, *The Bracelet of Garnets and Other Stories*, tr. by Leo Pasvolsky. New York: Scribner's Sons, 1917.

Kuznetsov, Anatoly, *Babi Yar*, tr. by Jacob Guralsky. New York: Dial Press, 1967.

Leonov, Leonid, *The Thief*, tr. by Hubert Butler. New York: Dial Press, 1931.

———, *The Badgers*, tr. by Hilda Kazanina. London: Hutchinson, 1946.

———, *Skutarevsky*, tr. by Alec Brown. New York: Harcourt, 1936.

———, *Invasion*. Moscow: International Literature, 1943.

Mandelstam, Osip, *Selected Poems*, tr. by C. Brown and W. S. Merwin. New York: Atheneum, 1974.

Mayakovsky, Vladimir, *The Bedbug and Selected Poetry*, ed. by Patricia Blake, tr. by Max Hayward and George Reavey. New York: Meridian Books, 1960.

———, *Complete Plays*, tr. by Guy Daniels. New York: Washington Square Press, 1968.

Nagibin, Yurii, *The Pipe Stories*, tr. by Shneerson. Moscow: Foreign Languages Publications, 1958.

Nekrasov, Victor, *Kira Georgievna*, tr. by Walter Vickery. New York: Pantheon, 1962.

Nikolaeva, Galina, *Harvest*. Moscow: Foreign Languages Publications, 1952.

Olesha, Yurii, *Envy*, tr. by T. S. Berczynnski and C. Rougle. Ann Arbor: Ardis Press, 1975.

Pasternak, Boris, *Poems*, tr. by Eugene M. Kayden. Ann Arbor: University of Michigan Press, 1959.

———, *Dr. Zhivago*, tr. by Max Hayward and Manya Harari. New York: Pantheon, 1958.

———, *Selected Writings*, tr. by Beatrice Scott. New York: New Directions, 1958.

Paustovsky, Konstantin, *The Golden Rose,* tr. by Suzanna Rosenberg. Moscow: Foreign Languages Publications, 1961.

———, *The Story of a Life,* tr. by Joseph Barnes. New York: Pantheon, 1964.

Pavlenko, Pyotr, *Happiness,* tr. by J. Fineberg. Moscow: Foreign Languages Publications, 1950.

Pilnyak, Boris, *The Naked Year,* tr. by A. Tulloch. Ann Arbor: Ardis Press, 1975.

———, *Mother Earth and Other Stories,* tr. by Vera Reck and Michael Green. New York: Praeger, 1968.

Platonov, Andrei, *The Fierce and Beautiful World,* tr. by Joseph Barnes. New York: E. P. Dutton, 1970.

Prishvin, Mikhail, *Nature's Calendar,* tr. by W. L. Goodman. New York: Pantheon, 1952.

Remizov, Alexsei, *The Clock,* tr. by J. Cournos. London: Chatto & Windos, 1924.

Sholokhov, Mikhail, *And Quiet Flows the Don,* with *The Don Flows Home to Sea,* Parts I and II, translation of *The Quiet Don* by Stephen Garry. New York: Knopf, 1941.

———, *Seeds of Tomorrow* (Vol. I of *Virgin Soil Upturned*), tr. by Stephen Garry. New York: Knopf, 1935.

———, *Harvest on the Don* (Vol. II of *Virgin Soil Upturned*), tr. by H. C. Stevens. New York: Knopf, 1960.

Shukshin, Vasily, *Snowball Berry Red and Other Stories,* tr. by Donald M. Fiene, Geoffrey Hosking, and others. Ann Arbor: Ardis Press, 1977.

Simonov, Konstantin, *Days and Nights,* tr. by Joseph Barnes. New York: Ballantine, 1962.

Sologub, Feodor, *The Little Demon,* tr. by John Cournos and Richard Aldinston. London: M. Secker, 1916.

Solzhenitsyn, Alexander, *One Day in the Life of Ivan Denisovich,* tr. by Thomas P. Whitney. New York: Crest Books, 1963.

———, *Matrena's House* and *For the Good of the Cause* and *Zakhar the Pouch,* tr. by Michael Glenny. New York: Farrar, Straus and Giroux, 1972.

———, *Stories and Prose Poems,* tr. by Michael Glenny. New York: Farrar, Straus and Giroux, 1971.

———, *The First Circle,* tr. by Thomas P. Whitney. New York: Harper & Row, 1968.

———, *Cancer Ward,* tr. by Rebecca Frank. New York: Dial, 1968.

———, *Candle in the Wind,* tr. by Keith Armes. Minneapolis: University of Minnesota Press, 1973.

———, *The Love Girl and the Innocent,* tr. by Nicholas Bethel and David Burg. New York: Farrar, Straus and Giroux, 1969.

———, *August 1914,* tr. by Michael Glenny. New York: Farrar, Straus and Giroux, 1972.

———, *The Gulag Archipelago,* tr. by Thomas P. Whitney. New York: Harper & Row, Parts I and II, 1974; Parts III and IV, 1975.

———, *Lenin in Zurich,* tr. by H. T. Willets. New York: Farrar, Straus and Giroux, 1976.

Tendryakov, Vladimir, *Three Novellas,* tr. by J. G. Garrard. New York: Pergamon, 1967.

Tertz, Abram, *The Trial Begins,* tr. by Max Hayward. New York: Pantheon, 1960.

———, *Fantastic Stories,* tr. by Max Hayward and Ronald Hingley. New York: Pantheon, 1963.

———, *The Makepeace Experiment,* tr. by Manya Harari. New York: Pantheon, 1965.

Tolstoy, Alexsei, *The Road to Calvary,* tr. by Edith Bone. New York: Knopf, 1946.

———, *Bread,* tr. by Stephen Garry. New York: Ryerson Press, 1938.

———, *Peter the Great,* tr. by Edith Bone and Emile Burns. New York: Ryerson Press, 1936.

Trifonov, Yurii, *The Students,* tr. by Ivy Litvinova and Margaret Wettlin. Moscow: Foreign Languages Publications, 1953.

Voinovich, Vladimir, *The Life and Extraordinary Adventures of Private Ivan Chonkin,* tr. by Richard Lourie. New York: Farrar, Straus and Giroux, 1977.

Voznesensky, Andrei, *Selected Poems of Andrei Voznesensky,* tr. by Anselm Hollo. New York: Grove, 1964.

Zamyatin, Evgeny, *The Dragon: Fifteen Stories,* tr. by Mirra

Ginsburg. New York: Random House, 1967.

———, *We*, tr. by Mirra Ginsburg. New York: Viking, 1973.

Zoshchenko, Michael, *Wonderful Dog and Other Tales*, tr. by Elisaveta Fen. London: Methuen, 1942.

———, *Nervous People and Other Stories*, tr. by H. Gordon and H. McLean. New York: Pantheon, 1963.

Index

About and Around (Abramov), 238

Abramov, Feodor, 238

Acmeism, 35-37

Adventure of a Monkey, The (Zoshchenko), 187

Afinogenov, Alexander, 179

Akhmadullina, Bella, 218, 220-221

Akhmatova, Anna, 36, 37, 38-41, 43, 60, 184, 187, 201, 204, 222, 223, 245

Aksyonov, Vasily, 225, 232, 279

Aldanov, Mark, 94

Aldington, Richard, 43

Aliger, Margarita, 204, 207

Amalrik, Andrei, 244

Andreyev, Leonid, 74, 78-81, 85, 90

Annensky, Innokenti, 36

Anti-Worlds (Voznesensky), 219-220

Armoured Train, The (Vsevolod Ivanov), 106

Arp, Jean, 67

Artamonov Business, The (Gorky), 84-85

Artist Unknown (Kaverin), 139

Artsybashev, Mikhail, 81

Arzhak, Nikolay (pseudonym for Yuri Daniel), 249, 251

Astafyev, Victor, 280

At the Top of My Voice (Mayakovsky), 54

August 1914 (Solzhenitsyn), 266, 267, 272-273

Averbakh, Leopold, 142, 143

Babayevsky, Semyon, 195

Babel, Isaak, 53, 55, 105, 112-118, 136, 176, 181, 201, 207

Babeuf, François, 172

Babi Yar (Evtushenko), 218

Bagritsky, Eduard, 176

Baklanov, Grigory, 228, 282

Bakst, L., 2

Bakunin, Mikhail, 52

Balmont, Konstantin, 3, 4, 8-10, 25, 81, 94

Balzac, Honoré de, 44, 84, 108

Bath House (Mayakovsky), 54

Baudelaire, Charles, 1, 3, 5, 10

Beardsley, Aubrey Vincent, 3

Beckett, Samuel, 135

Bedbug, The (Mayakovsky), 54

Bedny, Demyn, 97

Belinsky, Vissarion, 90, 276

307

Belov, Vasily, 238, 239, 279
Bely, Andrei, 4, 5, 14, 17, 20, 21,
    23-28, 31, 36, 48, 55, 56, 62,
    81, 94, 96, 100, 108, 136, 247
Benois, Alexander, 2, 3
Berberova, Nina, 95
Berdyayev, Nikolay, 19, 94, 223,
    277
Bergholtz, Olga, 184, 197, 201,
    246
Bezymensky, Alexander, 68
Bitov, Andre, 233
Blake, William, 3
Bloch, Jean-Richard, 145, 217
Blok, Alexander, vi, 4, 14, 17, 20,
    25, 28-35, 56, 58, 62, 64, 73,
    96, 131
Bogomolov, Vladimir, 282
Bokov, Nikolay, 254
Bondarev, Yuri, 225
Borges, Jorge Luis, 249
Borodin, Sergei, 181
Boswell, James, 31
Brecht, Bertolt, 285
Breton, André, 67
Brezhnev, Leonid, 244, 251
Brik, Osip, 48, 53
Brodsky, Joseph, 55, 218, 221-223
Bronowsky, Jacob, 211
Brown, Clarence, 42
Brown, Edward J., 143
Bryusov, Valery, 3, 4-8, 10, 14, 17,
    22, 35, 65, 81, 96, 138, 146
Buffon, George Louis, 174
Bulgakov, Mikhail, viii, 118-121,
    179, 201, 233, 234-238, 245,
    246, 293
Bunin, Ivan, 24, 74, 76-78, 85, 90,
    94, 201, 232, 255
Burlyuk, David, 46, 51
Bykov, Vasily, 225, 228
Byron, George Gordon, 10, 66

Cancer Ward (Solzhenitsyn), 265,
    270-272

Castro, Fidel, 218
Cement (Gladkov), 153-155
Chagall, Marc, 67, 174, 246
Chain of Koshchey, The (Pris-
    hvin), 175
Chalidze, Valery, 244
Chapayev (Furmanov), 151
Chavannes, Puvis de, 2
Chekhov, Anton, 76, 84, 90, 117,
    128, 129, 146, 205
Chernyshevsky, Nikolay, 147, 149
Chizhevsky, Dmitri, 10
Chukovskaya, Lidia, 262
Chukovsky, Korney, 201, 222, 262
Cities and Years (Fedin), 128-129,
    172, 191, 193
Cloud in Trousers (Mayakovsky),
    51
Cohen, Hermann, 63
Coleridge, Samuel, 10
Conrad, Joseph, 284
Cooper, James Fenimore, 176

Dali, Salvador, 67
Daniel, Yuri, 224, 243, 251, 262
Dante, Alighieri, 21, 268
Days and Nights (Simonov), 183
Degas, Edgar, 2
Derzhavin, Gavrila, 23
Diaghilev, Serge, 2
Dickens, Charles, 133
Dr. Zhivago (Pasternak), 207-217,
    293
Dostoyevsky, Feodor, 4, 12, 16, 22,
    24, 33, 46, 78, 100, 103, 128,
    130, 131, 132, 133, 134, 135,
    146, 148, 170, 172, 194, 201,
    209, 213, 227, 238, 246, 247,
    249, 251, 254, 276
Doyle, Arthur Conan, 176
Dreiser, Theodore, 145
Druggist's Island (Bitov), 233
Dudintsev, Vladimir, ix, 201, 202-
    204, 205, 207
Duel, The (Kuprin), 75

Duncan, Isadora, 59
Dyomin, Mikhail, 245

Eichenbaum, Boris, 48, 138
Eisenstein, Sergey, 63
Ehrenburg, Ilya, viii, 68, 95, 164, 169-174, 197, 198, 201, 204, 207, 233, 246
Eliot, Thomas Stearns, 42, 64, 136, 209, 247
Embezzlers (Katayev), 121
Engels, Friedrich, 145
English Pre-Raphaelites, 1
Envy (Olesha), 134-138, 139
Ermolayev, Herman, 163
Ernst, Max, 67
Esenin, Sergey, vi, 57-60, 63, 96, 138, 207, 245
Evtushenko, Evgeny, vi, 55, 217, 218-219, 220, 221, 224
Extraordinary Adventures of Julio Jurento and His Disciples (Ehrenburg), 170

Fadeyev, Alexander, 152-153, 159, 183, 187, 188, 189, 229
Falen, James, 118
Fall of Paris, The (Ehrenburg), 172
Fantastic Tales (Sinyavsky), 247
Fedin, Konstantin, 99, 128-130, 191, 192, 193, 204, 208, 243, 293
Fedorov, Nikolay, 216, 217
Feltrinelli, Giangicomo, 208
Fet, Afanasy, 5, 20, 24
Fierce and Beautiful World, The (Platonov), 229-230
Filosofov, D., 3
First Circle, The (Solzhenitsyn), 265, 268-270
Fitzgerald, F. Scott, 136
Five Evenings (Volodin), 286
Flaubert, Gustave, 114

Forever Flowing (Grossman), 259-260
Formalists, 49-50, 136
Frank, S., 277
Freud, Sigmund, 109, 126
Furmanov, Dmitri, 150-152
Futurism, 45-48

Galich, Alexander, 253
Gautier, Théophile, 6, 36
Gentleman from San Francisco, The (Bunin), 77
George, Stefan, 1, 3
Gerland, Brigette, 250
Gershenzon, Mikhail, 23
Gide, André, 133
Gippius, Zinaida, 3, 4, 14-15, 24
Gladkov, Feodor, 153-155, 201
Glenny, Michael, 284
Goethe, Johann Wolfgang von, 10, 21, 24, 66
Gogol, Nikolay, 11, 17, 31, 33, 100, 116, 120, 121, 125, 128, 130, 135, 190, 248, 249, 293
Going Under (Chukovskaya), 262-263
Golomstock, Igor, 250
Golovin, Ivan, 2
Goncharov, I. A., 4, 24, 76
Gorky, Maxim, 7, 35, 52, 74, 75, 81, 83-91, 96, 104, 106, 118, 128, 142, 144, 146, 149, 276
Goya, Y. Lucientes, 246
Gracq, Julien, 42
Graves, Robert, 236
Grin, Alexander, 175-176, 177
Grossman, Vasily, 259-260
Guests, The (Zorin), 199-200
Gulag Archipelago (Solzhenitsyn), 266, 273-276, 279
Gumilyov, Nikolay, 36, 37-38, 43

Haggard, Henry Rider, 176
Happiness (Pavlenko), 194-195
Harvest, The (Nikolaeva), 195

Hauptmann, Gerhart, 24
Hayward, Max, 40
Hegel, Georg Wilhelm Friedrich, 24
Heine, Heinrich, 10
Hemingway, Ernest, 136, 198, 218
Heredia, José Maria, 38
Herman, Yuri, 179
Herzen, Alexander 247
Hitler, Adolf, 172, 186
Hoffmann, E. T. A., 9, 99, 130, 138, 246, 247, 248
Holderlin, Friedrich, 3
Holy Well, The (Katayev), 233-234, 255
Hopkins, Gerald, 44
House on the Embankment, The (Trifonov), 228
Huxley, Aldous, 102
Huysmans, George Charles, 25

Ibsen, Henrik, 9, 25
Ilf, Ilya, 118, 176, 179
Ilyenkov, Vasily, 178
In Good Time (Rozov), 288
Inber, Vera, 184
Invasion (Leonov), 184
Ionesco, Eugene, 285
Isakov, I., 185
Islanders (Zamyatin), 101
Ivanov-Razumnik, R., 25, 58
Ivanov, Vsevolod, 83, 99, 105-107, 108, 112
Ivanov, Vyacheslav, 4, 20, 21-23, 30, 35, 42, 94
Ivarsk, George, 95

Jacobson, Roman, 48
Johnson, Samuel, 31
Joyce, James, 28, 48, 144, 146, 198, 209, 233

Kafka, Franz, 112, 136, 146, 233, 248, 249

Kandinsky, Vasily, vi, 47, 48, 50, 138, 220
Kant, Emmanuel, 170
Katayev, Valentin, viii, 83, 99, 118, 121, 178, 233-234, 255
Kaverin, Veniamin, 99, 138-140, 201, 204, 207, 230, 231
Kazakevich, Emmanuil, 207
Kazakov, Yuri, ix, 225, 231-232, 280
Keats, John, 28, 66
Kennan, George, 275
Kermode, Frank, 210
Khlebnikov, Velimir, 46, 47, 65, 67, 68, 138
Khodasevich, Vladislav, 62
Khrushchev, Nikita, ix, 188, 189, 201, 209, 224, 234, 240, 241, 243, 249, 251, 261
Kipling, Rudyard, 75, 176
Kira Georgievna (Nekrasov), 225-226
Klee, Paul, 220
Kline, George, 223
Kluyev, Nikolay, 57
Kochetov, Vsevolod, 189, 256
Korneychuk, Alexander, 184
Korolenko, Vladimir, 74-75, 85, 90
Kosygin, Alexey, 244, 251
Kron, Alexander, 204, 207, 230
Kruchonykh, Alexey, 47
Krymov, Yuri, 179
Kryukov, Feodor, 162-163, 164
Kuzmin, Mikhail, 43
Kuznetsov, Anatoly, 245
Kuprin, Alexander, 74, 75-76, 85, 94

Last Greeting, The (Astafyev), 281
Lawrence, D. H., 136
Leconte De Lisle, Charles Marie, 6, 38
Léger, Fernand, 169, 174
Lenin, Vladimir, viii, 53, 72, 88,

89, 93, 95, 133, 142, 145, 146, 149, 211, 267, 274
Leonov, Leonid, 99, 130-134, 135, 138, 183, 184
Leopardi, Giacomo, 10
Lermontov, Mikhail, 5, 17, 20, 28, 64
Leskov, N. S., 130
Levers, The (Yashin), 205
Lewis, Wyndham, 43
Libedinsky, Yuri, 97-98
Life and Adventures of Private Ivan Chonkin, The (Voinovich), 256-257
Light in the Window, The (Nagibin), 205
Live and Remember (Rasputin), 281
London, Jack, 75, 81, 176
Lower Depths (Gorky), 84-85
Lukacs, George, 145
Lunacharsky, Anatoly, 96
Luntz, Lev, 100, 138

Maeterlinck, Maurice, 4, 5, 25
Maguire, Robert, 108
Mailer, Norman, 78
Makar's Dream (Korolenko), 74
Makepiece Experiment (Sinyavsky), 247
Maksimov, Vladimir, 261-262
Malevich, Kasimir, vi, 43, 47, 138, 220
Mallarmé, Stephane, 1, 3, 5, 42
Malraux, André, 145
Mandelstam, Osip, vi, 36, 37, 41-45, 56, 61, 62, 138, 207, 219, 223, 252
Mann, Thomas, 209, 232
Marinetti, Filippo, 45, 46
Markov, Vladimir, 14, 95
Marshak, Samuel, 222
Marx, Karl, 60, 170
Master and Margarita (Bulgakov), 235-238, 246

Matrena's Home (Solzhenitsyn), 239, 241-242
Maupassant, Guy de, 114, 117
Mayakovsky, Vladimir, vi, vii, 46, 47, 50-57, 58, 62, 63, 64, 65, 67, 83, 138, 139, 143, 172, 207, 218, 245, 246
Medvedev, Roy, 163-164
Merezhkovsky, Dmitri, 3, 14-15, 16, 17, 94, 96
Merimée, Prosper, 176
Meyerhold, Vsevolod, 50, 55, 80, 138
Michaelangelo, Buonarroti, 3
Mikhailov, Sergei, 204
Miller, Arthur, 182
Miro, Joan, 220
Modigliani, Amadeo, 169, 174
Monet, Claude, 2
Moravia, Alberto, 292
Mother, The (Gorky), 86, 149
Mozart, Wolfgang Amadeus, 31
Muchnic, Helen, 133
Musil, Robert von, 233
My Sister, Life (Pasternak), 65

Nadson, Semyon, 24
Nagibin, Yuri, 205, 206, 220, 225, 231, 280
Naked Year (Pilnyak), 107-110
Nekrasov, Victor, 17, 24, 183, 225, 243
Nervous People (Zoshchenko), 125
Nesserer, Yuri, 220
Nietzsche, Friedrich, 21, 25
Nikolaeva, Galina, 195
Not By Bread Alone (Dudintsev), 202-204
Novalis, Friedrich, 3, 28
Nusinov, Isaac, 146, 188

Okudzhava, Bulat, 253
Olesha, Yuri, 134-138, 139, 181, 204

On the Island (Kazakov), 231-232
One Day in the Life of Ivan Denisovich (Solzhenitsyn), 239-241
O'Neill, Eugene, 84
Orwell, George, 102, 248
Osborne, John, 285
Ostrovsky, Alexander, 178

Pain Around My Heart, The (Bogomolov), 282-283
Panfyorov, Feodor, 178
Panova, Vera, 191, 193, 194, 198, 199, 285
Paustovsky, Konstantin, 176, 227, 293
Pasternak, Boris, vi, ix, 10, 50, 55, 62-66, 184, 207-217, 219, 223, 235, 250, 293
Pavlenko, Pyotr, 194-196
Pavlov, Ivan, 126
People, Life, Years (Ehrenburg), 173
Petersburg (Bely), 27
Petrov, Evgeny, 118, 179
Petty Devil, A (Sologub), 12-13, 82
Picasso, Pablo, 169, 174
Pilnyak, Boris, viii, 83, 99, 105, 107-112, 143, 181, 201
Piper, D. G., 139
Pit, The (Krupin), 75
Platonov, Andrei, 229-230, 245
Plehve, V. K., 72
Plekhanov, Georgy, 72
Pletnyov, V., 179
Poe, Edgar Allen, 1, 3, 9, 44, 78, 81, 138, 176, 249
Poggioli, Renato, 62
Pogodin, Nikolay, 179, 285,
Pomerantsev, Vladimir, 198, 201, 246
Potebnia, Alexander, 48
Pound, Ezra, 43
Prishvin, Mikhail, 174, 177, 230

Proletcult, 97
Proust, Marcel, 28, 39, 87, 144, 146
Pugachov, Yemelian, 59
Pushkin, Alexander, 5, 6, 9, 24, 33, 46, 50, 84, 147, 188, 217

Quiet Don, The (Sholokhov), 155-159, 272, 293

Rabelais, François, 114
Radek, Karl, 144
Radzinsky, Eduard, 285, 286
Rasputin, Valentin, 280
Razin, Stenka, 59, 109
Red Cavalry (Babel), 115-117
Red Laugh (Andreyev), 79
Remizov, Alexey, 81-83, 99, 108, 130
Requiem (Akhmatova), 41
Ribera, José de, 169
Rilke, Rainer Maria, 42, 62, 63, 66, 216
Rimbaud, Arthur, 1, 3, 5
Rimsky-Korsakov, Nikolay, 3
Road to Calvary (A. Tolstoy), 166-167, 192
Robbe-Grillet, Alain, 102
Rogers, Will, 97
Rolland, Romain, 145
Romains, Jules, 120
Rosetti, Dante Gabriel, 10
Rout, The (Fadeyev), 152
Rozanov, Vasily, 4, 14, 16, 17-18
Rozov, Victor, 285, 287-288

Sakharov, Andrei, 244
Salieri, Antonio, 31
Salinger, J.D., 226
Saltykov-Shchedrin, Mikhail, 190
Sartre, Jean Paul, 233
Scarlet Sails (Grin), 176
Schemann, Alexander, 276
Schopenhauer, Arthur, 78
Scriabin, Alexander, 3, 63

Scythians (Block), 35
Seasons of the Year (Panova), 198
Semuchatsky, Vladimir, 209
Serafimovich, A. S., 159
Serapion Brothers, 99, 100, 104, 106, 124, 126, 138
Sergeyev-Tsensky, Sergei, 182
Serov, Valentin, 2
Seven Days of Creation (Maksimov), 261-262
Seven That Were Hanged, The (Andreyev), 79
Severyanin, Igor, 45
Shakespeare, William, 10, 66, 215
Shalamov, Varlan, 258-259
Shaw, George Bernard, 145
Shelley, Percy Bysshe, 3, 10, 66
Shklovsky, Victor, 49, 50, 94, 99, 123, 138, 139, 204
Sholokhov, Mikhail, 155-164, 188, 189, 192, 201, 262, 272, 293
Shostakovich, Dmitri, 182, 222
Shukshin, Vasily, 238, 239
Shvarts, Yevgeny, 285
Silence (Bondarev), 227
Silver Dove, The (Bely), 26
Simon, Claude, 102
Simonov, Konstantin, 183, 184, 188, 208
Sinclair, Upton, 145, 198
Sinyavsky, Andrei, 224, 243, 250, 251, 262, 293
Slonim, Marc, 190
Slutsky, Boris, 221
Snow Masks (Blok), 32
Sologub, Feodor, 4, 10-14, 15, 24, 81
Solominka (Mandelstam), 44
Solovyov, Vladimir, 16, 18-21, 22, 24, 25, 30, 223
Solukhin, Vladimir, 230
Solzhenitsyn, Alexander, 162, 163, 239-242, 244, 251, 262, 264-277, 279, 293
Somov, Konstantin, 2

Sotnikov (Bykov), 229
Soupault, Philippe, 67
Stalin, Joseph, vii, viii, 89, 97, 104, 119, 138, 142, 160, 167, 168, 172, 173, 182, 185, 186, 188, 189, 191, 195, 197, 201, 229, 233, 234, 239, 246, 248, 268, 271, 280, 284, 285
Stanislavsky, Konstantin, 80, 84, 234, 284
Starry Ticket (Aksyonov), 226
Sterne, Lawrence, 99
Stevenson, Robert L., 176
Stories of Kolyma, The (Shalamov), 258-259
Story of a Life, A (Paustovsky), 177-178
Stranger, The (Blok), 31
Strindberg, August, 78
Strugatsky, Arkady, 257
Struve, Gleb, 95, 146
Struve, Peter, 277
Subotsky, Lev, 187
Sudermann, Hermann, 24
Surkov, Alexey, 184, 201
Swinburne, Algernon Charles, 3, 10

Tendryakov, Vladimir, 225, 232
Tertz, Abram (pseudonym for Andrei Sinyavsky), 246-249, 250
Thaw, The (Ehrenburg), 173, 174, 197, 200
Thief, The (Leonov), 130-131
This Is Moscow Speaking (Arzhak), 249-250
Tolstoy, Alexey, viii, 164, 165-169, 181
Tolstoy, Leo, 4, 16, 46, 50, 63, 75, 78, 79, 87, 90, 110, 116, 119, 133, 146, 148, 156, 192, 193, 209, 217, 264, 270, 276, 289, 293
Tomashevsky, Boris, 138
Tovstonogorov, Georgii, 285

Travelling Companions (Panova), 193

Trial, The (Tendryakov), 227-228

Trial Begins, The (Sinyavsky), 247

Trifonov, Yuri, 228, 280

Trip Back Home, The (N. Zhdanov), 205

Trotzky, Leon, vii, 61, 88, 95, 99

Tsvetaeva, Marina, vi, 60-62, 63, 65, 94, 204, 207, 223, 245

Turgenev, Ivan, 4, 24, 33, 76, 78, 129, 146, 148, 209, 293

Tvardovsky, Alexander, 185, 198, 201, 225, 238, 240, 241, 264, 266, 279

Tvardovsky, Alexander, 185, 198, 201, 225, 238, 240, 241, 264, 266, 279

Twelve, The (Blok), 34

Twelve Chairs (Ilf, Petrov), 121

Twenty Six Men and a Girl (Gorky), 84

Tynyanov, Yuri, 48

Tyutchev, Feodor, 5, 17, 20, 22

Ugly Swan (A. Strugatsky), 258

Vasily Tyorkin (Tvardovsky), 185

Vasnetsov, V. M., 3

Velasquez, Diego, 3

Verhaeren, Emil, 6

Verlaine, Paul, 3, 4, 66

Verne, Jules, 176

Verses on the Death of T.S. Eliot (Brodsky), 223

Veselovsky, Alexander, 48, 49

Vinci, Leonardo da, 17

Vinokurov, Evgeny, 221

Virgin Soil Upturned (Sholokhov), 160

Virta, Nikolay, 178

Vladimov, George, 254, 255

Voinovich, Vladimir, 256-257

Volodin, Alexander, 285-286

Voltaire, François Marie, 170, 248

Voronsky, Alexander, 106, 142, 143

Voznesensky, Andrei, 55, 218, 219-220, 221, 223, 224

Vysotsky, Vladimir, 253

We (Zamyatin), 102-104

Weidle, Wladimir, 95

Weil, Irwin, 88

Wells, H.G., 120

What Is To Be Done? (Chernyshevsky), 149

What Matters Most (Zamyatin), 101-102

White Guard, The (Bulgakov), 119

Whitman, Walt, 9, 10

Wilde, Oscar, 1, 3, 10, 25

Witte, Sergei, 73

Woolfe, Virginia, 233

Wordsworth, William, 10

Yakira, Peter, 252

Ysshin, Alexander, 205, 206, 279

Yavlensky, Andrei, 47

Yefremov, Oleg, 285

Yoncheventsky, Vasily, 182

Young Guard (Fadeyev), 183, 187

Yourcenar, Marguerite, 236

Zabolotsky, Nikolay, 66-69, 179, 204

Zalygin, Sergei, 238, 239

Zamoyskaya, Helen, 251

Zamyatin, Yevgeny, 55, 94, 99, 100-104, 108, 119, 131, 136, 143, 257

Zhdanov, Andrei, 40, 145, 187, 184

Zhdanov, Nikolay, 205, 206

Zhirmunsky, Victor, 48

Zhukovsky, Vasily, 10

Zoshchenko, Mikhail, 55, 83, 99, 118, 123-128, 187, 249, 293

Zorin, Leonid, 199, 285